The De Gaulle Republic

ROY C. MACRIDIS
Professor of Political Science
Washington University

BERNARD E. BROWN
Assistant Professor of Political Science
Vanderbilt University

The De Gaulle Republic

QUEST FOR UNITY

THE DORSEY PRESS, INC.

1960 – Homewood, Illinois

First Printing, July, 1960

Library of Congress Catalogue Card No. 60–14048

PRINTED IN THE UNITED STATES OF AMERICA

Preface

THIS IS A STUDY of De Gaulle's Fifth Republic—its origins, institutions, and chances of survival. After a long period of internal strife an attempt is now being made to forge a new unity, based on the national reality of France and its incarnation in the person of Charles de Gaulle. Our goal in this work has been to trace the origins of the new regime, subject to critical analysis its institutions and ideology, and show how the traditional political forces and divisions of Republican France continue to assert themselves.

Particular difficulties were encountered in preparing comparative electoral statistics. For the visual presentations we relied upon the excellent charts and maps in *Année Politique* and *Le Monde*. We also used the figures in Maurice Duverger, *Constitutions et Documents Politiques* (Paris, 1957), and consulted the publications of the Service des Affaires Politiques of the Ministry of the Interior, especially the *Liste des Candidats aux Elections Législatives,* November 23–30, 1958.

The major part of this book was written in 1959, and we have added a brief epilogue on the events of January–February, 1960. Initially each author was responsible for separate sections of the manuscript; however, cooperation became increasingly intimate so that what we present is truly a joint effort. We are both grateful to the Fulbright Commission for grants enabling us to study and teach in France in 1956–57 and again in 1958–59. Roy Macridis received liberal support from the Rockefeller Foundation enabling him to spend two years in France. To its trustees and to Dr. Kenneth Thompson he wishes to express his deepest thanks. Both Washington University and Vanderbilt University have facilitated our work with small grants for secretarial assistance. We wish to thank the officers and staff of the *Fondation Nationale des Sciences Politiques* of the University of Paris, particularly Professors Jacques Chapsal, Jean Touchard, Jean Meyriat, Alfred Grosser, Jean Meynaud, René Remond, Maurice Duverger, Serge Hurtig, and many others who gave generously to us of their time. A number of French political leaders

v

were also kind enough to be interviewed and provide us with information and documentation. Professor Benjamin Rivlin of Brooklyn College read the parts of the manuscript dealing with Algeria and the French Union. Professor Henry Ehrmann of the University of Colorado read the whole third part. Professor Renè Remond read the chapters on the referendum and the elections. They all made valuable suggestions. Dr. William E. Weld, Jr., then cultural attaché of the United States Embassy in Paris and Dean Robert Davril, head of the Fulbright Commission, were a constant source of friendly encouragement. Finally, our thanks to Mrs. Dorothy Conard, secretary of the Department of Political Science at Washington University, who typed or supervised the typing of the manuscript in its various stages. Of course our thanks to those who helped us in no way implies their approval of this book, for which we alone are jointly responsible.

Roy C. Macridis
Bernard E. Brown

St. Louis, Missouri
Nashville, Tennessee
   February, 1960

Table of Contents

Part Three. Gaullism in Action

Appendixes

Index

Abbreviations Used in Text

Political Parties and Movements: France

CANAC, *Comité d'Action des Associations Nationales d'Anciens Combattants*
MRP, *Mouvement Républicain Populaire*
PCF, *Parti Communiste Français*
PSA, *Parti Socialiste Autonome*
RGR, *Rassemblement des Gauches Républicaines*
RPF, *Rassemblement du Peuple Français*
SFIO, *Section Française de l'Internationale Ouvrière* (Socialist party)
UDCA, *Union des Commerçants et Artisans* (Poujadist)
UDSR, *Union Démocratique et Socialiste de la Résistance*
UDT, *Union Démocratique du Travail* (Left Gaullist)
UFD, *Union des Forces Démocratiques*
UFF, *Union et Fraternité Française* (Poujadist)
UGS, *Union de la Gauche Socialiste*
UNR, *Union pour la Nouvelle République*
USRAF, *Union pour le Salut et le Renouveau de l'Algérie Française*

Parties and Groups: Algeria

ALN, *Armée de Libération Nationale*
CRUA, *Comité Révolutionnaire pour l'Unité et l'Action*
DPU, *Dispositif de Protection Urbaine*
FLN, *Front de Libération Nationale*
MNA, *Mouvement National Algérien*
MTLD, *Mouvement du Triomphe des Libertés Démocratiques*
ORAF, *Organisation de Résistance d'Algérie Française*
OS, *Organisation de Sécurité*
PPA, *Parti du Peuple Algérien*
SAS, *Sections Administratives Spécialisées*
UDMA, *Union Démocratique du Manifeste Algérien*
UFNA, *Union Française Nord-Africaine*
UT, *Unités Territoriales*

Other Organizations

CRS, *Compagnies Républicaines de Sécurité*
CFTC, *Confédération Française des Travailleurs Chrétiens*
CGT, *Confédération Générale du Travail*
FO, *Force Ouvrière*

INTRODUCTION

The Quest for Unity

THE FIFTH REPUBLIC has come in the wake of a political upheaval that involved a temporary collapse of the regular
process of government. As in all previous cases, the new constitution
—the sixteenth the country has had since the revolution of 1789—
performs the traditional, one may say the ritualistic, function of
reasserting the unity and the continuity of a political society that
remains profoundly divided. Why so many constitutions? Why so
many sharp divisions about the nature of the ultimate form of the
body politic? Why so much disagreement upon the fundamental
bond of a society which in many other systems—both Anglo-Saxon
and European—is taken for granted?

These questions cannot be answered merely by analyzing the
articles of previous constitutions and pointing to institutional defi-
ciencies. It is true, for instance, that the Constitution of the Fourth
Republic consecrated the ascendancy of the Assembly: Dissolution
was hamstrung in many ways, the Council of the Republic attempted to assume some of the powers together with the name of its
formidable predecessor, the legislative process and even budget
making underwrote the supremacy of the Assembly and its committees, and the executive became again a "captive." This is all incontestable. But under different conditions the same constitution
could have led to a cabinet system in which the supremacy of the
executive and the prime minister would have been assured. In fact,
as was the case with the Third Republic through the device of the
décrets-lois, the Fourth Republic had concentrated through a number of similar devices enormous powers in the hands of the prime
minister and the cabinet. Many of these powers antedated the Algerian rebellion. The executive could by simple decree control

1

prices, regulate wages, reorganize the socialized sector of the economy, modify the status of the civil service, and reform the administrative services. He was given wide latitude to shape policy at home and abroad and to influence developments in Algeria and in the French Union.

But the Fourth Republic was characterized not only by cabinet instability but by the inability of the cabinet to use its immense powers in the realm of policy making. The possible area of decision making was progressively restricted and a handful of deputies exploited the internal divisions of the political parties in the National Assembly in order to block cabinet policy and paralyze decision making. They became permanent veto groups within the political system.

The political parties themselves progressively lost the bulk of their membership in the years after the liberation. The public was becoming disaffected from a system in which party pledges had no relevance to government policy. This alienation of the public from the political parties and the political system led eventually to the *alienation of the parties from the public.* The political parties became increasingly divorced from reality. In the "house without windows" and in their congresses they fought the old battles and argued fine doctrinal points while the growing pace of industrialization was transforming the nation and creating a host of new problems.

The most pervasive trait of French political history is that of a divided society in search of unity. Alexis de Tocqueville had noted that:

The word individualism, which we have coined for our own requirements, was unknown to our ancestors, for the good reason that in their days every individual necessarily belonged to a group and no one could regard himself as an isolated unit. Nevertheless each of the thousands of small groups of which the French nation was then composed took thought of itself alone; in fact there was, so to speak, a group individualism which prepared men's minds for the thorough-paced individualism with which nowdays we are familiar.

Group divisions within the French society are characterized by their multiplicity, their intense ideological character, and what may be termed the tenacity of group "memories." Divisions are regional, economic, religious, social, and political. They relate to the old quarrel of economic freedom versus *dirigisme,* the perennial *question scolaire,* the vague but ever-present conflict between Left and Right which reflects differences in tendency and style more than substance. Political ideologies and families, such as the Communists, the Socialists, the Radicals, the Christian Democrats, and the extreme Right, have developed their own vocabulary, style, literature, and press; these families in turn have fragmented into subgroups with differences among them that only the fully initiated can grasp.

Social and economic groups whose objective interests appear to have a common denominator are divided into small political and ideological splinters. The veterans, farmers, workers, artisans, and middle classes—merchants, teachers, students, and public servants —are all spread out among a great number of organizations with conflicting political affiliations and ideological outlooks. There is no other major political system where the multiplicity of professional and occupational groups is compounded to such an extent by the ideological element. The interest groups are "politicized," that is, impregnated with political attitudes. Hence, existing party divisions are sharpened and compromise is made more difficult.

Group divisions and the concomitant ideologies have been deeply registered in the historical consciousness of the French nation. Munich, the Resistance, and Marshal Pétain are living myths linked with others in the more remote past that influence attitudes with regard to contemporary problems and actions. Political events are automatically placed in certain historical categories in terms of which they evoke automatic reflexes. A strike reminds the bourgeoisie of the Popular Front (the return of De Gaulle was imperative for many, including the leader of the Socialist Party, for fear of the Popular Front); defensive measures taken by the state and the police recall to the workers repression by the "Versaillais." A number of commentators have already written lengthy statements to show the similarity between the constitution of the Fifth Republic and that of 1814 or the July Monarchy. The new National Assembly was compared to the *chambre introuvable* and it followed that De Gaulle might also be forced to resort to dissolution. Ideological divisions are projected through the multiparty system upon the Parliament and the executive. The Left and the Right are divided into splinter groups which reflect every conceivable point of view and whose perception of the present and the future is shaped by ideological commitments that belong to the past.

The demise of the Fourth Republic may be traced ultimately to lack of consensus in French society. Consensus is to be distinguished from uniformity. There may be differences, even fundamental ones, in a "consensual" society. But there is widespread agreement on the means through which certain goals can be accomplished. Basic political procedures or ideas (such as majority rule, parliamentary sovereignty, judicial review, federalism) will be respected by organized groups when they seek to attain their ends. A consensual political system presupposes a homogeneous political culture, which is not to be confused with social or political conformity. A homogeneous political culture denotes the existence of commonly shared traditions and ideologies concerning the *political process*. The "rules of the game" are not questioned.

The French political system is not consensual and has not been consensual ever since the Revolution of 1789. The French are not in agreement on the values of the state nor on political procedures to be used in the resolution of group conflicts. Every political regime thus far has represented the victory of temporarily dominant elements within the political culture. Each regime has been outfitted with a complete set of symbols and agencies, and all have finished by being overwhelmingly repudiated. Occasionally, at times of great national peril, unity has been achieved around the myth of "France." Yet, the content of national symbols has always given rise to disagreement—the interpretations of Jaurès and Maurras, Rénan and Daudet, being obviously incompatible. The "real France" has never been able to produce a "legal France" in its image.

The lack of consensus in France is illustrated by disagreement among the Republicans on constitutional reforms. With the possible exception of the period between 1905 to 1914, which André Siegfried considered to have been the "Golden Age" of the Third Republic, there was no decade in which the French were not at odds about their Republican Constitution. The "Grévy Constitution" was barely established when General Boulanger's movement for reform took an ominous turn. After World War I there were ill-fated attempts at reform by Millerand and Doumergue. No sooner had the Constitution of 1946 been adopted by a narrow margin than the movement for reform began again.

Demand for reform is not necessarily an indication of instability. The test of a political system is its ability to adapt in order to meet changing circumstances. A peculiarity of the French political system was that every group wanted reform but no agreement ever emerged. The form of government therefore became a source of discord adding another layer of division to the already existing ones. The perennial demand for reform by all groups and parties (except perhaps the Radical Socialists) was in itself an indication that the legitimacy of the Republic was being slowly undermined even among those attached to the Republic. Every political family lived under a roof which it considered to be badly in need of repair. For each one the Constitution was only a *pis-aller*, a temporary structure instead of a legitimate channel for the resolution and translation of conflict into decisions. The debates on constitutional reforms in the last year of the Fourth Republic and Pflimlin's final admission of the impotence of the system just before his resignation, invited a tribune of the people to assume full powers and reform the regime.

It is precisely when divisions are sharp and when no accepted instrument for overcoming them is available that the quest for unity in France emerges more imperative than ever before. It is then that a new constitution is sought in the name of national unity. The Gaullist solution in 1958 was another in a long line of efforts to provide legitimacy in the name of national unity, to reconcile the "legal France" with the "real France."

De Gaulle succeeded in directing the strong wave of nationalism into a Republican channel. He played the role of Rousseau's legislator in attempting to launch a new system embodying the national interest. He even used Rousseauian phraseology, representing himself as the embodiment of the national interest and integrity ever since the defeat of France in 1940. As he explained in a press conference, "I belong to everybody because I belong to no one." He is above the welter of interests and ideological conflicts. He represents the "general will" and not just "the will of all." In 1945 he failed to impose his views on the constituent assemblies and the nation. In 1958 he was given a second chance to create a genuine synthesis of the political traditions in France, as distinguished from merely registering the temporary victory of one political family.

Part One

The Collapse of the
Republic

CHAPTER I

The Fourth Republic

SINCE MAY, 1958, the Fourth Republic has been subjected to a constant barrage of criticism. During the days of crisis, Prime Minister Pflimlin made reform of the institutions of the Republic one of the major planks of his program. Indeed, he eventually used the question of reform as an excuse to turn power over to General de Gaulle. Even those who proclaimed their determination to defend the Republic at all costs made clear their lack of enthusiasm for the regime. During the debate on General de Gaulle's speech of investiture, Mendès-France criticized sharply the provisions of the Constitution of 1946, while defending the Republic. The Communists, who attempted to assert their leadership of the Republican forces, felt free to join the extreme Right in attacks on the Fourth Republic.

Yet, when the Constitution of the Fourth Republic was drafted, it seemed to conform to the profound historical traditions of the nation, and in effect represented a compromise among the principal political forces in France. The rapporteur of the constitution, Paul Coste-Floret (MRP), summed up the debate by declaring before the Constituent Assembly that the presidential regime might lead to dictatorship, while the Assembly regime would serve revolutionary purposes. The only solution was a balance between the legislature and the executive. "The presidential system condemned, the Assembly government discarded, we have no choice but to return to the parliamentary system." [1]

---

[1] Cited in Philip Williams's excellent analysis of the constitutional problem, *Politics in Post-War France* (London, 1954), p. 165. Among the best studies on the Fourth Republic, in addition to Williams, are the following: François Goguel, *France under the Fourth Republic* (Ithaca, 1952); Maurice Duverger, *The French Political System* (Chicago, 1958); Herbert Luethy, *France Against Herself* (New York, 1955); and

9

Stability of the Popular Vote

The constant turnover of cabinets and the existence of a multitude of political parties and parliamentary groups under the Fourth Republic has obscured an underlying political stability, a stability so profound that many French observers have used the term "immobility." Ministerial crises during the ten-year period following the expulsion of the Communists from the governing coalition in 1947 involved relatively minor shifts in emphasis among the parties of the Center, never any sudden alternation between Left and Right. Similarly, the broad divisions among the electorate tended to remain constant throughout the life of the three legislatures of the Fourth Republic.

The elections of October, 1945 and June, 1946 for the Constituent Assemblies revealed the existence of three large parties, each receiving approximately 25 per cent of the total vote, or between 4.5 and 5.5 million votes. The Communists, Socialists, and Popular Republicans (MRP) dominated the political scene during the period of constitution making and for the first year of the new legislature. In these two elections the Radical Socialists and allies, grouped loosely in a Rally of the Left Republicans, and the Moderates, each won between 2 and 2.5 million votes. The Communist vote remained remarkably stable in all succeeding elections, whereas the Socialists lost one million votes between the elections of October, 1945 and November, 1946, and the MRP dropped one half of its support between November, 1946 and June, 1951. The party founded by General de Gaulle in 1947, Rally of the French People (RPF), won 4.1 million votes in June, 1951, attracting support mainly from the former MRP bloc and the conservatives.

Viewing all three legislative elections of the Fourth Republic, it is possible to discern six fairly constant currents of party opinion, taking into account the reshuffling caused by the formation and decline of the RPF. On the Left, the Communist party consistently won between 5 and 5.5 million votes (or 25 per cent of the total). The Socialist party (SFIO) maintained itself at between 2.7 and 3.2 million votes. After a rapid decline in 1947 the MRP leveled off at approximately 2.7 million votes. The Radical Socialists and allied

André Siegfried, *De la troisième à la quatrième république* (Paris, 1956). For a bibliography of French political literature, see the article by the present writers, "The Study of Politics in France Since the Liberation: A Critical Bibliography," in the *American Political Science Review* (September, 1957), pp. 811–26.

groups gained some ground in 1956, and generally received around 2 million votes. The Independents, who were hurt by the RPF in 1951, averaged between 2.5 and 3.3 million votes. The main variation from the pattern was due to the sudden emergence of the RPF

STABILITY OF POPULAR VOTE UNDER FOURTH REPUBLIC

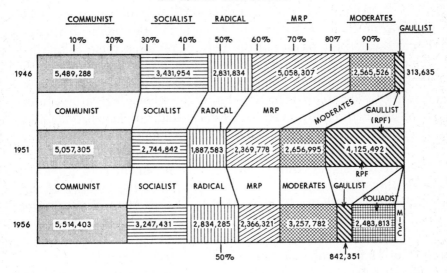

in the election of 1951 and then its decline in 1956. Its place on the Right was partially taken by the Poujadists, however, who polled over 2.4 million votes in 1956. The three members of the prewar Popular Front—Communists, Socialists, and Radical Socialists— together received an absolute majority of the votes in all elections under the Fourth Republic (58.9 per cent in 1946, 51.5 per cent in 1951, and 54 per cent in 1956). However, the differences between these parties, and within them, precluded any revival of the Popular Front.

Thus, there were three major currents (Left, Right, and Center) with at least two distinct party organizations within each category: Communists and Socialists on the Left, Popular Republicans and Radical Socialists in the Center, and Moderates or Independents and Gaullists or Poujadists on the Right. Each party could count on a solid core of support, with perhaps two million members of the electorate constantly shifting about between the parties or into abstention. The "floaters" (not always the same people, of course) tended to vote MRP in 1945–46, RPF in 1951, either Mendésist or Poujadist in 1956—and for the neo-Gaullist UNR in 1958. Between 80 and 90 per cent of the voters remained loyal to their parties throughout the Fourth Republic. The deadlock state resulted not from volatility of public opinion, but from deeply rooted divisions.

The Demoralization of Organized Opinion

All political parties of the Fourth Republic were incapable of realizing their programs. The evolution of the political situation either isolated the parties of the Left, or required them to sacrifice their ideals in order to participate in a coalition. The parties of the Right likewise had to compromise in coalitions, though they received considerable satisfaction during the second legislature. In the third legislature, however, a Socialist–Radical Socialist coalition (Republican Front) excluded the Independents from the cabinet.

Compromise and agreement among the parties traditionally take place at two stages: during an election and in the formation of a governing coalition. Under the Third Republic the practice of run-off elections (*ballottage*) permitted the forces of the Left, Center, and Right to regroup, generally in support of the candidates who won the largest number of votes on the first ballot. No possibilities for this kind of collaboration existed in 1946 since each party put forward lists, with the department as the basic electoral unit, and seats were awarded according to proportional representation. When the RPF began to score impressive victories in local elections after its creation in 1947, the leaders of the Center parties calculated that the system of PR would probably give the Communists and Gaullists together over 50 per cent of the votes *and seats* in the second legislature. In self-defense, then, they introduced a significant modification of the electoral law: Parties were permitted to form electoral alliances (*apparentements*) in each department. If any party, or coalition of parties, received a majority of the votes in that department, it would be awarded *all* of the seats which subsequently were to be divided among them. Coalitions were formed in eighty-five departments, primarily by the Radical Socialists, Socialists, and MRP. A majority was won in thirty departments. As a result the Communists and Gaullists together received 48.2 per cent of the national vote, and only 35.2 per cent of the seats. Electoral alliances thus proved to be of considerable importance, and certainly staved off the collapse of the Fourth Republic in 1951.

A great deal of controversy developed around the electoral system in the second legislature, with the Radicals demanding a return to the traditional system of single-member districts plus *ballottage*, the Communists defending the list system of PR without alliances, the MRP urging PR with alliance in a runoff, and so on. Parliament was unable to agree on any kind of reform, and Edgar Faure's dissolution of the National Assembly in December, 1955 produced an election based on the same procedure in use in 1951. This time the collapse of the RPF had reduced the danger to the Center parties, or at least so it was assumed, and a smaller number of alliances were registered (mainly between Radicals and either Socialists or MRP). The Socialists, Radicals, and some Social Republicans (former members of the RPF, led by Jacques Chaban-Delmas) actually drafted, signed, and promulgated a "Republican Front" program. A majority was obtained only in ten departments, so that the distribution of seats corresponded very closely to the national voting pattern.

The Left. In this competition for mutually profitable alliances, the Communists were completely isolated. After its expulsion from the cabinet in 1947, the party went through a "revolutionary" phase—resorting to violent strikes, demonstrations in the country, and obstructionism in Parliament. It continued to align its policies with those of the Soviet Union by opposing the Marshall Plan and military cooperation with other Western powers. The divisions between the Communists and the other parties of the Left became so great that collaboration in either electoral campaigns or in Parliament was out of the question. The Communists made strenuous efforts to break out of political quarantine by reviving the "united front" tactic after the death of Stalin. They offered support to Mendès-France in 1954, which was disdained. In 1955 Edgar Faure accepted Communist votes on a question of confidence, though he scorned the idea of a working alliance. It became customary for prime ministers to announce, with considerable moral indignation, that they would not take Communist votes into account on a question of confidence (that is, would resign if confidence were accorded because of Communist support). This automatically drove the balance in the Assembly to the Right. Systematic opposition or exclusion of one fourth the deputies greatly compressed the range of agreement and action open to the coalition cabinets.

The second party of the Left, the SFIO, participated intermittently in electoral and governmental coalitions along with other parties of the Left and Center. Such cooperation had become essential in 1947 in order to permit the formation of a government, once the Communists had gone into opposition. From 1947 to 1951 the Socialists formed one wing of the Third Force—an *ad hoc* creation of the Socialists, MRP, and Radicals designed to prevent either the Communists or Gaullists from coming to power. As a result of their participation in an essentially centrist coalition, the Socialists lost some working class and left-wing intellectual support. In spite of extensive electoral cooperation, the parties of the Third Force failed to hold on to their parliamentary majority in 1951. It became possible for the moderates to form a government with the aid of the MRP and Radicals. Elements of the RPF were soon attracted into the system. The Socialists, however, were alienated by the passage of the *loi Barangé*, which permitted state aid to religious schools. The SFIO entered the "Cure of Opposition" period that lasted until 1954 when it came to the support of Mendès-France without actually entering his cabinet. As a consequence of the election of 1956 the Socialists returned to power, forming a cabinet that included Radicals and Social Republicans with the support of the MRP and Independents. Thus, the Socialists managed to work out electoral agreements with the MRP and Radicals in 1951, and with the Radicals in 1956, yet remained hostile to cooperation with the Communists. Their choice of allies, perhaps forced by circumstances, reflected a trend in Socialist policy toward the Right. Socialist intellectuals were restive over the inability of their party to carry through a thoroughgoing transformation of French society when in power, or to block the Right when in opposition.

The Center. The Radical Socialists are traditionally the model of a "hinge party," equally ready to make alliances with parties of the Left or the Right depending not so much on the issues as on the chances for success. The party never developed a consistent program, and always claimed a privileged position in governing coalitions. Its lack of ideology made it a perfect buffer between the hard-pressed Left and the resurgent Right of the Fourth Republic. The very defects of the Radical party—lack of cohesion, loose organization, and absence of program—enabled it to facilitate the work of the Assembly in the never-ending business of finding new majorities on shifting issues.

In 1954 Mendès-France deliberately set about to transform the Radical Socialist party into an ideological movement, appealing especially to the forward-looking elements of the middle class. One of the staunchest defenders of the "hinge party" viewpoint, Martinaud-Déplat, was compelled to resign as administrative president. Mendès looked forward to an alliance between Socialists and Radicals, uniting the working and middle classes in a genuinely non-Communist Left coalition. However, other leading Radicals, including Edgar Faure, continued to favor the traditional tactic of working with both Left and Right, depending upon which way the wind blew.

Tension built up at the Radical Congress of November, 1955 when Mendès and Edgar Faure (then prime minister) locked horns ostensibly over the question of the single-member district electoral system, actually over the fundamental orientation of the Radical party. The Congress elected Mendès-France the first vice-president (Edouard Herriot being unanimously acclaimed president), but did not require the dissidents to resign. In December, Faure dissolved the National Assembly after being denied confidence by an absolute majority, thereby making it impossible for Mendès-France to carry through his reform of the party before the elections. The executive committee of the Radical Party thereupon expelled Faure and some of his associates—who fought the election under the banner of the RGR (Rally of the Left Republicans).

In October, 1956, a number of right-wing Radicals, led by André Morice, left the Radical Congress and party. Although Mendès was titular chief of the party, he was unable to introduce discipline into the parliamentary group. In June, 1957, he resigned his post at the head of the party. "In the party," he said, "there are struggles ahead. I shall be with you. But don't ask me to endorse an organization of the party which has been the source of so many disappointments." He was followed by only a dozen members of the Assembly. Under the leadership of Félix Gaillard and Bourgès-Maunoury, the Radical party resumed its former orientation—that of a hinge party, ready and eager to collaborate with other Center groups under almost all conditions. The Radicals subsequently formed and led two ministries. All the grandiose schemes for a "renovated Radicalism" were quietly laid to rest.

During the course of the Fourth Republic the Popular Republican Movement (MRP) evolved gradually from ideological Christian Socialism to the pragmatic politics of a Center party. The historic importance of the MRP was to eliminate the identity of Catholicism with the Right and make possible an alliance between Catholicism and Socialism. It included, however, a large number of conservatives who had voted MRP in order to check the Communists immediately after the Liberation and who switched over to the RPF and the Independents. The MRP vote dropped by half, but as a result it became a more homogeneous party. Still a number of tensions developed. The militants were for the most part Christian trade unionists and intellectuals, who infused the Movement with ideological fervor and a sense of social mission; but the party as a whole derived its main electoral support from the traditionally conservative and clerical western and northeastern departments. The deputies have tended therefore to be far more conservative than the militants. The position of the MRP as the "swinging" element of most coalitions under the Fourth Republic meant that considerations of power tended to predominate over purity of principle.

The Right. On January 20, 1946, General de Gaulle unexpectedly resigned as head of the government. After the text of the first constitution had been rejected by referendum, he expounded his constitutional views for the first time in a speech at Bayeux. The General's arguments in favor of a presidential regime were destined to become law of the land twelve years later. At the time, the electorate unenthusiastically approved the second draft of the constitution, and the Fourth Republic came into official existence. A Gaullist Union created by René Capitant for the election of November, 1946 received only 300,000 votes. In April, 1947, General de Gaulle personally founded the RPF, dedicated to the overhauling of the constitution. By the end of the year it won about 40 per cent of the vote in municipal elections. The voters flocking over to De Gaulle were offered a vision of a republic above the parties with a president, chosen by a large electoral college, incarnating the interests of France as a whole and arbitrating among the rival groups and public powers. The working class was to be reintegrated into the nation by a scheme of capital-labor associations. Communist influence would thus be diminished, the State would be rescued from the selfish groups, and a united nation would regain its influence in the world.

The followers of General de Gaulle suffered a series of disheartening setbacks. The Third Force succeeded in stabilizing the political situation and thereby averted new elections. A Radical, Henri Queuille, stayed in power for over twelve months (September, 1948 to October, 1949). The Gaullist movement lost momentum.

Modification of the electoral law further reduced the prospects of a Gaullist victory in 1951. There were only 120 RPF deputies in the second legislature—not quite enough to bring about General de Gaulle's return to power. Antoine Pinay formed a ministry in March, 1952 whose program won the support of a number of Gaullist deputies. An attempt to impose discipline on the RPF parliamentary group led to a split. In May, 1953, General de Gaulle, realizing that his movement had lost its cohesion, formally abandoned leadership of the RPF. He withdrew to Colombey-les-deux-Eglises to write his memoirs.

Activist opponents of the Republic had high hopes when Pierre Poujade, a bookseller from Saint-Céré in Lot, won a surprising victory in the election of January, 1956. Poujade had begun his political career as a defender of the interests of small shopkeepers, particularly in their spectacular clashes with tax collectors. His movement soon attracted the support of antiparliamentary and right-wing groups. Poujade's followers entered the campaign of 1956 with a vague program: "throw the rascals out," and then call a States-General Assembly to consider the grievances of the populace.

Poujade's "French Union of Fraternity" received 2,483,813 votes (almost 10 per cent of the total), winning 52 seats. UFF deputies, however, were ineffective in Assembly debates, and Poujade's popularity declined. In January, 1957, Poujade himself ran as a candidate in a Paris by-election. "How many times have you wanted to throw a bomb in the Assembly?" he asked his cheering followers. "Elect me, and I will be that bomb!" He lost by an overwhelming margin. Poujade established links with nationalist groups in Algeria and dissident army officers—for example, General Jacques Faure, who was placed under military arrest and then mildly disciplined for plotting to overthrow the regime. When General Faure ran as a Poujadist candidate in a Lyon by-election, he too suffered a crushing defeat. The frustrations of the activists found an outlet in street fighting and secret preparations for the violent overthrow of the Republic.

Perhaps the only major political party which succeeded in realizing a large part of its program under the Fourth Republic was the Independents (or Moderates). French conservatives have traditionally been distinguished by lack of organization in the country and in Parliament. By 1954 Roger Duchet created a National Center of Independents, and managed to bring about a measure of discipline among the deputies theretofore loosely allied as "Independents and

Peasants." They advocated a laissez-faire policy: reorganization of the nationalized industries, reduction of taxes, a balanced budget, stimulation of private investment, and, in general, creation of conditions favorable to capitalist development. In the second legislature the Independents were in a position to play a key role in the formation of coalitions, and were usually able to exploit differences among the other parties to their own advantage. "Immobilisme" meant very largely, if only by default, the *laissez faire* desired by moderates. Yet even the Independents felt frustrated by this immobility, especially in view of the growing sentiment of nationalism. From 1956 to 1958 they attached themselves fervently to the cause of French Algeria. The policy of a negative state which they found congenial in the economic realm was becoming inappropriate for the realization of military and national objectives in Algeria. Although Guy Mollet's Socialist cabinet pursued a nationalist policy, Duchet and his friends were increasingly restive over the trend of events in North Africa and the prospect of Socialist economic reforms.

When the Independents turned against Mollet's government, the circle was complete. By May, 1958 *every one* of the principal political parties had reason to feel deeply disillusioned. Their militants had no particular devotion to the institutions which somehow were held responsible for thwarting their aspirations. The morale of the Republic was at a low ebb.

The Record

The Fourth Republic emerged in 1946 into a world where the balance of power was completely transformed. Even those most affected by the idea of nineteenth century "French grandeur" realized in 1945 that power had slipped away from Western Europe and was now concentrated in the United States and the Soviet Union. In a speech at Bar-le-Duc in July, 1946, General de Gaulle frankly conceded that these two gigantic powers could not be rivaled by the individual nations of Europe. Yet, he went on to contend that the "old world" could bring about a new equilibrium. "Ancient Europe which, for so many centuries, was the guide of the universe, can constitute in the heart of a world tending to split in two, the necessary element of compensation and understanding." And of course Europe was to be led by the most powerful state on the continent—France.

General de Gaulle was expressing a widespread belief among his countrymen that a world from whose councils France was excluded could not be well ordered. During the period of *tripartisme* the French government tried to steer a middle course between the two Great Powers while reasserting its authority in the overseas territories. In 1947, foreign and domestic issues merged into one irreducible whole. The deterioration of relations between the Great Powers, coupled with the offer of Marshall Plan aid by the United States and opposition to this aid by both the Soviet Union and the French Communist party, compelled a choice in favor of cooperation with the Western powers. Yet the Third Force coalition considered itself not only a middle way between Gaullists and Communists, but also, in spite of formal acceptance of the European Recovery Program and NATO, a mediator between America and Russia. The longing of the regime to act an independent role in the world could never be realized: The Russian danger was too direct and the need for American credits likewise too pressing to allow for much freedom of maneuver.

The Fourth Republic's foreign policy reflected a contradiction between ideology and cold reality (that France was dependent for economic recovery and military protection on the United States). Decision makers seemed to view the contradiction as a question of time sequence: American aid would be accepted temporarily, until France recovered sufficiently to act independently. They shied away from an attempt to re-evaluate France's international position. When it was evident that Germany could not be prevented from regaining its sovereignty, an attempt was made by the French to neutralize German power within a European system. Shortly after the outbreak of the Korean War the United States determined to re-arm Germany. The French government, fearful of a German military force, proposed a scheme for a European defense community. But public opinion was too divided to accept merger of the armed forces of Western Europe, and France had the dubious honor of being the only state among the intended participants to reject its own plan. The result of French hesitation was the rearmament of Germany without effective international controls—exactly what the French feared most.

The same hesitations, deriving from a lack of fundamental agreement, manifested themselves likewise in France's colonial policy. In Indochina the French Army was committed to a hopeless battle. The claim of the Vietminh rebels for independence could not be entertained by the regime, since it would have violated the image of France as a great world power. Yet France lacked the strength to reimpose its sovereignty in Asia. A measure of realism led to a partition of Vietnam and, in North Africa, the grant of autonomy to Tunisia and Morocco in 1954 by the Mendès-France government. A *loi-cadre* for Africa in 1956 provided for home rule and paved the way for independence. These decisions were perhaps the most significant achievements of the Fourth Republic in the field of foreign policy. Nonetheless, the cabinets responsible for them were immediately accused by the Right of "abandoning" French interests.

The indecisiveness of the foreign policy of the Fourth Republic was another expression of the bitter internal divisions among the French people and parties. A pro-Western or even neutral policy required the cooperation of all the non-Communists—who were themselves in deep disagreement over the role to be played by France in the world. The leaders of the Center coalition never achieved a satisfactory definition of the goals of French policy, and continued to be affected by the old ideas of grandeur.

In domestic affairs, the Fourth Republic was successful in achieving economic development on the basis of moderate planning. A *Commisariat-général du plan* was created in 1946 to take stock of the French economy and suggest recommendations. Under the chairmanship of Jean Monnet the commission drew upon the advice of economists, technicians, and managers, and after a year of study urged rapid modernization. The Monnet Commission prepared a long-range plan providing for increased capital investments in six basic industries over a period of four years. By 1952 the goal had been substantially attained, with national production 45 per cent over that of 1938. In the next four years the plan called for broader investments in consumer industries, and again the targets were reached or surpassed. Productivity went up substantially, and the annual increase in national production averaged 10 per cent.

Over-all economic progress was incontestable (see accompanying figure). Aside from the dollar deficit and the relative gap between wages and prices, to the detriment of the working classes, an appreciable overhauling of French industrial and commercial structures was under way. The strength of the Poujadist movement was provided by marginal groups—individual merchants, artisans, and shopkeepers—who were being driven out of the market by more modern economic organizations. It was a desperate attempt to stop the irreversible trend toward industrialization and modernization. "Dynamic" France was winning over "static" France.

The benefits of industrialization trickled down to the farm and

ECONOMIC GROWTH BETWEEN 1949 AND 1957 *
(*In Percentages, with 1949 as Base Year*)

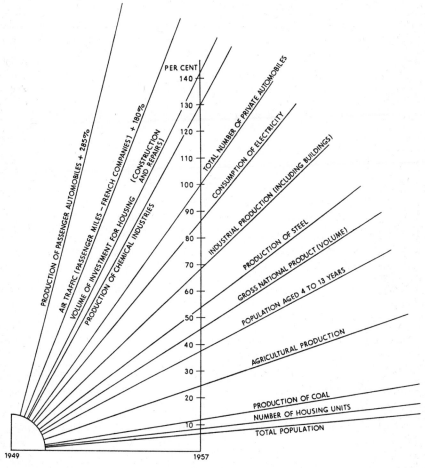

* From *Mouvement Économique en France de 1944 à 1957*, Institut National de la Statisque et des Études Économiques (Paris, 1958).

village, and generated the inevitable social friction. Artisans, small farmers, and local attorneys found it more difficult to make a comfortable living. The old *patron,* though by no means extinct, was giving place to the technician and the manager. In the nationalized areas of the economy and the public corporations—electricity, gas, railroads, aviation—technological progress often approximated and surpassed that of Western Germany and the United States. The use of fertilizers and tractors modified the traditional pattern of agricultural exploitation and raised the yield per acre of many crops. In 1949 there were 17,290 tractors; today there are more than 70,000. The wine growers and with them the powerful alcohol lobby faced increased competition from the dairy and fruit juice industries. New technical improvements, particularly refrigeration in the urban centers, are slowly changing shopping and consumption habits. The success of the "Quick Lunch" in France is the symbol of a major revolution! Thanks to the effort made by the much-maligned leadership of the Fourth Republic, the scars of World War II were healed, and France, despite the war of Indochina and the fighting in Algeria, is a prosperous country. Her population is not only growing but undergoing a drastic structural change. By 1970 France will be the country with the youngest age structure in Western Europe.

Yet the Fourth Republic failed in one crucial respect: It was unable to assure and enforce an equitable social distribution of the national income. Wage levels remained below their 1938 level until about 1951—in spite of American aid and economic growth. Since then the standard of living of the workers has risen gradually, but still lags behind the general rate of economic expansion. Family allowances and other social security benefits helped the low-income groups only to a limited extent.

A number of factors contributed to this discrimination against the working class. The trade-union movement was split into three main groups, with the Christian trade unions and the Socialist *Force Ouvrière* unable to cooperate with the larger, Communist-dominated General Confederation of Labor. This internal strife greatly reduced the militancy of the labor movement. In addition, the employers' organizations adopted a hard line toward wage demands. Profits were either reinvested in industry or distributed in the form of dividends—or were sent abroad. Above all, the State lacked the will or vigor to require redistribution of profits. In the first two years of the Republic, the Communist-Socialist-MRP coalition called for sacrifices by the workers to get the country's war-damaged economy back into production. The Third Force coalition in power from 1947 to 1951 depended on the votes of relatively conservative Radical Socialists and some Independents to stay in office. A program of social reform was not pressed since opposition in the Assembly would have brought down the government and possibly have led to new elections at a time when Gaullist sentiment was running high. After 1951 the Socialists were driven out of the governing coalition and the MRP gravitated toward the Right. The Mendès-France government was not in power long enough to undertake a program of social and economic reform. The "Republican Front" government of Guy Mollet gave lip service to the ideal of social reform, but became increasingly a captive of nationalist opinion, especially with regard to Algeria. When Mollet began to institute minor social and economic reforms and higher taxes to pay for the war in Algeria, he was overthrown by the adverse votes of the Independents, who had tolerated his government only because of its policy in Algeria.

The consequences of failure to enforce redistribution of income were serious. Communist claims appeared to be borne out in the eyes of the working class: The bourgeoisie was the chief beneficiary of the nation's economic progress, and the State was unable to provide for just shares for all. The workers and lower-income groups by and large remained faithful to the Communist party, while the Socialists gradually lost a good deal of their working class support. A vicious circle came into being. The existence of a strong Communist party condemned all of the Center and Right parties to live together, ruling out any program of action from which the conservative partners dissented. Inability to reform confirmed the attachment of the Communist supporters to their party.

The delicate balance on which the governments of the Fourth Republic reposed also made it difficult to deal effectively with marginal economic groups. Perhaps the most notorious example was the inability of the government to resist the demands of alcohol-producing groups. In the post-Liberation years, the State, through its *Service des alcools*, was annually purchasing over twice as much alcohol as the market could safely absorb. Twenty per cent of the state-owned stock was sold at premium prices to manufacturers of alcoholic drinks—at a time when the government was spending a considerable sum to fight the ravages of alcoholism. Out of desperation, the addition of alcohol to gasoline was required by law, though it had the doubly unfortunate effect of increasing the price and impairing the quality of the final product. Yet, the chief alcohol lobbies (beetgrowers, wine growers, commercial and home distillers) were able to prevent any significant reform. In May, 1953, the René Mayer government specifically staked its life on its request for special powers to cope with the situation—and was overthrown by the Assembly.

The same internal stalemate among the majority parties precluded any lasting solution of the problems posed by the poverty-stricken "free" (that is, private, and, in practice, predominantly Catholic) schools. By 1950 the educational system supported by the Catholic community (serving 20 per cent of the total school population) was deteriorating rapidly. Teachers' salaries were very low, and buildings were inadequate. Catholic organizations demanded state aid for the private schools, while all the lay parties rallied to the cause of the public schools. When the second legislature convened in June, 1951, the issue came up for debate. The MRP was driven into an alliance with the Right, and the Socialists went into opposition. Yet neither side had a sufficient margin to resolve the question once and for all. The Assembly voted a stop-gap measure, which provided financial aid to both the private and public schools in proportion to the number of students in attendance. Thus, the quarrel was perpetuated, adding to the internal divisions of the democratic parties.

The proclivity of the regime to postpone decisions as long as possible, and better yet, to avoid them altogether, is also illustrated by the problems of taxation and housing. Peasants, small shopkeepers, and professional people were able to evade a good deal of the taxation to which they were theoretically subject (though they complained the loudest whenever attempts were made to enforce the law), while big business firms, salaried civil servants, and the workers paid their share. Yet, the cabinets of the Fourth Republic were so constituted that an essential element of their support was in danger of fading away at the mere suggestion of tax reform. The regime stumbled along with a manifestly outdated, unfair, and unenforceable fiscal system. Feeble efforts to examine business records led to a movement of violent protest by shopkeepers, who were soon organized by Pierre Poujade. The success of the Poujadists in the 1956 elections in turn made even less likely any sound fiscal reform.

Vested interests proved powerful enough to prevent the State from entering the domain of housing and construction. Tenants who occupied prewar apartments insisted on legislation maintaining ludicrously low rents, while private contractors kept themselves busy building luxury apartment projects. Several hundred thousand residents of Paris alone occupy rooms in cheap hotels. State subsidies, when they finally materialized, were only partially used for lower-income housing. Inadequate housing laws contributed to the State's over-all failure to redistribute income after the Liberation.

The Fourth Republic managed to survive for some twelve years. The regime, crippled by basic divisions, was unable to take forceful steps and confront issues clearly. Its leaders became masters of compromise, equivocation, and procrastination. Issues of foreign policy, social legislation, colonial relations, education, and constitutional reform were never settled. Cabinet instability was itself an expression of this immobility since the same ministers simply changed posts and since the internal contradictions of all cabinets made action difficult. On the positive side, the Fourth Republic introduced some basic reforms that slowly modified the structure of the French economy. The regime was in no danger of collapse until it confronted one grave problem—Algeria—that transformed the indifference and even the alienation of the public into an imperative demand for action. French nationalism, nourished by many setbacks and defeats from 1940 on, exploded during the Algerian war. At this juncture the inability of the regime to act intensified popular discontent and strengthened the forces seeking to overthrow the Republic.

CHAPTER II

The Algerian Jmbroglio

THE HISTORY of French Algeria began with a slap. In the course of confused negotiations involving a consignment of wheat, the Dey Hussein asked the French Consul, Pierre Daval, why inquiries concerning this matter had not been answered. Daval replied that the French government considered it useless to write him. Hussein ordered Daval to leave his presence; Daval refused to budge; whereupon, on April 29, 1827, the Turkish Dey struck the French consul with a fly swatter. In February, 1830, after much deliberation, the French government decided upon a punitive expedition. More than honor was at stake from the French point of view. The prime minister, M. Polignac, saw the military action as part of a vast design in which "the influence of France will be established from the African shore of the Mediterranean to the heart of Asia." Thirty thousand men, under the command of General de Bourmont, debarked at Sidi-Ferruch on June 14, and occupied Algiers on July 5. Charles X wrote: "To take Algiers I considered only the dignity of France; to keep it, I shall consult only her interest." The conquest of Algeria proved to be long and costly. It was not until seventeen years later that the chief leader of Moslem resistance surrendered to the French, who suffered heavily during this period of guerrilla warfare. Sporadic outbursts of violence continued to take place long thereafter.[1]

The Two Communities

Algeria, in 1954, the year the rebellion broke out, was inhabited by two distinct communities: a population of Moslems, num-

---

[1] The best short history of Algeria is Gabriel Esquer's, *Histoire de l'Algérie* (Paris, 1957), especially Chapter 1. The citation from Charles X is in Colette and Francis Jeanson, *L'Algérie hors la loi* (Paris, 1955), p. 29.

bering about 9 million, along with approximately 1.2 million people of European origin. These two communities, which do not mix socially, are separated by their language, customs, traditions, history, religion, and level of economic development. Between 1 and 2 million Moslems participate in the modern economy created by the Europeans; the other 7 or 8 million eke out a living in a country whose outmoded agriculture can support less than half their number. They have, on an average, one eighth of the income enjoyed by those who have adapted to modern conditions. About 1 million Moslems are usually unemployed; 90 per cent of the total industrial and commercial activity of Algeria takes place in the European sector. Twenty-two thousand European farmers own three times as much property as do the 630,000 Moslem landholders. As for education, the same sharp contrast is evident between the two communities. In 1954 only 6 per cent of the men and 2 per cent of the women among the Moslem population were literate in French. One fifth of the Moslem boys and one sixteenth of the Moslem girls of school age attended classes. Not more than 7,000 Moslems progressed beyond the level of primary school instruction.

The 1.2 million Europeans constitute virtually a replica of the French economy: 30 per cent are engaged as technicians or workers in industry; 24 per cent in administrative and intellectual professions; 12 per cent in agriculture; 11 per cent in commerce; and 9 per cent in personal services. The so-called *colons* (which in the strict sense of the term means European landowner) number about 20,000—one third of whom own less than 10 hectares (about 25 acres) of land and live in relative poverty. According to Germaine Tillion:

There are around 12,000 "real colons," of whom 300 are rich and a dozen excessively rich. . . . With their families the 12,000 colons constitute a population of around 45,000 persons. The other Europeans—well over a million human beings—are specialized workers, civil servants, employees, taxi-drivers, mechanics, station-masters, nurses, shopkeepers, businessmen, and taken together they represent probably over three-fourths of the economic infrastructure of a country which could not survive their loss.

The two communities in Algeria are mutually suspicious. Historically, each has developed a sense of innate superiority over the other: The Europeans considered the Moslems fit only for manual, domestic, and servile labor—and hence opposed any attempt to extend

to them educational facilities and political rights. The Moslems had
a strong attachment to their traditional Islamic way of life, which
reinforced their separateness from the French community. This has
produced pervasive and persistent racial tension.

The social structure of the Moslem community has been subjected
to severe strains as a consequence of French rule. Over a million
Europeans (to which must be added 400,000 French troops in recent
years) are on the soil of Algeria. Contact between the two communities has made the Moslems painfully aware of their depressed living
conditions, without giving them the opportunity to achieve the
higher standard of living enjoyed by the Europeans. In a real sense,
the benefits of civilization (sanitary facilities, medical services, and
so forth) brought by the French have only served to worsen the
plight of the native population. The rate of population growth among
the Moslems, which had been kept down by the ravages of disease,
increased rapidly while agricultural resources remained the same.
The impact of modern civilization, therefore, has been to disrupt
the balance between population and resources.

The morale of the Moslem elite has been undermined by expo-
sure to European technology. Over 40 per cent of the adult male
Moslem population have been to France as members of the armed
forces or workers in French factories. Four hundred thousand are
employed in France, and their number is renewed constantly. Their
remittances to families in Algeria amount to about $90 million a year
(a certain percentage of which goes into the coffers of the anti-
French rebels). These men have seen and been influenced by a modern economy, whose achievements they would like to emulate. As
Germaine Tillion observes:

> One Algerian adult man out of two has lived in France and, in the
> background of the misery which he has before his eyes, he can evoke
> (and he does evoke) images of another world: happy children, well
> dressed, well washed, who nibble on bread and jam in coming back from
> school, busy housewives making their numerous daily purchases, and
> those warm and comfortable little kitchens that can be glimpsed
> through the windows. . . .

A small number of Moslems manage to become fully assimilated
in their new environment; they may even marry Frenchwomen and
settle down. The rest have lost the old traditions, are indifferent to
their former spiritual values, but are incapable of entering fully into
the modern world. Under these conditions, the *limited* extension of

Western techniques and education results mainly in dislocation of the native society.[2]

In all revolutionary situations two factors are found: the objective conditions of poverty and the growth of a conscious desire, translated into revolutionary action, to overcome it. Depressed conditions of life have been the accepted lot of the Moslems for many generations. The new factor today is the determination on the part of a political elite to work for radical change. Moslem university students, who constitute the major part of the political class, learn from their study of the Revolution and French history that violence may be necessary in order to achieve national independence and defend the liberty of a people. The principles of 1789 are accepted enthusiastically—and then applied to the present relations between France and Algeria. By November, 1954 the social tensions between the two communities had developed into a revolutionary situation, which had all the characteristics of twentieth century anticolonial movements. Thus, a small elite, exploiting the pent-up resentments of the underprivileged masses, spearheaded the struggle for national independence against the French.

The Independence Movement (1925-1947)

In 1925 a Moslem member of the Central Committee of the French Communist party, Hadj Abd el-Kaber, founded the *Étoile nord-africaine*. This organization, with headquarters in Paris, had as its objective the defense of "Moslem interests" in all of North Africa. It was soon taken over by a young Moslem Communist, Messali Hadj, who had served in the French Army, married a Frenchwoman, and attempted to reconcile the word of the Koran with the teachings of Karl Marx. The program of Messali Hadj at the time was one of militant Arab nationalism: complete independence of Algeria, withdrawal of the French Army, creation of an Algerian national army. The French authorities dissolved the *Étoile nordafricaine*, which continued, however, to function underground.

In 1930 an important event served to stimulate Algerian nationalism. To commemorate the centenary of "Algérie française," the French staged a colorful re-enactment of the 1830 invasion. Europeans, dressed in the costumes of the period, paraded their triumph

---

[2] The quotations are from Germaine Tillion, *L'Algérie en 1957* (Paris, 1957), pp. 16, 72. The figures cited on education and the economy in Algeria are from Tillion, pp. 68–69, and Raymond Aron, *L'Algérie et la République* (Paris, 1958), pp. 18–20.

before the descendants of the vanquished. Moslem sensibilities were further flouted by the holding of a Eucharist Congress in Carthage. Moslem students and intellectuals in Paris as well as in North Africa began to flock into the nationalist movement. In 1931, Ben Badis founded the *Association des Oulémas,* with the goal of reviving and modernizing Moslem culture. Schools were established throughout Algeria to teach the Koran and Arabic. Ben Badis' political program was simple: "Islam is my religion, Arabic is my language, Algeria is my country. . . . Independence is a natural right for every people of the world." Although Messali Hadj (who by this time had broken with the Communist party) continued to call for immediate and complete independence, most Moslem leaders, including Ben Badis, would have been content with a fuller measure of political and economic equality.

Ferhat Abbas, later the president of the Algerian revolutionary government, published the same year a collection of essays, *Le Jeune Algérien,* to "commemorate" in his own fashion the centenary of the French landings. The theme that runs throughout the essays is one of bitterness and resentment. Nonetheless, he cried out desperately his attachment to France, his desire to be recognized as fully French, even though a Moslem. "We are Moslems and we are French. We are natives and we are French. There are here, in Algeria, Europeans and natives, but there are only Frenchmen." He directed his criticism not against France, but at those who come between France and the natives, the real enemies of both Moslems and Frenchmen—the Spaniards, Italians, Maltese, and Jews! His goal was a union, a loyal understanding between Islam and France, between "our spiritual country and our intellectual country." Thus, in contrast to the *Oulémas,* Ferhat Abbas sought the future in an understanding, if not a cultural fusion, with France. In 1936 he reiterated his position in an eloquent passage that is frequently cited:

If I had discovered the *Algerian nation,* I would be a nationalist and I would not blush as if it were a crime. . . . And yet I would not die for the *Algerian Fatherland* because that Fatherland does not exist. I have not discovered it. I have interrogated history, I have interrogated the living and the dead; I have visited the cemeteries: no one spoke to me of it. . . . We have dispersed once and for all the clouds and chimeras in order to link definitively our future with that of France.[3]

---

[3] See Ferhat Abbas, *Le Jeune Algérien* (Paris, 1931), pp. 24, 116, 138. The passage on the Algerian nation is cited by Ch.-André Julien, *L'Afrique du Nord en*

The French authorities during this period made a few concessions to the native population: Moslem municipal councilors were permitted to participate in the election of mayors, and the right to vote was given to a small number of Moslems who had served in the French armed forces or who owned property, on condition that they abandon their personal status. Even these minor reforms aroused the bitter opposition of the Europeans in Algeria, and yet were considered totally inadequate by the Moslems.

The most important political reform envisaged by the French toward increased political participation of the native population was the Blum-Violette Bill in 1937. The bill would have granted French citizenship and voting rights to Moslems who had given proof of a certain degree of education or loyalty. Full French citizenship, without even these conditions, had previously been conferred on the Jews in 1871 and other foreigners (Maltese, Spaniards, Italians, etc.) in 1889. Even such nationalist advocates as Ben Badis welcomed and accepted the Blum-Violette Bill as a progressive measure. However, the Europeans of Algeria manifested such violent hostility that the bill was withdrawn by the government. As a result most Moslem leaders concluded that the goal of assimilation was unrealizable. Ben Badis called continually thereafter for the creation of an Algerian nation.

Messali Hadj, meanwhile, had attempted unsuccessfully to revive the *Étoile nord-africaine*. In 1935 he was jailed for encouraging military desertions. During the Popular Front, he returned to France (after a period in hiding) and was permitted to campaign openly for the nationalist cause. Messali then decided to devote his efforts to Algeria rather than all of North Africa. In March, 1937, he founded the *Parti du Peuple Algérien*. Although he was imprisoned, the PPA continued to function. A year later Ferhat Abbas set up the more moderate *Union Populaire Algérienne*. The PPA won some impressive victories in local elections, but was dissolved soon after war broke out.

The events of World War II provided a sudden stimulus to the movement for Arab nationalism. The French, especially the Gaullists, were almost compelled to promise equality to the Moslems in order to secure their cooperation in the war effort. In addition, the ideals

marche (Paris, 1952), pp. 110–11. The early development of the independence movement is treated in detail by Charles-Henri Favrod, *La Révolution algérienne* (Paris, 1959), pp. 66–71.

of national self-determination were espoused by the Western democracies, and Moslem leaders did not hesitate to evoke them.
French authority was severely shaken by the defeat of 1940—and
by the arrival in 1942 of American troops whose wealth of war
matériel made a strong impression on the local population. As a
result of the defeat by Germany and the Anglo-American presence,
the French could no longer enjoy the awe of the Moslems.

In December, 1942, General Giraud and Admiral Darlan asked
Moslem leaders to support the war effort. Ferhat Abbas seized the
occasion to present a petition, *Message aux autorités françaises*,
calling for a new statute in Algeria that would bring an end to racial
and religious distinctions. There was no response whatsoever on the
part of the French authorities. Within a few weeks, Ferhat Abbas
and twenty-seven other Moslem leaders signed the *Manifeste au
peuple algérien*—which proved to be the turning point in the history
of the Algerian independence movement. The Manifesto flatly repudiated the policy of assimilation, which was characterized as
merely a technique used by shrewd French politicians to maintain
the Moslem people in a condition of colonial servitude. In order to
obtain the "sincere support of Arab Algeria in the struggle for the
triumph of law and liberty," the Manifesto demanded that: the
colonial system be abolished; all peoples exercise the right of self-
determination; and that Algerian Moslems participate immediately
and effectively in the "government of their country." It also called
for the adoption of a special Algerian constitution in order to guarantee absolute equality for all inhabitants regardless of race or religion; a comprehensive agrarian reform to redistribute lands to
Algerians; the recognition of Arabic as an official language; freedom
of the press and of association; free and compulsory education for
children of both sexes; and separation of Church and State. In effect,
the Manifesto demanded a large measure of autonomy for Algeria
and full rights for the Moslems, but stopped short of the goal of independence. Ferhat Abbas later characterized the Manifesto as an
attempt to create "an Algerian State in which French and Moslems
would have equal civil rights, without questioning the *droit de
regard* [right of supervision] of France."[4]

The French at first accepted the Manifesto as a basis for discus-

---

[4] See Gabriel Esquer, *Histoire de l'Algérie, op. cit.*, pp. 61–65. Also Charles-
Henri Favrod, *La Révolution algérienne, op. cit.*, pp. 71–75, and Jacques Chevallier,
Nous, Algériens (Paris, 1958), p. 33.

sion. A proposal was submitted to General de Gaulle, suggesting the creation after the war of an Algerian state enjoying internal autonomy and universal suffrage without religious discrimination. General Catroux, the governor-general, categorically rejected the proposal, reaffirming the "French" character of Algeria. When Moslem representatives in retaliation refused to cooperate with French financial authorities, General Catroux proceeded to imprison a number of their leaders. The Moslem representatives hastened to assure Catroux and De Gaulle of their loyalty to France, and regretted the misunderstandings. The nationalist leaders were thereupon released, but the misunderstandings persisted.

In December, 1943, General de Gaulle, on behalf of the French Provisional government, hoping to stimulate recruitment of Moslems in the armed forces, promised to confer French citizenship on "Moslem élites," and to increase Moslem representation in Algerian deliberative assemblies. These measures were formally promulgated by an ordinance of March 7, 1944—characterized at the time by René Pleven, Commissioner for the Colonies, as "the most audaciously revolutionary act in a half-century of Franco-Algerian relations." It accorded all the rights of French citizenship, without loss of the personal status, to certain categories of Moslems: former officers, holders of University degrees, civil servants and employees of the State, and members of local assemblies. A law of October 4, 1946 added the veterans and high school graduates to the list. A system of two electoral colleges (three fifths of the total membership for French citizens—Europeans and Moslems with citizenship rights—and two fifths for the rest) was to be created.

The March, 1944 ordinance aroused strong opposition on the part of the European population since it might have led to infiltration of the first electoral college. Most Moslems also rejected the ordinance, since it provided for a political evolution based upon the discredited policy of assimilation. Its failure to please either side illuminated the political dilemma: autonomy (even with a link to France preserved) would have satisfied the Moslems, but was rejected by the Europeans; the maintenance of French rule was the demand of the Europeans; a policy of gradual integration and assimilation was repudiated by both groups. The reforms envisaged by the March, 1944 ordinance were never implemented.

In response to De Gaulle's gesture Ferhat Abbas founded the *Amis du Manifeste et de la Liberté*. The program of the "Friends" demanded the creation of an autonomous Algerian Republic with its own parliament, army, finances, and flag—but still federated with France. A parliament would be chosen by a single electoral college without distinction between Europeans and Moslems. By the end of the year it had 500,000 enrolled members.

Tension began to build up rapidly between the Europeans and the nationalists. In March, 1945 a Congress of the *Amis du Manifeste* recommended mass demonstrations for the day, which was obviously approaching, of victory over Germany. The police prepared to maintain order. On VE Day, May 8, the inevitable incidents led to riots, assassination of some Europeans, and eventually brutal police repression. According to official figures, there were 115 European and 1,500 Moslem victims. The nationalists claim that 45,000 Moslems were slaughtered. In spite of mass arrests carried out by the authorities, the leaders of the independence movement gradually rebuilt their organizations.

Upon his release from prison in March, 1946, Ferhat Abbas created a new political party as a successor to the "Friends of the Manifesto": the *Union Démocratique du Manifeste Algérien*. In June, 1946 UDMA elected eleven deputies to the French Constituent Assembly. Under the pressure of events, and particularly of the VE-Day incidents, Ferhat Abbas had become increasingly in favor of national independence, but nonetheless remained more moderate than the leaders of the *Parti du Peuple Algérien*. UDMA called for neither assimilation nor separation, but rather for the gradual development of a new Algerian democracy, "guided by the great French democracy." The goal was elimination of the colonial system, the abandonment on the part of the Europeans of racism, and the modernization of the Moslem religion. "Moslem nationalism is an anachronism. It is not necessary for men of the same country to be of the same religion. A Jewish or Christian Algerian must be the brother of a Moslem Algerian." [5] So, despite the bitter feeling engendered by the events of May, 1945, there were still reasonable leaders among the Moslems. It was an appropriate moment to make an effort for the reconciliation of the two communities. In August, 1947, the French Parliament began to debate a bill whose purpose was to

---

[5] Excerpts from the UDMA platform are in Charles-Henri Favrod, *op. cit.*, pp. 77–78. On the uprising of May 6, 1945, see *ibid.*, pp. 74–76, and Jeanson, *L'Algérie hors la loi, op. cit.*, p. 71. On the 1944 ordinance, Ivo Rens, *L'Assemblée algérienne* (Paris, 1957), pp. 72–75. For the wartime period and the Manifesto to the Algerian People: Esquer, *Histoire de l'Algérie, op. cit.*, pp. 79–86.

elaborate a new status and establish new political institutions for Algeria.

The Postwar "Settlement"

Since the conquest of Algeria the French have oscillated between two policies. One was to consider the territory a natural extension of the Metropolis, directly governed by central administrative agencies, and to which all laws made by Parliament were applicable. The second was to organize Algeria as a distinct territorial collectivity. In 1848 a decision was made in favor of central administrative control and assimilation. After some second thoughts under the Second Empire, the policy of assimilation was reaffirmed. A decree of October 24, 1870 organized Algeria into three departments of the French Republic. But once again it was found that the automatic application of French laws to Algeria was unsatisfactory, and a reaction set in against the policy of assimilation. The tendency since the turn of the century, and until the events of May, 1958, has been to take account of the "original personality" of Algeria and provide for a degree of administrative decentralization. The chief difficulty related to Moslem representation and the precise method of securing an "equitable" representation of the two communities.

Until the Second World War, all persons of French nationality in Algeria were either citizens (subject to French private law) or noncitizens (enjoying a personal status, that is, subject to Moslem law and religion). As has been seen, this division of the two communities was modified by the March, 1944 ordinance according citizenship (and voting rights) to certain categories of Moslems without at the same time requiring them to relinquish their "personal status." This entailed the existence of two groups and two electoral colleges: Europeans *and* "assimilated" Moslems to whom full citizenship had been granted, and Moslems on whom such rights had not been conferred. The creation of an Algerian Assembly representing both colleges was envisaged.

During the debate in the National Assembly, spokesmen for the Europeans in Algeria insisted on the creation of two *equal* and *homogeneous* colleges (one for French and another for all Moslems), which would have required elimination of all Moslems from the first college. René Pleven put the case for the Europeans bluntly: "We firmly believe that there is no social peace possible in Algeria without the double college, a double college which remains such as it is, and does not become one day a single college." That is, if Moslems were permitted to enter the first college by virtue of a continuing extension of citizenship rights, the parity (and, in fact, supremacy) enjoyed by the Europeans would be upset or destroyed.

A Moslem deputy seized the occasion offered by the debate to denounce efforts being made to spread Christianity in Algeria. When Rightist deputies interrupted, M. Boukadoum cried out: "Don't forget that I am Algerian before everything else!"

ON SEVERAL RIGHTIST BENCHES: You are French before everything else.
M. BOUKADOUM. I am an Algerian Moslem before everything else.
M. BENTAIEB. Don't speak of religion!
M. MUSMEAUX. If you consider Algerian Moslems as Frenchmen, then give them all the rights of Frenchmen.
M. LOUVEL. Let them first say that they are French! [6]

This barren dialogue between Moslem and French deputies underlined the complexity of the problem confronting the National Assembly.

The Socialist prime minister, Paul Ramadier, was faced with the difficult problem of holding together his majority on the Algerian issue. Ever since the departure of the Communist ministers in May, maintenance of his cabinet in office depended on the unity of Socialists, MRP, and Moderates. This coalition threatened to break up over Algeria. The Socialists, supported by the Communists and Moslem deputies, favored a large measure of Algerian autonomy, while the MRP and Moderates insisted on guarantees for the rights of the Europeans in Algeria. The prime minister offered assurances that the government would insist on giving the Europeans a veto in the envisaged Algerian Assembly. On August 18, General de Gaulle issued a press statement on the Algerian question, which strengthened the hand of the Center and Right. In order to maintain French sovereignty in Algeria, De Gaulle recommended that the first college be homogeneous (that is, all the Moslems who had been enrolled as a consequence of his ordinance of March, 1944 should be transferred back to the second college). The essential problems of Algeria, said De Gaulle, are economic, social, and cultural—not po-

---

[6] *Journal Officiel, Assemblée Nationale,* August 20, 1947, p. 4457. See also the remarks of General Aumeran, *ibid.,* August 19, 1947, p. 4422. The best historical summary of the legal status of Algeria is in Ivo Rens, *L'Assemblée algérienne, op. cit.,* pp. 9–11. The René Pleven quotation is from *ibid.,* p. 76.

litical. "Sovereignty of France: that means we must not permit the fact that Algeria is of our domain to be questioned under any form, neither from within nor from without."

Ramadier managed to work out a compromise without alienating his own party. But when Algeria was defined to be a "group of departments," the Moslem deputies withdrew in protest and refused to participate in the debate or vote. All Moslems already registered in the first college were permitted to remain there—with the exception of high school graduates (who had been admitted earlier). The final vote on September 2 was by the sizable majority of 325 to 86.

The new law, known as the "Algerian Statute," promulgated on September 20, 1947, contained the traditional formula that: "Algeria constitutes a group of departments endowed with civil personality and financial autonomy," but added the phrase, "and a particular organization." It established a governor-general, a central administration under his direction, a council of government, and a representative Assembly—making Algeria quite different from any other "group of departments" in the French Republic. Article 2 of the Statute provided that: "Effective equality is proclaimed among all French citizens. All French nationals in the departments of Algeria enjoy the rights which inhere in the quality of French citizenship and are subject to the same obligations, without regard to distinctions of origin, race, language or religion." After stressing that this "effective equality" applies particularly to political rights, the Statute (Articles 30 and 31) proceeded to establish an Algerian Assembly consisting of two separate colleges, each with sixty deputies, and each representing vastly *unequal* portions of the population (one million Europeans compared to nine million Moslems).

However, inasmuch as a certain number of Moslems were permitted to remain in the first college (63,000 Moslems out of a total of 532,000 registered), there was a possibility that Moslem representatives in the first college would join the solid bloc of Moslem deputies in the second college, and be in a position to outvote the Europeans. As a safety device Article 39 provided that, at the request of either the governor-general, the finance committee, or one fourth of the members of the Assembly, votes shall be made by a two-thirds majority of all members—unless there is a simple majority in *each* of the colleges. The Europeans were thus given a built-in veto power over the decisions of the Assembly.

The Statute also proclaimed a number of reforms long demanded by Moslem leaders, including: abolition of the *communes mixtes* (communes with a majority of natives, but administered by an agent of the governor-general), the recognition of Arabic as an official language and the teaching of Arabic at all levels of the educational system, the same separation of Church and State for the Moslem religion as for all others, the extension of suffrage to Moslem women, and abolition of military government in some of the territories. However, these measures were to become effective only by a vote of the Algerian Assembly—in which the Europeans had a veto. In fact, none of these reforms was ever adopted.

The Statute of 1947 was designed to please the party groups in the National Assembly, not the communities for whom it was intended. As already mentioned, none of the Moslem deputies in the National Assembly, not even those elected with administration support, took any part in the vote. The reaction of the Europeans was as hostile as that of the Moslems. One of their spokesmen, Boyer-Banse, was so enraged that he addressed a letter to the Minister of the Interior (whom he termed the Minister of Foreign Affairs), containing a sarcastic threat: "If France, by abandoning us, were to dishonor herself, we would be reduced to bringing our case before the United Nations as an abandoned people."[7]

The Europeans had received two safeguards in the Statute of 1947: the double college, and the two-thirds vote in the Algerian Assembly. However, three safeguards are obviously better than two, so they proceeded to arrange elections within the second college in such a way as to make sure of the docility of the Moslem representatives. According to the Statute, the 120 members of the Assembly were to be elected, one third at a time, every three years. The first elections took place in April, 1948, under the direction of Governor-General Marcel-Edouard Naegelen, a Socialist. Naegelen, who viewed Moslem nationalism as if it were a kind of perverted pro-German Alsatian autonomy movement, determined to preserve the integrity of the French Republic at all costs. He made it clear that democratic liberties were to be enjoyed only by democrats, and

---

[7] The Boyer-Banse statement is cited by Ch.-André Julien, *L'Afrique du Nord en marche, op. cit.,* p. 321. For a summary of parliamentary negotiations over the 1947 Statute, and the text of General de Gaulle's press statement, *cf. Année Politique, 1947,* pp. 148–52, 359–60. For the text of the Statute, and commentary: Ivo Rens, *L'Assemblée algérienne, op. cit.,* pp. 262–75; Charles-Henri Favrod, *La Révolution algérienne, op. cit.,* pp. 79–80; and Esquer, *Histoire de l'Algérie, op. cit.,* pp. 85–86.

that terrorists could expect no quarter. Prefects and subprefects were instructed to find "suitable" candidates, and get them elected.

The results would have put even Tammany Hall to shame. Out of the sixty Moslem deputies in the second college, forty-three were elected as "Independents" with administration support, as opposed to only nine MTLD and eight UDMA. Thirty-two Moslem nationalist candidates were arrested (virtually all later became leaders of the FLN), and their meetings prohibited. Armed forces were deployed on election day, ballot boxes were stuffed, voters intimidated, and newspapers seized. An MRP deputy, Jacques Fonlupt-Espéraber, who witnessed these fraudulent proceedings, wrote to the Minister of the Interior in 1949: "It is not the voters who have chosen the elected officials; they have rather been *designated* by the *administration.*"

In February, 1951, the second election for the Algerian Assembly was boycotted by the MTLD (which thereby gave up its nine seats), while the UDMA lost one of its seats. It was estimated that of the sixty members of the second college, only seven or eight Moslems were in the opposition. All the others represented the administration, and only a dozen of these had a personal following of any sort. That is, two thirds of the Moslem deputies were nothing more than creatures of the administration. Among the interesting results of this election: at Port-Gueydon, out of 23,677 voters registered in the second electoral college, 23,671 voted—giving 23,645 votes to the administration candidates, and nine votes to a Communist. The fraud during the legislative elections of June 17, 1951 for the French National Assembly was equally extensive. Eighty per cent of registered Moslems were declared to have voted. In Algiers, where fraud is relatively difficult, an official administrative list received 42 votes out of a total of 7,233. But in the "mixed commune" of Chélif the official list received 10,225 out of 12,166. In one district of Djelfma, candidates of the MTLD, UDMA, and Communist parties failed to receive a single vote, while the official list received 800 votes—or 300 more than the 500 registered voters. All requests to the *Conseil d'État* to invalidate elections that took place under such conditions were rejected. Similar pressure was applied by the administration during the third, and last, election for the Algerian Assembly in February, 1954. "In Algeria," concludes Charles-André Julien, "electoral fraud is an institution of the State considered legitimate in order to defend the cause of French sovereignty."

Fonlupt-Espéraber pointed out, at the tribune of the National Assembly, that the "prefabrication" of successful candidates was conducted without discernment or intelligence. It would have been superior tactics, he respectfully suggested, even if not superior morality, to manufacture 53 per cent majorities instead of the usual 98 or 99 per cent. He observed that genuine elections had never taken place in Algeria:

We have brought into this so-called Algerian Assembly sixty Moslems with or without *burnous* [cloaks] * who, for the most part have been chosen by the administration, not always from among the best, and over whom the members of the first college exercise such authority and pressure that the administration always has some fifty votes in reserve.

No one, he concluded, has ever dared claim that these men represent the Moslem population of Algeria.

The *colons* and the administration were so pleased with their discovery that rigged elections afforded a kind of "democratic" justification of their political predominance, they failed to appreciate the disastrous long-term consequences. The Moslems lost all hope of realizing their goals by parliamentary means. "The French Republic has cheated," asserted an UDMA leader. "It has duped us." The Moslem masses were literally thrust out of the legal political system and into the ways of violence. The rebel leaders (many of whom had presented themselves as candidates during the elections of 1948, only to find themselves arrested) were so embittered, they rejected thereafter all offers from the French promising "free elections." In 1956 Ferhat Abbas, in a reply to Guy Mollet's call for a cease-fire to be followed by free elections, remarked plaintively: "The free elections that are intentionally proposed for us to reject, would be elections prepared by the ultras, with their prefects, their mayors, their judges, their police commissioners, and four hundred thousand troops to run them." The *colons* gained a temporary tactical advantage but lost a precious opportunity of winning the confidence of the Moslem elites.[8]

The record of the Algerian Assembly shows lamentably meager

---

* That is, assimilated or not.

[8] The citations by Fonlupt-Espéraber are in: Ivo Rens, *op. cit.*, p. 95; J.O., *Assemblée Nationale*, July 29, 1955, p. 4518 and October 11, 1955, p. 5024. Ferhat Abbas' remarks on free elections are quoted by Charles-Henri Favrod, *op. cit.*, p. 204. The electoral frauds in Algeria are treated in Ch.-André Julien, *L'Afrique du Nord en marche, op. cit.*, pp. 326–34; Charles-Henri Favrod, *op. cit.*, pp. 80–82, 87, 148–49; and Ivo Rens, *op. cit.*, pp. 92–107.

accomplishments. The Assembly elected in April, 1948 consisted of the following members: in the first college—40 Algerian Union and RPF, 13 Independents, 2 Radical Socialists, 4 Socialists, and 1 Communist; in the second college (elected under conditions already described)—43 "Independents" (those supported by the administration, and known popularly as "yes-men"—*beni-oui-ouis*), 9 MTLD, 7 UDMA, and 1 Socialist. On April 22, 1948 the Algerian Assembly held its first meeting. Governor-General Naegelen addressed the members on the historic importance of this Assembly, the first to be elected in Algeria on the basis of "universal suffrage." As is traditional in French parliamentary practice, the senior member ("doyen d'âge") called upon the four youngest members (two from each college) to act as secretaries. However, the youngest Moslem deputy had in fact just been imprisoned for "remarks injurious to French sovereignty." Exclaimed the next youngest Moslem, M. Ferrouki: "The position for which you have designated me belongs rightfully to one of my colleagues, M. Demaghlatrouss, who has just been arrested, scarcely half-an-hour ago, at the entrance to this Assembly!" Whereupon, all the MTLD deputies left the hall in protest. Ferhat Abbas then was prevented from reading a statement by the presiding officer and all the UDMA deputies withdrew. Tension between nationalists and Europeans, which flared up in symbolic fashion the very first day on which the Algerian Assembly met, was a persistent feature of its deliberations.

The Assembly concerned itself almost entirely with budget economies, reduction of local taxes, and securing increased financial aid from the Metropolis. The outbreak of the rebellion led to the disruption and finally to the demise of the Assembly. When members of the first college lambasted the Mendès-France cabinet for its policy of "abandon," representatives of the government were forbidden to reply on the grounds that "politics" was irrelevant to the debate.

On January 20, 1955, about forty members of the second college, meeting separately, issued a declaration protesting against arbitrary arrests. They also demanded "integration" of Algeria with France. One month later the new governor-general, Jacques Soustelle, proclaimed that the official policy of the government was now "integration," and called upon the Assembly to approve a number of reforms in this sense. The day before the Assembly's scheduled meeting a caucus of sixty-one Moslem parliamentarians, including forty members of the second college, rejected integration as defined by Soustelle, and decided to boycott the Algerian Assembly after making the following declaration:

The immense majority of the population is presently won over to the Algerian national idea. Faithful interpreters of their will, the undersigned elected officials believe it their duty to orient their action towards the realization of this aspiration.

Even the Moslems chosen by the administration were no longer dependable. The governor-general thereupon postponed the date for the meeting of the Assembly, on the ground that many of its members had been subject to "constraints and pressures." Subsequently the French government cancelled the legislative elections in Algeria for the National Assembly scheduled for January 2, 1956. Finally, on April 12, 1956 the Algerian Assembly was dissolved. It was destined never to meet again.[9]

In retrospect, the Algerian Assembly was a failure. It never got around to adopting a single one of the reforms envisaged by the Statute of 1947, such as the abolition of the mixed communes, organization of instruction in Arabic, and extension of the suffrage to women. Above all, the Assembly never became a bridge between the representatives of the two communities. The double college system and the manipulation of elections by the administration discredited it in the eyes of the Moslems. The nationalists were denied representation in the Assembly, and the few that managed to get elected were prevented from voicing their point of view. The parliamentary experiment having proved inadequate, leadership of the nationalist movement devolved upon the advocates of force.

The Armed Insurrection

The revolutionary leaders had stepped up their political activity immediately after the repression of May, 1945. The *Parti du Peuple Algérien* created an underground apparatus, the paramilitary *Organisation de Sécurité* (O.S.), which was extended over the entire territory of Algeria. Ben Bella, who had received four citations while serving in the French Army as an adjutant, created an O.S. network in Oranie. In 1948 he was transferred to Algiers in order to supervise liaison between military units and political leadership. A year later he became chief of the entire O.S., devoting him-

---

[9] The painful incident of April 22, 1948 is recalled by Ivo Rens, *op. cit.*, pp. 114–15. The history of the Assembly is appraised by Rens, *ibid.*, pp. 225–44. See also, Charles-Henri Favrod, *op. cit.*, p. 80.

self exclusively thereafter to military preparations for the rebellion. The French prefects were aware of the existence of this military network by the spring of 1950. Ben Bella himself was arrested, but escaped to Cairo shortly thereafter.

Meanwhile, there were the inevitable disagreements among nationalists regarding the advisability of continuing to engage in parliamentary activity and the precise moment for unleashing an armed uprising. In March, 1954, after two years of debate, a Revolutionary Committee for Unity and Action (CRUA) was created in order to prepare for an immediate armed rebellion. When the fighting broke out on November 1, 1954, CRUA transformed itself into the Front of National Liberation (FLN) and issued a statement to the Algerian people on the aims of the rebellion.

The FLN proclaimed as its goal a "democratic and social Algerian State within the framework of Islamic principles," but respecting all fundamental liberties "without distinction of race or creed." It promised that upon the realization of Algerian independence all "honestly acquired" interests would be protected. Frenchmen in Algeria could either remain French and be treated as foreigners, or take Algerian nationality and enjoy the same rights and duties as the others. "The links between France and Algeria will be defined by an accord between the two powers on the basis of equality and respect for each other." The French government was then called upon to enter into negotiations for peaceful liquidation of the colonial system.

The O.S. emerged as a regular Army of National Liberation (ALN), whose troops are in uniform and subject to standard military discipline. Algeria is divided into six zones (Willayas), each of which is subdivided into military sectors. A representative of the FLN is attached to each command post. Soldiers and their wives receive small monthly stipends. In November, 1954 the armed forces numbered probably less than a thousand. In spite of French reprisals in the months that followed, new recruits flocked to the ALN. In August, 1955 a rebel offensive was launched in the area of Philippeville, resulting in assassinations and provoking a French counteroffensive. In 1956 Ferhat Abbas, abandoning his advocacy of moderation, fled Algeria to throw in his lot with the FLN. The only important Moslem leader to stay out was Messali Hadj, who founded a rival National Algerian Movement. By 1956 the ALN had expanded greatly. Its exact size is a matter of conjecture; estimates range from

7,000 to 130,000. There is probably a well-organized core of several thousand, along with numerous irregulars. General de Gaulle revealed in a press conference that in four years of war the French Army has killed over 77,000 rebels, while suffering 7,200 casualties of its own. If the ALN has lost that number of men and continues to hold down half a million French troops, its strength must be estimated liberally.[10]

On September 19, 1958 the FLN proclaimed the Provisional Government of the Algerian Republic, with Ferhat Abbas as president of the Council, and seventeen ministers (of whom five have been captured by the French). The principal headquarters of the government are at Tunis. Delegations are also maintained at cities throughout the Middle East, and in the principal capitals of the world. An administrative network functions throughout most of Algeria, and even in metropolitan France itself, assuring the FLN of revenue, recruits, and supplies. This government has been officially recognized by Tunisia, Morocco, Egypt, Communist China, and several communist countries of East Europe.

The conflict that has raged in Algeria since 1954 is essentially between two nationalisms. On the one side are the Algerian nationalists—inflamed and dedicated as only a people in search of a State can be. They equate French sovereignty with colonial inequality and speak of the French Army as the "army of occupation." On the other side are the French nationalists, profoundly convinced of their right to extend modern civilization over a backward country, whose people in turn should be grateful for this opportunity. Every argument produced by one side immediately provokes an emotional reaction by the other. If the Moslems claim the right to self-government, the French consider their language and culture directly in danger; when the French point to the economic progress accomplished under their direction, the Moslems rejoin that it has been made at their expense. In the crucible of war, each nationalism has become an armed vision.

---

[10] De Gaulle's statement on casualties may be found in *Le Monde*, October 25, 1958. See also the summary in *Le Monde*, November 1, 1958. The FLN's proclamation is reprinted in Charles-Henri Favrod, *op. cit.*, pp. 169–72. On the evolution of the armed insurrection: *ibid.*, pp. 83–86, 88–96, 105–18; Jacques Chevallier, *Nous, Algériens, op. cit.*, pp. 79–98; and "Algeria—Midsummer 1958," *World Today* (August, 1958), 326–38.

CHAPTER III

The Impact of Algeria

THE ALGERIAN UPRISING of November, 1954 was part of a pattern: The Moslem population of all North Africa was inflamed by nationalist sentiment, inspired by successful independence movements elsewhere in the world, and determined to oust the French. In neighboring Tunisia a national resistance army had been fighting the French in open warfare for over two years, while in Morocco terrorism broke out after the French deported the nationalist Sultan Mohammed V in favor of the more pliable Mohammed Ben Arafa in 1953. The French Army, weakened by the demands of the Indochina War, was unable to restore order in either Tunisia or Morocco. In July, 1954 Prime Minister Mendès-France determined to salvage what he could in the two protectorates by making a sweeping grant of autonomy, on condition that French interests were safeguarded. Accompanied by Marshall Juin, whose presence was calculated to win the confidence of French settlers and appease Rightist opinion in France, he flew to Tunisia in order to consult with the Bey. "The internal autonomy of the State of Tunisia," declared the French Prime Minister upon his arrival "is recognized and proclaimed without reserve by the French government."

A Tunisian government, formed by the nationalist Neo-Destour party, was invited to enter negotiations with the French government in September. Although a great many difficulties cropped up during the conferences, eventually the Tunisian nationalists ordered their armed bands to cease operations. The atmosphere in Morocco was also improved by the release of political prisoners and announcement of economic reforms. The French settlers immediately accused Mendès-France of "selling out," but were unable to find enough

45

allies in the Assembly to block the new policy. However, French nationalists drew a hard-and-fast line at Algeria. Morocco and Tunisia were technically "protectorates," while Algeria was juridically part of the French Republic. French nationalists might begrudgingly admit the legal possibility of dealing with a Tunisian government, but denied that the Republic could negotiate diplomatically with its own citizens (that is, the Algerian Moslems). French political leaders determined to "integrate" Algeria with France rather than follow the precedents established in negotiations with the Tunisians and Moroccans.

The Integration Debate

Integration, for the ultras of Algeria, meant simply the elimination of all distinctions and barriers between France and Algeria. The term was also used by elements of the army, and others, to designate the granting of complete equality of rights to Moslems in Algeria. The policy gradually worked out by the National Assembly in a series of *lois-cadres* (framework laws) contained features of both viewpoints. An attempt was made to devise an institutional structure within which Moslems could participate increasingly in the government of Algeria along with the Europeans, but which at the same time would preserve French sovereignty there.

One curious proposal for integration on both levels was "personal federalism," proposed notably by Marc Lauriol, a professor of law at the University of Algiers, and since 1958 a deputy from Algeria. As the term indicates, he rejected the classical form of federalism based on division of powers between territorial entities. The problem in Algeria, according to Lauriol, is mutual respect and association of two communities who live in the same geographic area. He proposed the creation of a national Parliament consisting of two sections: a metropolitan section of 600 deputies, elected by all French citizens wherever they reside; and a Moslem section of 100 deputies elected by "Moslem Frenchmen" who maintain their personal status. The Moslem section would be exclusively sovereign for all matters concerning Moslem law; both sections would deliberate jointly on matters involving France and Algeria; all other matters would be left to the metropolitan section.[1] This ingenious proposal would clearly have protected the interests of the Europeans, but had

---

[1] Marc Lauriol, *Le fédéralisme et l'Algérie* (Paris, 1957), *passim*.

no appeal to the Moslems. The degree of autonomy to be enjoyed by them would have been subjected to the overriding power of the French.

The leading interpretation of integration was that developed by Jacques Soustelle on the basis of his experience as governor-general of Algeria in 1955. Soustelle rejected federalism since, under the conditions then prevailing, it would have led directly to "secession." Above all, he was firmly opposed to the creation of an autonomous Algerian Assembly with its seat at Algiers. Such an Assembly would simply and inevitably proclaim the separation of France and Algeria. For this reason, as governor-general he recommended the liquidation of all embryonic elements of an Algerian state that had been brought into being by the 1947 statute.

The integration advocated by Soustelle recognized the "originality" of Algeria as a province of France. In the economic and social domain, it meant the complete fusion of Algeria's economy, industry, and currency with that of France. But the essential element of integration is political: that all citizens of Algeria, Europeans and Moslems alike, have equal rights and duties—accompanied by a certain amount of administrative autonomy on a local level. "Between all the French of Algeria, whatever might be their ethnic origin, whatever their creed, in the same way as between them and their fellow citizens in France, there must reign equality of rights and of duties for all—from Dunkerque to Tamanrasset." The supreme decisions for Algeria must be made by the Parliament and executive of France, in which all Algerians are fairly represented. "As for the sovereignty of the whole, it suffices, to be equitable, that Algeria has its share in Parliament, by the same right as any other province represented in the Assemblies, in proportion to its population." In other words, instead of one million Europeans confronting a permanent majority of nine million Moslems in Algeria, nine million Moslems would face a majority of forty-four million Frenchmen.

Integration precipitated a bitter controversy in the country. One of Soustelle's most eloquent critics, Raymond Aron, warned that the application of the principles of integration would lead inevitably to a catastrophe, in view of the differences between the population of France and North Africa. Economically, he argued, integration would require huge sacrifices on the part of the French people, including a sharp reduction in their standard of living; politically, it would bring an intransigent bloc of Moslem deputies into the National Assembly.[2] However, the country as a whole was not prepared to abandon one million compatriots on the other side of the Mediterranean. Objective consideration of the problem was ruled out by the identification of the French presence in Algeria with the cause of French nationalism.

The Breakdown of Political Balance

The cabinet crisis has been sometimes described as a normal, even indispensable feature of the French political system. It has often been pointed out that the Republic inherited from both the Old Regime and Bonaparte an efficient, highly centralized civil service; in order to prevent the utilization of the vast power of the bureaucracy for partisan purposes, the National Assembly must impose continuing responsibility upon the political heads of the executive. At the same time, factional groups that would ordinarily compromise their differences within one major party in the United States and Britain, work together as separate political parties in a cabinet coalition. Majorities in the Assembly shift according to the issues; the cabinet crisis becomes then a technique of adjustment enabling the Assembly to deal with *ad hoc* problems. In normal times the French parliamentary system works better than is realized by most of its critics.

But after the outbreak of the Algerian rebellion, the relations among the parties and between Assembly and government became increasingly embittered. Between November, 1954 and May, 1958 five cabinets lost the confidence of the National Assembly—Mendès-France in February, 1955, Edgar Faure in December, 1955, Guy Mollet in May, 1957, Bourgès-Maunoury in September, 1957, and Félix Gaillard in April, 1958. Instead of enabling a new majority to work out a new policy, each crisis made it more difficult for coalitions to be formed on the basis of a specific program. The balance of political forces and of the classic French parliamentary system broke down completely over the Algerian issue.

---

[2] Jacques Soustelle's position on integration is defined in his *Aimée et Souffrante Algérie* (Paris, 1956), pp. 36–37, 92–93, 161, 207, 242–46. For the exchange of views between Aron and Soustelle, *cf.* Raymond Aron, *L'Algérie et la République, op. cit.,* pp. 14–39, and Jacques Soustelle, *Le drame algérien et la décadence française, Résponse à Raymond Aron* (Paris, 1957), pp. 26–27. See also Alfred Fabre-Luce, *Demain en Algérie* (Paris, 1958), pp. 32–33.

The first crisis—stemming from a vote of no confidence in the Mendès-France government—demonstrated that the Assembly was hostile to any policy that smacked of "negotiations" with the rebels. Mendès himself had affirmed his intention to undertake a "limited" repression of the rebellion, reminding the Assembly that the settlement in Indochina alone made possible the transfer of troops to Algeria. One of the champions of the Europeans in Algeria, René Mayer (Radical deputy from Constantine) at the time even congratulated the government on the rapidity with which it had taken measures to protect the population. Nonetheless, certain elements of the governing coalition—in particular Radicals and Social Republicans—were uneasy over the implications of the talks with Tunisia. When a full-scale debate on North African policy took place on February 2, the Independents and nationalists accused the government of provoking trouble in Algeria by its weakness in Tunisia. Exclaimed General Aumeran, a spokesman for the Right: "The arrival in power of Mendès-France, his action in Tunisia, his declarations and those of the Minister of the Interior have unloosed in the three departments of Algeria a terrorist movement of unprecedented magnitude." Enough Radicals and former Gaullists joined with the Independents, MRP, and Communists to refuse confidence to Mendès-France by a vote of 319 against, 273 for, and 22 abstentions.

Theoretically, the Rightist critics should have been given the opportunity to form a government; in fact, they did not have the votes. The crisis was resolved by Edgar Faure, who approved the North African policies of his predecessor, yet had the confidence of the moderates and the Right on economic affairs. Obtaining the support of the Radicals, MRP, Independents, and Gaullists, Faure was invested by a vote of 369 to 210 (Communists and Socialists). Mendès-France's program of conciliation and reforms was continued, but with a different parliamentary base: The Socialists went into the opposition, and their place was taken by the MRP, Independents, and Gaullists. The crisis followed the usual pattern of minor adjustments within the Assembly; one Radical was substituted for another as prime minister, and he continued the same policy with only slight modifications as a concession to the Right. Indeed, the Faure government received comfortable majorities on Algeria, eventually going down to defeat over the unrelated question of electoral reform. But the Algerian problem was not resolved in the

interim, and greatly complicated the task of the party leaders in all
subsequent negotiations for the formation of a cabinet.[3]

In the campaign that followed the dissolution of the Assembly in
December, 1955, the Algerian issue figured prominently. A "Republican
Front" electoral alliance was formed by the Mendésist Radicals,
the Socialists, the UDSR, and a few Gaullists. Mendès called
determinedly for an end to the war in Algeria by negotiations, and
demanded that the "monstrous feudal interests be put in their place
by an assertion of the national will." Speaking at Marseilles, he outlined a program to "save the French presence in Algeria": genuinely
free and strictly controlled elections, and promulgation of reforms.
Guy Mollet also spoke about the necessity of bringing to an end
"this cruel, imbecillic war."

In the Assembly that emerged from the elections of January 2,
1956 no governing coalition was possible without the support of the
Socialists. Consequently, the President asked Guy Mollet to form a
government, which was mainly based on the Republican Front electoral alliance. Mollet's government received the confidence of the
Assembly by a vote of 420 (including Communists and MRP) to
71 (Poujadists and Independents), with 83 abstentions (mainly
Independents). In May disagreements which had been rumored
for some time broke out into the open. In a letter to Mollet, Mendès-
France criticized at length the policy of the government in Algeria.
He submitted his resignation as minister without portfolio, but requested that the other Radical ministers remain in the cabinet in
order to avert a crisis.

The defection of the Mendésist Radicals, unrest within the Socialist party itself regarding Algeria, and renewed hostility by the
Communists, coupled with the opposition of the Right to Tunisian
and Moroccan independence and new tax measures required by the
war, threatened to undermine Mollet's parliamentary position. But,
in the summer of 1956, following Egyptian seizure of the Suez Canal
and open declaration of support for the Algerian rebels, a wave of
nationalist fervor swept over France. A kind of "sacred union," excluding only Communists and Poujadists, came into being and sustained the Socialist cabinet for almost a year. Mollet was also helped

---

[3] On the Mendès-Faure crisis, *Année Politique, 1955,* pp. 10–22. An excellent
defense of the French parliamentary system is in Henry Bertram Hill, "The Reliability
of France in the European System," *Modern France* (ed. E. M. Earle) (Princeton,
1951), pp. 478–83.

by the weakness of his principal political opponents. The repression of the Hungarian Revolution by Russian troops caused profound resentment, and isolated the Communist party; the influence of Mendès-France, who had become one of Mollet's leading critics, was neutralized by the divisions of the Radical party; even the Poujadists were split by their leader's telephone instructions to "his" deputies ordering them to vote against the military action in Egypt.

It was not until March, 1957 that Mollet's parliamentary position began to deteriorate seriously. The Moderates and Right continued to support his Algerian policy, but were increasingly upset by his economic program (which was in large measure, of course, a consequence of the very war they themselves demanded). The government survived a general debate only by virtue of the abstention of the Independents. Mollet's majority crumbled, not directly on Algerian policy, but rather on the economic consequences of conducting the war. The Independents wanted Mollet to call a halt to his program of social legislation (including a proposal for extensive medical insurance, and also the envisaged reform of the educational system), and to stop colonizing the administration with members of his party. "All you expect from me, then," replied Guy Mollet, "is my Algerian policy and nothing else." The lines hardened. Roger Duchet wrote in *France Indépendante* that his friends could no longer encourage "errors and extravagance" in economic matters. Confidence was refused the government in May by a vote of 250 against (Communists and Poujadists, joined by 64 Independents and Peasants), 213 for (Socialists, MRP, Social Republicans, and some Radicals), with 70 abstentions (including 32 Independents and Peasants, and 28 Radicals).[4]

Despite the urgency of the Algerian problem, it is symptomatic that the last year of the Fourth Republic began with a typical kind of cabinet crisis, provoked by issues of economic policy. The positions of the parties during the period of President Coty's deliberations threw an interesting light on the nature of coalition government in France. Guy Mollet offered Socialist "toleration" of a government of the Right—which would then be required to adopt, under Socialist pressure, reforms in Algeria and a "social" policy if it wished to continue in office. For fifteen months the SFIO implemented a policy of the Right in order to avoid a crisis; they now hoped to turn the

---

[4] On the Mollet period: *Année Politique, 1956,* pp. 12–24, 41–49, 59–61, 78–82, 103–5, 112–19 and *Année Politique, 1957,* pp. 1–3, 29–32, 52–55.

tables by compelling the Independents to carry out their social and economic program. The Right, which thoroughly enjoyed its privileges as holder of a veto power, refused to accept the offer. Pierre Pflimlin, the leader of the MRP, was the first to attempt to form a government, but he withdrew because of the opposition of the Socialists and Radicals. Coty then called upon Bourgès-Maunoury, a Radical with long experience as minister. Bourgès-Maunoury, refusing to commit himself to a detailed economic program, talked vaguely of a "new statute" for Algeria. He gave satisfaction to the Right by maintaining Robert Lacoste in Algeria and appointing André Morice Minister of Defense; he pleased the Socialists by keeping Albert Gazier as Minister of Social Affairs and endorsing the Socialist program of social and educational reform. Confidence was finally voted on June 12 by an unimpressive majority.

There was no majority, however, in the Assembly for any policy but that of continuing the pacification in Algeria, which had to be paid for somehow by increased taxation. Little then was accomplished by the crisis of May, 1957, except to shift to a new cabinet the responsibility of resolving problems over which the Assembly appeared to be deadlocked.

The new government lasted only three months. It proved impossible to work out a compromise between the Left and the Right over the nature of Algerian "integration" with France. The Prime Minister convoked a Round Table Conference of all "national" political groups in a futile attempt to achieve agreement. Most patriotic organizations in Algeria urged their representatives and friends in the Assembly to vote against the government. On September 30 the cabinet was refused confidence by 279 to 253, with Independents and Radicals split on the vote.

During the month-long crisis that followed the overthrow of the Bourgès-Maunoury government, it became clear that there was no majority capable of formulating coherent policy on economic problems and Algeria at the same time. Antoine Pinay, leader of the Independents, agreed to form a ministry, only to be denied investiture because of Socialist opposition by a vote of 248 to 198. Coty turned to Guy Mollet, who this time formed a cabinet with the participation of MRP, Radicals, and Social Republicans. This offered the Independents an opportunity to take their vengeance by voting against Mollet, whose investiture was thus rejected by a vote of 290 to 227. Since neither Independents nor Socialists would per-

mit the other to govern, the only solution lay somewhere in the
Center. Coty called upon the young Radical Minister of Finance,
Félix Gaillard, who quickly secured the cooperation of Socialists,
MRP, and Independents, and on November 5 was invested by 337
to 173 (Communists and Poujadists), and 20 abstentions (Mendésist Radicals and some Independents). The only result of the crisis
was to bring the MRP and Independents into the new cabinet.
But, since the support of both groups had been necessary all along,
in fact little was changed. The inability of the National Assembly to
evolve a policy on Algeria was again underlined.[5]

The utter futility of the cabinet crisis was illustrated by Gaillard's
position on the proposal to devolve limited powers upon an Algerian
entity. His predecessor, now Minister of the Interior, had been overthrown specifically on this issue. Yet, in his speech of investiture,
Gaillard announced his intention to take up, submit to the Assembly, and stake the life of his government on that very proposal
—which was subsequently approved by the Assembly with only
minor modifications. A thirty-five day crisis had been provoked
over details of the future operation of a "federative" executive and
assembly that everyone knew was destined never to materialize. Perhaps the most important consequence of this particular crisis was
the nomination of a Gaullist, Jacques Chaban-Delmas, as Minister
of Defense. One of the young men brought into his cabinet was Léon
Delbecque, who later helped organize the revolt in Algeria.

The intensity and length of cabinet crises in the Third Legislature
was due mainly to the discord among the democratic parties, who
together disposed of only a narrow majority. The elections of January 2, 1956 produced an Assembly in which, out of 600 deputies,
about 200 were either Communist or Poujadist. Thus, the Assembly
included a strong body of deputies on which no government could
depend. Defection of a marginal group of forty to fifty deputies,
added to the Communist and Poujadist vote, could force a government out of office. Divisions over Algerian, social, economic, and
foreign policy problems rendered the formation of a majority coalition virtually impossible. The clash of Socialists and Independents,
particularly on economic problems, precipitated an over-all stalemate. Yet the Fourth Republic had survived stalemate before. "Immobilisme" had not been fatal before 1958 because problems had

---

[5] The Mollet-Bourgès and Bourgès-Gaillard crises are summarized in *Année
Politique, 1957*, pp. 54–65, 87–117.

somehow taken care of themselves without the active intervention of the State. But Algeria did not take care of itself. The rebellion gathered strength, the economy was burdened by the interminable war, and above all, half a million French troops were tied down in Algeria. The impotence of the regime aroused a feeling of national outrage (akin to the frustration of American opinion during the Korean War). The people became increasingly dissatisfied with their government, and more receptive to the propaganda of antiparliamentary movements.

Failure of Policy

The immediate reaction of the French government to the outbreak of fighting in Algeria was to counter with military measures. Jacques Soustelle, who had been appointed governor-general in Algeria by Mendès-France and continued to serve there under Edgar Faure, won official endorsement of his plan for capital investment, reforms, pacification, and "integration" as an alternative to both independence and assimilation. In fact, the Faure government had time only to declare a "state of emergency" enabling civil and military authorities to take exceptional security measures. The confusion of French policy was illuminated by announcement simultaneously of completely contradictory policies: gradual application of the 1947 statute; acceptance of Soustelle's program of integration (which involved repudiation of the 1947 statute); and consideration of a new charter for Algeria providing for greater autonomy! [6]

Serious attention was first devoted to the need for a political program in Algeria during the election campaign of December, 1955 and in negotiations for a cabinet in the first weeks of the new legislature's existence. While a Republican Front government was being formed in Paris, tensions continued to build up in Algeria. Moslem leaders petitioned the National Assembly to recognize the existence of an Algerian nationality, while European patriotic groups expressed their determination to fight Soustelle's plan for integration. The program of the leaders of the Republican Front, Guy Mollet and Mendès-France, was also anathema to them. Both men talked of genuinely free elections, to be held within a limited period (Mendès mentioned six months) for an Algerian Assembly with which negoti-

---

[6] On the Algerian policy of the Faure government: *Année Politique, 1955,* pp. 199–202, 205–10, 232–34, 275–78, 291–93.

ations could be conducted. In his speech of investiture before the National Assembly on January 31, Mollet stated his intention to proceed without undue delay to hold a "genuine popular consultation through free elections *in a single college.*" His program found no more support among the Moslems than it did with the Europeans of Algeria. Ferhat Abbas immediately declared that only the FLN (and not some future Algerian Assembly) was qualified to negotiate with France.

After his investiture, Mollet left Paris for a visit to Algiers. The European elements were whipped up by a violent campaign against the principle of a single college, and especially in opposition to the nomination of General Catroux as resident minister. A number of Poujadist deputies and nationalist leaders arrived in Algiers ahead of Mollet, and cooperated with local patriotic groups in manifesting against the person of the Prime Minister. When Mollet attempted to place a wreath before the Memorial to the Dead, he was attacked by the mob. The Prime Minister was profoundly shaken, and impressed by the passion of the crowd. He later declared in the Assembly: "This painful manifestation was however . . . the expression of highly respectable sentiments: devotion to France, anguish at being abandoned." [7] General Catroux resigned and was replaced by Robert Lacoste. Three years afterward Guy Mollet admitted that at the time he had underestimated the virulence and danger of the right-wing groups.

Upon his return to Paris, Mollet broadcast an appeal for a cease-fire, promising that "free and loyal" elections would follow three months after its acceptance. The policy of the government, which became known as the "triptyque," involved three distinct stages: cease-fire, elections, and negotiations. The cease-fire would lead to a surrender of arms by the rebels; the elections were to allow the Algerians to designate spokesmen with whom the French would negotiate (though in what sense was never made clear) regarding the future of Algeria. The FLN replied that French recognition of an Algerian government must precede a cease-fire, and that this Algerian government would thereupon organize the elections. The Socialist government was thus caught in a crossfire of criticism: The Europeans rejected outright the single college while the FLN refused to lay down its arms without being recognized by the French.

---

[7] *Année Politique, 1956,* pp. 22–29, 180–87.

In an effort to secure agreement in the Assembly and also appease international opinion, the Prime Minister several months later made an important "declaration of intent" regarding Algeria. The principles to guide the daily direction of Algerian affairs were: strict equality between all inhabitants of Algeria, coexistence of the communities and respect for their legitimate rights, and the shaping and delimitation of the "personality of Algeria" while maintaining links with France. Mollet, arguing that regional autonomy corresponded more closely to Algerian reality than a national state, insisted on the importance of allowing the "Algerian personality" to express itself on a local level. Above all, France would conserve the permanent power of *arbitration* between the two communities there so that neither one could exploit or oppress the other. The Europeans in Algeria again objected that Mollet's plan, especially the single college, would lead inevitably to their expulsion; the Moslems remained skeptical concerning the promise of a single college; and the FLN insisted on independence. Official policy was in an impasse: It had no influence on the course of events in Algeria, yet no majority existed in favor of any striking new initiative.[8]

Mollet's successor, Bourgès-Maunoury, was caught in the same crossfire between Left and Right, European nationalists and Moslem rebels. Following the precedent set by his predecessors, he promised to introduce a *loi-cadre* (framework law) permitting the progressive establishment of new institutions in Algeria first on a local, then a departmental, and finally on a regional basis. Each region would become a provincial political entity, eventually participating in an "Algerian whole." When elections would become possible, representatives of the population were to have the opportunity to discuss and amend the *loi-cadre*. This was the reform about which debate in the National Assembly revolved for the next eleven months. The cabinet itself was badly split over the nature and application of the principle of a single college, and the extent to which executive and legislative powers would be devolved upon Algeria.

The major points of the *loi-cadre* proposed by the government were: (1) A single electoral college, within which minorities would receive a minimum guaranteed representation—the electoral procedure to be used was not specified; (2) the French Republic would act as "permanent arbiter" between the two communities; (3) Alge-

---

[8] Mollet's Algerian policy is conveniently summarized in *Année Politique, 1956*, pp. 185–86, 210–12, 502–5, and *Année Politique, 1957*, pp. 211–14, 230–32.

ria would be divided into a number of territories endowed with administrative autonomy; (4) a "federative" Parliament would be created at Algiers, with jurisdiction over purely local affairs.

The reform had no chance whatsoever of winning over the Moslem population, yet the mere suggestion of a single college and a federative Parliament led to the defection of the Right and the overthrow of the cabinet. The Gaillard government's only contribution to a redefinition of Algerian policy was to add to this unrealistic proposal a few qualifications which would afford supplementary guarantees to the Europeans. The amended *loi-cadre* (referred to by the wits as the "loi-cadavre") was finally adopted by the National Assembly amid general indifference.[9]

Debate in the National Assembly was artificial and irrelevant, since proposals were designed to placate the political parties at home rather than come to grips with the Algerian problem itself. The Center governments could not agree on a program of genuine internal autonomy, nor on a policy of liberal reforms, nor on war without reforms. They staggered along, unable to repress the insurrection by force alone, equally unable to win over the Moslems with promises of improvements. Contradictions within the Assembly forced the system to a halt at a time when public opinion was swept by a wave of nationalism, and insistently demanded a firm lead.

The Gaillard government had neither the opportunity nor the will to work out a distinctive Algerian policy. It was thrown off balance almost immediately after taking office by a sudden worsening of Franco-Tunisian relations. Complicated negotiations had been in progress ever since Mendès-France's Carthage Declaration of July 31, 1954, and particularly since the protocol of March 20, 1956 recognizing Tunisia's independence. Conventions were to be drawn up by the two countries defining France's role in foreign and military policy, and guaranteeing the interests of French settlers.

Tunisia, in the view of the French military, had become a "privileged sanctuary" for the Algerian rebels. It was estimated that between 12,000 to 15,000 rebel troops were quartered or in training in Tunisia. Significant quantities of arms were flowing out to the rebels across the border. Robert Lacoste expressed a prevalent view in declaring that without these arms, "the affair would soon be over." He later stated that between December, 1957 and February, 1958

---

[9] On the *loi-cadre: Année Politique, 1957*, pp. 84–86, 90–93, 121–22, 239–42, 244–48, 256–59; and *Année Politique, 1958*, pp. 250–52.

the FLN received over 18,000 rifles, machine guns, mortars, and bazookas through Tunisia. On several occasions in the latter part of 1957, rebel bands sortied out of Tunisia for lightning raids on French positions, and were then pursued back into Tunisian territory by the French Army. Meanwhile, the French garrison in Tunisia of 15,000 men was virtually bottled up, unable to prevent arms shipment to the rebels or the training of the FLN army. French nationalists were infuriated by the indignities to which their country was being subjected by a former protectorate.

One of the pressing issues confronting the Gaillard government was whether to join with the United States and Great Britain in filling a Tunisian request for a thousand light arms. The Bourgès-Maunoury government had already refused to provide the arms, for fear that they might find their way into the rebel camp. The Tunisian president, Habib Bourguiba, thereupon threatened to accept arms and other aid from the countries of Eastern Europe. Under American and British pressure, the French government reconsidered its position, and finally announced on November 12 that it would furnish the arms, provided that the Tunisians guarantee they would never be turned over to the rebels and that no aid would be accepted from the Communist bloc. Bourguiba rejected these conditions as being incompatible with Tunisian sovereignty. The United States and Britain immediately shipped the rifles and machine guns over strong French protests. Gaillard declared before the National Assembly that the Allied decision was an unfriendly gesture and might destroy the Atlantic Alliance. Rightist leaders accused the government of weakness and subservience. The Independents in Gaillard's cabinet began to waver in their support of the Prime Minister.

In January another border incident aroused French nationalists. A rebel detachment ambushed a French patrol, killing fourteen men and taking five prisoners. It then retreated into the area around Sakhiet-Sidi-Youssef. Observers speculated that the FLN may have provoked the incident in order to disrupt Franco-Tunisian relations. Powerful voices in France and Algeria called out for stern measures to put Bourguiba in his place. Gaillard informed the National Assembly that "the attitude of the Tunisian government is inadmissible." Matters came to a head on February 8, when a French aerial squadron bombarded Sakhiet-Sidi-Youssef after several aircraft had previously been fired on by FLN units in the town. An international Red Cross team happened to be in the area at the time, and reported many civilian casualties. Bourguiba reacted by recalling his ambassador in Paris, forbidding French troops in Tunisia from leaving their bases, and demanding the total evacuation of all French forces. One of the most significant aspects of the crisis was the request of the Tunisian ambassador for an interview with General de Gaulle before leaving his post. He thought it his duty, he explained, "to meet with the man who incarnates the true conscience of France." The General listened to the grievances of the ambassador, and expressed his hope that Franco-Tunisian cooperation would not be compromised. Whatever may have been the military reasons for the attack on Sakhiet, the result was precisely what the French dreaded most: the internationalization of the North African problem. Bourguiba announced his decision to bring the affair before the Security Council of the United Nations.

In order to head off an embarrassing confrontation in the Council, the United States and Great Britain on February 17 offered their good offices to both France and Tunisia. Although the parties eagerly accepted the offer, the chances for success were slight. Gaillard wished to use the "good offices" to eliminate sources of friction between France and Tunisia—if possible, by securing international supervision of the frontier in order to cut off the flow of military supplies to the rebels. On the other hand, Bourguiba hoped that the United States and Britain would become directly involved in the Algerian situation, and might be able to impose a settlement. Numerous meetings between the American and British representatives (Robert Murphy and Harold Beeley) with Bourguiba and Gaillard resulted after a month in only limited agreement.

The good offices provoked an outburst of anti-British and anti-American feeling in France, and strengthened the militant patriotic groups. Right-wing deputy Le Pen exclaimed in the Assembly: "Of the two dangers which threaten us, the Soviet and the American, the second is the closest." The nationalists accused Gaillard of being a tool of the United States. "Where is French policy decided?" thundered Soustelle. "If it is in Washington, then what are we doing here . . . ?" Deputies from all sides of the Assembly denounced "internationalization" as an attempt by the United States to squeeze France out of North Africa for the benefit of the giant oil companies.

In vain did Gaillard try to reason with the Assembly, to warn against blaming foreigners for all of France's troubles:

> By a majority, you are going to refuse confidence and open a crisis: for how long? On what majority will a new government be able to count tomorrow? What will be the social, financial, economic consequences? And what will be the new policy of the new government?

But it was too late for counsels of moderation and reason. Gaillard and his government were refused confidence on their foreign policy, April 15, by 321 votes to 255 (77 Independents and Peasants out of 111, and 17 Social Republicans out of 20 joining the Communists, Poujadists, and followers of Mendès-France and Mitterand in opposition). The extremes once again had combined to defeat a government, to whose policies there was no real alternative in the Assembly. For the third time in less than a year the Independents had overthrown a government—in spite of their insistence on constitutional reforms to strengthen the executive! [10]

On April 26, the President turned to a leader of the Center-Left, M. René Pleven (UDSR), after Georges Bidault had been compelled to renounce. Pleven negotiated with the parties for an "Algerian Charter," and agreement on a program of economic austerity. The MRP and Radicals decided to enter the cabinet, but the Socialists pledged only their support, not their participation. Pleven proceeded with his plans, and on May 7 formed his cabinet. He chose André Morice, who had split the Radical party in 1956 and symbolized a "tough" line in Algeria, as Minister of Defense. The Radicals voted unanimously to withdraw their support for Pleven, who thereupon abandoned his attempt to form a cabinet. The overthrow of Gaillard, coupled with the failure of Bidault and Pleven, revealed that the Assembly would countenance neither a policy of "abandon," nor one of force, in Algeria. Signs multiplied that the Socialists, MRP, and Radicals were considering a more "liberal" approach to the Algerian problem.[11]

President Coty on May 8 designated the man who seemed most clearly to represent the spirit of the Assembly: Pierre Pflimlin. The MRP leader had recently advocated a political solution in Algeria, though he added that negotiations were possible only on the basis

---

[10] The course of Franco-Tunisian relations and the "good offices" are treated in *Année Politique, 1958*, pp. 16–19, 39–43, 245–50, 312–15, 327–32.

[11] On the negotiations leading to the designation of Pflimlin: *Année Politique, 1958*, pp. 44–56.

of a military situation favorable to France. The Independents agreed, by a narrow margin, to participate, along with the MRP, Radicals, and UDSR. Pflimlin proposed to present his government to the National Assembly on May 13. But across the Mediterranean preparations were made for a mass rally to protest his investiture.

CHAPTER IV

The Thirteenth of May

ALGERIA on the thirteenth of May presented all the characteristics of a revolutionary situation: a proliferation of conspiratorial groups which worked up the Algerian population to a fever pitch over the danger of being "abandoned"; a police force and militia in Algeria largely made up of elements of the very population that wished to overthrow the regime; an army profoundly demoralized by the task of crushing a rebellion in the absence of clearly defined political objectives; a large number of generals and officers who had entered into dissidence; and a Minister of National Defense who nourished the plot to destroy the Republic of which he was supposed to be the "defender." During the eventful day of May 13 an insurrection took place. Public buildings were occupied, and the forces of order—the army and police—fraternized with and then joined the rebels. Within twenty-four hours a revolutionary "Committee of Public Safety" was in control of the city of Algiers and most of Algeria.

A mood of restiveness if not treason had been rampant among the French of Algeria for several years. Conspiracy has been a characteristic element of Algerian politics since World War II when agents of Vichy, the Free French, the Allies, and the Axis swarmed in Algiers. After the nationalist rebellion broke out in 1954, a number of secret societies were formed by French activists, drawing frequently from the wartime conspiratorial cadres. The insurrectionist tendencies of the European population were thus channelled through a series of parallel organizations, which were united in their opposition to the regime but lacked any other clear-cut purpose. A second and distinct conspiratorial network was created by Gaullists, mainly in the Metropolis, who planned to use an uprising in Algeria as a means of bringing about General de Gaulle's return to power. The activists and the Gaullists were the spearhead of the "revolution." Other groups—in particular the veterans and certain elements of the military and police forces—were sympathetic and provided much-needed support at critical moments. In brief, the uprising of May 13 was prepared by the Gaullists and activists, facilitated by the psychological services of the army, accepted by the generals, and finally taken over by the Gaullists.

The Gaullist Network

Charles de Gaulle had been disappointed with politics as a result of his RPF experience. He withdrew into solitary pride and bitterness at Colombey-les-deux-Eglises, worked at his memoirs, received a few visitors from time to time. His political influence seemed to be on the decline after the breakup of the RPF in 1953. In a press conference on July 2, 1955, De Gaulle confirmed the general impression that he was retiring from politics. In a last phrase, however, he left his followers some hope that his ideas concerning reform of the State might yet be realized. "Without being able to foresee which factor or event will provoke a change of the regime, one can believe that the shock ('secousse') will come. This time it must not be the corollary of a catastrophe, but the signal of renovation." He terminated the press conference, which many thought was in the nature of a political testament by saying, "*Au revoir* . . . and perhaps for a long time."

In 1956, in order to take a well-deserved rest after his literary labors, he traveled throughout the French Union. Speaking in public for the first time in two years, he was accorded a warm welcome everywhere. Distinguished visitors, ambassadors, parliamentarians, top-grade civil servants began to make the pilgrimage to Colombey, or to confer with De Gaulle at his Paris headquarters, rue de Solférino. The old RPF leadership—Debré, Soustelle, Michelet, Frey —concluded that the General's return was possible. De Gaulle himself seemed little disposed to abandon his memoirs and solitude. In February, 1958, after the raid on Sakhiet in Tunisia, De Gaulle received Houphouet-Boigny (a leader of the Ivory Coast and a member of the cabinet), Robert Lacoste, and the Tunisian ambassador, all of whom seemed to believe that his intervention was necessary to arrest the deterioration in the relations between France and North Africa and the disintegration of the French Union. Each visi-

tor had his own view of De Gaulle's attitude. Some were convinced
that only De Gaulle could grant independence to Algeria; others,
that only he could maintain French sovereignty there. Men of the
Left began to think of him as the sole hope, men of the Right clung
to him as a barrier against the Left. The General received them all,
refused to be bound to any particular formula, kept a judicious
silence on key points, and waited serenely.

In 1957 two members of De Gaulle's personal *cabinet,* Olivier
Guichard and Jacques Foccart, began to establish contacts with
activists, dissident elements of the army, and others who were
plotting to overthrow the regime. They worked closely with Michel
Debré and Jacques Soustelle in order to produce the conditions
under which Charles de Gaulle would willingly return to power.[1]

De Gaulle's views, as expressed to many political personalities
who made the pilgrimage to Colombey in the period immediately
preceding the events of May, 1958, may be summarized as follows:

On the Fourth Republic. He categorically refused to accept any
responsible position in the existing regime. The Fourth Republic
could not resolve any of the important problems facing France;
it could neither wage war successfully nor negotiate peace fruit-
fully. Yet, in view of the general apathy of French opinion, the
regime could probably last a long time.

Recent Evolution of Opinion. However, there appeared to be a
general awakening of opinion recently. If a new political consciousness, due to the pressure of events and the "paralysis of the regime,"
were to express itself, he would "face his responsibilities and take in
hand the reins of the nation." He did not wish to express himself on
political questions because his views were always misinterpreted—
by the Right, which lacks the quality of generosity; by the Left,
which ignores the necessity of power. However, if it really became
necessary, he "would not refuse to make a declaration."

On Algeria. His views were ambiguous. He favored "generosity
and liberalism"—but not "capitulation"; the maintenance of the
French presence—but not a refusal to undertake negotiations. He
hoped that France would remain in Algeria "sufficiently" so that one

---

[1] In general, see Bromberger, *Les 13 complots du 13 mai* (Paris, 1959), chap. 1.
The summary of De Gaulle's views which follows is based on: Soustelle's letter to
Alain de Sérigny, reprinted in the latter's *La révolution du 13 mai* (Paris, 1959), pp.
8–9; Bromberger, *op. cit.,* pp. 25–26; and the record of an interview granted by General
de Gaulle to leaders of the *Comité d'Action des Associations Nationales d'Anciens
Combattants* (CANAC), kindly made available to the authors by that organization.

day she might renew her influence in North Africa. He was reserved on the question of integration because he doubted that the Moslems favored it. On the other hand, "pacification" should be waged energetically and be accompanied by a great social, educational, psychological, and political effort.

On the Possibility of Returning to Power. He was skeptical about the possibility of being asked to return to power. He was convinced that the political parties would unite against him. But he felt, nonetheless, that it was possible to act on French opinion by insisting on the need for France to recover her national "independence." He believed that an appeal to national sentiment could bring about the *psychological shock* which might permit the renovation of the institutions of the nation. In April he reluctantly admitted to Chaban-Delmas that he would take power if offered to him, but expressed doubt that the system would ever permit it.

Early in May the military attaché to the president of the Republic, General Ganeval, called De Gaulle's chief aide, Colonel de Bonneval, asking for a rendezvous. On behalf of President Coty he asked under what conditions De Gaulle would consider forming a government. The inquiry was kept secret, since there would have been a hostile reaction in Parliament if it were known that the president was even thinking of De Gaulle. A reply was given three days later. De Gaulle did not wish to be invested in the ordinary manner prescribed by the constitution and parliamentary practice. He insisted that his investiture must clearly signal the advent of a new regime. The president of the Republic was to write a formal letter requesting De Gaulle to form a government. None of the preliminary negotiations to form a cabinet would be required. De Gaulle would not present himself before the Assembly, and the investiture would be voted in his absence.

President Coty concluded that these conditions would not be accepted by the party leaders nor by the Parliament. Dismissing the De Gaulle possibility at that time, he continued his discussions with René Pleven and then Pierre Pflimlin. However, the exchange of views between Coty and De Gaulle was of crucial importance: It demonstrated to the General that the regime was far closer to the brink than he had previously been willing to believe, and it testified to the existence of a Gaullist alternative in the mind of the president of the Republic. It also strengthened the conviction of Delbecque, Soustelle, and other Gaullist militants that, in the event of an "appeal by the nation" (which they undertook to arrange), De Gaulle would not refuse to act.[2]

The Gaullists who sought to bring about the return of their chief were bound together in a network of personal relations. Their contacts were facilitated by common membership in the political organizations that remained in place after the collapse of the RPF (particularly the Social Republican party). The most important instrument of mass action available to the Gaullists was the Union for the Safety and the Resurrection of French Algeria—*Union pour le Salut et le Renouveau de l'Algérie française* (USRAF)—created by Jacques Soustelle in March, 1956 in order to "save French Algeria." USRAF was originally patronized by a number of important political personalities, including five former governor-generals of Algeria. The leadership consisted of a president (Soustelle), six vice-presidents (notably Georges Bidault, André Morice, and Alexis Thomas), and three councilors (including Léon Delbecque).

USRAF's stated goal was to modify the climate of opinion regarding Algeria. Soustelle proclaimed time and again that members of all parties were welcome, so long as they subscribed to the essential belief that French sovereignty must continue to be exercised over Algeria. As he declared before USRAF's first General Assembly in February, 1958:

> We are a League, that is to say a group of men who can have on all levels, political, philosophical, confessional, syndicalist, etc., the most diverse ideas, but who have joined together to act on one particular level and for a common program.

In fact, the Gaullists rapidly became the dominant political element of the organization.

USRAF was probably the most powerful and successful single pressure group in the history of the Fourth Republic. In 1956 it succeeded in coordinating and directing the activities of twenty-four veterans' groups for the cause of "French Algeria." In August, 1957 a link was established between USRAF (exercising political leadership) and the Veterans' Action Committee (which asserted that its two million members were behind the cause of French Al-

---

[2] The negotiations between Coty and De Gaulle were made public by Bromberger, *Les 13 complots du 13 mai, op. cit.*, pp. 11–27. The attitude of Algerian extremists was expressed in Alain de Sérigny's editorial, "Il faut en sortir," *Echo d'Alger*, May 11–12, 1958, where he invoked De Gaulle's name for the first time. See also Raymond Dronne, *La Révolution d'Alger* (Paris, 1958), p. 51, and Paul Gerin, *L'Algérie du 13 mai* (Paris, 1958), p. 82.

geria). USRAF conducted a vigorous public relations campaign, constantly applying pressure upon the state. It launched a program of "solidarity," linking cities and towns in Algeria and France; it proposed that full integration be tried in a pacified section of Algeria; and above all it held mass rallies, published brochures, and distributed literature. The official USRAF bimonthly organ, *La Vérité sur l'Algérie*, had a circulation of 25,000. Over a million USRAF posters were distributed throughout France, carrying such slogans as: "The loss of Algeria will be a new Sedan," "The loss of Algeria will be the loss of a job for one out of five French workers," and so forth.

USRAF also engaged in clandestine activities, exploring the possibility of creating a situation (the "psychological shock") that might bring about General de Gaulle's accession to power. In great secrecy underground Committees of Public Safety were set up throughout France and Algeria. In March, 1958 Alain de Sérigny secured Soustelle's consent to create an Algerian branch of USRAF. Although Algerian opinion was already "enlightened," De Sérigny later explained, it was necessary to introduce in Algeria a certain amount of "cohesion and pragmatism."[3]

The conspirators had a precious advantage in their plot against the regime: The Minister of National Defense, Jacques Chaban-Delmas, approved of their objective. A general in the Resistance at the age of 29, president of the Social Republican parliamentary group, and mayor of Bordeaux, he had stated as a condition for his participation in cabinets that he reserved complete freedom to campaign for the return of General de Gaulle. Chaban-Delmas organized a private network of young colonels to report on the state of morale in the army, and to disseminate his directives. The ministry which he headed became a nerve center for the plot to overthrow the regime.

The key man in the May revolt was USRAF's councilor, secretary-general of the Social Republican Federation in Nord, Léon Delbecque. Chaban-Delmas brought Delbecque into his cabinet to coordinate the psychological warfare program. For this purpose, Delbecque established an office in Algiers—which became the

---

[3] Alain de Sérigny, *La révolution du 13 mai, op. cit.*, p. 6. USRAF's central execu tive was formally elected at the first General Assembly, February, 1958. *Cf. La Vérité sur l'Algérie, passim*, and p. 22 for Soustelle's statement. The goals of USRAF are discussed *ibid.*, January 1, 1957, p. 7, and May, 1957, p. 5.

"antenna" of the ministry. Delbecque set himself two parallel tasks: to organize dissident army officers, particularly those in charge of psychological warfare, and to forge the unity of patriotic and veterans' groups in Algeria. The plan was to trigger a massive nonviolent civilian demonstration, which would provoke the intervention of the military against the regime in order to prevent bloodshed. A Committee of Public Safety would be installed, with Soustelle at its head. The army would be compelled to appeal to De Gaulle as the sole means of arbitrating differences between Algiers and Paris. The plot called for the circumvention and possibly the arrest of the two key military figures, General Salan and General Massu, who were considered men of the "system."

Delbecque faced a formidable task in attempting to unify and then rally Algerian public opinion behind De Gaulle. In fact, the Algerians had always been more Pétainist than Gaullist. They reproached De Gaulle for allowing Communists in the government, nationalizing industries, and inciting natives to wild dreams of independence by his Brazzaville speech. As Soustelle noted in his memoirs of the war years:

> For many French of North Africa, if the National Revolution [of Pétain] had not existed, it would have been necessary to invent it. Troubled by hatreds of class, races and castes . . . our North Africa offered a fertile soil for the propaganda of the Marshal. Nowhere in France or the Empire was this propaganda so blatant.

The "street" in Algiers belonged to the activists. The problem confronting the Gaullists was how to utilize for their own purposes the militants at the disposal of the extreme Right. Delbecque's major contribution was the creation of a *Comité de Vigilance,* including most of the patriotic and veterans' groups, staffed and led by reliable Gaullists. Among the organizations represented were the Veterans' Action Committee (Arnould and Martin), the student groups (Lagaillarde), USRAF-Algerian branch (Professor Muller), the Poujadists (Dr. Lefebvre and Goutallier), and the "national" political parties—Morice Radicals, Independents, and MRP. Colonel Thomazo also participated, thus serving as a liaison with the army. Without Delbecque's knowledge, however, some of the activists leaders met separately after each session of the Committee in order to concert their action independently of the Gaullists.

The evolution of the cabinet crisis forced the pace of events. On May 12 Alain de Sérigny attempted to bring Soustelle back to Algiers, so that the revolt would have a political chief. Soustelle tried unsuccessfully to receive De Gaulle's authorization, then decided to remain at the National Assembly for the investiture debate. But he sent Delbecque to Algiers with final instructions: Continue a vigilant mass demonstration all night until the investiture vote is announced; in the event of Pflimlin's success, unleash such a clamor that the army will be compelled to intervene and take power. Since the vote on Pflimlin would probably be delayed until early in the morning of the fourteenth, the Vigilance Committee at Algiers prepared their "clamor" for the afternoon of the same day. The scenario was to unroll, however, in a slightly different fashion. Some of the actors refused to play the roles assigned them in the script.

Delbecque was the buckle that bound together the various groups seeking to overthrow the regime or bring De Gaulle to power: restive elements in the army, the Algerian activists, veterans' groups, and USRAF. "It is correct," he stated later, "that I was the organizer of the Movement of the Thirteenth of May. . . . I made it my business to be in the right place, at the right time, to exploit in General de Gaulle's favor the upheaval that was bound to take place."[4] The Gaullists, in fact, helped stage the uprising of which they later took advantage.

The Veterans

Almost 20 per cent of the French population are either veterans or "war victims" (including four million holders of veterans' cards, one million resistance fighters, and numerous war widows, civil victims, deportees, and internees). Veterans' associations have proliferated, and are based on military units, ideological and social affinities, geographic origin, and even types of disability. They have not acted with any degree of unity on political matters, however, since the veterans themselves mirror the political divisions of the nation.

Under the prodding of USRAF in 1956, twenty-four veterans' associations (less than half the total number) agreed to work together for the cause of "French Algeria." On July 7, 1957 their representatives took a solemn "patriotic oath" in Algiers, to oppose by all

[4] Cited by Paul Gérin, *L'Algérie du 13 mai, op. cit.,* p. 81. On the role of Chaban-Delmas and Delbecque, and the Gaullist plan, *cf.* Bromberger, *Les 13 complots du 13 mai, op. cit.,* pp. 39–51, 105–14, 151–62, 210. Soustelle's acid remarks on the French of North Africa are in his *Envers et contre tout* (Paris, 1947), vol. 1, p. 419.

the means at their disposal any measures endangering *l'Unité française* (that is, the union of Algeria and France). The following month leaders of these groups created a Committee of Action of the National Association of the Veterans—CANAC. Nineteen veterans' associations eventually adhered to CANAC.* "This Action Committee," it was resolved, "has as its mission the safeguard by all means of the national heritage. With regard to Algeria, it will act in close liaison with USRAF." In September, 1957 the corresponding veterans' groups of Algeria established a local Action Committee, which claimed 400,000 members (half of whom were Moslems). One important veterans' group remained outside the new organization: the Veterans of Indochina, a well-knit group hostile to De Gaulle and in favor of seizure of power by the army.

Immediately upon its establishment, CANAC began to participate in politics as a particularly vigorous pressure group. In the first few months of its existence, veterans' delegations were frequently received by ministers and the presidents of political groups in the National Assembly. CANAC also sent numerous letters to deputies and senators calling for defeat of the *loi-cadre*, integration of Algeria with France, and a hard line toward Tunisia. During this period the veterans employed a courteous, almost deferential tone in their dealings with members of Parliament and the government. A harder line was adopted after a meeting between members of CANAC's executive committee and General de Gaulle in March, 1958.

The interview was requested by the secretary-general of the organization, Alexandre Sanguinetti, "in order to express anguish at the degradation of the French State," and to tell the General why the present situation might be the prelude to a "new June 1940." The meeting took place on March 27. General de Gaulle was typically vague in his remarks, but he made an important statement which impressed the delegation: "The General deems that the Action Committee has made a start in . . . reclaiming independence for France and that it must persevere because it is the only way to provoke one day the *psychological shock* permitting the renovation of the nation's institutions." [5]

---

* The most important were, the *Union Nationale des Combattants, Anciens du Corps Expéditionnaire Français en Italie, Association des Combattants de l'Union Française, Association Nationale des Combattants Parachutistes, Rhin et Danube,* and the *Union Nationale des Combattants d'Afrique du Nord.*

[5] The record of the interview with De Gaulle, along with press communiques, letters to editors, deputies, ministers, etc., were made available to the authors by

The veterans' new, tough policy was expressed in a letter of April 14 to all deputies, calling upon the nation to reassert its independence regardless of the sacrifices that might be necessary. A warning was issued: "The Veterans will consider null and void any abandon or concession made by the government and Parliament that infringes upon the rights of the French people, who are the sole legitimate sovereign." In Algeria the local agents of CANAC along with other patriotic groups organized a mass protest rally on April 26. Fifteen thousand persons swore an oath, transmitted to the prefect and widely publicized: "All the French of Algeria . . . take an oath before their dead to oppose by all means the formation of a government of abandon. They require the formation of a government of national safety, for only such a government is capable of restoring the grandeur of the country."

When the Gaillard crisis was on the point of being resolved by the appointment of Pflimlin, CANAC sent an open letter to the *ministres et ministrables:* "You are pathetic! Go! Admit it, gentlement, you are incompetent. . . . So gentlemen, make a noble gesture. Leave with honors and a pension if you wish, but have pity. Go, so that France may live. Do not force us to drive you out!"

In spite of those threats, the millions of veterans in whose name CANAC spoke were not prepared to march against the Republic. The majority of shock troops were under the command of extreme right-wing groups whose goal was to bring the army, not De Gaulle, to power. CANAC and the Gaullists were to be outflanked on the right by the activists. Yet, the "ripeness" of the revolutionary situation was to a large extent their work.[6]

Activists and Shock Troops

The existence of antirepublican activist groups has been a perennial feature of French political history since the Revolution. They have always manifested particular virulence at times when the authority of republican government was low, for example, after the scandals of the 1880's and 1930's. General Boulanger, Paul Deroulède, Léon Daudet, Charles Maurras, Colonel de la Rocque,

---

CANAC. On the Algerian veterans, see *Le Bled*, April 16, 1958. A Gaullist deputy later commented: "Only an event of great importance could create the shock that would permit General de Gaulle's return. That event could only come from Algeria." Raymond Dronne, *La révolution d'Alger, op. cit.,* p. 51.

[6] The pronouncements of CANAC were publicized by the *Echo d'Alger*, May 9 and 10, 1958. The patriotic oath of April 26 is reprinted, *ibid.*, April 27–28, 1958. In general, see Bromberger, *Les 13 complots du 13 mai, op. cit.,* pp. 200–211.

and Jacques Doriot were representative leaders of the extreme Right during the course of the Third Republic. The general decline of the French government's prestige, combined with a powerful wave of nationalism in public opinion, caused a proliferation of activist groups under the Fourth Republic.* Although these groups glorified a romantic kind of action-for-the-sake-of-action, in many cases they attracted a significant number of intellectuals. Their commandos consisted mainly of veterans who had served in the paratroops, special armored units, or in Indochina, along with a mixed lot of resistance fighters and Vichyites. This diversity in membership and goals made impossible the creation of a central organization. The activists in both France and Algeria had varying ideologies but no clear political goal, numerous chiefs but no leader.

One of the most important of the Algerian secret societies was the French Union of North Africa (UFNA), created in 1955 by Boyer-Banse and Robert Martel. It boasted 15,000 active adherents and a disciplined force of "One Thousand" armed men. Its leaders were in close contact with several extremist groups in France, notably the Veterans of Indochina. The most notorious activist group in Algeria was Dr. Kovacs' Resistance Organization of French Algeria (ORAF), in which Poujadists participated. Among the many friends and allies of Dr. Kovacs was the Poujadist general, Jacques Faure. Assigned to Algeria in October, 1955, General Faure created the *Unités Territoriales,* consisting of reservists who served, in uniform, three days a month. Preaching openly the necessity of a military dictatorship in France, General Faure set about practically by himself to organize a *putsch* in Paris and Algiers. The Territorials, to which the *colons* and ultras flocked, were to play a key role in his plans. General Faure's indiscretions led to his arrest in December. His punishment was light—thirty days in confined quarters, after which he was given a command in Germany.

In the fall of 1956, Kovacs and other activists arrived at the conclusion that the commander of the French forces in Algeria, General Salan, was "soft" and ready to "sell out Algeria," and should be

---

* Some of the more important groups in France included: the *Mouvement Jeune Nation,* Jean-Baptiste Biaggi's *Confédération Nationale des Combattants Volontaires de la Résistance* and *Volontaires de l'Union française,* the *Anciens d'Indochine,* Tixier-Vignancourt's *Rassemblement national,* the *Phalange française,* Dorgère's *La Défense Paysanne* and Pierre Poujade's *Union pour la défense des Commerçants et Artisans.* The most influential right-wing journals were *Aspects de la France, Rivarol, Jeune Nation,* and Poujade's *Fraternité Française.*

replaced by a more cooperative commander in chief. They determined to bring about this change of command by the simple expedient of killing Salan. After Faure's arrest, Kovacs proceeded to carry out his fantastic scheme. Late one afternoon, when General Salan was usually at work, two rockets were launched at his office from homemade bazookas. The General happened to be elsewhere at the time, and the rockets took the life of his chief adviser. Investigation soon brought to light the responsibility of the activists. Kovacs and his aides were arrested, but were not brought to trial until after De Gaulle's advent to power.[7]

The dismantlement of Kovacs' ORAF after the bazooka incident did not noticeably affect the strength of the activist groups. The Poujadists and the university students (led by Pierre Lagaillarde), who were charter members of Delbecque's Vigilance Committee, entered into a formal alliance with Martel's UFNA. These three groups were counted on by Delbecque to mobilize the population; they agreed among themselves to work with the Gaullists up to a point—and then to act strictly on their own behalf. They determined to seize the Governor-General's building on the thirteenth, and compel the army to "take over" before the Gaullists were ready.[8]

As it turned out, the minuscule activist groups made a contribution to the uprising that was all out of proportion to their actual strength. They unquestionably furnished an element of spontaneity, a spark which led to the seizure of power ahead of time. But in the final analysis the revolt of May thirteenth was possible only because the army was willing to enter into dissidence.

The Armed Forces

There were two chief ingredients in all of the Algerian plots: the mass uprising, to be timed with some significant political event in France, leading to the occupation of public buildings; and the army, which would be expected to take a stand against the regime. But the army, by its nature, reflected the political divisions of

---

[7] On the bazooka plot, cf. Bromberger, loc. cit., pp. 95–104; Pierre Popie, "Comment fut préparée la journée du 13 mai," Le Monde, May 30, 1958; and the record of the trial, reported in Le Monde, October 11 through 17, 1958. Kovacs fled the country while on bail. He was condemned to death in absentia and his accomplices received prison terms. For the secret societies, see Bromberger, op. cit., pp. 74–84.

[8] The role of the students and activists is treated in Bromberger, op. cit., pp. 108–14, 163–78; Alain de Sérigny, La révolution du 13 mai, op. cit., pp. 63–69; Jean Ferniot, Les Ides de mai (Paris, 1959), pp. 16–17; and Paul Gérin, L'Algérie du 13 mai, op. cit., pp. 52–54.

the nation itself. Units made up of draftees, for example, and commanded by reserve officers, could not be counted on to associate themselves with an insurrection. The problem facing all conspirators was how to secure the involvement of *portions* of the army, which would then force the rest of the army to follow suit in order to preserve its unity. In the calculations of the conspirators, three military forces could be relied on for friendly cooperation: the Detachments for Urban Protection (*Dispositif de Protection Urbaine*—DPU), the Territorial Units (UT), and the paratroops.

The DPU came into existence as a consequence of the "Battle of Algiers." In January, 1956 Resident Minister Robert Lacoste delegated all police powers in the city of Algiers to General Massu, whose paratroops launched a cleanup operation in the Arab quarters. After the rebel apparatus in the Casbah had been destroyed by the paratroops, Massu in turn delegated the police powers to Colonel Godard and his adjutant, Lt. Colonel Trinquier. These two officers created the DPU in order to relieve and carry on the work of the paratroops in Algiers. It consisted of European volunteers who acted as police auxiliaries. Its 6,000 members wore emblems, carried arms, traveled about freely day and night, and had the power of arrest. All Moslems in Algiers were subject to minute police control and supervision. Every building in the Casbah had an agent who reported on tenants and visitors. For every group of buildings there was a "chef d'ilôt," who acted as a liaison with the military. If the presence of a rebel agent was reported, troops were on the scene in short order. The Casbah network was staffed and supervised by the "bleus"—former rebel terrorists, outfitted in blue uniforms, who received their freedom only after volunteering for this kind of police work. The participation of masses of Europeans in the demonstrations of May 13, and later of both Europeans and Moslems in the "festival of fraternization," was largely secured by the efficient apparatus of the DPU, under the direction of junior officers in the psychological services of the army.

The *Unités Territoriales* were organized and commanded (until his arrest in December, 1956) by General Jacques Faure. They consisted of 30,000 to 40,000 Europeans who, after completion of their military service, remained in the reserve. The Territorials, armed and in uniform, were given security and police work (searching for bombs, guarding buildings, blocking off sectors) in the localities in which they resided. A few units, equipped with tanks, eventually were able to function as an autonomous mechanized force. Since all of its members were European residents of Algeria, the Territorials possessed in an unusual degree a common political purpose. One of the commanders of the Territorials was Colonel Thomazo, who was taken into the confidence of all the various plotters against the Republic since his armed men would obviously have an essential role in the revolt. He was the link between the high command and the extremists: Each counted on him to keep the other in line in the event of a showdown.[9]

The third military force counted on by the conspirators—the paratroops—was destined to play a key role in the actual seizure of power. The paratroops emerged during the Algerian war as a *corps d'élite*. They achieved enormous popularity among the Europeans in Algeria for their daring exploits and success in repressing terrorism in the city of Algiers. At Delbecque's request, a crack unit—the Third Regiment of Colonial Paratroops under the command of Colonel Trinquier—was called back to Algiers on May 11 for the ostensible purpose of "maintaining order." When students and activists prepared to storm the Governor-General's building two days later, the regular security police were replaced by these picked paratroops.

The Supreme Commander of Armed Forces in Algeria, General Raoul Salan, was the focal point of all the conspiracies. The Gaullists, distrustful of Salan, worked diligently for his replacement by a more reliable officer. On the other hand, the activists were divided. Some were convinced that Salan was losing Algeria by timid tactics, but most of them wanted the army and its Supreme Commander to take power. Salan himself seemed content with the role of a "republican general," leaving political affairs to cabinets and resident ministers. He was distinctly less popular than the colorful General Massu.

The continuing cabinet crisis forced Salan out of his customary political neutrality. After several meetings with a number of generals and the outgoing resident minister, Robert Lacoste (who warned that a "diplomatic Dien Bien Phu" was in preparation),

[9] See Bromberger, *op. cit.*, pp. 123–25; *Le Monde*, May 16, 1958; Jacques Duquesne, *L'Algérie, ou la Guerre des mythes* (Paris, 1958), pp. 152–55; and Ferniot, *Les Ides de mai, op. cit.*, pp. 46–55, and Pierre Popie, *op. cit., Le Monde*, May 30, 1958.

he dispatched the following telegram through the chief of staff to
the President of the Republic:

The present crisis reveals that the political parties are profoundly divided over the Algerian question. The press leads one to believe that the
abandon of Algeria will be envisaged by diplomatic procedures, starting
with negotiations for a cease-fire. I remind you of my conversation with
M. Pleven, in the course of which I expressly stated that the only provisions of a cease-fire could be the following: "France, confirming its appeal
for a cease-fire, invites the rebels in Algeria to surrender their arms as
soon as possible, and guarantees a generous amnesty, and their return
into a rejuvenated Franco-Moslem community."

The Army in Algeria is troubled by the feeling of its responsibility. . . . The entire French Army would be outraged by the abandon of
the national heritage. *It would be impossible to predict its reaction of
despair.*

I ask you to please call the attention of the President of the Republic to
our anguish, which only a government firmly determined to maintain our
flag in Algeria can relieve.

General Salan had taken a serious step: In effect he claimed a veto
power over the investiture of a cabinet. His telegram was immediately distributed to the officers of the army in Algeria.

General Ely, the chief of staff, was now convinced that the army
in Algeria was ready to support Soustelle and De Gaulle in the event
of an uprising, and that the paratroops were prepared to descend
on Paris if required in order to prevent the investiture of a "government of abandon." On May 12 he wrote a letter to De Gaulle, informing him of the danger that the army would assume directly a political
role by opposing the next government, which could lead to the
secession of Algeria from France. He appealed to De Gaulle to save
the unity of the army and the nation. This letter apparently persuaded General de Gaulle that the regime was really disintegrating,
and that his intervention was not only possible but necessary.

At the same time, Pflimlin sent to the military leaders in Algeria
a text of his investiture speech. In it the prime minister–designate
envisaged the possibility of negotiations at some future date concerning a cease-fire with the rebels (which repeated previous official
pronouncements, without going as far as General de Gaulle was to
go several months later in inviting Algerian representatives to Paris).
At that moment, however, even a mild reference to negotiations
provoked outright hostility. According to Alain de Sérigny, the
generals "were unanimous in declaring that their conscience forbade

them to risk the life of a single man in order to arrive at such a result." [10]

The Seizure of Power

On May 10, 1958 the patriotic groups in Algeria made a firm decision: to oppose by all the means at their disposal the impending investiture of Pierre Pflimlin as prime minister. The cabinet crisis caused by Félix Gaillard's resignation was already in its third week. Ardent defenders of the Algerian cause, like Georges Bidault, had failed in their attempts to form a government. Rumors were spread that Pflimlin intended to negotiate with the FLN for a cease-fire and to seek the good offices of Tunisia and Morocco. The influential editor of the *Echo d'Alger* summed up the feeling that prevailed among the Europeans of Algeria: "If Pflimlin is invested, we are lost."

The Vigilance Committee in Algiers dispatched an audacious telegram to Pierre Pflimlin on May 10: "The Committee invites you to abandon the idea of constituting a government that would be inapt in the present situation given the dangers which menace the country, and implores you to make room for the rapid formation of a Government of Public Safety." It then issued a proclamation to the people of Algeria: They were to consider themselves "mobilized in the service of Algeria" in the battle against a "government of abandon." The Committee decreed a general strike for the thirteenth of May, to culminate in a mass protest rally at the very moment Pflimlin was supposed to confront the National Assembly. "On May 13, at 1:00 P.M., all activity will cease in the city. The entire population of our communities will assemble *en masse* to manifest its opposition to an inacceptable investiture *at the very hour when the National Assembly is to meet.*" It was expressly stated that "the rally would affirm the determination of Algeria to see the establishment of a Government of Public Safety."

The original purpose of the May 13 demonstration, then, was openly political: to exert pressure on the National Assembly in order to forestall the selection of Pierre Pflimlin as prime minister, and if possible to bring about the designation of a Government of Public

---

[10] Alain de Sérigny, *La révolution du 13 mai, op. cit.*, p. 44. General Salan's telegram of May 9 is reprinted in *Année Politique, 1958*, pp. 529–30 (our italics). On the role of General Salan, cf. Bromberger, *Les 13 complots du 13 mai, op. cit.*, pp. 114–27, 137–38, 151.

Safety. This kind of mass action had become part and parcel of political life in Algiers during the previous several years. On numerous
occasions a governor-general or resident minister encouraged popular manifestations in Algeria as a means of strengthening his position
vis-à-vis Paris.

At a meeting of the Veterans' Action Committee (CANAC) in
Paris on the same day of May 10, one of the conferees suggested
that the veterans pay tribute to the three French prisoners whose
execution had just been announced by the FLN. The association
decided to organize a manifestation in both Paris and Algiers on
May 13. The Algerian affiliate of CANAC then took the initiative in
calling for this demonstration, and secured the approval of the
authorities. The ceremony in Algiers was scheduled also on May 13,
at the *Monument aux Morts,* and was to be attended by the military.
So two separate actions were to take place in Algiers on the thirteenth
of May: a general strike culminating in a political demonstration;
and a ceremonial honoring the three dead prisoners, to which the
authorities pledged their support and participation. The high-ranking officers who agreed to attend the ceremony expected it to be
dignified and silent.[11]

On the afternoon of May 13 a large crowd of perhaps 100,000
people completely filled the square in front of the Memorial to the
Dead. Spirits were stimulated when students on their way to the
rally took time off to sack the American Cultural Center. The crowd
chanted slogans, sang, and promised death (usually by hanging) to
several well-known politicians. A loudspeaker mounted on an automobile blared out a message of the Vigilance Committee: The
Pflimlin government was one of "abandon," and only a "Government
of Public Safety" would be recognized in Algeria. In the late afternoon, when it appeared that the "political" part of the rally was
over, a military delegation led by Generals Salan and Massu made

---

[11] The most informative source on the events of May is Merry and Serge Bromberger, *Les 13 complots du 13 mai.* The Bromberger brothers, well-known journalists,
interviewed many of the participants in this drama. Although their book is undocu-
mented, none of the persons discussed therein have challenged its accuracy (with the
exception of a *Force Ouvrière* leader who was alleged to have conferred with
Michel Debré). On the preparation of the manifestation of May 13 in Algiers, see
Bromberger, pp. 139–49; the *Echo d'Alger* for May 11, 12, and 13, 1958; Alain de
Sérigny, *La révolution du 13 mai, op. cit.,* pp. 22–25; and Pierre Popie, "Comment fut
preparée la Journée du 13 mai," *Le Monde,* May 30, 1958. According to de Sérigny,
Robert Lacoste expressed to Senator Rogier in Paris his hope that during the planned
demonstrations of May 13 the Algiers City Hall would be taken by assault and Mayor
Jacques Chevallier ejected. On this controversial point, see de Sérigny, *op. cit.,* p. 38;
Le Monde, July 30, 1958; and Jacques Chevallier, *Nous, Algériens, op. cit.,* p. 152.

its way amid great confusion to the Memorial to the Dead and de-
posed flowers. The ceremony was thus terminated and the officers
left.

At this point the leaders of the conspiratorial societies gave the
long-awaited signal. Several hundred university students led by
Pierre Lagaillarde, and other demonstrators (mainly members of
Martel's "One Thousand" and the Poujadists—but *not* including
the Gaullist forces) raced to the Forum, a large open area in front
of the Governor-General's building. Actually, the high school students, sensing that something was up, dashed there and were first
on the scene. They assembled before the gates of the building and
demanded to be let in. A thin line of Republican Companies of Security (CRS) stood guard. Suddenly, the CRS were ordered (by
whom has never been made clear) to retreat into the building. The
men of the Third Regiment of Colonial Paratroopers who replaced
them allowed their lines to be forced. The demonstrators then invaded the building, ransacked the library, broke windows, smashed
furniture, and threw dossiers out of the windows. Within half an
hour the upper floors were occupied by rioters.

The generals then appeared on the scene, and tried at first to persuade the rioters to go home. After failing to restore order, they decided to join forces with the insurgents. Army officers and civilians
appeared on the balcony of the Governor-General's building to
proclaim the creation of a Committee of Public Safety. General
Massu sent a telegram to President Coty:

> Inform you creation civil and military Committee of Public Safety at
> Algiers, under my presidency ["sous ma présidence, moi, général
> Massu"], in reason gravity situation and absolute necessity maintain
> order. We demand creation, at Paris, of a Government of Public Safety,
> sole capable of preserving Algeria, integral part of Metropolis.

The formation of the Committee of Public Safety was the most
original feature of the Algerian uprising. The suggestion was made
during the course of agitated discussions between General Massu
and a small number of manifestants who had gained the balcony
and were haranguing the masses in the Forum. It included Pierre
Lagaillarde, president of the Algerian students' association, and
others who had never been active in politics before. When asked
whom he represented, one replied simply: "La foule!" (the mob).
In the confusion, a young man told General Massu it was necessary
to create a representative organ capable of canalizing the manifestation. Massu later declared: "I looked at General Salan, who heard

this. He said nothing. I had only thirty or forty seconds for reflection. I resolved to accept in order better to control the action of this committee." He then requested the addition of representative Moslems along with leaders of the Vigilance Committee.

In fact, the idea of *salut public* had been circulating in Algeria and France for some time. The call for a Government of Public Safety was launched, with much fanfare, by Jacques Soustelle immediately after the fall of the Gaillard government. Said Soustelle on April 15: "I am no prophet, but what I wish is that the crisis should permit a step to be taken, as great a step as possible, toward that which seems to me indispensable, a Government of Public Safety, a government of union in a truce among the parties." He added, of course, that only General de Gaulle was qualified to undertake this task.

The phrase, "salut public," which continually recurred thereafter in the propaganda of the Gaullists, soon dominated political debate in Algeria. The theme was sounded by Soustelle in a press conference of April 25, by the Veterans' Action Committee in a letter of May 3 to all deputies, by Georges Bidault in a speech of May 7, and by Alain de Sérigny in an editorial of May 9 in the *Echo d'Alger*. On May 10, a number of patriotic organizations presented a declaration to Robert Lacoste, to be forwarded to President Coty: "The French of Algeria . . . ask the President of the Republic to affirm his authority as Chief of State by putting an end to the quarrels of the parties, by the immediate formation of a Government of Public Safety." And during the riots of May 13, a loudspeaker mounted at the headquarters of the army newspaper *Le Bled* harangued the crowd to the effect that decisions not emanating from a Government of Public Safety would be considered null and void. The currency of the phrase *salut public*, then, would indicate that the creation of a Committee of Public Safety was not quite as spontaneous as at first appeared.[12]

The timetable of the "revolution" had been altered by the sudden

---

[12] General Massu's explanation of how the CSP was formed may be found in the *Echo d'Alger*, May 15, 1958. A slightly different version is given by Jean Ferniot, *Les Ides de mai, op. cit.*, pp. 35–36. For de Sérigny's account see his *La révolution du 13 mai, op. cit.*, pp. 61–62. Soustelle's press conference statement is in *Echo d'Alger*, April 17, 1958. Michel Debré called for a Government of Public Safety in USRAF's *La Vérité sur l'Algérie*, January 1, 1957—but this was the only time the phrase was used during the entire period of the journal's existence (July, 1956 to February, 1958). The phrase was invoked frequently by the *Echo d'Alger* after Soustelle's declaration, for example, in the issues of April 24, 25, and 26 and May 3, 8, 9, 10, and 14, 1958.

independent initiative of the extremists in storming the Governor-General's building. The Committee of Public Safety, instead of being an emanation of the Gaullist-controlled Vigilance Committee, was a haphazard creation—a "soviet." The Gaullists were forced to move swiftly. Delbecque and his allies infiltrated the Committee of Public Safety, and maneuvered the army officers into position behind De Gaulle. In the end, the activists, who scored the first blow, were themselves elbowed out of the way.

It appears that the army high command was not directly responsible for the events of May 13, which were engineered by the Gaullist and activist groups. A number of junior officers collaborated with these groups, with the knowledge of some of their superiors. The actual seizure of public buildings by the activists, ahead of the Gaullist schedule, took the generals completely by surprise. All high-ranking officers on the scene attempted to disperse the mob. Both Massu and Salan tried to persuade the demonstrators that their violence was out of place. During the discussions which led to the creation of the Committee of Public Safety, Massu and Salan, obviously unprepared and confused, improvised their actions. Massu's quick decision to accept and head a Committee of Public Safety placed him at the forefront of the insurrection—whereas it had never been the intention of any of the plotters to assign him an important role. Although not directly implicated in the uprising, both Massu and Salan, once involved, fully accepted the consequences. They immediately characterized Pierre Pflimlin's duly invested government as one of "abandon," asked for De Gaulle's "arbitration," demanded a Government of Public Safety, and finally prepared to extend the movement of "national renovation" from Algeria to France.

CHAPTER V

The Coming of De Gaulle

ON THE MORNING of May 14 the Republic had two governments: a Committee of Public Safety in Algiers, invested by a mob, and a Council of Ministers in Paris, headed by Pierre Pflimlin, duly invested by the National Assembly. Within three weeks the government in Paris capitulated. The crisis, which culminated in Charles de Gaulle's accession to power, went through three distinct stages: (1) an initial period of confusion, with each side attempting to win over the other; (2) a trial of strength—the army prepared to invade the Metropolis while the government, after trying to work out an arrangement, prepared to defend the Republic; (3) the abdication of the regime, highlighted by President Coty's message to Parliament in favor of General de Gaulle.

Confusion and Accommodation (May 13-17)

On the evening of May 13, the National Assembly was engaged in debate over the investiture of Pierre Pflimlin. What was the position of the prime minister–designate, judged so dangerous by the army and the Algerian patriots? Said Pflimlin: "The day when the rebellion, having lost all hope of success, is ready to give up fighting, the government will, if our country's interest seems to call for such an initiative, choose the most favorable moment to suggest talks with a view to a cease-fire." He added that his government was ready to ask for additional appropriations in order to increase the war effort. He explicitly pointed out that truce talks could not be subordinated to any political conditions. "The talks could not take on the character of a negotiation involving the status of Algeria. Their purpose will be to determine the general conditions for a cease-fire." Elections would be held only after calm was re-established, truce talks were conceivable only as the expression of a French victory, and the bond between Algeria and France was never to be subject to question. The role of Morocco and Tunisia was alluded to in a particular sense: that these friendly powers might persuade the Algerian rebels to accept the above conditions. In short, Pflimlin's declaration on Algeria differed in no way from the official policy of his predecessors.

Soon after the investiture speech was read, news of the Algerian uprising reached the Assembly, throwing the debate into an uproar. "The National Assembly will be called upon, this very night, to assume its responsibilities. For my part, I am ready to assume mine," declared Pflimlin. He hastened to the Hotel Matignon to confer with Gaillard and members of the outgoing cabinet. The prime minister–designate was placed before two alternatives: to withdraw in favor of a cabinet of national unity, probably headed by Mollet and including Independents and Socialists; or to persevere, obtain the investiture, enforce republican law, and bring the army under control. The majority of the members of Pflimlin's party, along with some Radicals, encouraged him to persevere. Others, however, including, notably, leaders of the Independents and Guy Mollet talked vaguely about the disadvantages of Pflimlin's investiture, but did not propose an alternative. Pflimlin offered to withdraw if any other solutions were suggested; otherwise, he refused to lay down his burden. "I do not wish to create a vacuum at this perilous hour. It would be criminal to leave France without a government under present circumstances." The Socialist and Radical groups informed Pflimlin of their support. The MRP leader determined to carry through. Just before addressing the Assembly, Pflimlin gave his consent to an exceedingly important decision by the outgoing prime minister, Félix Gaillard: to confer civil powers on General Salan in order to control the Algerian situation.

In the early morning of the fourteenth, Pflimlin addressed the Assembly again. "At Algiers, some Frenchmen whose anguish I understand, whose anxiety I appreciate, have let themselves be led to commit serious acts, and there also were military chiefs to take, I say it with deep regret, an attitude of insurrection against republican law." Yet he had just consented to vest civil powers in those very military chiefs! "Assume your responsibilities," concluded Pflimlin, "we are perhaps at the brink of civil war, whose beneficiaries will doubtless be these people [pointing to Communists] with whom nothing can ever reconcile me."

Disregarding Pflimlin's broad hint, the Communists abstained rather than vote flatly against his investiture. If Communist abstentions had been added to the hostile vote of 129, which would normally have been the case, Pflimlin's investiture would have been by the razor-edge margin of eight votes. The opposition consisted of Poujadists, Social Republicans, Independents, and right-wing Radicals. Mendès-France and Mitterand joined Radicals, Socialists, and MRP in support of the government. Had there been no uprising in Algeria, it is almost certain that Pflimlin would have failed to receive a majority.

The Council of Ministers met immediately to adopt a number of measures for the defense of the Republic: Communications between Algeria and France were cut; aircraft forbidden to fly to Algeria; shipping directed to avoid Algerian ports; the Ministry of Finance instructed to stop payments in Algeria. The order was also given for the arrest of activist leaders in Paris, and for a closer police guard around Jacques Soustelle. Pflimlin obtained from President Coty an address to the army of Algeria, in which the chief of state called upon the army not to divide Frenchmen in the face of the enemy. "Chief of the armies by virtue of article 33 of the Constitution, I give you the order to continue to do your duty ["rester dans le devoir"], *under the authority* of the Government of the French Republic." [1]

Pflimlin maintained contact with General Salan by telephone. The Prime Minister assured Salan that his government had no intention of "selling out" Algeria; on the contrary, he repeated that he was prepared to step up the war effort. The General asked authorization to send two officers to Paris in order to inform the cabinet about the political situation in Algeria. Both sides seemed to be offered the prospect of compromise leading to the restoration of legality. In Paris it was not quite sure whether the army had instigated the rebellion or was seeking to control it.

The high command at Algeria was equally confused and embarrassed. Shortly after the news of Pflimlin's investiture reached Algiers, General Massu personally read to the crowd an inflammatory communiqué of the Committee of Public Safety: "We inform the population of Algiers that Pflimlin's *government of abandon* has

---

[1] Quotations from Pflimlin's declarations before the National Assembly are in the *J.O., Assemblée Nationale*, May 13, 1958, pp. 2255, 2272, 2273 (our italics).

just been invested, thanks to the complicity of Communist votes." He then called on De Gaulle to speak out for the creation of a Government of Public Safety:

In any event the Committee of Public Safety *which I represent* continues to assure liaison between the population and the army, and *assumes power until the final victory*. . . . We decree as of now the mobilization of all French energies in the country's service, and we ask you to be ready to respond to the first call issued by the Committee of Public Safety."

Quite a different posture was struck by General Salan later on the same day in a communiqué to the population of Algiers, duly posted in public places. He announced his assumption of military and civil powers (as indeed had been authorized by the prime minister) in order to maintain order. The population was urged to return to their occupations in calm, dignity, and discipline. Salan made it clear that authority resided in the supreme commander, not in any extralegal insurrectionary organization: "The Committee of Public Safety constituted under the pressure of events to affirm the will of the Franco-Moslem populations to remain French, assures the liaison between these populations and the high command *which transmits its order to it.*" The army appeared to be searching for a way back to legality.

The activists suspected that they were being bypassed. In defiance of Salan's directive that work be resumed, instructions went out to continue the strike, fill the Forum, keep the demonstration going. The Territorial Units took up positions outside the doors of the Committee of Public Safety, face to face with the paratroops. The generals became uneasy. General Allard attempted, unsuccessfully, to have the Territorials withdrawn and dissolved. In the afternoon General Massu held a press conference, whose tone contrasted sharply with the earlier declaration. He talked of his surprise and anger at the rioting, related how he decided, in the space of thirty seconds, to sponsor and head a Committee of Public Safety—for the sole purpose of avoiding bloodshed. "Since its creation, the Committee of Public Safety has explained that its goal was to restore order. I think this goal has been attained." He condemned the pillaging of the government headquarters, the continuation of the general strike and the mobilization of the Territorials. "I want to avoid bloodshed. I am not an insubordinate General. . . . There can be no question of creating at Algiers an insurrectional government. . . . Power belongs *to General Salan and he is the emanation of the government*. If the

Committee forgets it, it will be dissolved." [2] But the Committee of Public Safety had no intention of disappearing. Delbecque asserted that the Pflimlin government would not be recognized; Gaullists took over the radio; tension built up between the activists and the army. The tenuous balance was upset on May 15 by another force: General de Gaulle at last intervened.

On the morning of May 15, General Salan visited the headquarters of the Committee of Public Safety. Delbecque immediately directed him to the balcony, introducing him to the population. Salan congratulated the people on their determination to save French Algeria, expressed his confidence in victory, concluding with, "Vive l'Algérie française!" Salan withdrew, saw Delbecque (who, some observers claim, motioned him back with a pistol), returned to the microphone and shouted the vital phrase: *"et vive De Gaulle!"* The crowd took up the cry. Pflimlin had failed in his effort to control the army.

De Gaulle's staff announced that a communiqué would be issued that afternoon. General de Gaulle, profoundly affected by the events, was ready to act. His brief declaration gave new hope to the dissidents in Algeria.

The degradation of the State leads infallibly to the estrangement of the associated peoples, uneasiness in the Army, the disintegration of the nation, the loss of independence. For twelve years France, at grips with problems too difficult for the regime of the parties, has been in the throes of this disastrous situation. Today, before the ordeals which mount anew, let it be known that I hold myself ready to assume the powers of the Republic.

Pflimlin reacted energetically to the double threat posed by the army and De Gaulle. Guy Mollet entered the cabinet as vice-premier, Jules Moch as Minister of the Interior. The government asked the Assembly to declare a state of emergency (after realizing that a state of siege would only accord full power to the very military against which it had to protect itself). "I ask the republican and national majority of Parliament," said Pflimlin, "to unite around the government which, in the hour of peril, has the burden of defending republican law."

The Assembly voted the government's bill for a state of emergency by the overwhelming margin of 461 to 114. The Communists were

---

[2] The statements of Massu and Salan at Algiers may be found in Ferniot's, *Les Ides de mai, op. cit.,* pp. 32–36; Alain de Sérigny, *La révolution du 13 mai, op. cit.,* p. 76; Bromberger, *op. cit.,* pp. 219–20. Our italics in the quotations above.

now voting with the government for the defense of the Republic. Some Independents who had voted against Pflimlin's investiture supported the motion for a state of emergency. As one of their spokesmen, Guy Petit, put it: "I am ready to accord the government the exceptional powers that it requests in order to preserve republican order, which alone is legitimate." The Minister of Defense, Pierre de Chevigné (MRP) transferred out of Paris several generals suspected of plotting with their colleagues in Algiers. General Ely, after vainly attempting to persuade Pflimlin and de Chevigné to give way for a Government of Public Safety, himself resigned—but remained in touch with his successor and the army.

In spite of this display of firmness, some advocates of "republican defense" began to survey the prospects of a Gaullist solution. One of the first to attempt to establish a contact between the government and De Gaulle was Guy Mollet. During the course of the debate on May 16, Mollet addressed three extremely important questions to De Gaulle: (1) Do you recognize the present government as the sole legitimate government of the nation? (2) Do you disavow the promoters of the Algerian Committees of Public Safety? (3) Are you ready, if called upon to constitute a government, to present yourself before the National Assembly, and to withdraw if you fail to be invested? That evening, as if in answer, De Gaulle scheduled a press conference for May 19.[3]

Meanwhile, in Algeria, the "festivals of fraternization" took place. For the first time masses of Europeans and Moslems joined hands at the Forum. Its impact on French public opinion was profound. Many wondered whether a providential solution had not perhaps been found for the Algerian problem, and began to look with sympathy upon the men of May 13.

The Trial of Strength (May 18-26)

As has been noted, one of the serious weaknesses of the right-wing groups who instigated the demonstrations in Algeria was the lack of effective political leadership. On May 17, Jacques Soustelle, eluding his police guard, succeeded in reaching Algeria. He received at first a cool reception. Salan and Massu at this time

---

[3] Quotations by Pflimlin, Petit, and Mollet are from the *J.O., Assemblée Nationale*, May 16, 1958, pp. 2364, 2375, 2368–69, in that order. Mollet's questions to De Gaulle are reported by Ferniot, *op. cit.*, p. 70 and Bromberger, *op. cit.*, p. 243. De Gaulle's press declaration of May 15 is reprinted in *Année Politique*, 1958, p. 534.

thought that Pflimlin could be persuaded to retire in favor of De Gaulle, and that Soustelle's presence in Algeria would only complicate matters. Also, Salan held his supreme civil and military powers from the government. He could not delegate any part of them to Soustelle without breaking definitively with Paris. The military attempted to keep Soustelle's arrival secret. Delbecque and the Committee of Public Safety, however, immediately alerted the population, which demonstrated in his favor. Salan had no alternative but to accept Soustelle as his chief political adviser. The Algerian revolution was now in Gaullist hands.

Although no specific powers were devolved upon Soustelle, this was nonetheless the turning point in relations between the government and the army. Until Soustelle's arrival, Pflimlin and Salan could still hope for some kind of arrangement. But as soon as Salan joined up with Soustelle, the regime was directly challenged. Up to then, the army had sought to limit and control the uprising; from this point on, the army became a full participant in the rebellion. The trial of strength between army and government was engaged.

On May 18 General Massu dispatched two officers to Pau (the training center for paratroops) to offer General Miquel command of a military operation against the government. The object of the operation, which received the name "Resurrection," envisaged an armed assault upon the government in Paris. In order to carry out this mission, General Miquel was to dispose of the following military forces: 1,500 paratroops from Algeria headed by General Massu, 2,500 paratroops in training at Pau, a tank unit stationed at the outskirts of Paris, and the North African troops quartered in France. In addition, agents of the army undertook to organize the CRS (whose officers assured the army of their total support), the 20,000 policemen of Paris (who formed secretly a Committee of Public Safety headed by Jean Dides), and thousands of veterans who were to be furnished with paratroop uniforms. The adhesion of the CRS and the Paris police alone guaranteed the success of the Resurrection. However, there were differences of opinion within the army on both tactics and goals. Some officers tended to favor a genuine *coup* which would disperse the Assembly and simply turn power over to De Gaulle; others hoped that the mere threat of military action would suffice to bring De Gaulle to power by legal means.

Apprised of these military preparations, the government began to organize its defenses. Jules Moch concentrated the CRS in Paris, unaware that most of the men were ready to join up with the army. He also requested a vast quantity of small arms from the Minister of Defense, which led to the rumor that the government might arm the workers. Moch later denied any such intention.

In this supercharged atmosphere, De Gaulle held his press conference on May 19 at the Palais d'Orsay. The General spoke grandly, vaguely about the future of Algeria, criticized the "regime of the parties," commended the army for having maintained order in Algeria. He then talked of his own role. The moment has come, he said, when he might once more be directly useful to France:

Useful because I am a solitary man, because I am not involved with any party or organization, because for six years I have engaged in no political activity, for three years I have made no declaration, because I am a man who belongs to none and who belongs to all. Useful, how? Well, if the people so desire, as in the previous great national crisis, at the head of the government of the French Republic.

But the delegation of exceptional powers, he pointed out, would itself have to be exceptional; he could not accept the ordinary procedure of investiture. A question was posed by Maurice Duverger: "Some people are fearful that if you come to power, you might infringe on the public liberties." To which De Gaulle reacted quickly: "Have I ever done so? On the contrary, I restored them when they had disappeared. Do you think that at the age of sixty-seven I am going to launch on a career of dictator?" Without specifically answering the question posed by Mollet several days earlier, he expressed his "great esteem" for the Socialist leader, reminding his audience also of the social progress accomplished by his government in 1944–45 (nationalizations, family allowances, planning, and so forth [4]).

In the meantime, Pflimlin tried to maintain the appearance of an accord with Salan. "Between the government and the authorities of Algeria," he assured the Assembly, "contact has never been broken. We will take all possible measures in the next few days to reestablish normal relations, to assure everywhere the complete return to legality." In the face of the rebellion, the National Assembly devoted its energies to a resolution praising the very army which

---

[4] Cf. *Année Politique*, 1958, pp. 534–36. On Operation Resurrection, see Bromberger, *op. cit.*, pp. 273–312. In a campaign speech on November 24, 1958 in Oran, General Miquel stated: "As of May 14, in accord with General Salan, I was chief of a clandestine resistance movement for the whole of France. It is therefore I who carried De Gaulle to power." (*Le Monde*, December 6, 1958.)

threatened its existence. Even the Communists joined in the unanimous resolution: "The National Assembly considers it a duty to express to our soldiers *and to their chiefs* the deep gratitude of the nation for the services rendered to the country under the flag of the Republic." Those to whom the resolution was addressed replied by invading Corsica.

On May 23 General Salan signed an order authorizing several agents, including Pascal Arrighi, to ascertain whether the people of Corsica were ready to create Committees of Public Safety and rally to the Algerian rebellion. A Corsican Committee of Public Safety had already been formed and had secured the participation of activist elements and the cooperation of a detachment of paratroops stationed in Corsica. A unit of CRS, sent in great haste to the island by Jules Moch, offered to collaborate with the paratroops in maintaining order. The prefecture of Ajaccio was taken over without any opposition. The next day a plane brought an assortment of journalists and delegates from Algiers, including Léon Delbecque, Roger Frey, and Alain de Sérigny. There was one tourist: Colonel Thomazo, who happened to be at the airport when the plane was loading, and decided impulsively to go along. He remained in Corsica one month as its military governor.

The rebellion of Corsica infuriated the Prime Minister. In addressing the Assembly, Pflimlin said that he could understand how the people of Algeria might fear being cut off from France. "For the events of Corsica, no justification, no excuse can be invoked. . . . If certain Frenchmen doubted the existence of a conspiracy directed against republican institutions, the events of Ajaccio must have opened their eyes." He warned the Assembly that further operations were probable, that the government would use vigorously all the means at its disposal against the insurgents.

Jules Moch set about immediately to crush the rebellion in Corsica. Three delegates of the Ministry of the Interior were instructed to leave at once for the island. However, since the navy had difficulty finding a seaworthy ship, the project had to be abandoned. Moch then scraped together a force of 1,000 CRS. But the military aircraft were all reserved for the paratroops, civil aircraft would be unable to land in Corsica, and the navy again couldn't put its hands on the necessary ships. Even if transport were arranged, it remained exceedingly doubtful that the police would fight the paratroops. The measure finally taken by the government against the rebels was derisive: by a vote of 395 to 150 the parliamentary immunity of Pascal Arrighi was lifted. Yet the government studiously refused to condemn General Salan, who had signed an order of mission for Arrighi, and who continued to exercise the full powers vested in him by the prime minister. The events of Corsica made it evident that the Fourth Republic, incapable of preventing the invasion of one of its departments, in effect was without defense.[5]

The Regime Abdicates (May 27-June 2)

All of the leaders of the regime, including the prime minister, the vice-premier, and the president of the Republic, were now convinced that only De Gaulle's accession to power could avert a military invasion of the mainland. The question was how and under what conditions it would take place.

A contact had already been established between the cabinet and the General on May 22 when Antoine Pinay, with Pflimlin's encouragement, paid a personal call at Colombey. Pinay returned with the conviction that De Gaulle wished to act in complete legality. The General's chief aide suggested to Guy Mollet and Maurice Schumann separately that to save the Republic a meeting between De Gaulle and the Prime Minister would be essential. There was an initial confusion when Mollet and Pflimlin, both actually in favor of a meeting with De Gaulle, refused to be put in the position of "betraying" the other. Guy Mollet, profoundly shaken by the Corsican revolt, on May 25 wrote a personal letter to General de Gaulle. He confessed his inability to understand why De Gaulle did not condemn the preparations for a putsch. To a visitor he reportedly declared the same day, in a voice choked with emotion: "Adieu! We will perhaps never see each other again. I shall be killed on the barricades at the head of the miners of Nord!"

The following day De Gaulle was informed that the envisaged military operation was scheduled for the night of May 27. He immediately sent a note to Mollet, in answer to his letter, suggesting the utility of a direct contact; the General also dispatched a note to Pflimlin proposing a secret meeting. The Prime Minister and the General were unable to arrive at an accord. De Gaulle wanted

---

[5] On the Corsican operation, *cf.* Pascal Arrighi, *La Corse, atout décisif* (Paris, 1958), pp. 83–124, and Bromberger, *op. cit.*, pp. 339–54. For Pflimlin's gesture to Salan, and his reaction to the events of Corsica, see *J.O., Assemblée Nationale*, May 20, 1958, p. 2390 and *ibid.*, May 26, 1958, pp. 2476–77.

Pflimlin simply to resign, at which point he would accept the powers
of the Republic. Pflimlin tried to persuade him that the Assembly
was not favorably disposed toward him, that only the General's
prior condemnation of the military *coup* in preparation could clear
the atmosphere. De Gaulle refused on the ground that, out of power,
he was unable to stop the putsch; he would make such a declaration only if he were at the head of the government. The two men
separated in agreement only that they might meet again. De Gaulle
returned to Colombey early on the morning of Tuesday, May 27.
He found a message that Resurrection would definitely be unleashed
the following evening. He thereupon made the following statement:

> I began yesterday the regular procedure necessary to the establish-
> ment of a republican government. In these conditions, any action from
> whatever side it might come, which places in question the public order,
> might have serious consequences. Even in making allowance for circum-
> stances, I cannot approve such actions. I expect the ground, naval, and
> air forces now in Algeria to remain exemplary under the orders of their
> chiefs, General Salan, Admiral Auboyneau, General Jouhaud. To these
> chiefs, I express my confidence and my intention to establish contact with
> them immediately.

General Miquel shortly thereafter received instructions from Algiers
to suspend operations.

The communiqué was sent to Pflimlin by special messenger.
The Prime Minister was indignant; he had not committed himself
during the talks with De Gaulle to transfer power to him. He only
later discovered the real reason for the communiqué. But the National Assembly was stupefied by De Gaulle's statement that he had
begun the process of investiture. How could any such procedure
be started without its knowledge, and indeed while a duly invested
cabinet continued to receive massive votes of confidence? François
Mitterand demanded to know whether the government planned to
disappear with the first wind blowing from Colombey. "The Prime
Minister," he cried out, "has duties with respect to his majority. His
majority has taken risks for him and before history, when it invested
him on the night of May 13th. He is bound by a contract." [6] The
Socialist parliamentarians voted by 111 to 3 not to support the can-
didature of General de Gaulle "under any circumstances."

---

[6] *J.O., Assemblée Nationale*, May 27, 1958, p. 2534. On the Mollet-Pflimlin-De
Gaulle parleys, *cf.* Bromberger, *op. cit.*, pp. 355–92, and Ferniot, *op. cit.*, pp. 98–103,
113–26.

That evening Pflimlin informed the Assembly of his meeting with De Gaulle.

The President of the Council, for his part, has not at any time forgotten that, having been invested by the National Assembly he could remit only in your hands the mandate that you entrusted to him. . . . For the government, the path of duty is clearly laid out: we will not create a power vacuum.

But it remained unclear whether Pflimlin's object was simply to persuade the General to disavow the Algerian revolt, or to prepare his advent to power. There seemed to be much truth in the observation made by Jean de Lipkowski:

Mister Prime Minister, it is not you who abandon power, it is, alas! power that abandons you. . . . If you have had to ask General de Gaulle to intercede between you and your legions, it is because already you can secure obedience only through an intermediary.[7]

In the early hours of May 28, Pflimlin met with his cabinet. The Prime Minister drew up a balance sheet: It was impossible to avoid civil war unless General de Gaulle was brought to power by legal means. On the other hand, the cabinet had the moral obligation to stay in office in order not to create the "vacance de pouvoir." The only solution was to offer President Coty the cabinet's *conditional* resignation—to take effect when the obstacles to De Gaulle's investiture were overcome. President Coty accepted the decision, which was immediately announced to the press. That afternoon a mass rally, inspired by the Socialist party, was held at the *Place de la République* in Paris. Socialists and Radicals were in the parade—along with many Communist leaders. Communists made up the majority of the manifestants, estimated at about 200,000.

While the Left demonstrated in Paris, President Coty received an ultimatum from Algiers. The invasion of the Metropolis was now set for May 30; it would be called off only if De Gaulle were in power. That same day Coty requested the presidents of the National Assembly and the Council of the Republic, André Le Troquer and Gaston Monnerville, to confer with General de Gaulle in order to negotiate a procedure for his investiture. The discussion between De Gaulle and Le Troquer was stormy, and had unfortunate repercussions. The president of the National Assembly insisted that

---

[7] The interventions by Pflimlin and de Lipkowski are in the *J.O., Assemblée Nationale*, May 27, 1958, pp. 2535, 2538.

De Gaulle make a personal appearance before the Assembly. The
General spoke of full powers for two years—while Le Troquer
contended that a period of three months was the maximum
in his opinion. Monnerville hastened to suggest six months. Le
Troquer argued also that revision of the constitution was out of the
question. The conferees parted in anger, without any meeting of
minds. The stalemate seemed to be complete.

The following morning Coty decided to present the National
Assembly with a stark choice: either invest General de Gaulle with
full powers, or accept his own resignation as president of the Republic. If the Assembly refused to accept his advice, an alternative
was possible under the constitution: Le Troquer, president of the
National Assembly, would replace the president of the Republic in
the event of the latter's resignation. As soon as Algiers was notified
that Coty intended to threaten the Assembly with his resignation,
General Miquel was once again instructed to postpone Resurrection, but to keep his troops in readiness. On the afternoon of May
29, Le Troquer hastily read Coty's message to the Assembly.

Coty first recalled his persistent efforts to secure far-reaching
reforms of the constitution. "Here we are now on the brink of civil
war. After having fought the enemy for forty years, are Frenchmen
tomorrow going to fight Frenchmen?" There is now no time, he
said, to undertake the customary leisurely survey for the designation
of a prime minister.

In this hour of danger for the country and the Republic, I have
turned toward the most illustrious of Frenchmen, toward the one who, in
the darkest years of our history, became our leader for the reconquest of
freedom, and who, having thus forged national unity, refused dictatorship and restored the Republic.

Coty then related that consultations between the presiding officers of the two chambers and General de Gaulle revealed the existence of serious obstacles. "I respectfully ask General de Gaulle to
confer with the Chief of State and to examine with him that which
is immediately necessary, within the framework of republican legality, for the formation of a Government of National Safety. . . ." If
this initiative were to fail, Coty announced his intention to resign.

The reaction of the Socialists to the message was almost unanimously hostile. De Gaulle's claims, as reported by Le Troquer, appeared excessive. At this point, a sensational bit of news circulated
among the deputies: An exchange of letters had taken place between

Vincent Auriol and General de Gaulle; the latter's response was reasonable, quite different from the position reported by Le Troquer. The former president of the Republic had written that De Gaulle could not think of forcing the Republic to capitulate before a putsch, to which he would then owe his investiture; or of accepting the support of the Pétainists while renouncing that of the working class. De Gaulle replied that although the Algiers rebels invoked his name, he was in no way involved in their machinations. There followed a crucial paragraph testifying to his respect for legality:

As I would never consent to receive power from any source other than the people, or at the very least their representatives (as was the case in 1944–45) I fear that we may be heading toward anarchy and civil war. In that event, those who, by a partisanship which to me is incomprehensible, will have prevented me from saving the Republic once again while there still was time, will bear a heavy responsibility; as for myself, I will only nurse my sorrow until my death.

The Socialist group wavered. It voted to accept Auriol's letter as a basis for negotiations with De Gaulle. That afternoon General de Gaulle finally made the trip to the Elysée. President Coty solemnly requested that he form a government, volunteering to see party leaders on his behalf. The President then insisted on two capital points: the Parliament must adjourn itself for six months (no question of two years), and the prime minister–designate must honor the National Assembly with an appearance before it. De Gaulle agreed. The paratroops did not descend on Paris that night.

General de Gaulle, especially anxious to secure the support of the SFIO, received Vincent Auriol and then a Socialist delegation consisting of Guy Mollet and Maurice Deixonne. When Auriol expressed concern that the referendum might take on the character of a plebiscite, De Gaulle replied with great emotion that he failed to understand why some republicans lacked confidence in him. Could he not have engineered a *coup d'état* in 1944? Did he not retire from public life, simply and with dignity, in 1946? Could he not at that very moment lead an irresistible attack against the regime? Auriol was profoundly affected. De Gaulle spoke of his liberal ideas concerning the French Union, and stated that all colonies would be offered a free choice between independence and a community with France. Mollet and Deixonne returned to their group completely under the spell of "un très grand monsieur." The Socialist parliamentarians by a vote of 77 to 74 approved De Gaulle's investiture. The General, meanwhile, received leaders of all national parties at the Hôtel Lapérouse. On Sunday, June 1, for the first time since December 1945, General de Gaulle entered the National Assembly.[8]

He read a statement, dryly, unemotionally. If invested, the government would ask full powers for a period of six months. He promised that a reform of Article 90 of the constitution would be submitted to the Parliament so as to enable the government to revise the Constitution of the Fourth Republic. Once confidence is granted, the Parliament would recess until the date of its next ordinary session. "Thus the government of the Republic, invested by the national representatives and given the means of action, will be able to answer for the unity, integrity, and independence of the country."

The debate which followed took place in De Gaulle's absence. Mendès-France, who was the first to speak, analyzed the defects and vices of the Fourth Republic, chief among which was its inability to emancipate the colonial territories. He announced his refusal to vote investiture under the threat of military force, but promised his support in the future if the General were to break with the reactionaries. Maurice Deixonne and Tanguy-Prigent reflected the hesitations and divisions of the Socialist group. François Mitterand launched a bitter attack on the antidemocratic forces which had propelled De Gaulle to power. "The presence of General de Gaulle signifies, even in spite of himself, that henceforth vehement minorities will be able to act with impunity and assault democracy." The government should have taken as its model, exclaimed Mitterand, the resolution and integrity of Abraham Lincoln in the face of secession. The National Assembly accorded its confidence by a vote of 329 for, 224 against. Among the 83 deputies joining the Communists in opposition were a number of Radical Socialists led by Mendès-France, and a majority of the Socialist deputies (49 opposed, 42 in favor).

After voting confidence, the Assembly had now to delegate full legislative and constituent powers to the government. Another appearance by the Prime Minister was necessary to bring the issue to a rapid vote. On the evening of June 2, General de Gaulle came once

---

[8] Coty's message is in the *J.O., Assemblée Nationale*, May 29, 1958, p. 2556. For Coty's decision and the Le Troquer-Monnerville-De Gaulle interview, *cf.* Bromberger, *op. cit.*, pp. 389–413, and Ferniot, *op. cit.*, pp. 138–52. The Auriol-De Gaulle correspondence is reprinted and discussed by Ferniot, *op. cit.*, pp. 159–63, Bromberger, *op. cit.*, pp. 415–28, and *Année Politique*, 1958, pp. 538–39. For De Gaulle's talks with Socialist leaders, *cf.* Bromberger, *op. cit.*, pp. 432–34.

again to the Palais Bourbon. He went out of his way to assure some of his critics (the reference was obviously to Mendès-France) that he remained profoundly attached to them because of past associations—and hoped their personal relations would be continued in the future. He informed the Assembly, however, that if the government's bill for the revision of the amending clause of the constitution was not accepted, he would resign that very evening.

This time De Gaulle remained in the hemicycle, seemingly fascinated by the play of ideas and forces. When Jacques Duclos alluded to his proposal as a "plebiscite," De Gaulle reminded him that the Communists helped prepare the referenda out of which came the Fourth Republic. "We made these referenda together. Did the Republic disappear?" De Gaulle defended his conception of a referendum as perfectly compatible with the Republic. The Assembly was intrigued and captivated. "Because you understand that if I have formed the government, it is so that the Republic may continue!" The deputies burst into vigorous applause. "It is a pleasure and honor to find myself in your midst this evening," concluded the General. "After the 'operation sedition' that we experienced, we witnessed this evening 'operation seduction,'" observed a Communist deputy. The Assembly voted itself out of existence, 350 to 163. The regime welcomed its demise almost with a sense of relief.[9]

Republican Defense

In the final analysis, the regime chose to abdicate. Was there any alternative? The government could have persisted in vigorous defense of republican legality: court martial of dissident officers, blockade of Algeria, arrest of conspiratorial leaders in France, reconquest of Corsica, and in the event Operation Resurrection were actually launched, repression of rioters attempting to seize public buildings and armed opposition. From the tribune of the National Assembly on May 20, Mendès-France urged Pflimlin to defend the Republic with acts, not words: "Your strength, Mr. Prime Minister, doubtless greater than you believe, is your legitimacy. . . . But that strength and that legitimacy vindicate themselves and subsist only by action." He called upon the prime minister to inspire himself

---

[9] De Gaulle's declaration is in *J. O., Assemblée Nationale*, June 1, 1958, p. 2576, followed by debate, pp. 2577–92. For De Gaulle's second appearance, and interventions, *ibid.*, June 2, 1958, pp. 2618, 2623, 2624. Also Bromberger, *op. cit.*, pp. 429–39, and Ferniot, *op. cit.*, pp. 178–85.

on the model of the convention. "Do not invoke the weakness of your means. It has happened, in other times, that the Republic doubted some of its agents and some of its generals. But it relied on the people."

Unfortunately for the advocates of republican defense, the government did not have at its disposal the necessary force. Jules Moch relates that when he read De Gaulle's statement, "I have begun the process leading to the formation of a government," he heaved a sigh of relief, certain that there would be no attack that night. Moch's sense of relief is quite understandable, especially in the light of a later revelation. At the critical moment, "Out of nine officers commanding the military regions, four at least—who had authority over forty departments—did not conceal the fact that they were of one mind with Algeria. The super-prefects wondered under these conditions whether they were going to be arrested or whether they would do the arresting." The Minister of the Interior, an unflagging advocate of opposition to the rebellion, has since also commented on the state of morale among the two chief forces available to the Republic, the CRS and the police.

During the fortnight of anguish spent at *Place Beauvau* [Ministry of the Interior], I experienced a feeling of humiliation in noting the inefficiency of the police—that of Paris particularly: orders badly or not at all executed; misleading information furnished; commissioners shunning their duties; policemen personally participating or inciting participation in manifestations that they had been given the mission to suppress. . . . The *gendarmerie mobile* had the complexes of the army; it was not reliable. Even the CRS, once the pillar of the public order, to whose reconstitution I devoted myself in 1947, comprised units that were tired and contaminated by a long stay in the capital.[10]

The Minister of National Defense was not obeyed by the army, the Minister of the Interior had no police, the Minister of Aviation could not control the movement of military aircraft, the Minister of the Navy could not find any ships, the Minister of Algeria could not show his face in Algiers, the Minister of the Sahara could not go to the Sahara. Had the army decided to launch its invasion of France, given the defection of the police and the CRS, the outcome would not have been in doubt.

---

[10] Jules Moch, "De Gaulle d'hier à demain," *La Nef* (July–August, 1958), p. 10, and quoted by Ferniot, pp. 140–41. Mendès-France's exhortation is in *J.O.*, *Assemblée Nationale*, May 20, 1958, p. 2402.

The public forces having failed the government, one other alternative was theoretically possible: to form a Popular Front, arm the workers and democrats, declare a general strike, throw up barricades, and fight for the Republic in the best nineteenth-century tradition. Both Moch and Mollet at times thought of falling back on the "healthy democratic forces of the nation" as a last resort. The Minister of the Interior issued instructions to all prefects that, if unable to continue their functions, they were to take to the *Maquis*, keep in touch with the ministry by radio, and organize republican defense as best they could!

The divisions of the Left, however, which had largely contributed to a deadlocked system, ruled out this course of action. The gap between the Communists and the rest of the Left—aggravated by decades of mutual recrimination and political in-fighting—was too great to be bridged. The Socialists had more in common with De Gaulle than with the Communists. De Gaulle in power meant at least that the SFIO would continue as an organized party, even if in the opposition. The Popular Front implied the arming of a working class and inevitable Communist control. The Socialist leaders feared a possible repetition of the *coup de Prague*. Apart from doctrinal and political considerations, it was most improbable that the workers, Communist as well as Socialist, were prepared to fight or even resort to a general strike in order to block De Gaulle's return to power. The protest strikes and mass rallies were either total failures or manifested a notable lack of militancy. The five million electors who voted Communist were not ready to die on the barricades.

The forces of republican defense also lacked a head. Probably only one man in the National Assembly could have forged unity among the disparate groups of the Left: François Mitterand. But Mitterand was out of power, and all these in power were resolved to block him. Pflimlin and Mollet, who were entrusted with the conduct of affairs, considered Mitterand a greater danger than De Gaulle. The role of René Coty was crucial. Had the presidency been occupied by a forceful Republican, it is barely possible that the Center parties could have been galvanized into action. In 1947 President Vincent Auriol encouraged the leaders of the democratic center to resist the demands of General de Gaulle. Auriol declared at the time that he would not be the "Hindenburg of the Fourth Republic." But in 1958, the "Guardian of the Constitution," President Coty, wanted nothing more than to deposit his staggering burden in the hands of General de Gaulle. The presidency turned out to be not the shield, but the weakest link, of the constitution. The regime had neither the means nor the will to undertake its own defense.

Broadly speaking, power had been seized in Algeria and extended over France. The followers of De Gaulle strove to bring about the General's return—which seemed to them impossible by normal parliamentary processes; the extremists and activists of Algeria wanted the army to overthrow the Republic and rule the nation directly; the army was willing to intervene in political affairs, if necessary, but in the end deferred to De Gaulle. The Thirteenth of May was a chain reaction, in which all these groups were successful in achieving at least their initial goals. The activists, finding the "opening" they sought, incited the army to a state of insurgency; the army, already an administrative and political force in Algeria, prepared to invade the mainland rather than "abandon" Algeria; and General de Gaulle was called in by leading members of the regime to save the forms of republican legality.

If De Gaulle had not offered himself as a way out to the military chiefs in Algeria, would they have persisted in their disloyalty to the Republic? The regime might have been able to resist the army without De Gaulle behind it, as it had previously resisted De Gaulle without the army behind him. But it could not affront a combination of the two.

CHAPTER VI

The Army and the Nation

THE TREND of French military thinking concerning both tactics and strategy since the outbreak of the Algerian rebellion in November, 1954 has led to the alienation of the army from the State. In 1954 the French Army had just been thoroughly reorganized on the basis of the experience of World War II. Emphasis was placed on mobility, fire power, air-ground liaison, and logistics. The French Army was prepared to carry a share of the burden of Western defense, within the framework of the NATO alliance.

The army began its Algerian campaign as if it were a conventional battle: Forces in Algeria were speedily organized, and ordered to strike hard at rebel concentrations. Armor rolled ahead of motorized troops, punitive expeditions were carried out—but the results, to the disappointment of the authorities in Paris, were meager. Wherever the army struck in strength, the rebels simply disappeared. Within a year, virtually the entire French Army was engaged in Algeria; only small garrisons were left in Germany and France. Draftees and reservists were used (a measure never resorted to during the Indochina war), fresh credits were voted, and still the fighting flourished. Four hundred thousand French troops—approximately one soldier for every five adult male Moslems—did not suffice to stifle the rebellion.

A profound malaise was evident throughout the officer corps, due to a number of factors that antedated the Algerian rebellion. The collapse of 1940 had been a disastrous blow to morale. French armed forces played a very limited role in the Allied victory of 1944–45, in spite of the pretensions of biographical and historical accounts. The defeat in Indochina, though humiliating, was tempered by the knowledge that the army was not able to bring to bear its full might. But Algeria was different. The nation gave all that was

101

needed, from a military point of view—conscripts, money, supplies. Yet the war continued, and the redeeming victory sought by the army since 1939 remained as elusive as ever.

French officers found discussion on world strategy at NATO increasingly unreal. The Allies contemplated exclusively military operations involving techniques of modern warfare, while the French Army was deeply engaged in guerilla warfare. The officers contended that they were fighting a different kind of war, calling for new tactics. The result was a preoccupation with guerillas, development of psychological services, and reorganization of the army, all of which led to increased involvement of the army with politics.

The Theory of Revolutionary Warfare

The essence of the army's new doctrine was the distinction between modern warfare (which has been left, for all practical purposes, to the NATO allies), and the kind of warfare faced by French forces in the overseas territories. "In Indochina, Morocco, and Tunisia," declared Colonel Lacheroy, "the French Army has been directly engaged with adversaries conducting a revolutionary war." The goal of revolutionary warfare, he pointed out, is to seize power by virtue of the active support given to military units by a politically indoctrinated population. These techniques of the new warfare, developed according to Lacheroy by the Bolsheviks, had been used in pure form by the Viet Minh in Indochina.

A study group of French officers reported in 1957 the results of two years of reflection on the Indochina experience. They concluded that the real strength of the Viet Minh lay in the unity of political, psychological, and military action bringing about the *organization of the population.* The same techniques, according to the study group, were adopted by the Arab nationalists in North Africa, including the use of a "privileged sanctuary" as a base of operations. "M. Bourguiba," exclaimed one contributor to an army publication, "thinks of himself as the Mao Tse Tung of the FLN."

The master plan of the rebels required first the creation of a political organization, whose agents infiltrated selected areas of the country. After gaining the confidence of the people, they established a full-fledged administration—collecting taxes, administering justice, recruiting supporters. When the population had been won over, the area became a zone or base of operations for the rebel bands. The study group emphasized that revolutionary warfare is not directed at geographic or military objectives, but at the population. The rebellion could not be defeated by arms alone so long as the rebel organization remained intact and received the aid of the people.

The central idea used by the FLN to seduce the masses is *independence for an Algerian nation* (and as a corollary, criticism of France and spreading of doubts concerning French determination to remain in North Africa). Malcontents are kept in line by the use of terror. But the French specialists in psychological warfare did not consider the revolutionary war a spontaneous movement on the part of enthusiastic masses in favor of national independence. This, they claimed, was only a slogan used by a totalitarian political organization to conquer power. "There is no political solution in a revolutionary war," warned Commandant Hogard, "the legal power is condemned either to victory or disappearance." [1] In a revolutionary war, the French specialists concluded, the goal should be to destroy the rebel political organization, and to replace it with a new political organization directed by the army. In order to win a revolutionary war, the "forces of order" must eventually secure the support of the population for themselves. How was this to be accomplished? In effect, by copying the techniques used by the Communists in Indochina and the FLN in Algeria, placing these techniques at the service of a different goal, and marshaling the superior power of the French nation.

Consequently, the army needed a doctrine with which to win over the masses. The only theme capable of counteracting the rebel idea of independence was France—and the "universal values" incar-

---

[1] The best general introduction is Colonel Lacheroy's chapter on "La guerre révolutionnaire," in *La Défense nationale* (Presses Universitaires, 1958), pp. 307–30, and the same author's preface to a collection of articles on revolutionary warfare, in the *Revue Militaire d'Information* (February–March, 1957), pp. 7, 10. The use of Bolshevik techniques by the Viet Minh and Arab nationalists is discussed in "La guerre du Vietminh," *ibid.* (February–March, 1957), p. 35; Captain A. Soyris, "La révolution Tunisienne," *ibid.* (February–March, 1957), pp. 65–76; Lucien Poirier, "Un instrument de guerre révolutionnaire: le FLN," *ibid.* (December, 1957), pp. 7–33 and (January, 1958), pp. 69–92; Claude Delmas, "Les événements d'Afrique du Nord," *ibid.* (July, 1958), p. 100; and Commandant Jacques Hogard, "Cette guerre de notre temps," *Revue de Défense Nationale* (August–September, 1958), 1304–19. Military tactics required by pacification are analyzed in J. Hogard, "Guerre révolutionnaire et Pacification," *Revue Militaire d'Information* (January, 1957), 7–24. For the army's view of the FLN's ideology (i.e., independence): J. Hogard, "Tactique et stratégie dans la guerre révolutionnaire," *ibid* (June, 1958), p. 24; J. Cayol, "Les armes de la pacification," *Le Bled*, March 12, 1958, pp. 16–17, and J. Hogard, "Le soldat dans la guerre révolutionnaire," *Revue de Défense Nationale* (February, 1957), 215–20.

nated by the French presence. The army should therefore inform and educate the population as part and parcel of its military action. It was the task of the Psychological Services (5th Bureau) of the Army to build up faith in France, to exploit the weaknesses and contradictions in the rebel ideology. Measures were also to be adopted to institute a new and progressive social order within which the native population could achieve a more satisfactory way of life.

The key idea in the army's appeal to Moslems came to be *integration* but in a particular sense—Algeria is an "integral" part of France and her people, sharing the universal values embodied by France, were to become full French citizens. The young officers never concealed their antipathy to the reactionary policies of the *colons*, who overthrew a series of governments at the very intimation of reforms providing a single electoral college for both Europeans and Arabs. The last issue of *Le Bled* before May 13 denounced the capitalists of Algeria, who contributed to the FLN in the hope of buying protection, and hailed the "popular elements" who were determined to remain in Algeria come what may. Army officers, *Le Bled* continued, "feel closer to a proletariat attached to its soil and flag than to a capitalist ready to sell his soul in order to save his money and investments. . . . Coming from the middle class, the military cadres no longer have fortunes. If they have been fighting for nearly twenty years, it is because they are defending a heritage without price: their country and their honor." The military press repeated time and again that successful prosecution of the war in Algeria absolutely precluded a return to the *status quo ante*, that a new equilibrium should be created in order to afford Moslems a sense of participation in national life. And, of course, it was the army alone that was capable of creating these new conditions.

Finally, in order to keep the Moslem masses immune from subversion, they should be *organized*. The army ought to substitute its administration for that of the enemy. It was indispensable to establish labor, professional, social, and sport associations in order to integrate individuals into a coherent, dynamic, social whole. For example, the army set up a center for the formation of Algerian youth whose purpose was to take in charge all young people between the ages of 12 and 20 for physical and political education. Teams of French doctors and social workers established health services in the back country, making a special effort to reach and influence Moslem women. Social centers were founded for Moslem veterans, who were then encouraged to continue serving France. Schools were opened throughout Algeria by the military. Public meetings were held in villages once weekly, as part of the military program. The Communist technique was deliberately adopted of first discussing local questions which interest the audience directly, then bringing up large political issues. These public meetings were frequently organized by specially trained "traveling officers" ("officiers itiné-rants").

The Psychological Services considered it of special importance to "humanize" administration. The regular civil service, they contended, was out of touch with the native population. Army observers pointed out that in 1954 the French administration had no contact whatsoever with the bulk of the Moslem population. On the other hand, the rebel cadres, even though relatively inefficient, inspired confidence because they lived among the people. The army's chief agencies, in dealing with the problem of "underadministration" in Algeria, were the *Sections Administratives Specialisées* and the *Sections Administratives Urbaines* (SAS and SAU). As of July, 1958, troops assigned to the 592 SAS and SAU posts included 884 officers and 2,343 enlisted men. Over 300 schools were opened by SAS units, with 684 soldiers teaching 39,508 pupils (compared to 418 soldiers and 23,000 pupils in May, 1957). The SAS teams also established infirmaries and organized new communes. Hundreds of thousands of Moslems (reaching a total of one million by April, 1959) were evacuated from insecure regions, and placed in "regroupment centers" under the direct administration of the Psychological Services of the army. Thus, the SAS *encadred* the population, directing its activities, instilling faith and confidence in France, spreading consciously a political ideology. As the army's Algerian journal, *Le Bled*, observed in paying tribute to SAS officers: "It is significant to see the simultaneous intensification of military and political action, each supporting the other to the point that one can no more imagine military success without political success than political success without military success."[2]

---

[2] For the army's Psychological Services see "Les officiers itinérants," *Message des Forces Armées* (November, 1957), and J. Hogard, "Tactique et stratégie dans la guerre révolutionnaire," *Revue Militaire d'Information* (June, 1958), pp. 23, 29–30. On the army's hostility towards the colons, cf. *Le Bled*, May 14, 1958, p. 3 (this was written before the events of May 13), and Ximenes, "Essai sur la guerre révolution-naire," *Revue Militaire d'Information* (February–March, 1957), p. 22. The quoted tribute to SAS officers is from an editorial in *Le Bled*, March 26, 1958, p. 3. On the

Of course, all the while it was necessary to continue military operations against the guerrillas. But as the pacification campaign developed, the military effort was best served by deconcentration of forces and the assignment of delimited zones of operations to small units. The Algerian campaign became primarily a "war of captains and lieutenants."

A frequently cited example of the army's expanded role was a region of Kabyl, with a population of about 10,000. The area was placed in charge of an officer with special training in psychological warfare, after security was established. Under his direction, the army organized self-defense forces of Harkis (Moslems who serve under the French flag), built schools (staffed by soldiers) for 900 children, and established infirmaries where natives received free treatment by army physicians. The psychological officers have tended to become political commissars—indoctrinating shock troops, spreading the army's message, organizing the population. The ability of the 5th Bureau to mobilize thousands of Europeans and Moslems at short notice for any purpose was effectively demonstrated during the events of May.

Urban terrorism, particularly grave in Algiers, Constantine, and Oran, caused a further extension of the political rule of the army. On January 7, 1957 all police power in the city of Algiers was vested in the army, which was given the responsibility of restoring order to a city wracked by terrorism and threatened by a general strike. The task was successfully undertaken by the 10th Division of paratroopers, under the command of General Massu. Each paratrooper was given the authority to arrest any individual, Moslem or European, and to hold him in "a special place" without informing the civil authorities. It has been reported that 3,000 persons so arrested in the first nine months of 1957 have never been heard from since. Numerous others, eventually released, claimed to have been tortured.[3]

SAS, see also: Captain A. Souyris, "Les conditions de la Parade et de la Riposte dans la guerre révolutionnaire," *Revue Militaire d'Information* (February–March, 1957), pp. 101, 105; *Le Bled*, September 3, 1958, p. 9; and Jacques Duquesne, *L'Algérie, ou la guerre des mythes* (Paris, 1958), pp. 50–64.

[3] For a technical analysis of tactics required by this new form of warfare, see Captain H. Martin, "Guerilla, guerre en surface, guerre révolutionnaire," *Revue Militaire d'Information* (August, 1957), pp. 7–22 and (November, 1957), pp. 61–71; and J. Hogard, "Le soldat dans la guerre révolutionnaire," *Revue de Défense Nationale* (February, 1957), p. 227. Also Jean Ferniot, *Les Ides de mai, op. cit.*, pp. 46–55. The Kabyl experience is described in "A l'épreuve des faits," *Message des Forces Armées* (February, 1958). On the expansion of the military's domain in Algeria, and for a report on missing prisoners, see J. Duquesne, *L'Algérie, op. cit.*, pp. 25–30.

The enormous expansion of the army's administrative duties, and especially the violation of procedural safeguards in dealing with rebel prisoners or sympathizers, aroused much comment among liberal elements in France and deep misgivings on the part of the democratic party leaders. There was a real danger of a breakdown of communication and understanding between public opinion at home and the army in the field. The army became increasingly sensitive to criticism. When it was made to appear that politicians at home might endanger its achievements in Algeria, the army was readily persuaded by extremists and Gaullists to act in what it conceived to be its own and the nation's interest.

The Army's Political Theory

The defeat of 1940, along with De Gaulle's determination to carry on the war from London, shook the army profoundly. Every officer was confronted at the time with a political choice: to accept the leadership of Marshal Pétain or join the Gaullist camp; to march in Syria with Dentz or Catroux; to collaborate with or resist the Japanese in Indochina; to follow Darlan, Giraud, or De Gaulle in Algiers. The unity of the army suffered considerably as a consequence of the wartime quarrels. Those who had been faithful to Pétain, Darlan, or Giraud were understandably not on good terms with the Gaullists and those who had entered the army from the Resistance. The case of De Gaulle himself was symbolic: a general who flouted orders, refused discipline, challenged his superiors, even was condemned to death *in absentia* for treason—and who was finally vindicated, receiving all the honors a grateful nation could bestow. If one general could appeal from the regime to the nation in 1940, why could not other generals do the same in 1958?

The impact of the army's political duties in Algeria necessitated the abandonment of its former role of strict neutrality. It sought a more intimate association with civilian authorities and participation in the formulation of policy. General André Zeller gave voice to a widespread feeling when he declared that the army had gone beyond the point where it could sacrifice itself only out of duty or discipline. He called for a "political army," in the sense that the traditional estrangement between regime and army be eliminated. But the assumption was still that the State occupies the supreme position in the hierarchy of command: It is the State which defines the objectives of national policy, lays down the moral obligations of the army, and gives it a mission. The army claimed only the right to be heard.[4]

The logic of the Algerian war soon led the army beyond mere participation. The creation of an administrative network in Algeria brought the army into conflict with civil authorities. Who was to have the final say in the domain of police action, communal reorganization, propaganda, education, and recreation—the local army officers responsible for pacification or representatives of the Republic? In fact, the civil authorities retreated and withdrew all along the line. The resident minister's delegation of police power to the army in January, 1957 symbolized the inability of civilians to cope with the staggering security and political problems of Algeria.

General Salan revealed in June, 1958 that ever since taking command of the armed forces in Algeria he had desired unity of civil and military power. Under whose direction, the military or the civilians, should this unity be forged? "As regards the subversive war in which we are immersed, I have always thought that only the army, with its innumerable antennae in the population and its intimate contacts with all, could successfully manage the affair." Besides, added Salan, the civil administration is affected by political and partisan considerations, whereas the army is concerned only with the national interest!

But the Algerian war required more than administrative unity on a local level: It could not be successfully waged, concluded a number of army officers, unless the rebels were convinced that France would never capitulate. It was the duty of the army, then, to bring to an end the encouragement and aid being received by the rebels from "certain elements" in France and to define great objectives for the nation to follow. Thus, the roles of the State and the army were reversed: It was now the duty of the army (uncontaminated by partisan squabbling) to formulate the goals and obligations of the nation (heretofore misled and confused by political quarrels). As Commandant Hogard expressed it in January, 1957:

The soldier of today can no longer, as in times when wars were 'national,' neglect political considerations. As a Frenchman and as a soldier, he believes that he has the duty and the right to cry out to his compatriots: "This struggle is a struggle to the death, and we warriors can conquer

[4] See General André Zeller, "Armée et politique," *Revue Militaire d'Information* (April, 1957), pp. 506–14; and Raoul Girardet, *La Société militaire dans la France contemporaine, 1815–1939* (Paris, 1953), p. 119, and chaps. 1, 2, and 7.

only if you consent to look upon the true face of the enemy, only if you
accept the necessary transformations and sacrifices in order to beat him,
in short, only if France finds again its determination of Clemenceau's
time."

And if the army provides for schools, attends the sick, administers
municipalities, runs the economy, holds aloft national ideals, then
what useful purpose is served by parliaments, cabinets, and prefects?
In its last issue before May 13, *Le Bled* called for a complete revision
of political conceptions, and demanded the creation of "a Government of Public Safety, without which France will go to its suicide." [5]

After the victory of May 13, the army staked out enormous claims
over traditional political territory. One young officer even attempted
to erect the army's pretensions into a general political theory, drawing freely from Machiavelli. His statement, published in the *Message
des Forces Armées,* reflected the new political vocation of the officer
corps.

Politics is fundamentally the affair of the Prince. . . . In order to
assist him in his duties, the Prince disposes (apart from his functionaries,
simple emanations of himself, inevitable multiplication essential to a
modern State) of three corps having their personal ethic and whose role
depasses in grandeur the human expression of their activity. These are
the Magistracy, guardian of the law; the Police, protector of individuals;
the Army, rampart of the collectivity. And of the three the most exacting
for its members, who are expected to give their all because it is the defender of the most general interest, *the one whose calling is therefore essentially political, is the Army.*

The anonymous officer, to whom it did not occur that Parliament
might have a valid role to play, went on to explain the theory behind
the army's participation in the May 13 coup: If the Prince fails to
exercise his authority, then one of the three public bodies must fill
the gap. This was done in May by the army, because it had the keen-
est appreciation of the gravity of the situation. The intentions of the

---

[5] The quotation is from J. Hogard, "L'Armée française devant la guerre révolutionnaire," *Revue de Défense Nationale* (January, 1957), p. 78. See also *Le Bled,*
May 14, 1958, p. 3. General Salan's statement was made in an interview originally
accorded to *La Voix du Nord,* reprinted in *Le Bled,* June 18, 1958, p. 4. "The treasonable elements" in France are not only the Communists, but all those who advocate
negotiations in Algeria. In a thinly disguised reference to the liberal newspaper *Le
Monde,* one army officer reported: "In some sectors of Algeria, intelligence officers
summarize the evolution of subversion by indicating the number of copies of a great
Metropolitan daily which are sold in their zone: 'chez moi cela va mal, la vente du
. . . a augmenté; chez moi cela va mieux, la vente du . . . a baissé.'" J. Hogard,
"Tactique et stratégie dans la guerre révolutionnaire," *R. Mil. d'Information* (June,
1958), p. 33.

army are pure because they are national rather than political. The army seeks only to promote the principles of hierarchy, order, and authority—the basis of all human society. "Faithful to its political calling, rising above castes and clans, maintaining a keen sense of national well-being, conscious above all of the defense of the community, the Army intends to remain for the Prince his most reliable and most impartial support." [6]

Bit by bit, the Army developed an ideology (rudimentary but adequate for the purpose of seizing power) out of its experiences in Algeria. It believed only too gladly that the politicians were responsible for the "loss" of Indochina, Morocco, and Tunisia. It concluded that the State must be totally reformed, and that the army—selfless custodian of the general interest, unsullied guardian of the ideals of the nation—must assume the primary responsibility for renovation. The conditions were created by the young officers in charge of Psychological Services, the impulse was given by the activist groups, and at the moment of decision the generals accorded their endorsement. Without the army there could never have been a Thirteenth of May.

For the first time since Louis Napoleon, the French Army participated in a *coup d'état.* The army's responsibility for the events of May, 1958 was, if anything, greater than in December, 1851. On December 2, 1851, the generals merely carried out the orders of their legitimate chief, the President of the Republic (and even so, with considerable hesitation and soul searching); in 1958 the generals deliberately ignored the injunctions of the President of the Republic to obey constituted authority. In 1851 the army took no initiative in the plot to overthrow the Second Republic; in 1958 elements within the army created and exploited the revolutionary situation. The Second Empire was not dominated by the military; once Napoleon's coup succeeded, the army reverted willingly to its traditional role of political passivity. But in Algeria the army entered the Committee of Public Safety, arrogated to itself "the political destinies of French Algeria," and sought to impose its will on Paris. Activists in the army felt duty-bound to destroy a regime whose parliamentary squabbling appeared to endanger national unity.

The weakness of the Fourth Republic was beyond debate—as witnessed by the failure of any important social group to rally to its

---

[6] "Du rôle politique de l'Armée," *Message des Forces Armées* (October, 1958). See also *Le Bled,* January 22, 1958, p. 16.

defense. But the army's particular criticism is not entirely convincing. French military disasters after World War II were certainly not due to any refusal on the part of the National Assembly to supply credits, matériel, or men. Inability to adapt rapidly to the requirements of revolutionary warfare in Indochina and North Africa was largely due to the doctrinaire attitude of the high command and the inflexibility of French Army structure. The army was at least partially to blame for the failure to arm native troops under their own officers, for a paternalistic attitude toward local populations, and for disregard of morale factors. As François Mitterand has pointed out, in the winter of 1954 the army wanted to withdraw all forces from l'Aurès in order to be able to mount a grand offensive in the spring —thereby abandoning 120,000 inhabitants to the rebellion. This would have been a fatal error in the conduct of a "revolutionary war"—and was hardly the product of a civilian mentality.[7]

Democratic government necessarily assumes the supremacy of civil over military authority. In states with democratic traditions it is unthinkable that the army would openly challenge this assumption. Only in relatively backward or undeveloped countries, where practice in self-government is limited, are armed forces expected to play a specifically political role. The most significant feature of May 13 is the direct involvement and complicity of the army, in a country generally considered to be one of the bastions of democracy on the continent of Europe.

The army not only came out in opposition to the parliamentary institutions established by the Constitution of the Fourth Republic (which, it was commonly admitted, had failed to provide for effective government), it threw down a challenge to the very idea of republican government and sought justification in a totalitarian philosophy. On the basis of its experience in Indochina, the army concluded that control of the media of communication and propaganda was the key to power, and that ideals—any ideals—could be manufactured at will. Indoctrination of the masses with a particular point of view was simply an engineering problem to be resolved by manipulative processes. Viewing the Algerian rebellion essentially as an issue of force whose outcome would be determined by the loyalty

---

[7] François Mitterand, "L'Armée dans le système," *La Nef* (July–August, 1958), pp. 16–19. On the army's role during the Second Empire, see Raoul Girardet, *La Société militaire dans la France contemporaine, op. cit.*, pp. 133–44. Note also the comments on the army's actions in 1958 by Raymond Aron, *L'Algérie et la République, op. cit.*, pp. 89–90, and Maurice Duverger, *Demain la République, op. cit.*, p. 131.

and support of the Moslem masses, it proposed in blatant fashion to shape their thinking by using the totalitarian techniques of the enemy. The population, consequently, had to be "organized." Over *one million* Moslems have been herded into resettlement camps, where they are directly governed by the army. Those not in camps are watched, and if possible administered, by SAS officers or police agents in liaison with the army. In dealing with terrorists and re-fractory elements of the Moslem population, the army has not re-coiled from the use of torture on a large scale. Although military spokesmen at first tried to minimize the extent to which these proc-esses were used, it was finally held to be necessary in the prosecution of a guerrilla war. One liberal Catholic intellectual, after presenting a moving account of the torture techniques regularly employed by the French Army in Algeria, raised the agonizing question whether the real victor of World War II was not after all Adolf Hitler.

Criticism of the army's actions by intellectuals and party spokes-men in France exasperated a number of officers, who developed a "stab-in-the-back theory"—that the war in Algeria would long since have been won were it not for political sabotage on the home front. Some officers concluded that victory over the rebels was possible only on one condition: that the army project its control over France, do away with Parliament and the "regime of the parties," take over all media of communication—in effect, create a totalitarian system. The events of May 13 did not have this extreme result, but this is not proof that the antirepublican elements in the army have abandoned their hopes. The circumstances were such that General de Gaulle was able to preserve the semblance of republican legality and rally support from all groups of the population, including the army. How-ever, the army continued after his return to exercise far-reaching functions in Algeria and remained a vigorous force, while the inter-nal divisions of French society may well continue into the future. As long as the Algerian war goes on, the Republic is in grave danger.

The continuation of the Algerian war points up the weakness of the military outlook. One of the basic postulates of the French Army specialists in revolutionary warfare is that political movements (for example, for national independence) can be reduced to mere tech-nical manipulation of the masses by skilled elite groups. Colonel Lacheroy has contended that the concept of independence "has no innate meaning to the brave peasant or the village artisan, because never has he, or his father, or his father's father, or his grandfather's father had any interest in the question." [8] None of the army spokesmen ever mention the possibility that national independence movements might be part of a historical process, or that the ideal of independence could be a legitimate aspiration on the part of non-European peoples.

Basically, the French Army was assigned a task far beyond the capacity of even a ferociously determined and united French nation: to reverse the tide of revolt by Asian and African peoples who had been conquered in the preceding century. The "techniques of revolutionary warfare" worked successfully for the Viet Minh because the idea of national independence corresponded to the hopes and desires of the population. The same techniques, had they been used by the French in Indochina, would not have produced the same results. While a pro-French attitude can be manufactured for some elements of a native population, it is illusory to assume that propaganda and control of media of communication can arrest the independence movement.

By considering the Algerian problem to be one of force and manipulation of docile populations, the French Army left the rebels no alternative between surrender and victory—thus excluding political solutions. Both sides were thus driven to apply the lessons learned from Mao-Tse-Tung and the Communists in their effort to win the elusive battle for domination.

---

[8] Colonel Lacheroy, "La guerre révolutionnaire," in *La Défense nationale, op. cit.,* pp. 309, 318. On the question of torture in Algeria, see *Année Politique, 1957,* pp. 30, 35–36, 40; Pierre-Henri Simon, *Contre la torture* (Paris, 1957), especially pp. 72–93, 105–14; Pierre Vidal-Naquet, *L'Affaire Audin* (Paris, 1958), and Henri Alleg, *The Question* (London, 1958). The army's view of the controversy is exemplified by Colonel de Rocquigny, "Le terrorisme urbain," *Revue Militaire d'Information* (February, 1958), p. 81.

Part Two

The New Constitution

CHAPTER VII

The Perennial Constitutional Debate

THE CONSTITUTION of the Fifth Republic originated in a sweeping delegation of constituent powers to General de Gaulle's newly invested government. In derogation of the provisions of Article 90 * the enabling act of June 3, 1958 provided "the constitution will be revised by the government formed on June 1, 1958." It was specified in the act that the following principles ought to serve as the basis for the new constitution: universal suffrage, which remains the source of political power and from which, or the organs chosen by it, executive and legislative power derives; an effective separation between the government and Parliament so that each performs its functions under its own responsibility; responsibility of the government before Parliament; independence of the judiciary so that the basic liberties defined in the preamble of the Constitution of 1946 and the Declaration of the Rights of Man be safeguarded. A new organization of relations between the Republic and the peoples associated with it was envisaged. The act outlined briefly the procedure to be followed for the elaboration of the constitution. It involved the examination of the text by a constitutional consultative committee and by the *Conseil d'Etat,* and finally popular approval in a referendum.[1]

---

* Article 90 of the Constitution of the Fourth Republic provided for a cumbersome method of constitutional revision. The initiative for reform was to come from the National Assembly. A proposal for revision voted by Parliament was to be submitted to a referendum, unless there was a majority of three-fifths in favor in both assemblies or a majority of two-thirds in the National Assembly. The Communists controlled some 150 votes out of a total of 596 and the other parties could not arrive at an agreement.

[1] *Recueil,* p. 5. (For an explanation of abbreviated titles, see references at end of chapter.)

This authorization enabled General de Gaulle's government to elaborate the text of the Constitution of the Fifth Republic in an attempt to put an end to the constitutional instability that has plagued the nation ever since the Revolution. Thus, the France that emerged from the Revolution of 1789 has had on the average a constitution at least every fourteen years: limited monarchy (1789); a republic establishing an assembly government (1792); a directorate (1796); the Consulate and the Empire (1801); the restoration of the monarchy (1814); a return to limited monarchy (1830); the Second Republic (1848), which degenerated into one-man rule and the return of the Empire (1852); the Third Republic (1875); an authoritarian system (Vichy 1940–44), and the Fourth Republic (1946).[2]

This constitutional instability, whose most pervasive feature is the lack of legitimization and institutionalization of any form of government, is a reflection of persistent incompatibilities that the body politic has been unable to surmount in the last century and a half. Its causes must be sought in the interstices of the social system—in the relations between classes and the manner in which power is claimed or exercised by them. A constitution, as Aristotle observed, is but a map that shows the broad contours of power in any given system. Constitutions in France, however, tend to be only makeshift arrangements, temporary compromises permitting the various forces to continue their warfare. Yet the more divided the body politic appears to be, the more the emphasis upon a constitutional document in order to cement the loose social and political bonds. In urging adoption of the new constitution De Gaulle asked the French to vote for it in order to re-establish national unity.

The broad delegation of constituent powers to General de Gaulle's government was also prompted by the ineffectiveness of the Fourth Republic and the events of May 13. Cabinet instability, coupled with the inability of the National Assembly to make decisions on urgent postwar problems, provoked a widespread movement of reform for the reinforcement of the executive.

The debate over the constitutional causes of cabinet instability led to the review of the more basic shortcomings of the Fourth Republic, particularly the division of the body politic into a great number of political parties. It was generally agreed that mere reform of the electoral system would be inadequate since multipartism

---

[2] See *Duguit, et al., Les Constitutions.*

had existed under a great variety of electoral systems. In fact it was doubtful that any solution could be found. Hence the search for parliamentary institutions that recognized the inevitability of multipartism without allowing it to thwart effective government. A number of political leaders and students, realizing that the two-party system, which is responsible for the success of the British parliamentary institutions, could not be duplicated in France, sought a solution in a presidential system. A president elected by direct popular vote would assume the traditional prerogatives of the executive. Thus, in a divided society there would be an element of unity, stability, and decision making. Even opponents of presidential government generally agreed that the excessive powers of the Parliament should be curbed, and that parliamentary procedure should be accordingly "rationalized." Many of the provisions of the new constitution concerning the Parliament and legislative-executive relations stem from a long debate that antedates the Fourth Republic.

A personal element related to the quest for leadership also played an important role in the formulation of the new constitution. In the last years of the Fourth Republic the greatness of France was hardly reflected in a dignified manner, to say the least, in the spectacle of a weak President of the Republic constantly in search of a prime minister. Ever since his self-imposed exile, De Gaulle was the only person in whom the demand for unity, national independence, and leadership could find anything approaching a broad consensus. The constitution is tailor-made to fit De Gaulle.

The Background of the Debate

On August 25, 1944 General de Gaulle entered Paris and was asked to proclaim the Republic on behalf of the people. He refused, pointing out that the French State had never ceased to exist. His own account of the occasion is perhaps one of the most illuminating footnotes on French political history. While he was waiting at the outskirts of Paris, he writes in his *Memoirs*, he was visited by a messenger from the Prefect of Paris with the information that the capital was in the hands of Resistance forces. He immediately asked the messenger to return to Paris and inform the Prefect that his intention was not to go to the *Hôtel de Ville* where the Council of the Resistance and the Committee of the Liberation of Paris were in permanent session. He would rather go to the "center," which was the Ministry of War—the logical center for the government and for the French commanding staff, "not because I did not want to establish contact with the leaders of the Parisian insurrection" he adds. "I wanted to make it clear that the State, after the tribulations that could neither destroy it nor enslave it was returning home." [3]

The incident and De Gaulle's attitude illustrates a basic cleavage in French political ideology and attitude dividing the Right and Left, which accounts to a great extent for constitutional instability. According to the Right, the State embodies the legitimate interests of the people; while according to the Left, these interests are identified only with the people. The Right contends that the State represents, in Burkian fashion, the immutable interests of the political society standing above particular forms of government. The legitimacy of the State springs from the reality of the French nation and French history. The Left, on the other hand, sees precisely in a popular mandate the source of political power and as a result considers a republic as the direct emanation of the popular will, sovereign and unlimited, to be the only legitimate form of statehood.

Neither of the two points of view could ever be institutionalized in pure form. Concessions had to be made by the conservatives to the exigencies of representative government and popular elections. Republicans had in turn to compromise with the needs of political authority and temper direct popular rule accordingly. After the establishment of the Third Republic, the conflict between these two points of view became a confrontation between legislative omnipotence in the name of popular sovereignty and a strong and stable executive in the name of State authority. The Constitution of the Third Republic was a compromise: The executive (President of the Republic and the cabinet) represented the elements of authority and stability, whereas the Chamber of Deputies incarnated the popular will. The balance, however, was upset by legislative encroachments upon the prerogatives of the executive, which led in turn to repeated efforts to reinforce the executive. Thus, constitutional conflict and revisionism became a permanent part of the republican institutions. Indeed, the movement for constitutional reform became a perennial debate.

On two occasions in the early years of the Third Republic the exercise of executive power or the demand for constitutional reform in order to give to the executive larger powers were tantamount to a

---

[3] *Mémoires*, Vol. II, pp. 302–3. For some shrewd comments see A. Frossard, *Histoire Paradoxale de la 4 ième République* (Paris, 1946).

direct threat to the Republic: In 1877 when President MacMahon attempted to thwart a Republican majority by dissolving the Chamber of Deputies, and a decade later when General Boulanger advocated drastic constitutional reform. In both cases the conservative forces desired the restoration of the monarchy. In both cases it was the Republic that was in danger. The republican forces were led to equate the Republic with a strong legislature and a weak executive. The right of the executive to dissolve the Parliament became a dead letter, while the standing orders of the Chamber of Deputies and the Senate progressively underwrote the supremacy of the legislature and its powerful committees in practically all matters of policy, including appropriations and the preparation of the budget. In the twentieth century, the republican reflexes held firm despite the growing realization that a legislature divided into many parties could not formulate policy.

Suggestions for the reform of the system came almost invariably from the Right, but in a form that no longer questioned the republican institutions. For instance, the proposals of Tardieu, Millerand, and Doumergue in the interwar years were addressed primarily to the reform of parliamentary procedure. In most cases they envisaged the introduction of simple rules of procedure aimed at restoration of a balance between the legislature and the executive. Most important among them were: the right of dissolution at the discretion of the prime minister; the creation of an Office of the Prime Minister enabling him to discharge more effectively his growing responsibility for policy initiation and coordination; strict control of interpellations —to prevent the deputies from putting in jeopardy the life of the government at any time; limitations of the powers of the legislative committees that had become for all practical purposes miniature parliaments; the organization of the parliamentary debates in a manner that would give priority to government proposals; limitations of the powers of the Senate, and finally, the elimination of the initiative of private members in proposing finance bills. All these reforms, drawn largely from British experience, aimed at strengthening the executive within the frame of the parliamentary institutions.

Summing up the problems of parliamentary government in France and suggesting a number of reforms, René Capitant, in a succinct pamphlet written in 1934,[4] pointed out that in order to "give" France a government and reintroduce a genuine parliamentary system in

---

[4] René Capitant, *La Réforme du Parlementarisme*.

which "the government governs and the Parliament controls" it was sufficient to attribute to the prime minister the right to dissolve the Chamber of Deputies and to maintain the single-member electoral system with runoffs (*ballottage*). In this manner he hoped that a majority would emerge. "Parliamentarism," he continued, "does not call for a representation of opinions and interests but for elections which create a government." [5] It was not therefore a question of undermining the sovereignty of Parliament but rather of transferring the sovereign powers of Parliament to a government that enjoyed its support. In fact, he concluded, the concentration of all powers in the hands of Parliament was a salutary development that facilitated their transfer to a cabinet, as the British experience showed. "The separation between the executive and the legislature is an erroneous idea." [6]

Thus, Capitant, who later became an important figure in De Gaulle's provisional government and one of the founders of the RPF in 1947, proposed to establish a cabinet system. Parliamentary sovereignty would remain intact, but the executive, supported by a strong majority, would govern effectively. Central to his thesis was the creation of stable and coherent majorities—a prerequisite for all modern parliamentary democracies. The logic of his argument was perhaps the only one that could provide for a compromise between the theories of the Left and the Right. It simply posited that *if* in a parliamentary system there is a majority, then the strength of the executive emanates directly from Parliament, that is, from the will of the people as expressed in elections. But what if no such majority could result from an electoral consultation?

The Left became increasingly intransigent in equating an omnicompetent assembly with the Republic. They still feared that efforts to strengthen the executive might endanger the Republic itself and the privileges that the deputies and the senators had concentrated in their hands. In the Third Republic the formation of cabinets was an undertaking in which the political weight of each political group had little relation to its numbers. The formation or the resignation of a government often depended upon small marginal groups of twenty or thirty deputies. Many deputies felt, despite the assertion of collective supremacy, that the government was the real center of power, and they wanted to maintain the conditions for participating

---

[5] *Ibid.*, p. 10.
[6] *Ibid.*, p. 15.

in it. Such conditions existed only as long as there was no threat of dissolution and the cabinet remained at the mercy of the political parties and groups. Therefore a stubborn resistance developed to any reform. In the guise of parliamentary sovereignty, the deputies were defending a *status quo* that gave them direct control over and participation in the cabinet. Compared to a British backbencher, a French deputy was a feudal lord and he was not prepared to abandon his privileged position.

In the last decade of the Third Republic, the reluctance of the parties, particularly those of the Left, to enact the needed reforms accounted to a great extent for the virulence of the antiparliamentarian and antirepublican movement that reappeared in the years preceding the events of May 13, 1958. For if the parliamentary institutions, as they stood, were equated with the republican tradition, then an attack against them involved an attack against the Republic. The manner in which the institutions functioned, however, intensified the attack. Parliament, unable to legislate because of the absence of cohesive majorities, had to delegate broad powers to the executive, but held fast to its powers of life and death over the cabinets. So while it was losing its supreme prerogative—legislation—it maintained over the cabinets a control that in the eyes of the public seemed increasingly capricious and arbitrary. Given the urgency of the situation confronting the country in the thirties, Parliament appeared an incoherent and divisive force. Many became convinced that an effective and stable government had to be sought outside of Parliament, perhaps even outside of the Republic itself. Thus, the constitutional debate in the last years of the Third Republic had come back to its starting point. Once more the demand for a strong government took a character that threatened the Republic. The Right was returning to the theory according to which the authority of the State must be derived from some source other than public opinion, whereas the Left, now that the Republic appeared to be in danger, fell back once more upon the Jacobin theory of legislative omnicompetence. The crisis of the parliamentary institutions became once more a crisis of the regime.

Reform of the Constitution and the Resistance

During the Resistance period we find the same pervasive conflict on the nature of constitutional reform. Two novel factors should be mentioned, however. First, with the exception of the Radical Socialist party whose political strength was negligible at the time of the Liberation, *all* political parties and groups were against returning to the institutions of the Third Republic. Second, the Communists, who had until then paid little attention to matters of constitutional reform, except to defend the Republic in the thirties in the name of the Popular Front, emerged as the most articulate exponents of the Jacobin republican tradition. As was so often true in the past, when the time came to formulate measures for institutional reform, wide differences appeared that stemmed from divisions in the body politic. Innumerable projects reflected the two sides in the French constitutional debate: a strong executive and assembly government. The first was proposed in the speeches of General de Gaulle and the projects prepared by some of his assistants or avowed sympathizers; the second, by the Communists—when finally they were provoked to state their position. Socialists, Moderates, Radical Socialists, and even the liberal Catholic group that formed the MRP oscillated between the two.

General de Gaulle, who has been so often portrayed as a rigid and uncompromising political leader, showed remarkable acumen. He avoided for a long time any explicit commitments regarding the future structure of the State. During the war he seemed to favor the establishment of a new Republic in which popular sovereignty and parliamentary government were to be maintained. But what kind of parliamentary government? What were to be the relations between the executive and the legislature? Beyond favoring a "government able to govern," De Gaulle, so eloquent in his envisaged proposals for social and economic reform, remained remarkably taciturn. For instance, as late as March, 1944, in a speech before the Provisional Consultative Assembly in Algiers promising "free, direct, and general elections," he declared:

> The new regime must have representatives elected by all men and women. . . . It will function in a manner very different from that which paralyzed the Parliament of the Third Republic. The government, to which the confidence of the national representatives will confer the executive power, will be in a position to use it with the force and stability required by the authority of the State and the greatness of France in the world.[7]

But he considered his role and that of his provisional government to be primarily that of custodian of the national interests of France;

---

[7] *Discours et Messages* (Paris, 1946), p. 422.

after the Liberation the new institutions would be made by the people and their representatives. Indeed he went beyond this by pointing out time after time that his provisional government would "give an account" to the representatives of the people as soon as free elections had been held.

A "strong government" a "government that governs" but a "responsible" government ready to account for its acts to the nationally elected representatives—didn't this suggest the parliamentary system advocated by Capitant, who now advised De Gaulle? Both Left and Right found in these statements what they were seeking. The emphasis upon the role of the national representatives was an echo of the Jacobin theory of legislative supremacy. But the notion of a strong government, even if a responsible one, was equally compatible with the conservative point of view.

It was after the liberation of France, in connection with the imminent election of a Constituent Assembly, that De Gaulle criticized sharply the notion of assembly government and opted for a balanced organization of the public powers. It was unthinkable, he pointed out, that an Assembly elected to make a new constitution should have absolute and unlimited powers. He proposed that its duration be limited to seven months. In addition to its constituent powers it should nominate the president of the government, ratify treaties, and vote the budget. The government, he conceded later, was to remain responsible before the Assembly and could be overthrown by a vote of censure requiring an absolute majority. The Assembly would be able to initiate laws concurrently with the government.[8] There was to be no derogation of the principle of cabinet responsibility and no qualifications to the basic tenets of parliamentary government. A remark made by General de Gaulle on September 4, 1945 on the occasion of the seventy-fifth anniversary of the Third Republic, gave heart to the heirs of the Jacobin tradition. After pointing out the weakness of the executive that was responsible for a state of permanent political crisis in the last years of the Third Republic, De Gaulle criticized the Senate. Though a second chamber was "certainly necessary," the Senate had enjoyed "the abusive right of blocking indefinitely the decisions of the lower assembly and blocked urgent reforms, especially on social matters." [9]

Between the elections of October 18, 1945 and his resignation on

---

[8] *Ibid.*, pp. 699.
[9] *Ibid.*, p. 661.

January 20, 1946, General de Gaulle's views remained consistent. Two incidents gave him the opportunity to present more fully his views and his acceptance of parliamentary government. The first occurred when the Communists insisted on at least one of the key ministries of his cabinet—War, Foreign Affairs, or Interior. From a political standpoint their demand could not be contested since they were the largest party in the Constituent Assembly and De Gaulle had promised to form a cabinet of national unity. But De Gaulle had been unanimously nominated president of the government by the Assembly and considered it to be his prerogative to choose his ministers. To accede to the Communist demands would be, in his opinion, a distortion of the nature of the executive function and in effect a return to the practices of the Third Republic in which the groups determined the composition of the cabinet. "The independence, the cohesion, the authority of the government" would be endangered, he asserted. "I come before the national representatives," he declared before the Constituent Assembly, "to return the mandate given to me." [10] His resignation was refused and he was allowed to determine the composition of his cabinet. But at a moment when his popularity was at its highest there could not have been a more unexceptionable parliamentary gesture.

In December, 1945 the Assembly attempted to reduce the government's envisaged military appropriations. General de Gaulle again stated the case for parliamentary government in the clearest possible fashion. "The Constituent Assembly," he pointed out, "has the totality of the legislative power. . . . It has the power to follow the government it likes or, if it does not like it, to let it go or make it go. . . . These powers are not contested and in my opinion cannot be contested. . . ." But "there is also a government." He reminded them that its composition and its program had been accepted. The situation, he said, should be clarified. "Does the government have your confidence—yes or no? You will either vote the credits or you will not, in which case the government will retire from office. There is no more democratic way." [11]

But De Gaulle went even further. Before a hushed Assembly he pointed out:

. . . it is a general conception of government, and of its relations with the national representatives, that separates us. . . . We have begun to

---

[10] *Ibid.*, p. 702.
[11] *Ibid.*, pp. 714–15.

reconstruct the Republic. You will continue to do it. No matter how you do it I think I ought to say in all conscience, and undoubtedly this is the last time I am speaking in this place, that if you do it without taking into consideration the lessons of our political history of the last fifty years and more particularly of what happened in 1940, if you do not take into consideration the absolute necessity of the authority, dignity, and responsibility of the Government, you will create such a situation that one day or another, I predict, you will regret bitterly having started on the road you are about to take.

The Assembly hesitated to overthrow De Gaulle and voted only a token reduction of the military appropriations.

De Gaulle's speech at the Assembly was criticized with indignation not only by the Communists but by the Socialists as well. His threat to resign was denounced as blackmail that if tolerated would lead to the abdication by the Assembly of its powers. If De Gaulle stays in office he should "acquire the habits of democracy," said André Philip, one of the Socialist party's leading authorities on the constitution.[12] The Socialists and the Communists were again identifying the Republic and parliamentary institutions with assembly government. They were unwilling to tolerate a strong, even if responsible government, much less a presidential or semipresidential system. De Gaulle's action was consistent with the British cabinet type of parliamentary government. Yet, as had been pointed out by his adviser, Capitant, parliamentary government cannot function without large national parties. If De Gaulle were committed to parliamentary government did he also cast himself in the role of party leader? Rather than put his immense prestige and popularity at the head of a political movement in order to influence the preparation of the new constitution, De Gaulle resigned.

Many of General de Gaulle's followers in the underground had considered the idea of presidential government. Retrospectively, however, the most important study was the one prepared by a special study group—the *Comité Général d'Etudes* (CGE) [13]—appointed by De Gaulle's representative in occupied France. It was composed of a number of political leaders and jurists with Michel Debré as *rapporteur*. The committee took into consideration a proposal made by another leading Gaullist, Blocq-Mascart, on behalf

---

[12] Quoted by Gordon Wright, *The Reshaping of the French Democracy*, pp. 127–28.
[13] *Guetzévitch*, pp. 287–97; and for a discussion, Nicholas Wahl, "Aux Origines de la Nouvelle Constitution."

of a Resistance group, the O.C.M. (*Organisation Civile et Militaire*), advocating an outright presidential government.

The form of democracy proposed by Debré was a parliamentary system based upon a separation of powers between the executive, composed of the chief of state and the cabinet, and the legislature. The role of the executive was to govern and that of the legislature to safeguard individual liberties and "inspire and control" the government. A President of the Republic would be chosen by an electoral college guaranteeing his independence and authority vis-à-vis the legislature. A president elected for "a period of twelve years" would give to French institutions the "keystone" they had lacked. In addition, the work of the parliamentary assemblies should be "rationalized" in order to correct four capital errors of the past: the excessively long legislative sessions, the interminable budgetary debates, the proliferation of committees that literally suffocated the government, and the abusive practice of interpellations. The government would have to retire in case of an adverse vote in an annual debate engaging the responsibility of the government. Otherwise it would remain in office for the balance of the year. The government was to have the discretionary right of dissolution and calling of elections. It could legislate by decree on all matters except those that were explicitly reserved to Parliament. Parliamentary sessions were to be short and the deputies were to be deprived of the right to introduce bills involving an increase in expenditures or reduction of revenue.

The report by Debré brought the Communist party out into the open on matters of constitutional reform. Speaking for the Central Committee, Georges Cogniot laid down the party's official position.[14] Debré's report and the drafts of the constitution that had been prepared by Blocq-Mascart were denounced as "Cromwellian." It was up to the people to decide what their constitution would be and for a Constituent Assembly to prepare one. The Communists favored increased parliamentary control over the government. It was the lack of such control, not its excesses, that accounted for the paralysis of the institutions of the Third Republic. They suggested greater popular control through the acceptance of an imperative mandate and the recall of the elected representatives.

The Communist position was spelled out in detail in the draft of

---

[14] Quoted by Gordon Wright, *op. cit.*, p. 38.

the constitution the party presented to the Constituent Assembly some two years later. National sovereignty was to reside in the people and be implemented by direct responsibility of the deputies by means of recall; the elective principle was to be extended to all departmental and local administrative posts; the National Assembly alone would exercise all the legislative power and have the initiative in the preparation and the elaboration of the budget. The President of the Republic, with very limited powers, was to be elected by the National Assembly and would nominate the ministers in accordance with the vote of the National Assembly. The cabinet and the prime minister would not enjoy the right to issue *décrets-lois* and to dissolve the Assembly. Finally, a novel institution would be established—a bureau, elected by the National Assembly, composed of twenty-five members, sitting in permanence, convening the Assembly and pronouncing the cloture of the legislative session. When the National Assembly was not in session the bureau would have all its powers of control over the government. The president of the bureau would succeed the President of the Republic if the latter were "momentarily" unable to perform his functions or in case of death until the election of a successor.[15]

Thus, by falling back upon the appealing doctrine of popular sovereignty the Communists presented themselves as the champions of the Jacobin tradition. The government belonged to the people and its delegates. Close and daily scrutiny of the government by the Parliament was indispensable. The legislature was to become a direct emanation of the general will unhindered by any scheme of separation of powers. It was clear that the bureau envisaged in the Communist draft was only a different name for the Praesidium of the Supreme Soviet and that the Communist constitution was attempting to do away with all obstacles that the Right wished to erect to block their way to power—a strong President of the Republic, a bicameral legislature, and an executive with some autonomous powers.

While the various national Resistance groups were busily debating constitutional reform, a committee appointed by Marshal Pétain was in the process of elaborating a new constitution. The final document, prepared in 1944 in accord with the delegation of constituent powers to Marshal Pétain by the law of July 10, 1940, was

---

[15] The draft of the constitutional project of the Communist Party is in *Les Projets Constitutionnels Français, Notes Documentaires et Études* (Paris, April 3, 1946), pp. 15–20.

presumably to be submitted to the people immediately after the Liberation, thus maintaining a continuity with the Third Republic. Pétain's constitution bears a remarkable similarity to the Debré project. It endorsed a republican form of government and the traditional individual guarantees. It provided for an enlarged electoral college for the election of the chief of state—the President of the Republic—composed of the members of the legislature and representatives of municipal units. The president, elected for a term of ten years, was to be "the *'arbitre'* of the superior interests of the country . . . and, if necessary maintains through the right of dissolution a continuous circuit of confidence between the nation and the government." He was given the traditional prerogatives that the President of the Republic had under the Third Republic: nomination of the prime minister, the power of pardon, command of the armed forces of the nation, and execution of laws. He was to have the power to dissolve the lower house with the accord of the Senate, as under the Third Republic. Dissolution, however, was to be automatic if three successive cabinets were overthrown by the lower house. All his acts were to be countersigned except that of nominating and revoking the prime minister.

The legislature was to be bicameral, elected by the people on the basis of universal and equal suffrage, but the fathers of three or more children were to be given more than one vote. The project of Pétain, like that of Debré, aimed at "rationalizing" parliamentary procedure: a smaller number of deputies; shorter sessions—not to exceed six months; the introduction of a personal vote; the replacement of the permanent legislative committees by *ad hoc* committees; abolition of the right of the deputies to initiate expenditure. In contrast to Debré's scheme, there was to be no incompatability between a cabinet and a legislative post and a vote of censure against the cabinet was freely allowed to intervene during the debate.[16]

The similarity between the Pétain constitution and the Debré project shows the identity of the views of the French Right on matters of constitutional reform. Both authors were primarily concerned with the reinforcement of the executive branch by enlarging the electoral college of the President of the Republic, adding to his prerogatives, and rationalizing the parliamentary procedure. Although Debré did not go so far as to give to the President of the Republic the

---

[16] *Duguit, et al., Les Constitutions*, pp. 386–94.

power to dismiss the prime minister, he envisaged a serious curtailment of the legislative competence of Parliament.

Both projects cast the president in the quasi-monarchical role of *arbitre,* embodying the supreme interests of the nation and political irresponsibility. The persistent trait of French conservative thought has been to strengthen the executive outside of the Parliament and in terms of a theory of representation that evades the issue of responsibility to the people. Gaullism and Pétainism were not so far apart when it came to matters of constitutional reform.

*   *   *   *   *

In the years of the Resistance and immediately after the Liberation, the Right and the Left assumed their traditional postures. The Left, led now by the Communists and often followed by the Socialists and some Center groups, favored an assembly government, similar in substance if not in form or name to the institutions of the Third Republic. There were obviously serious differences in their ranks regarding the specific implementation of assembly government, but they agreed on the need for legislative supremacy. The Right, on the other hand, was in favor of a strong executive within the context of parliamentary institutions, if properly "rationalized." Despite disagreements over presidential government or a cabinet government in which the powers of the legislature were to be qualified, the Right stood united in support of reinforced executive authority.

Theoretically, it was possible to work out a compromise along the lines suggested by Capitant: strong executive leadership based upon a parliamentary majority. The absence of such a majority, however, drove both sides farther apart. For the Left, the reinforcement of the executive meant a design to govern against Parliament. For the Right, the unity that could not derive from Parliament had to be provided by an executive with independent powers. Compromise failed because, in addition to ideological differences, neither side could create the indispensable political prerequisite for the development of a genuine parliamentary government—a majority. General de Gaulle might have used his prestige in the months after the Liberation to lead a political movement. Instead, very much like Pétain, he refused to consider himself a political leader deriving his strength from popular mandate—as is the case with the president of the United States or the prime minister in Great Britain. Though he argued until the time of his resignation for parliamentary government and behaved in accordance with its rules, he failed to act according to its logic by assuming political leadership. When he finally agreed to head a political movement—the RPF—the historical opportunity had been lost.

De Gaulle's unwillingness to assume political leadership seemed to indicate that he had never accepted parliamentary government in earnest and instead hoped for an executive whose authority was independent of the people. The Left thereafter considered him the exponent of a theory of government that was traditionally associated with the Right. On the other hand, the failure of the electorate to produce a majority reinforced the conviction of the Right that "assembly government" meant political chaos and led it inescapably to favor a new constitution endowing the executive with independent powers. After 1946, General de Gaulle seemed to endorse this point of view.

Further References

Citations in this chapter and Chapters VIII, IX, X, and XI are made from the following sources:

L. Duguit, H. Monnier, and R. Bonnard, *Les Constitutions et les Principales Lois Politiques de la France Depuis 1789* (7th ed.; Paris, 1952) (referred to as *Duguit, et al., Les Constitutions*). This compilation includes Pétain's constitutional project.

H. Michel and B. Mirkine-Guetzévitch, *Les Idées politiques et sociales de la Resistance* (Paris, 1954) (referred to as *Guetzévitch*). This source book with good commentaries includes a draft of the Debré project of 1944.

No publication of the collected speeches of General de Gaulle for 1958 has appeared. We have referred the reader to accounts given in *Le Monde* and have checked against the microfilm collection of all his speeches available at the Fondation Nationale des Sciences Politiques. For his utterances before June 1, 1958 and notably between 1940 to 1950 we have used Charles de Gaulle, *Discours et Messages 1940–1946* (Paris, 1946) (referred to as *Discours et Messages*) and *La France Sera la France, Ce que Dit; ce que Pense le Général de Gaulle* (RPF ed.; Paris, 1950) (referred to as *La France Sera La France*) which reproduces his most important utterances between 1946 to 1950.

Recueil des Textes relatifs au Référendum Constitutionnel du 28 septembre 1958, du 3 juin 1958 au 7 septembre 1958 (referred to as *Recueil*) (Paris: Imprimerie de l'Assemblée Nationale, 1958). It includes the original government project and the modifications brought to it by the CCC, and the final text as it was submitted to the referendum. It also includes all decrees issued for the organization of the referendum.

Ordonnances portant lois organiques et ordonnances relatives aux Pouvoirs publics (Paris: Imprimerie des Journaux Officiels, No. 1119, 1959) (referred to as *Lois Organiques*). It includes all the basic ordinances taken by the government of General de Gaulle by virtue of the delegation of power given to him by Article 92 of the constitution.

The best analytical studies of constitutional reform in France are: R. Capitant, *La Réforme du Parlementarisme* (Paris, 1934). Gordon Wright, *The Reshaping of the French Democracy* (New York, 1948), particularly chaps. 1 and 2; *Revue Française de la Science Politique*, Vol. IV, No. 4 (October–November, 1954); and Nicholas Wahl "Aux Origines de la Nouvelle Constitution," *Revue Française de la Science Politique*, Vol. 12, No. 1 (March, 1959), pp. 30–66, and the bibliography cited. For background material the publications of André Tardieu, especially *Le Souverain Captif*, and Léon Blum, particularly his *Réforme Gouvernmentale* (1919) and *A L'Échelle Humaine* (1944) are important. Also Debré, *La Mort de l'État Républicain* (1947), and *La République et ses Problèmes* (1952).

CHAPTER VIII

The Movement for Reform

The Reformette of 1954

THE NEED to revise the Constitution of the Third Republic was overwhelmingly endorsed by the people in the referendum of October 21, 1945. Eighteen and a half million voted for revision and only 700,000 wished to see the country return to the prewar institutions. Yet the Constitution of the Fourth Republic was only a modified version of the Third, reflecting the lowest possible common denominator of agreement among the various political groups. It was adopted by some nine million votes against eight million. About eight million voters abstained. Political power was vested in the representatives of the sovereign people. It was made extremely difficult for the prime minister to appeal over the heads of the National Assembly by means of dissolution and elections. The executive remained, as under the Third Republic, a creature and an agent (*commis*) of the legislature.

As soon as the Constitution of the Fourth Republic came into effect the movement for reform began. Most of the resolutions introduced between 1946 to 1950 dealt with the manner in which the prime minister was invested, the freedom of the deputies to introduce bills involving additional expenditures, and the right of dissolution. The most comprehensive proposal for reform was made by Michel Debré in June, 1949, providing for separation of powers between the executive and the legislature and an enlarged electoral college for the President of the Republic—a resolution motivated at the time by the electoral successes of the Gaullists.

The following year the "government parties"—Socialists, MRP, and Radicals—agreed on a limited constitutional reform. A resolution

134

to this effect was passed on November 30, 1950 by the National Assembly and on January 26, 1950 by the Council of the Republic. It was only on December 7, 1954—almost four years later—after long debates and innumerable compromises and reconsiderations that reform was enacted. The most important change was to make the investiture of the prime minister possible by a relative majority—a return to the "old and tested" principles of the Third Republic. The right of the prime minister to close the session of the National Assembly was reintroduced, but only after the National Assembly had sat for seven months. The powers of the upper chamber were increased. No effort was made to reinforce the position of the prime minister and the cabinet vis-à-vis the Parliament by making dissolution effective or by giving to government the power to set the parliamentary order of business and organize the deliberations of the National Assembly. Nor was there an attempt made to cope with one of the most pressing issues—the creation of a new constitutional framework for the relations between France and her colonies. The "reformette" of 1954, as it was aptly called, failed to deal with the basic problems of executive leadership, cabinet stability, and colonial policy.[1]

The adoption of the "reformette" only strengthened the movement for constitutional reform. After the fall of the Mendès-France government, Christian Pineau stated on February 10, 1955, in his investiture speech, that if invested his government was ready to proceed with "the examination of all measures, including constitutional reform, for the purpose of improving the functioning of the parliamentary institutions." One week later, Edgar Faure, in his investiture speech that followed Pineau's unsuccessful effort, repeated that the reform of the metropolitan institutions and of the French Union should come under re-examination. He was the first prime minister to institute round-table conferences in which most of the parliamentary leaders (excluding the Communists) and former prime ministers participated. Difficulties in North Africa, however, and ulti-

---

[1] For the movement of reform in the period of the Fourth Republic see Philip Williams, *Politics in Post War France* (1958); François Goguel and Georges Gallichon in *Revue Française de Science Politique*, Vol. IV, No. 4 (Oct.–Dec., 1954), pp. 674–708, 793–835; D. W. S. Lidderdale, *The Parliament of France* (London, 1951); M. Duverger, *The French Political System* (Chicago, 1958); Michel Debré, *La République et ses Problèmes* (1952); *Ces Princes Qui Nous Gouvernent* (1957).

On the reform of 1954 see François Goguel, *Revue Française de Science Politique*, Vol. 3 (July, 1955), pp. 485–502; Roy C. Macridis, "A Note on the Revision of the Constitution of the Fourth Republic," *American Political Science Review* (1956), pp. 1011–22; Roy Pierce, "Constitutional Revision in France," *Journal of Politics*, Vol. VIII (1957), pp. 221–48.

mately the dissolution of the National Assembly put an end to this endeavor.

In October of the same year President René Coty reminded his fellow citizens that the observation of Caesar on the politically volatile nature of the Gauls (*in consiliis capiendis mobiles*) was still valid. The flexibility of the parliamentary institutions, he conceded, may well be adapted to the national temper. The President's generation had known of literally hundreds of ministries. But the previous generation had witnessed revolutions and *coups d'état*. "Fuses that blow," he said, "are preferable to houses that burn." But it was equally true that the parliamentary institutions should be renovated and brought up to date to meet the needs of the time. The reform of the State was the "key to all other reforms." Guy Mollet, who formed the first government of the third legislature after the elections of January 2, 1956, pledged to support all efforts by Parliament to reform the institutions.

The need for reform was also proclaimed with increased urgency by all political parties in 1956. The MRP national congress, held in May, demanded "a comprehensive reform for the purpose of establishing a real parliamentary system giving the government, at the time of investiture, the required powers and length of time to enable it to govern . . . and assuring through the mechanism of automatic dissolution a balance between parliament and government." The UDSR–RDA congress in October asserted in its resolution that the party "continues to be opposed to the Constitution of 1946" and stated that constitutional reform was more imperative than ever. It called for the unqualified right of dissolution and investiture of the prime minister for a fixed period of time. The RGR proposed investment of the cabinet with the powers to govern for a minimum period of two years, automatic dissolution in case of an adverse vote on the question of confidence, and the revision of the standing orders of the National Assembly in order to improve its working methods. The Social Republicans called for government stability through a system of separation of powers with a strong president. The Poujadists demanded an overhaul of the existing institutions through the convocation of the States General. The Independents, in the national congress of the party, proclaimed "the urgent necessity of establishing a new and modern Republic." They favored governmental stability through the adoption of automatic dissolution, the elimination of the right of deputies to introduce bills involving expenditures, shorter legislative sessions, and reform of the legislative procedure of the National Assembly in order to limit it only to the deliberation of the general principles of bills.

After the fall of Guy Mollet's government in May, 1957, every prime minister or prime minister-designate promised constitutional reform. Bourgès-Maunoury, in his investiture speech on June 12, 1957, said "the reinforcement of the executive appears to be a pressing need in the light of ten years of experience. It should lead to a revision of the constitution." In October of the same year after the overthrow of the Bourgès-Maunoury cabinet, Antoine Pinay, one of the leaders of the Independents, affirmed in his investiture speech that "recovery cannot take place except by a government which is assured of a minimum of stability." To establish such a government "we all know that we must reform the constitution. I believe that such a reform must be a very comprehensive one." Guy Mollet, who tried to form a government after Pinay had failed, repeated almost these very same phrases. "The revision of the constitution has been under consideration for a number of months. Many bills and resolutions have been introduced. The appropriate committees have examined them. Everything leads to the conclusion that new devices to strengthen the executive must be sought not only in the revision of the constitution but also in the reform of the standing orders of the National Assembly." He promised to organize a round-table conference with the participation of the leaders of the various parliamentary groups. His government, he added, would be ready to submit specific proposals and stake its life upon their acceptance. Félix Gaillard, who finally succeeded in forming a government, was equally outspoken in his investiture speech of November 5, 1957. "We shall seek to establish the healthy functioning of the Parliament. . . . In January, 1958 the Assembly will discuss the reform of the constitution." Finally, the last government of the Fourth Republic under Pierre Pflimlin made constitutional reform the cornerstone of its program. Pflimlin resigned to make room for General de Gaulle only after he had secured the passage of a comprehensive resolution in favor of constitutional reform.[2]

The appropriate committee of the National Assembly (*Commis-*

---

[2] The citations from the resolutions of party congresses, the pronouncement of the President of the Republic, and the investiture speeches of the prime ministers or prime minister-designate come from *Année Politique*, 1955, 1956, and 1957 in the following order: 1955, pp. 589, 590–93, 599–600; 1956, pp. 459–60, 470, 475–76, 458, 457, 477–78; 1957, pp. 524, 529, 533, 538.

sion du suffrage universel, des lois constitutionnelles, du Règlement et des pétitions) considered a vast number of proposals for reform involving practically every article of the constitution: abolition of Article 13, prohibiting the delegation of law-making powers to the executive (which for all practical purposes had been set aside by legislative practice); incompatibility between ministerial functions and a parliamentary mandate; personal vote; shorter parliamentary sessions; the requirement that a motion of censure should be accompanied by a statement of policy; the elimination of the initiative of deputies to introduce expenditures and so on. From the very start constitutional reform suffered from the evils it was attempting to correct: fragmentation and diversification so characteristic of the work of the National Assembly. Every group introduced resolutions for reform. Members of the same cabinet discovered that they were the authors of resolutions that either differed radically from those proposed by other members of the cabinet or were diametrically opposed to proposals they themselves had introduced earlier. Thus, Félix Gaillard, as prime minister, was arguing vehemently against "automatic dissolution" in case of an adverse vote on the question of confidence only to be reminded by Paul Reynaud that two years previously he had introduced a proposal in favor of automatic dissolution!

The inability of Parliament to reach a decision was due primarily to the clash of the two concepts of government already discussed. Constitutional reform to strengthen the executive would immediately provoke a *crise de conscience* among the Republican groups and a cascade of amendments to protect the Assembly. The French parliamentarians were thrown into a panic at the very suggestion that the cabinet should have the discretionary power of dissolving the Assembly in case of an adverse vote on general policy or on specific legislative texts; or that bills would be considered adopted unless there was an absolute majority against the government. They called for cabinet stability, but would not contemplate effective measures of executive leadership.

Action by Parliament was also extremely difficult because of the nature of the majority required by the amending clause—three fifths of both chambers or two thirds of the National Assembly. Even this majority could have been attained had it not been for the issue of electoral reform. The Independents and the Radicals advocated a majority system, while the Communists, MRP, and the Socialists were in favor of proportional representation. Although it was likely that some Socialists would abandon proportional representation, the MRP became increasingly intransigent. The Radicals and the Independents killed constitutional reform by linking it with electoral reform. The MRP pressed for constitutional reform without making any concession on electoral reform. There were perhaps two distinct majorities—one for constitutional reform and another for electoral reform—but there was no majority for both.

A Presidential System?

As has been said, the constitutional projects of both Marshal Pétain and Michel Debré envisaged the establishment of a President of the Republic chosen by a large electoral college with considerably increased prerogatives. In both proposals the president was to represent the interests of the nation, exercise *arbitrage,* and perform important leadership functions. In the middle of 1956 a presidential system was advocated by Georges Vedel and Maurice Duverger,[3] both professors of the Law School of the University of Paris. Vedel recommended a genuine presidential system patterned after the American model; Duverger wished to preserve the essentials of the parliamentary system while modifying drastically its functioning in the direction of executive leadership and authority.

Professor Vedel argued that France is characterized by a marked fragmentation of opinions and attitudes which is translated into a multiparty system and a multigroup Assembly. Precisely because the Assembly was a mirror of public opinion it was singularly unable to produce stable governments with internal cohesiveness and a political program. The cabinet was both the creature and the prisoner of the Assembly. Thus, one canon of a parliamentary system, that governments be able to function effectively, was sacrificed to another, that legislative assemblies be truly representative of the people. The problem was how to maintain the representative character of the Assembly and at the same time provide for a government

[3] The views of Georges Vedel and Maurice Duverger were presented in *Revue Banque et Bourse,* Supplement 13 (May, 1956), "L'Instabilité Gouvernmentale," and *Le Monde,* April 12, 13, May 6, 18 and June 12, 1956, respectively. Duverger's views were more fully developed in his *Demain la République* . . . (1958). The article of Maurice Thorez appeared in *L'Humanité,* May 19, 1956. Duchet's article is in *Le Monde,* June 2, 1956. For a general review of Vedel's and Duverger's arguments, François Goguel, "Vers une Nouvelle Orientation de la Réforme Constitutionnelle," *Revue Française de Science Politique,* Vol. VI, No. 3 (June–September, 1956), pp. 493–507.

with the ability to perform its functions in matters of national defense, foreign policy, and economic planning. Vedel concluded that a solution could be found only in one way—the adoption of a presidential system similar in broad outlines to that of the United States.

In support of his thesis, Vedel pointed out that the American Congress resembles in certain respects the French legislature. It is a body representing a society divided into economic, social, regional, and ideological blocs. The Republican and Democratic labels cover indiscriminately a number of political groups, he contended. In fact, the Americans have a multiparty system which is highlighted by the lack of party discipline in Congress. However, it is the president who governs, not Congress. He is elected by the people, is independent of Congress, and symbolizes the national interest over and above the welter of particularisms represented in the legislature. It followed that the introduction of a presidential system in France would have the double merit of leaving the representative character of the Assembly intact, while at the same time providing for a government which the National Assembly, like the American Congress, cannot produce. Thus, Vedel proposed: a president elected by an absolute majority of the French people, embodying the executive prerogatives, not responsible to the legislature and appointing his own cabinet; and a legislature, faithfully representing all shades of French opinion, retaining the traditional prerogatives in matters of legislation (budget, treaties, and so forth). Only in case of persistent conflict between the two branches did he envisage a dissolution of the legislature and national elections for a new Assembly and a new president at the same time. But this was almost an afterthought. He believed that slowly the two would develop a *modus vivendi,* "like husband and wife."

Duverger agreed with all the reasons advanced by Vedel. He added that it was now necessary for the French Left to face up realistically to the need of a strong executive. The specters of Napoleon, MacMahon, and Boulanger and the shadow of Doumergue and De Gaulle should not continue to haunt the republican conscience and condemn the Republic to impotence. He was concerned, however, that the presidential system advocated by Vedel might lead, in the event of a conflict between the two branches, to a prolonged stalemate. He suggested that a President of the Republic be maintained as the head of the State, but that a prime minister be elected directly by the people. The prime minister would concentrate in his hands the totality of the executive power and be responsible to the National Assembly. The key to his proposal was that in the event of an adverse vote on the question of confidence dissolution would be automatic. The country would then be asked in a general election to vote at the same time for a prime minister *and* a new legislature. He hoped thus that the various parliamentary groups would be forced to coalesce in favor or against policies and leaders and hence that the way would be paved toward the creation of a two-party system. For both authors the central problem of modern democracy is to involve the people in the affairs of state. Their respective reforms aimed to create an executive that would derive its power directly from the people and would thus be able to exercise political leadership on their behalf.

The proposals made by both Duverger and Vedel were based upon a superficial view of the American system and underestimated the importance of the two parties in the electoral process. The choice of a president is almost invariably made between two candidates nominated by the two major parties irrespective of their internal differences. Thus, the election of a president by the whole nation has been greatly simplified. Vedel's proposal that a president be elected by an absolute majority with as many ballots as may be necessary might not be necessarily effective. It took thirteen ballots for the National Assembly and the Council of the Republic to elect the last president, René Coty. The French electorate might be just as reluctant to compromise. The hope voiced by Vedel that a *modus vivendi* between the president and the legislature would develop seems also unduly optimistic. In the United States the president disposes of important advantages in his relations with Congress and he is the leader of the party which very frequently has a majority in both houses of Congress. His position cannot be easily duplicated, unless the automatic dissolution suggested by Duverger modified the configuration of public opinion and led to the creation of a two-party system. Otherwise, as Raymond Aron pointed out in a different connection, automatic dissolution might create a situation similar to that of the last years of the Weimar Republic.

Both the Left and the Right rejected overwhelmingly the proposals of Duverger and Vedel in favor of a strong executive, but for diametrically opposed reasons. For the Left, a president or a prime minister deriving his powers from universal suffrage was a potential Bonaparte. Maurice Thorez took particular pains to refute Du-

verger's arguments by reiterating the traditional Communist position against Cromwellian adventures and in favor of direct democracy. On behalf of the Independents and Moderates, Roger Duchet
disposed of the theories of Duverger and Vedel in an article entitled "A l'Ombre d'un César." The Communists had nothing to gain
by reinforcing a "bourgeois executive," while the Right feared a
president and prime minister who, deriving their legitimacy from a
popular mandate, might threaten their interests and upset the *status
quo*. Underlying the opposition was the fear on all sides that the
executive might be transformed into an instrument of popular will
overshadowing the representative assemblies.

The National Assembly in Action

Basic disagreements produced a feeling of futility. Only a
mere handful of deputies attended the great debate on constitutional reform under the Gaillard cabinet early in 1958—only a few
months before the fall of the Fourth Republic. "After all we are debating these issues as if we were in committee," quipped the *rapporteur* Coste-Floret, looking at the empty banks of the Assembly. Gaillard began the defense of his project by apologizing for speaking at
such a "late and lonely hour." "I have been listening to this debate
for twenty-five years," exclaimed Paul Reynaud.[4] During the debate,
which lasted over ten full legislative days, more than seventy-five
amendments were introduced from the floor. The government was
compelled to modify its original proposals and finally to put the question of confidence for the acceptance of an amended version of its
text.

The original proposal introduced by Gaillard provided that whenever the prime minister put the question of confidence on a legislative
text, the bill would become law unless a motion of censure was introduced against the government and voted. It specified that to be acceptable such a motion of censure should state an alternate program
and name the prime minister's successor. It further stipulated that
such a motion could be carried only by absolute majority so that all
blank votes or abstentions would count for the government. Thus it
was hoped that legislation could be passed not when there was a
majority for a given policy or a given text, something which was becoming increasingly difficult, but rather whenever there was no abso-

---

[4] For a good summary of the debate, *Année Politique*, 1958, pp. 20–22; 28–29, 33.

lute majority against. If censure were voted under these conditions after the first eighteen months of the legislative term, the prime minister could dissolve the National Assembly.

In the long and tedious debate that followed, the deputies voiced their anxieties. Paul Reynaud objected that bills would become laws without majority support and that the government would be free to put the question of confidence on all the provisions of a bill, thus depriving the National Assembly of the right to scrutinize each article separately. This was a "strait jacket." He continued, somewhat inconsistently, by pointing out that if such a reform were enacted, the National Assembly would make sure to invest the least dynamic political leader as prime minister from whom a promise not to dissolve would be secured in advance. "Dissolution must be automatic or there is no dissolution," he said. He questioned the effectiveness of forcing the opposition to state a program in a motion of censure. The deputies would have little difficulty in getting around this requirement with a vague policy statement, such as "we are in favor of peace and the well-being of humanity." Three former prime ministers, Reynaud, Faure, and Pleven, introduced an amendment providing for separate votes on the question of confidence and the motion of censure with complicated procedures allowing the Assembly to reject a bill without overthrowing the cabinet. The power of dissolution was also made subject to important limitations. At this point the debate became so confused that the government readily agreed to send its bill back to committee together with all amendments and counterproposals.

The report of the committee presented by the *rapporteur* (Coste-Floret) and endorsed by the government was a synthesis of the various points of view. The most important of the government proposals —that the opposition be required to designate a successor to the prime minister and that a bill become law unless a motion of censure against the government was voted by an absolute majority—were dropped. A new formula for dissolution was introduced by the committee. There could be no dissolution within the first eighteen months. If, however, in the two years following the investiture of a prime minister a motion of censure were voted, dissolution would be automatic—but not quite. Two conditions were attached: first, the prime minister should have announced prior to the vote of the National Assembly that in case of an adverse vote he would dissolve, and second, the President of the Republic would have the last word in accepting or rejecting dissolution. It was only in the last year of the legislative term that the prime minister could dissolve the National Assembly at his discretion.[5]

The revision of Article 17, depriving the deputies of the right to introduce bills increasing expenditures or diminishing revenue, was passed with only the Communists voting against. An amendment, however, introduced by Triboulet, a Social Republican, providing that the cabinet could not put the question of confidence on bills but only on matters of general policy was adopted. At this point the Prime Minister, Gaillard, intervened to make the committee's report a question of confidence. The vote on the first reading of the whole text was 308 against 206, four tenths of a ballot over the required majority of three fifths! It was a tenuous victory, especially since the project included an article stating that "the provisions of the present constitutional law will not become effective unless the electoral law is abrogated and a new law is voted that will determine the new electoral system and the new standing orders of the National Assembly".

What exactly did the reform accomplish? The matter has only historical interest, but it throws some light on the manner in which the faction-ridden Assembly worked. The text finally adopted differed little from past practices. Four years of debate led again to a reform project that was superficial. The right of dissolution remained carefully circumscribed, and the position of the prime minister vis-à-vis the National Assembly was as precarious as ever. The reform did not make it any less likely that negative majorities could continue to overthrow the cabinet with impunity. The various amendments, or rather the *jeu de massacre*, to use the expression of the Minister of Justice, Lecourt, had led to a text that bore little resemblance to the government's original proposal. "We believe," said the Prime Minister, "this constitutional reform, no matter how incomplete, marks a progress or at least a chance for progress." Declared tersely Paul Reynaud, "We have nothing." [6]

Constitutional reform became a primary objective of the Pflimlin government of May 13. In his investiture speech Pflimlin reiterated, like all his predecessors, the urgency of this matter. "On March 21," he stated in the resolution proposed by his government, "the Na-

---

[5] The debate on the Gaillard proposal took place between February 12 and March 19, 1958. The text of the committee's final report on which the government put the question of confidence in *2e rapport supplémentaire, 3ième legislature 1957–58, No. 6840, Annexe au procès-verbal de la séance du 8 mars 1958, Journal Officiel.*

[6] In general see *Année Politique*, 1958, pp. 28–29, 33.

tional Assembly revised the constitution in a limited but useful manner. . . . Yet it was evident that more was required in order to give strength and efficacy to the republican institutions. . . . The crisis of the nation indicates the urgency of profound reforms." In the previous year France had been without a government for three months, he pointed out, and added that it was futile for a government like his about to be formed to ask for or expect a long stay in office. He simply declared that it was his intention to "create the proper conditions [for cabinet stability] for the future" and to do so he promised to undertake "a comprehensive and coherent reform of the executive power." [7]

While the army was preparing an assault upon the Metropolis the National Assembly devoted its time to a debate over constitutional reform. On May 26 a government resolution was accepted by the Committee on Universal Suffrage and reported to the floor together with some fourteen other proposals. The resolution simply stated that there was need to reform Articles 9, 12 (second paragraph), 45, 48, 52, and 92 in addition to reconsider the revision of Articles 17, 49, 50, 51, and 90 already decided under the Gaillard government. It was voted by 408 against 185 votes, with the Communists voting in favor in order not to give the government a pretext to resign and thus make room for De Gaulle! If the Communists had abstained, the vote in favor would have been 258. If they had voted against, there would have been no majority. A few hours later Pflimlin resigned.

The Last Stand

General de Gaulle's first step was to cut through the Gordian knot by requesting the reform of Article 90 and the delegation of constituent powers to his government. Many deputies felt that they were being asked to re-enact the scene that had been played at Vichy on July 10, 1940 when Parliament granted to the "government of the Republic under the authority and the signature of Marshal Pétain all powers to promulgate by one or more acts a new constitution of the French State." The memories of Vichy lay heavily over the deliberations of the National Assembly.

---

[7] Pflimlin's investiture speech in *Année Politique*, 1958, pp. 530–34. His proposal for constitutional reform, *Rapport No. 7188, Projet de loi tendant à la révision des certains articles de la constitution, Journal Officiel* (May 26, 1958).

The bill submitted by General de Gaulle [8] stated in its preamble that the new constitution was to respect universal suffrage, maintain the responsibility of the government before Parliament, and establish effective separation between legislature and executive. It went before the same committee that had examined the Gaillard proposals and Pflimlin's last-minute suggestions and was returned with a number of modifications. The committee recommended that the principles enumerated by De Gaulle's government be incorporated into the main body of the text. It also tried to preserve certain traditional parliamentary prerogatives. For instance, it provided that "the powers of the President of the Republic derive from universal suffrage *and* the elected Assemblies." It recommended that "the government propose an electoral system for the elections of the National Assembly offering a choice between a majority and a proportional system, that is submitted to the people in a referendum." The elaboration of the electoral system was then to be made "by law." Finally, it was suggested that the draft of the new constitution to be prepared by the government should be examined "within a period of three months by Parliament after it had been submitted to the Bureau of the National Assembly." To be adopted it should receive an absolute majority of the members composing the two chambers. If the project was not ratified by Parliament "within a period of three months or if it did not receive the requisite majorities then the government could submit it to the people in a referendum."

General de Gaulle made a number of concessions. The government incorporated the basic principles in the first article of the text; specified the role and the composition of the Constitutional Consultative Committee to which the draft of the constitution would be submitted; stated explicitly that the text would be elaborated by the Council of Ministers and that it would go before the *Conseil d'État* for a final check before it went to the people. But that was as far as he was willing to go. He did not want to resort to a referendum against Parliament as he might be forced to do if the amendments of the committee were accepted, because it would never occur to him to set the people against their representatives! But he made the amended text a ques-

---

[8] De Gaulle's proposal in *Rapport No. 7233, Assemblée Nationale Projet de loi constitutionelle modifiant l'article 90 de la Constitution, Session ordinaire, etc., Journal Officiel,* (June 1, 1958); the committee counterproposals, in *Rapport No. 7239, Assemblée Nationale, etc.* (June 2, 1958); the government concession in *Lettre Rectificative, etc.* (June 3, 1958).

tion of confidence and received 356 against 163 votes—well over the requisite three fifths. The vote in the Council of the Republic was a mere formality. A little more than twelve years after his resignation from the presidency of the government General de Gaulle was back in power and the road was clear for the elaboration of a new constitution—that of the Fifth Republic.

CHAPTER IX

The Making of the New Constitution

The Gaullist Inspiration

BEFORE GENERAL DE GAULLE resigned from the presidency of the government on January 20, 1946, he warned the members of the Constituent Assembly that evil days awaited them if they failed to learn the lessons of political history:

> There are two conceptions of government and they cannot be reconciled. Do you want a government that governs or an omnipotent Assembly that sets up a government only to carry out its wishes? The obvious formula in my opinion is that of a government that assumes alone, I repeat alone, the whole responsibility of the executive power . . . If the Assembly refuses all or some of the means the government considers necessary to carry out the responsibility of the executive power, well . . . then the government resigns.[1]

The controversy was the same one that plagued the Third Republic— what should be the respective spheres of the legislature and the government? The granting of confidence to a cabinet meant simply to the advocates of assembly government the constitution of a team that was to be an agent of the National Assembly. For De Gaulle, on the other hand, the expression of confidence was a solemn act comporting the establishment of a government with an autonomous sphere of action.

After his resignation De Gaulle moved gradually toward what some considered to be a presidential system. His ideas were fully developed in three important pronouncements between June and

---

[1] *Discours et Messages,* p. 716.

September, 1946: the Bayeux [2] and Epinal [3] speeches of June 16 and September 29, 1946, respectively, and a declaration issued when the Second Constituent Assembly began consideration of the text that was destined to become the Constitution of the Fourth Republic.[4] In the Bayeux speech he outlined his ideas for the first time in a comprehensive manner:

> The rivalry of the parties takes in our country a fundamental character, which leaves everything in doubt and which very often wrecks its superior interests. This is an obvious fact that . . . our institutions must take into consideration in order to preserve our respect for laws, the cohesion of governments, the efficiency of the administration and the prestige and authority of the State. The difficulties of the State result in the inevitable alienation of the citizen from his institutions. . . . All that is needed then is an occasion for the appearance of the menace of dictatorship.

To avoid the menace and possibly the success of a dictatorship whose dynamism would contrast so sharply with the immobility of the Republic and the apathy of the people, De Gaulle outlined the following institutional arrangements:

1. The legislature, executive, and judiciary must be clearly separated and balanced.
2. Over and above political contingencies there must be a national "mediation" (*arbitrage*).
3. The voting of the laws and the budget belongs to an assembly elected by direct and universal suffrage.
4. A second assembly, elected in a different manner, is needed to examine carefully the decisions taken by the first, to suggest amendments and propose bills.
5. The executive power should not emanate from the Parliament. Otherwise the cohesion and authority of the government would suffer, the balance between the two powers vitiated, and the members of the executive would be merely agents of the political parties.
6. A President of the Republic (*Chef d'État*), embodying the executive power above political parties, should be elected by a college, which includes the Parliament but is much broader than Parliament, in a

---

[2] For full text, *Ibid.*, p. 721–27.

[3] For full text, *Ibid.*, pp. 740–47.

[4] The two best statements on the preparation of the constitution are François Goguel, "L'Élaboration des Institutions de la République dans la Constitution du 4 Octobre 1958," in the *Revue Française de Science Politique*, Vol. IX, No. 1 (March, 1959), pp. 67–100, and Nicholas Wahl, "The French Constitution of 1958, the Initial Draft and its Origins," *American Political Science Review*, Vol. LII, No. 2 (June, 1959), pp. 358–82.

manner that will make him also the President of the French Union. It is for him to direct the work and the policy of the government; promulgate the laws and issue decrees; preside over the meetings of the Council of Ministers; serve as a mediator above the political contingencies; invite the country to express its sovereign decisions in an election; be the custodian of national independence and the treaties made by France, and appoint the prime minister in accord with the political orientation of Parliament and the national interest.

The Bayeux speech has remained the Gaullist charter in all matters of constitutional reform. Its basic principles were reiterated in all the national assizes of the RPF since its founding in 1947: restriction of the prerogatives of the legislature; a strong President of the Republic; a separation of powers between the executive and the legislature so that the former would not emanate "directly or indirectly" from the latter. On April 24, 1947 De Gaulle pointed out:

> . . . the separation of powers is the basis of democracy. . . . For France, given our divisions which are, alas! multiple and profound, the separation of powers is an absolute necessity. . . . We must have a regime in which the executive, legislative, and judiciary are separated in their attributions, in their personnel, and in their responsibilities so that there can be a real government, a real Parliament and real justice.[5]

In his last press conference, on June 30, 1955, prior to his temporary retirement, De Gaulle summed up his position:

> The State needs a head—a Chief of State—elected by a broader electoral college, with specific attributions and with the ability to exercise the role of national "arbitrage". . . . There must be a separation of powers so that the government, the Parliament, and the judiciary will have distinct origins and their proper jurisdiction and responsibility. . . . Nobody should be a parliamentarian and a minister at the same time, that is a judge and party, controller and controlled.[6]

Three authors, all of whom assumed important political positions in the Fifth Republic—Maxime Blocq-Mascart, Léon Noël, and Michel Debré—in numerous publications elaborated the Gaullist position. In December, 1955 Noël, in his *Notre Dernière Chance*, undertook a critical survey of the accomplishments of the second legislature of the Fourth Republic and concluded with a chapter entitled "What Is to Be Done?" The Constitution of the Fifth Republic reproduces almost everything he advocated: incompatibility between ministerial and legislative posts, reinforced powers of the

---

[5] Cited by Léon Noël, *Notre Dernière Chance* (Paris, 1956), p. 179.
[6] The full text in *Le Monde,* July 2, 1955.

president, a "rationalized" Parliament, a division of the legislative function between the Parliament and executive in a manner that gives to the latter large legislative powers. Even detailed suggestions pertaining to the number of deputies and of parliamentary committees were followed.

Early in 1958, Blocq-Mascart [7] published a new statement with a preface by Michel Debré. The book appeared actually only a month before the May 13 uprising. Once more Blocq-Mascart advocated a presidential system and a federation of the metropolitan departments, Algeria, and all the various overseas territories. In his preface to the book Debré demanded an immediate change of the regime. Parliamentary government as practiced in France had degenerated into assembly government:

> It is the Assembly which is the government; it is the Assembly which is the law; it is the Assembly which is the State. . . . [But] behind the façade of the absolute sovereignty of Parliament, one can perceive reality: the division of power among the political parties which are the government, the law and the State; and because of this, there soon will be no government, no law, no state. [8]

Many saw in his attack against the political parties the most dangerous aspect of Gaullist revisionism. De Gaulle had been consistently critical of the *régime des partis*. He had stated earlier "we do not wish to have the public powers belong—I say belong—to those feudal lords (*féodaux*) that call themselves parties." [9] The very term *Rassemblement* given to the Gaullist movement in 1947 was meant to distinguish it sharply from the parties—to incarnate national unity as opposed to factionalism. In his press conference of June 30, 1955, De Gaulle pointed out that after failing to realize the renovation of France at the time of the Liberation he had made a second unsuccessful attempt through the *Rassemblement*. "I was blocked by everything organized to protect the vested interests: political parties, the press, business, interest groups, and trade unions. It is classic," he concluded, "for feudalism to oppose the reinforcement of the state." [10]

Michel Debré's *Ces Princes Qui nous Gouvernent*, published in 1957, was in the nature of a detailed footnote to De Gaulle's state-

---

[7] *La Prochaine République Sera-t-elle Républicaine* (Paris, 1958).
[8] *Ibid.*, pp. iii–iv.
[9] Quoted by Léon Noël, *op. cit.*, pp. 179–80.
[10] *Le Monde*, July 2, 1955.

ments. In it he identifies the *Princes* that govern France as the leaders of the political parties, the press, the trade unions, and the business corporations. Through the fiction of parliamentary supremacy, they maintain an artificial division of public opinion and deprive the nation of political authority. "One must seek for and organize power outside of Parliament." Where can it be situated?

> The answer is clear: it cannot be situated anywhere else but around the chief of state elected by a much broader electoral college of which the Parliament is only a part. . . . The office of the prime minister must remain, but the collective responsibility of the cabinet, as well as the responsibility of every minister, exist only vis-à-vis the chief of state. It cannot be brought into play before the Parliament except under conditions and in terms of a procedure that are very exceptional.[11]

Thus, during the last years of the Fourth Republic, as was the case in the Resistance, avowed Gaullists undertook a critical examination of the domestic institutions and advocated a far-reaching constitutional overhaul. The Gaullist leaders, well aware of Parliament's inability to enact constitutional reforms, helped create a revolutionary situation in order to bring about a change of the regime and the establishment of a new constitution. Many of them recalled that De Gaulle in his last press conference had not excluded the possibility of his return. On the contrary, he had hinted that a shock (*secousse*) would not be the beginning of a catastrophe but "the signal of reorganization" (*redressement*).

When the shock occurred and De Gaulle agreed to return to power there was no question but that his ideas on constitutional reform and those of his followers would be implemented. Michel Debré, as Minister of Justice, and his associates were ready.

The Preparation of the New Constitution

The constitutional law of June 3 stipulated that, in preparing the constitution, the government was to seek the advice (which had no binding character) of a specially designated Constitutional Consultative Committee approximately two thirds of whose members were to be nominated by parliamentary committees and the other third appointed by the government. The constitutional text was to be drafted by the Council of Ministers and examined by the *Conseil d'État,* whose opinion was required. The final text was to be sub-

---

[11] *Ces Princes Qui nous Gouvernent,* pp. 173–74.

mitted to the people. The following stages in the preparation of the constitution were thus envisaged: the drafting of a document by the Council of Ministers under the over-all responsibility of General de Gaulle; the deliberations and suggestions for modifications by the Constitutional Consultative Committee; the redrafting of the text by the Council of Ministers in the light of the suggestions of the Consultative Committee; the presentation of the text to the *Conseil d'État,* and finally the preparation by the government of the definitive text that was to be officially submitted to the people. The constituent organs were exclusively the government, under the presidency of General de Gaulle, and the people, whose only option was to vote Yes or No to the proposed text. The recommendations of the Consultative Committee and of the *Conseil d'État* were in no way binding upon the government.

The first draft was prepared by the government in seven weeks. It was submitted to the Consultative Committee on July 29. The deliberations of this body lasted sixteen days. Its opinions and amendments were transmitted to the government on August 14 and published in the *Journal Officiel* on August 20. This was followed by a new round of governmental conferences before a text was referred to the *Conseil d'État* on August 27. The opinion of the *Conseil d'État* was given on August 29, and the final text of the constitution, to be voted on in the referendum, appeared in the *Journal Officiel* on September 4. The elaboration of the constitution took only three months.

It will be the task of future historians to trace in detail the manner in which the final draft of the constitution came into being and to attempt to assess the role played by the various members of the government, including General de Gaulle. The suggestions of the Consultative Committee in the form of a number of counterproposals have been published,[12] but there is no available public record of its deliberations and of the examination of the draft by the *Conseil d'État.* The government began its work with one obvious commitment—to incorporate in a new text the Gaullist revisionist ideas.

A small group headed by Michel Debré began its work aided by a number of experts most of whom came from the permanent administrative bodies, particularly the *Conseil d'État.* The Bayeux speech was the source of inspiration. A draft prepared by Michel Debré and

---

[12] *Recueil,* pp. 12–49.

some of his more intimate associates after consultation with General de Gaulle was placed before the group. Debré presided over all meetings of the various study groups that were set up and followed his draft through deliberations at all other levels—interministerial committees, the full cabinet, the Consultative Committee, and finally the *Conseil d'État*. When progress became slow at the early stage he and a small group of "experts" reworked his draft and prepared, in a period of one week, what became the final government version.

Debré's first project provided for a presidency patterned after the model of the Bayeux speech and limited cabinet responsibility to the National Assembly (it would come into play but once a year) The prerogatives of the National Assembly were seriously qualified. Legislative functions were enumerated with the proviso that everything not specifically granted entered within the scope of executive decree. When Parliament was not in session, the totality of lawmaking power would belong to the executive—that is to say, some seven out of twelve months. Only four nonspecialized legislative committees were to be allowed. Debré's project was rounded out by a Senate, including representation of the various professions, a Constitutional Council with powers of judicial review, and a "federation" for the French Union.

The interministerial committee on the preparation of the constitution, under the presidency of De Gaulle, included experienced parliamentarians such as Jacquinot, Pflimlin, and Guy Mollet. The committee toned down some of the more extreme provisions of the Debré draft. The general rule of responsibility of the government to Parliament was restored, though under stringent conditions: The number of permanent legislative committees was increased to six, and the right of the government to legislate when Parliament was not in session was curtailed. Curiously enough, the ministerial committee maintained the incompatibility between parliamentary and ministerial posts and accepted a limitative definition of Parliament's legislative competence. The ministerial committee also introduced the provision according to which a government bill becomes law unless a motion of censure is voted by absolute majority of the National Assembly. It qualified somewhat the emergency powers of the President of the Republic, gave explicitly to the prime minister the power to "direct the governmental activity," and strengthened the position of the government vis-à-vis the legislature by specifying that it could oppose any amendment from the floor which had not been first referred to the appropriate legislative committee. Most of the suggestions made by the ministerial committee thus involved matters of detail. The structure proposed by Debré, particularly the provisions relating to the President of the Republic which followed the instructions of General de Gaulle, remained unaltered. Though the contributions of the ministerial committee may have been important, as François Goguel has argued, they were inspired by the desire to "rationalize" Parliament and perhaps to strengthen the cabinet. A draft incorporating the suggestions of the committee received the final approval of the Council of Ministers and was submitted to the Constitutional Consultative Committee.

The Consultative Committee was composed of thirty-nine members. Sixteen had been elected by a majority vote (thus excluding the Communists) by the Committee of Universal Suffrage of the National Assembly, ten were elected in the same manner by the corresponding committee in the Council of the Republic, and thirteen were appointed by the government.[13] The political orientation of the members nominated by the committees of the Parliament was clearly right of center. Out of the twenty-six parliamentarians there were eight Independents and Moderates, five Socialists, three MRP, one Radical Socialist, one Radical dissident, two Social Republicans, three RGR, and four deputies from French Africa (Lamine-Gueye, Senghor, Tsiranana, and Lisette). With the exception of one deputy, Coste-Floret, who abstained, all the others had voted for the delegation of constituent powers to General de Gaulle. It was a friendly but well-chosen group in that it included the members of the National Assembly and the Council of the Republic who had been most active in debates on constitutional revision. Among them were such stalwarts as Coste-Floret and Pierre-Henri Teitgen, who had played an important role in the drafting of the Constitution of the Fourth Republic, and Edmond Barrachin and Bruyneel, who pleaded for constitutional reform throughout the last years of the Fourth Republic.

The Consultative Committee was convened on July 29 and, after electing Paul Reynaud president, divided itself into two working

---

[13] Among those appointed by the government there were two professors of the University of Paris (M. Waline and G. Charbonnet), one member of the *Conseil d'État* (no other than Blocq-Mascart), two members of the Council of the French Union (one of whom was Roger Frey, a leading Gaullist), a former ambassador (Léon Noël, the present President of the Constitutional Council), and Paul Reynaud.

groups—one dealing with the constitutional provisions for France, the second with the French Union. All resolutions were debated and voted upon, however, in plenary meetings. A number of the provisions of the government project that departed radically from the institutions of the Third and Fourth Republics preoccupied and disturbed many of the members of the committee. On August 9, when it appeared that the committee was contemplating the preparation of a substitute text, General de Gaulle spent two hours with its members and answered questions in a manner that appeared to satisfy them. His comments shed significant light on the intention of the framers. He assured them that the prime minister could not be revoked by the President of the Republic and that it was only for the president to invoke the emergency powers. He stressed the exceptional character of this provision and reminded them of the situation that confronted President Lebrun in 1940. He also pointed out that if the situation created by the May 13 events had deteriorated further there were no adequate provisions in the constitution to meet the emergency. He remained adamant on the question of the incompatibility between ministerial functions and the parliamentary mandate. Those who control must be sharply differentiated from the persons controlled, he said, repeating almost textually from his press conference of June 30, 1955.

The most important contribution of the committee was in connection with the section devoted to the "federation" between France and her overseas territories. (For a detailed discussion see Chapter XI.) Otherwise it made only minor suggestions in the form of specific counterproposals or recommendations that were debated without being adopted but which were transmitted to the government. Some of its proposals were accepted by the government. They provided that all political parties be required to respect the democratic principles of the constitution, that the electoral college of the president be enlarged, and that the emergency powers of the president be exercised only when it was impossible for the other constituted governmental authorities to function.

On the other hand, some of its counterproposals and suggestions were not accepted. The committee criticized sharply the rule of incompatibility on the grounds that it might dry up the recruitment of personnel of ministerial caliber. It suggested that a parliamentarian who became a minister be permitted to secure a temporary leave of absence instead of resigning his mandate. It proposed that the electoral regime be adopted only after popular consultation. It found the enumeration of the legislative powers too limitative, proposed that in case of discord between the two assemblies the National Assembly should be given the "last word," but insisted on the responsibility of the government before both chambers. The bulk of the provisions concerning the role and functions of the president, the relations between the government and the Assembly, and the "rationalization" of the parliamentary procedure were left virtually intact.

The consideration of the committee's report necessitated a new round of cabinet meetings, and the new draft went before the *Conseil d'État* for its opinion. This body added a phrase to Article 4, requiring that political parties respect the democratic principles of the constitution, stating that "parties are to exercise their activities freely." It also proposed that a provision should be inserted allowing for the future extension of the legislative competence of Parliament by "organic law." Both suggestions were accepted by the government.

The Brief for the Constitution

During the course of the deliberations of the *Conseil d'État* Michel Debré submitted orally on August 27 a brief on behalf of the government. It is perhaps the most important single statement of the theory behind the new constitution. Said Debré:

> The object of the constitutional reform is clear. First and above all [it is] to reconstruct a state power. It is in the superior interest of our security and of world equilibrium to save and renovate what we traditionally call the overseas France. . . . The first purpose that dominated our project was to remake the parliamentary regime; the second was to establish, around France, a Community.[14]

Debré, after rejecting assembly government, explained in some detail why a presidential system could not be adopted. First, the law of June 3 did not authorize the government to establish it. But in any case there were two obstacles: (1) The president was also the President of the Community, including France's former colonies—which prevented direct popular election; (2) it would not be possible to elect a president by direct and universal franchise in a country with as many internal divisions as France. He concluded in favor of a

---

[14] All citations from Michel Debré's speech before the *Conseil d'État* on August 27, 1958, *La Nouvelle Constitution* (Tours, 1958).

parliamentary system. He described the innovations introduced by
the constitution. Most of them related to the office of the president,
the rule of incompatibility between cabinet posts and the parliamentary mandate, and the rationalization of the parliamentary
procedure. The latter had been endorsed by many political groups in
the Fourth Republic and its origins could be traced to the Third Republic. It involved shorter sessions, a division between legislation
and rule making, a wider scope to the executive to legislate by decree, and reorganization of the legislative and the budgetary procedure in a manner that gave the government a controlling position.
Certain rules that normally were part of the standing orders of the
Parliament were put into the constitution: personal vote of the deputies, the length of time for which the presidents of the National
Assembly and the Senate were elected, the preparation of the order
of business of the National Assembly, and so on. But why all these
detailed provisions, asked Debré. Why not attempt to create a
strong executive by giving it the right of dissolution vis-à-vis a unicameral legislature in the hope that it would develop in the direction
of the British parliamentary type? His answer underlined the perennial dilemma of the French body politic:

Ah, if only we had the possibility of seeing tomorrow a constant and
clear majority, it would not have been necessary to establish an upper
chamber whose role is to support the government against an Assembly
which attempts, because it is so divided, to invade its sphere of action.
. . . There would be no need to attempt to establish order and stability
by cutting the ties that united the parties with the government. . . . It
would not be necessary to regulate so carefully the motion of censure.

And then the crucial conclusion that goes far toward explaining the
new constitution.

Because in France government stability cannot result from elections
held under any type of electoral system it must be the result of constitutional regulation. This is what gives to our constitutional project its decisive character and its historical justification.

The circle was squared. A stable parliamentary system was to
be manufactured in which the government could govern without
majority support!

The solution to the problem was to be found also in a Senate
that had powers equal with the National Assembly and in a strong
President of the Republic—the "keystone of the arch" of the new
parliamentary system. The president is the chief of state with the

traditional prerogatives of the executive. "He is in our France, where fundamental divisions prevail, the superior judge of the national interest." It is because of the superior and detached role of the president that his election must be assured in a manner that does not reflect or aggravate the basic divisions of French society. Hence the need of an electoral college different and broader than that of the Third and Fourth Republics, but restricted at the same time.

After mentioning that constitutions set down only the broad limits within which men govern, Debré concluded that the new constitution provided the best possible opportunities for men of good will to govern in accordance with the national interest. Stating that this was the last chance for France to remain a great nation and at the same time a democracy, he rested his case.

CHAPTER X

The Structure of the New Constitution *

The Legal Framework

THE LANDSCAPE of the new constitution is a familiar one. The executive power is shared by the President of the Republic and the prime minister with his Council of Ministers. The legislative power is vested in the National Assembly and Senate. The government is responsible before Parliament. The French Union is transformed into the Community. The Economic Council, an advisory body representing the various professional organizations, becomes the Economic and Social Council. The High Council of Justice and the High Court of Justice are reconstituted. The old Constitutional Committee is replaced by the Constitutional Council with somewhat broader powers of constitutional review. Some new features are: a habeas corpus clause, a provision requiring political parties to adhere to the democratic principles of the constitution, and a revised amending clause. The major innovations of the constitution lie in the manner in which the institutions are to function.

The Executive: The President of the Republic and the Government. The presidency of the Fifth Republic is a reaction against the development of the office since 1875. The framers wished to give to the president the prestige and prerogatives that would enable him to provide for the continuity of the State, to cement the bonds of the Community, and to supervise the functioning of the constitution. In the words of Michel Debré, he is to be the "keystone of

---

* For the text of the constitution see Appendix A.

the arch" of the new Republic—both the symbol and the instrument of reinforced executive authority. To accomplish this the framers modified the manner in which he is elected and strengthened his powers.

The president is elected by an enlarged electoral college which, in addition to the members of the Parliament, includes the municipal councilors, the general councilors, and the members of the assemblies and the municipalities of the overseas territories and Republics. It is composed of approximately 81,500 electors (excluding for the time being the municipalities of Algeria) of whom some 5,000 represent the 35 million inhabitants of the member states of the Community.

Under the Third and Fourth Republics, the president as the chief of state was irresponsible. His only personal act was the designation of the prime minister. But even this was carefully circumscribed by parliamentary tradition. The president was expected, whenever a cabinet crisis occurred, to consult the outgoing prime minister, the presidents of the two assemblies and of the various parliamentary groups, and often some of the former prime ministers before asking a political leader to form a government. All his other acts had to be countersigned by a responsible minister or the prime minister.

The Constitution of the Fifth Republic maintains the irresponsibility of the president but at the same time gives him personal powers that he can exercise solely at his discretion. It gives him also the power to make decisions concerning all matters related to the Community and allows for a virtual veto power over a large, even if ill-defined, area of policy making.

The president designates the prime minister. Though it is presumed that such a designation will be made with an eye to the existing party configuration in the National Assembly, it is a personal political act. The president virtually chooses the prime minister when we take into consideration his other powers, and particularly his power of dissolution of the National Assembly. Under the practice of the Fourth Republic, dissolution of the Assembly could take place only under very stringent conditions upon the request of the prime minister. The role of the President of the Republic was simply to sign the dissolution decree presented to him by the prime minister, if and when the conditions for dissolution were met. In the new constitution, dissolution is a discretionary act of the president. He can dissolve at any time, on any issue, and for any

UNIVERSAL SUFFRAGE — SENATORIAL AND PRESIDENTIAL ELECTORS —
(Municipal councilors and general councilors—81,000–110,000)

LEGISLATURE

EXECUTIVE

PRESIDENT OF THE REPUBLIC

Elected for 7-year term by members of Parliament, departmental councils, municipal councils, special delegates selected by municipal councils and towns of over 30,000 at rate of 1 for each 1,000 in excess of 30,000, and assemblies and municipal representatives of member states of Community. Total electoral college for election of De Gaulle, Dec., 1958, 81,671. National mediator and commander in chief. Nominates to all civilian and military posts; issues all executive orders, decrees, and ordinances; negotiates and ratifies treaties; asks for second deliberation on legislative bills; convenes legislature for extraordinary session; nominates members of cabinet; initiates constitutional revision; has power to pardon; presides over council meetings.

Personal Powers

Nominates prime minister; dissolves Assembly; refers bills to Constitutional Council for examination of constitutionality; calls referendum; issues decrees with force of law; nominates 3 of 9 members to Constitutional Council; can send messages to legislature; invokes state of emergency and rules by decree. President of Community; not responsible to Parliament.

PRIME MINISTER AND CABINET

Prime minister proposes cabinet members to President for nomination; "guides policies of nation"; directs actions of government and is responsible for national defense; issues decrees and makes nominations in lieu of President by delegation; presides over cabinet meetings; proposes referendum; has law-initiating power. Members of cabinet cannot retain legislative mandate. Prime minister is responsible before Assembly.

SENATE

306 members—Algeria, 31; Sahara, 2; overseas departments, 7; France, 255; other, 11. Mandate: 9 yrs. Renewable by thirds every 3 yrs.

Elected indirectly by municipal and general councilors and members of National Assembly. Approximate size of electoral college, 110,000. Majority system, but PR for 7 departments with largest population.

Functions

Full legislative powers jointly with Assembly. Bills must be approved in identical terms by both houses unless prime minister, in case of disaccord, asks lower house to vote "definitive" text. Otherwise Senate has full veto powers.

Cannot introduce a motion of censure and force government out of office.

NATIONAL ASSEMBLY
(552 Members)

Mandate: 5 yrs. Elected directly by equal and universal suffrage. Has law-initiating powers concurrently with government.

Limited Legislative Powers

Legislates on civil rights, nationality, status and legal competence of persons, penal law and procedure, taxation, electoral system, organization of national defense, administration of local government units, education employment, unions, social security, and economic programs. Authorizes declaration of war. Can initiate constitutional revision. Can delegate above powers to cabinet—votes organic laws. (All other matters fall within rule-making power.) Can overthrow cabinet by: (1) an adverse vote on programmatic declaration of government (relative majority); (2) a motion of censure introduced by 56 members voted by absolute majority—same signatories cannot introduce another motion during same legislative session; (3) a motion of censure on a legislative text under conditions as described in (2) —may be introduced by same signatories more than once.

Can question cabinet one day a week. Meets in regular sessions for a total that does not exceed 6 months. Cannot have more than 6 committees. Ratifies peace treaties, commercial treaties, treaties pertaining to international organizations, involving state

THE FRENCH FIFTH REPUBLIC

JUDICIARY

HIGH COURT OF JUSTICE

Composed of members of Assembly and Senate in equal numbers. Judges President of Republic for high treason and members of government for criminal offenses.

HIGH COUNCIL OF THE JUDICIARY

Nine members designated by President of Republic.
Presided over by President of Republic. Proposes nomination of judges and exercises disciplinary function

CONSTITUTIONAL COUNCIL

Composed of 9 justices and all ex-presidents of Republic. Three justices each appointed by presidents of Republic, Senate, and Assembly.

Functions

Supervises presidential elections and declares returns.
Supervises referendums and proclaims results.
Examines and decides on contested legislative elections.
On request of prime minister or presidents of Republic, Assembly, or Senate examines and decides on constitutionality of pending bills, treaties, and legislative competence of Assembly.
Examines automatically constitutionality of standing orders and organic laws.
"Consulted" on emergency legislation of President of Republic exercised under Article 16.

THE ECONOMIC AND SOCIAL COUNCIL

Elected by professional organizations.
Designated by government for 5 yrs. as specified by "organic law."
Composed of representatives of professional groups (205 members for French Republic and overseas departments and territories, 24 members represent Community).
Gives "opinion" on bills referred to it by government. "Suggests" reforms.
"Consulted" on over-all government economic plans.

REFERENDUM

Called on specific matters by President of Republic.

---

expenditures, modifying dispositions of legislative nature, relating to status of persons, requiring cession or acquisition of territory.
Votes budget submitted by government. If budget is not decided with Senate within 70 days, may be issued by decree.
Cannot introduce bills involving increased expenditures and decrease in revenue.
Agenda set by cabinet, and all government bills have priority for debate.

reason. There is only one limitation—he cannot dissolve twice within the same year—and one formality—he must "consult" with the prime minister and the presidents of the two legislative assemblies.

When the institutions of the Republic, the independence of the nation, the integrity of its territory, or the execution of international engagements are menaced in a grave and immediate manner and the regular functioning of the public powers is interrupted, the president may take measures necessitated by the circumstances (Article 16). Again this is a personal and discretionary act. The president is required only to inform the nation by a message and to "consult" the Constitutional Council. The National Assembly, however, reconvenes automatically and cannot be dissolved during the emergency period.

The constitution also vests explicitly in the president other powers that he can exercise at his discretion. He has the nominating power for all civil and military posts and, unless it is otherwise provided by an organic law, he signs all decrees and ordinances prepared by the Council of Ministers. He can raise the question of unconstitutionality on a bill or on a law before the Constitutional Council. The president also enjoys all the prerogatives that were vested in the office in the past. He presides over the meetings of the Council of Ministers, receives ambassadors, and sends messages to Parliament. He may ask for the re-examination of a bill or some of its articles, which cannot be refused; promulgates laws within fifteen days after their enactment; negotiates and ratifies treaties, and is kept informed of all negotiations leading to the conclusion of international agreements; and he is commander in chief and presides over the Committee of National Defense.

Finally, the president can bring certain issues before the people in a referendum:

> The President of the Republic on the proposal of the government . . . or on joint resolution by the two legislative assemblies . . . *may* submit to a referendum any bill dealing with the organization of the public powers, the approval of an agreement of the Community or the authorization to ratify a treaty, that without being contrary to the Constitution would affect the functioning of existing institutions [Article 11].

The calling of a referendum is however a personal act of the President of the Republic. He may elicit or refuse it depending on the circumstances.

The president, as was the case under the Fourth Republic, is president of the Community (formerly called the French Union). But, in contrast to the Fourth Republic, he has direct personal powers to act and legislate on all Community affairs without any responsibility to Parliament or corresponding power on the part of Parliament to intervene. He utilizes the various organs of the Community as he sees fit and issues all decisions concerning Community matters under his own name.[1]

The Domain of the "Veto" Power. The constitution explicitly consecrates the large influence of the president over the functioning of the institutions and policy making:

The President of the Republic shall see that the Constitution is respected. He shall ensure, by his arbitration, the regular functioning of the governmental authorities, as well as the continuance of the State.

He shall be the guarantor of national independence, of the integrity of the territory, and of respect for Community agreements and treaties [Article 5].

Mediation is a personal act involving the exercise of judgment. As a result, the president is given implicitly a veto power on almost every conceivable aspect of policy. He may refuse to sign a decree or to make a nomination; he may dissolve or threaten to dissolve the National Assembly and call for a referendum. His position in the Community gives him a direct influence over decisions in all other matters. He becomes an integral part of policy making and policy execution despite the fact that he is politically irresponsible.

The list of presidential prerogatives is thus an impressive one. The framers, while rejecting presidential government, wished nonetheless to establish a president who can act on his own. In matters of war, foreign policy, the preservation of internal peace, and the functioning of the institutions, his powers are overriding and he can bring them to bear upon every type of policy and decision. His acts thus have a political content. He can no longer remain an "irresponsible head of the State" like the British Crown.

The Government. The government, composed of the prime minister and his ministers, "determines and conducts the policy of the nation" and is "responsible before the Parliament." Special recognition is accorded to the prime minister. He "directs" the action of the government and is "responsible" for the national defense. He "assures the execution of the laws and exercises the rule-making power"

---

[1] For details, see Chapter XI.

—but on condition that all decrees and ordinances are signed by the President of the Republic (Articles 20 and 21). He determines the composition of his cabinet, presides over its meetings, and directs the administrative services. He defends his policy before the Parliament, answers questions addressed to him by the members of Parliament, states the over-all program of the government in special programmatic declarations, and puts the question of confidence.

Many of these powers lend themselves to future expansion. The prime minister may find it tempting to seek the support of Parliament in order to oppose the President of the Republic. He may invoke his political responsibility to cope with the impressive array of weapons that the constitution gives to the President of the Republic. Thus, a conflict between a "responsible" prime minister and an "irresponsible" president is likely to occur under certain conditions.

The Legislature.   The Parliament of the Fifth Republic is, as in the past, bicameral. It consists of a National Assembly and a Senate. The first, elected for five years by universal suffrage, is composed of 552 deputies (465 from Metropolitan France, 67 from Algeria, 4 from the Sahara region, 10 from the overseas departments, and 6 from the overseas territories). The Senate, elected for nine years is composed of 306 members (255 from Metropolitan France, 31 from Algeria, 2 from the Sahara region, 7 from the overseas departments, 6 from French citizens living abroad, and 5 from the overseas territories). The Senate is elected indirectly by the municipal councilors, the departmental councilors, and the members of the National Assembly. One third of its membership is renewed every three years. The two chambers have equal powers except in two respects—the traditional prerogative of the lower chambers to examine the budget first is maintained, and the Senate cannot introduce a motion of censure and bring about on its own initiative the fall of the cabinet. The government, however, if it so desires, may invoke its responsibility before the Senate, presumably with all the consequences that it entails. The new Senate was designed primarily to limit the powers of the National Assembly. It can block the decisions of the lower house and under certain circumstances exercises an absolute veto.

Article 45 specifies that every bill "is examined successively in the two assemblies with a view to the adoption of an identical text." But if there is continuing disagreement on the text of a bill after two readings by each assembly, the prime minister can convene a joint conference committee consisting of an equal number of members of the two chambers with the task of proposing a compromise text. This text may be submitted by the government for the approval of the two assemblies. It is only in case of a persistent discord between the two assemblies that the prime minister *may* ask the National Assembly to rule "definitively." Thus, the National Assembly has the last word and the Senate a veto power, depending upon the attitude of the government. If the government and the Senate are in accord, the senatorial veto is ironclad. The Senate can be overruled only if there is an agreement between the government and the National Assembly.

A Rationalized Parliament. The new constitution establishes a "rationalized Parliament" in a number of ways. Only two sessions of the two assemblies are allowed—two months and a half from October to December and about three months and a half from the last Tuesday of April to the end of July. The first session is to be devoted to the budget and the second to major legislative texts. Extraordinary sessions may take place at the request of the prime minister or of a majority of the members of the National Assembly "on a specific agenda." They are convened and closed by a decree of the President of the Republic. The lawmaking functions of the Parliament are restricted to matters limitatively defined in the constitution. The government can legislate on all other matters by simple decree. The legislative agenda is no longer the outcome of interminable debates between the president of the National Assembly, the presidents of the parliamentary groups, and a government delegate. The government now fixes the order of business. The vote of the deputies is personal. Only under specific conditions can there be a vote by proxy, and it is stated that "no deputy can receive more than one proxy." Attendance at the debates is obligatory, and unauthorized absence entails sanctions. The president of the National Assembly is elected for the whole legislative term, thus avoiding annual elections that in the past placed him at the mercy of the various parliamentary groups. The Senate elects its president every three years.

The Parliament can no longer establish its own standing orders. They must be approved by the Constitutional Council before they become effective. The number of parliamentary committees is reduced and their functions carefully circumscribed. Only six committees are allowed by the constitution. It is further stated that the government text of a bill and not the committees' amendments and counterproposals, as under the Fourth Republic, come before the floor. The government has the right to reject all amendments and to demand a vote on its own text.

All these provisions are directed against "Assembly government." By putting rules into the constitution that are essentially of a procedural character, it was hoped to limit Parliament to the performance of its proper functions of deliberation and to protect the executive from legislative encroachments. The new rules reflect a genuine desire to correct some of the more flagrant abuses of the past and are consistent with the strengthening of the executives in modern democracies. Some of the rules, however, are designed to weaken Parliament, for instance, the limitative enumeration of matters on which Parliament can legislate, and the manner in which the relations between the government and Parliament are established.

Relations between Parliament and Government. Four major provisions of a general character determine the nature of the relations between Parliament and the government: (1) the incompatibility between the parliamentary mandate and a cabinet post, (2) the manner in which the responsibility of the cabinet before the Parliament comes into play, (3) the distinction between "legislation" and "rule making," and (4) the introduction of the "executive budget."

The Rule of Incompatibility. Article 23 of the constitution is explicit: "The 'office' of member of government is incompatible with the exercise of any parliamentary mandate." Thus, a member of Parliament who joins the cabinet must resign his mandate for the balance of the legislative term. He is replaced in Parliament by the person whose name appeared together with his on the ballot—the *suppléant.* Nonparliamentarians may become cabinet members, which was the rare exception in the Third and Fourth Republics. Despite the rule of incompatibility, cabinet members sit in Parliament and participate freely in the debates.

The purpose of the rule was to introduce a genuine separation of powers and to discourage parliamentarians from trying to become ministers, which was one of the major causes for the high rate of cabinet turnovers. It was also the avowed intention of the framers to establish a government that would be better able to resist pressures emanating from parliamentary groups and thus be in a position to give its undivided attention to its duties.

Responsibility of the Cabinet before the Legislature. The responsibility of the cabinet to the legislature comes into play in a number of ways. After the prime minister has been nominated by the President of the Republic, he presents his program before the National Assembly and, through a minister, before the Senate. This programmatic statement calls for a vote in favor or against. In the first case, the cabinet, to use the terminology of the Fourth Republic, is "invested," while in the second case, the prime minister must submit his resignation to the President of the Republic. A vote by simple majority against the prime minister and his program is all that is required to dismiss the government at this stage. In the course of the year the prime minister may, at his discretion, make before the National Assembly "declarations of general policy," which may or may not, at his discretion, give rise to a vote.

After the cabinet has been invested, its responsibility to Parliament can be engaged in the following manner: The National Assembly (but not the Senate) has the right to introduce a motion of censure, which must be signed by one tenth of the members of the National Assembly. The vote on the motion takes place forty-eight hours after it has been introduced. The motion is lost unless it receives an absolute majority of the members composing the National Assembly. Blank ballots and abstentions count for the government. If the motion is carried, the government must resign; if the motion is lost, then its signatories cannot move another one in the course of the same legislative session.

The prime minister may, after consultation with the cabinet, stake the life of his government on any general issue of policy or on any given legislative text. Although the constitution does not use the term, this is equivalent to putting the "question of confidence." In the first case, the declaration of a general policy is presumed to be accepted unless there is a motion of censure voted under the conditions mentioned previously. In the second case, the bill becomes law unless a motion of censure is introduced and voted according to the same conditions, but with one difference: The same signatories may introduce a motion of censure as many times as the prime minister stakes his government's responsibility. Thus, if the motion is carried by an absolute majority, the bill does not become law and the government resigns. If, however, the motion is lost, and it is lost even if carried by a relative majority, then the text becomes law and the government stays in office. This was the essence of the Gaillard project.

"Law" and "Rule Making." The constitution provides, in accord-

ance with the canons of parliamentary government, that "law is
voted by Parliament." Members of Parliament and of the government can introduce bills and amendments. The scope of law making, however, is defined in the constitution (Article 34) to include:

> . . . the *regulations* concerning:
> civil rights and the fundamental guarantees granted to the citizens for
> the exercise of their public liberties; . . .
> nationality, status and legal capacity of persons, marriage contracts,
> inheritance and gifts;
> determination of crimes and misdemeanors as well as the penalties
> imposed therefor; criminal procedure; . . .
> the basis, the rate and the methods of collecting taxes of all types; the
> issuance of currency; . . .
> the electoral system of the Parliamentary assemblies and the local
> assemblies; . . .
> the nationalization of enterprises and the transfer of the property of
> enterprises from the public to the private sector; . . .
> [and the] fundamental *principles* of:
> the general organization of national defense;
> the free administration of local communities, the extent of their juris-
> diction and their resources;
> education;
> property rights, civil and commercial obligations;
> legislation pertaining to employment, unions and social security.

Parliament must also authorize the declaration of war and the continuation of the state of siege beyond a period of fifteen days.

This enumeration of legislative power is limitative and cannot be
enlarged except by an organic law. Article 37 makes this point clear.
"*All other matters,*" it states, "*than those which are in the domain of
law fall within the rule-making sphere.*" It goes even further, "Legislative texts pertaining to such matters may be modified by decree."
Thus, past laws dealing with matters that are now declared by the
constitution to be beyond the powers of the legislature can be modified by simple decree. They are "delegalized." The same article and
other provisions of the constitution ensure the distinction between
legislation and rule making for the future by a series of safety devices. If a bill is debated before the Parliament and the government
contests the Assembly's competence, the bill is referred to the Constitutional Council. If a bill is enacted by Parliament but there are
doubts about the Parliament's jurisdiction, the President of the
Republic, the prime minister, or one of the presidents of the two

assemblies can bring it before the Constitutional Council before it is promulgated. If a bill is passed and promulgated, even then it can be brought before the Constitutional Council on the ground that it deals with a matter that was beyond Parliament's competence. Finally, the government can modify in the future by simple decree a law passed by the legislature, provided the Constitutional Council decides that the Parliament exceeded its competence in passing it.

The constitution provides expressly that all lawmaking power enjoyed by Parliament may be delegated to the executive. The system of *décrets-lois* of the Third Republic and analogous practices of the Fourth are thus enshrined in the constitution. "The government may for the execution of its program ask Parliament to authorize it to take by ordinances, within a limited period of time, measures which are normally reserved to the domain of law [Article 38]." Such ordinances come into force as soon as they are promulgated, but they are null and void if a bill for their ratification is not submitted by the government before Parliament within a prescribed time, or if the ratification of the bill is rejected.

The Budget. The constitution introduces the "executive budget." The budget is submitted by the government to Parliament. Proposals stemming from members of Parliament "are not receivable if their adoption entails either a diminution of public resources or an increase in public expenditures [Article 47]." No bill entailing diminution of resources or additional expenditures is receivable at any time. These provisions date back to the proposals made in the period of the Third Republic by Gaston Doumergue, André Tardieu, Léon Blum, and other political leaders.

Safeguards buttressing the executive character of the budget have been written into the constitution. If forty days have elapsed after the budget has been submitted and the National Assembly still has not "decided" on the bill on a first reading, then the government may take the budget before the Senate, which is to make a decision within fifteen days. If it does, then the bill is returned to the National Assembly. In case of disaccord between the Senate and the National Assembly a conference committee between the two chambers may be set up at the discretion of the government. But "if Parliament has not decided within seventy days" after the introduction of the budget, then "the budget bill can be promulgated and put into effect by simple ordinance." [Article 47, par. 2 and 3] Thus the government may be able to bypass Parliament in case the latter has failed to reach an agreement.

These then are the great lines of the constitutional structure: strict bicameralism giving the Senate a genuine veto even over budgetary policy if it has the support of the government; a division between lawmaking and rule making that in effect gives to the executive broad legislative powers; the possibility that bills become law unless there is an absolute majority against the cabinet rather than a majority for the bill; delegation of lawmaking power to the executive; priority to the government bills before Parliament; a mechanism restricting the use of the motion of censure; the ever-present threat of dissolution; numerous devices in the hands of the President of the Republic and the prime minister to suspend legislation by appealing to the Constitutional Council and, finally, the possibility of a referendum on certain matters. The only concession made to Parliament is the provision for a period on one day a week in which deputies and senators question the cabinet members.

Other Constitutional Organs and Principles. The new constitution re-establishes an Economic and Social Council, with consultative and advisory powers, representing the most important professional interests in France and in the Community member-states. As under the Third Republic, a High Court of Justice, whose members are elected by the National Assembly and the Senate, may try the President of the Republic for high treason and the members of the government for criminal offenses committed in the exercise of their functions. A High Council of the Judiciary, presided over by the President of the Republic, nominates judges to the higher judicial posts, is consulted about pardons by the President of the Republic and rules on disciplinary matters involving the judiciary. The same section of the constitution (Article 66) provides what purports to be a writ of habeas corpus clause. "No one may be arbitrarily detained. The judicial authority, guardian of individual liberty, assures the respect of this principle under conditions provided by law."

The most striking innovation is a Constitutional Council composed of nine members who serve for a period of nine years. Three are nominated by the President of the Republic, three by the president of the National Assembly, and three by the president of the Senate. They are renewed by a third every three years. In addition, all former Presidents of the Republic are members ex officio.

A variety of powers has been devolved upon the Constitutional Council. It supervises the presidential elections and the referendums and proclaims the results; it is the judge of the validity of all contested legislative elections, thus avoiding bitter and long controversies in the legislative assemblies. It is the ultimate court of appeal on the interpretation of the constitution on a limited number of matters. Thus, all bills, including treaties, may be referred to it, before their promulgation, by the President of the Republic, the prime minister, or one of the presidents of the two assemblies. A declaration of unconstitutionality suspends the promulgation of the bill or the application of the treaty. It is the judge of the constitutionality of all standing orders and organic laws, which go before it automatically. It is, finally, the guardian of legislative-executive relations in all matters concerning the respective legislative competence of the two branches.

The constitutional review provided by the Constitution of the Fifth Republic differs from the American practice in two important respects. First, it is limited to certain specified categories of cases involving the relationship of governmental organs, and second, it is brought into play only upon the request of four officers of the Fifth Republic—the president, the prime minister, and the two presidents of the legislative assemblies. Review applies only to pending bills. A law cannot be attacked for "unconstitutionality" except under the specific and very restrictive terms of Article 37—that is, only when it is claimed by the government that the legislature exceeded its competence in enacting it. In contrast to the American practice, the Constitutional Council is the guardian of the constitutional provisions regarding executive-legislative relations with particular reference to lawmaking rather than the ultimate court of appeal for the protection of the law of the land at the request of an individual against legislative or administrative infringements.

As regards the amending process, the constitution provides that initiative belongs to the President of the Republic on the proposal of the prime minister and to the members of Parliament. An amendment proposed by the two legislative assemblies by simple majorities becomes effective only after it is approved in a referendum. A proposal stemming from the president and approved by the two chambers by simple majorities may go, at the president's discretion, either before the two chambers, meeting jointly in a congress, in which case a three-fifths majority is required, or it may be submitted to the people in a referendum. Thus, the revision of the constitution that emanates from the government may either go before the congress or the people, while a proposal stemming from Parliament must always be submitted to the people in a referendum.

In a number of cases the constitution provides for the enactment of organic laws to implement certain of its articles. They are laws dealing with matters of exceptional importance—the electoral system and the organization and functioning of governmental institutions, such as the Economic and Social Council, the High Court of Justice, and the Constitutional Council. For all these organic laws the constitution requires a special procedure. A bill intended to become an organic law is not debated for fifteen days after its introduction. The two chambers must agree on an identical text. If they fail to reach an agreement the government may ask the National Assembly to decide "definitively," but the National Assembly can do so only by absolute majority. Organic laws dealing with the organization or the powers of the Senate must receive the assent of this body. In all cases they go automatically before the Constitutional Council and must be found to conform to the constitution before they are promulgated.

The Constitutional Machinery: An Analysis

Every constitution is an expression of the political history of a country and an attempt to reinterpret and redirect it in the light of new political imperatives. It is also a creature of circumstances often shaped in answer to immediate needs and perhaps even the aspirations of individual political leaders. The major objective of the framers of the Constitution of the Fifth Republic was to correct the institutional defects of the past and to create a strong and stable executive. One of the most predominant themes of French politics has been the identification of a republic with assembly government. Executive leadership has been sought outside of Parliament never with Parliament. The framers of the new constitution hoped to avoid the perennial clash between executive and legislature while preserving the principles of representative government. The constitution was also elaborated under the pressure of the events of May 13 and to realize the ideas of General de Gaulle. In the same manner in which the Constitution of 1946 was made by the parties *against* De Gaulle, the new constitution was made *for* De Gaulle by his followers.

Every constitutional document formulates a pattern of relations between governors and governed and in so doing both reflects and establishes the center of political gravity. The new constitution recognizes the supremacy of universal suffrage and the sovereignty of the people, subject to a number of qualifications. Though the electorate is given, in the referendum, the means of participating in decisions, and though the President of the Republic may appeal to the people by dissolving the National Assembly or holding a referendum, great emphasis is put on indirect elections. Some commentators have already referred to a "senatorial constitution" in which the center of political gravity lies, as in the Third Republic, with the notables who constitute the electoral college for choosing the president and the senators. Out of five of the important decision-making organs of the constitution—the President of the Republic, the prime minister and his cabinet, the Senate, the National Assembly, and the Constitutional Council—only one, the National Assembly, is elected by direct, equal, and universal suffrage.

The framers of the constitution also "rationalized" the parliamentary system so as to avoid the re-establishment of assembly government. A bicameral system was introduced to prevent the ascendancy of the lower house, and efforts were made to protect the executive against the whims of the legislature. In every single case the framers were attempting to cope with the evils of the past, set up a new pattern of relations between the governors and the governed, and prevent an interpretation of their text that would lead to the return of the very forces and practices they wished to extirpate from French political life.

It is doubtful that these goals have been attained. The framers created a divided legislature and a divided executive, thereby running the serious risk of fragmentation instead of a separation of powers, and drove a wedge between decision making and political responsibility. The constitution seems to invite conflict rather than provide a means for its resolution. It is very doubtful that the president can play the ultimate role of a mediator in such conflicts since *arbitrage* means, in essence, the making of political decisions without assuming political responsibility. On the contrary, the office of the president will likely undergo drastic changes in the course of time. There will be a powerful tendency for it to become a responsible instrument of policy making or another organ—the prime minister or the National Assembly—will assume this role. The precedents established by General de Gaulle and especially by his successor will be crucial for the particular development of the office.

A Divided Executive.   The President of the Republic holds the totality of the executive power. Supreme judge of the national interest, ultimate arbiter in case of conflicts, with the power of dissolution and the freedom to decide on a referendum, he nominates the prime minister and is commander in chief and in charge of foreign policy. Indeed the only explicitly recognized prerogative he lacks is that of dismissing the prime minister. The prime minister and his cabinet, in turn, retain important attributions. Together with his cabinet, the prime minister "determines and guides the policies of the nation." Once nominated by the president, he is responsible only to the National Assembly.

As long as the president and the prime minister see eye to eye on issues of policy they can together bring to bear their immense powers upon the National Assembly. Executive leadership may well prove to be the rule and cabinet stability the result—unless, of course, there is a majority in Parliament against their policy. The president, in order to save the prime minister, will dissolve the National Assembly, thereby identifying himself with a policy, in which case two hypotheses may be envisaged: A favorable majority is returned and the policies of the president and the prime minister are endorsed; or a majority is returned against the prime minister. In both cases, the political responsibility of the prime minister *and* the president before the electorate have been engaged. If the electoral verdict is unfavorable, the only alternative left for a President of the Republic who has associated his fortunes with a prime minister in a national election is, to repeat Gambetta's old battle cry, to "give in or get out" (*de se soumettre ou de se demettre*).

The president and the prime minister, as long as they are in agreement, have ample weapons available to prevent this extreme situation from developing. The National Assembly can be controlled by means of the numerous constitutional devices, especially if the Senate cooperates. But there is also the possibility of a conflict between the president and the prime minister on an important national issue —the organization of defense, a treaty, the secession of a member of the Community, or the settlement of Algeria's political status. Although the president does not have the power to dismiss the prime minister outright, he can make the exercise of governmental functions so difficult for the prime minister (by refusing nominations, sending messages that are contrary to the investiture speech of the prime minister, declining to issue decrees decided in the Council of Ministers, threatening to bring certain policy issues before the people, and so on) that he can force him to resign. But the prime minister is responsible before the National Assembly and may be tempted to put his case before this body. The National Assembly may side with the prime minister and refuse to "invest" any other prime minister appointed by the president. This was known under the Third Republic as a "ministerial strike." The president will then be forced either to give in or to dissolve the National Assembly and call for elections in which his responsibility will be directly engaged. If the Assembly, on the other hand, sides with the president against the prime minister, presidential leadership will derive from legislative support and the independence of the president will be accordingly qualified. The stubborn imperative of political responsibility cannot be evaded. The president will either have to assume directly and openly responsibility for his actions and seek approval through the use of referendums or dissolution of the National Assembly and elections, or he will once more become an irresponsible head of the state, performing ceremonial functions while another organ—the prime minister—assumes the role of executive leadership. The system will evolve in the direction of a presidential or a cabinet government.

The framers of the constitution have designed, however, a number of barriers to prevent the development of the system in either direction. They cast the president in the quasi-monarchical role of mediator and, by providing for a restricted college for his election, sought to dissociate him from the very source that would legitimize his authority and transform the office into an instrument of government, as is the case with the American president. The framers of the constitution also erected obstacles to the development of the system along the lines of British parliamentary government, in which the prime minister and his cabinet concentrate in their hands the totality of executive power. The prime minister who is responsible before the National Assembly is deprived of the means of exercising effective political leadership: He cannot dissolve the National Assembly and ask for popular endorsement of his policies. He can only try to bolster his position by seeking the support of the National Assembly against the president. If he does so, he may have to pay a heavy ransom to the National Assembly that will amount to a return to assembly government that characterized the preceding regime. Unable to make a clear-cut choice between a parliamentary system with strong cabinet prerogatives and a presidential system, the framers created a hybrid system in which executive authority remains divided and separated from the people.

A Divided Legislature. The new constitution reintroduces a rigorous bicameralism which amounts to a return to the institutions of the Third Republic. The Senate is on an equal footing with the National Assembly in lawmaking, but lacks the power to bring about, on its own initiative, the fall of the cabinet by introducing and voting a motion of censure. Chosen indirectly by a body of electors which roughly corresponds to the electoral college of the president, it is bound to have an orientation different from that of the National Assembly, reflecting the interests and the pressures of the rural sectors of the population. If the government turns to the Senate in order to block the lower house on financial policy or other legislative matters, the prime minister will have to become increasingly attuned to the policies of the Senate, before which he is not technically responsible, and bypass the National Assembly, to which he is responsible. The new Senate may revive the practices of its predecessor in order to reinforce its position and influence the policies pursued by the prime minister. It may indeed find ways and means of securing effective control over the life of the government. The election of both the president and the Senate by approximately the same body of electors has a political logic which the senators cannot fail to perceive. They exert strong influence, if not control, over the municipal councilors by whom they are elected and who comprise the bulk of the presidential electoral college. When the senators begin to play a crucial role in the election of the president, they may attempt to make this office their instrument and wrest from the government prerogatives that are not given to them by the constitution.

Fragmentation or Separation of Powers. The separation of powers is based upon the liberal principles of the eighteenth and nineteenth centuries. By separating powers and allowing each one to act as a check upon the other, it was hoped to create a framework in which the government could not become the instrument of the majority and invade personal and property rights. In the twentieth century the principle has been attenuated in favor of majority rule. In all contemporary systems there has been an increasing concentration of powers in the hands of a popularly elected and responsible executive, brought about by the emergence of political parties that have become the vehicles through which popular participation is elicited and channeled into policy. The parties have been responsible for the development of cabinet or of presidential governments that bridge the separation between legislature and executive and create strong, stable, and effective government. The framers of the French Constitution, as has been seen, conceded that the secular divisions of the French body politic did not allow for majorities to coalesce. Yet they established institutions whose overt purpose is to discourage their formation and even to protect the government against a majority whose absence they deplored.

In the new constitution, powers are confused rather than separated. The executive is internally divided into two organs; bicameralism is a design to thwart the lower and only truly representative assembly; the president has political functions without being responsible, and the prime minister has subsidiary executive functions exercised under the control of the National Assembly, to which he is responsible. The National Assembly in turn may see its will paralyzed by a Senate which cannot enforce the responsibility of the cabinet and the prime minister. Within each power there are distinct and separate organs whose result, if not design, is to lead to a confusion that makes it difficult for issues to be clarified and majorities formed. This discourages public participation and allows for a group of leaders and administrators to govern in terms of the national interest as they conceive it.

One of the basic criticisms of the framers against the Fourth Republic was that the confusion of political parties and groups and the manner in which cabinets were formed and overthrown obscured the issues of political accountability and led to apathy and alienation of the public. Had they been genuinely concerned with involving the people directly with the State they could have created a president elected by universal suffrage in whose name executive power could be exercised on behalf of the people. Responsibility for policy initiation, foreign affairs, defense, and the budget would be clearly focussed upon the president. Or they could have deprived the president of all personal prerogatives and required the countersigning of all his acts by a responsible prime minister, so as to constitutionalize a cabinet government. The president might have maintained the right of referendum and perhaps the use of emergency powers provided by Article 16, but the very logic of cabinet government would have meant that even these powers could not be used except with the consent of the prime minister. In either case, the structure would have an internal logic. Popular participation would have been invited by concentrating public attention on a given leader or party. It would have encouraged majorities and minorities to be formed around policies and men and might have paved the way to new party alignments. As it stands, the constitution may well perpetuate the confusion of responsibilities and the alienation of the public so characteristic of the Fourth Republic.

It is for these reasons that the proponents of a presidential system, like Georges Vedel, and of a strong and responsible cabinet, like Duverger, criticized the new constitution. In their opinion it dissociates the people from their government and blocks the development of party leadership. It may lead to a government without majority support and perhaps even to one that may attempt to govern against the majority. The disregard of popular sovereignty runs counter to the needs of positive government in a modern democracy. The same point is made by René Capitant, a Gaullist and perhaps the most articulate exponent of constitutional revisionism under the Third and Fourth Republics. He wrote:

It is clear that the framers made a fundamental error which vitiates their constitutional structure. Inspired by the legitimate desire to limit the sovereignty of the National Assembly, which was the source of all evils of the previous regime, they were misled in the course they followed. Instead of attempting to go beyond representative government by limiting parliamentary sovereignty in terms of popular sovereignty, clearly enunciated and better organized, they thought they had found the solution in a multiplication of the number of representative organs. . . . In the new constitution three organs have a representative character, the National Assembly, the Senate, and the President of the Republic. The government, which is not elected and does not represent the nation, must govern by taking into consideration the political orientation of these three organs which all have means of exercising their sovereign influence. This is the classic scheme of separation of powers, especially in the form it took in France under the July Monarchy. . . . The proposed system is liberal rather than democratic.[1]

---

[1] René Capitant, in Léon Hamon, *De Gaulle dans la République,* p. xviii.

The Center of Political Gravity

The framers, as has been noted, both endorsed and qualified the principle of modern democratic systems—direct universal suffrage. Two governmental organs—the President of the Republic and the Senate—are elected indirectly by a college whose bulk consists of mayors and municipal councilors who assist the mayors in the conduct of municipal affairs. Thus, presidential elections in France are totally unlike elections for the American president in which the "electors" are chosen expressly for the purpose of electing the president. For instance, the electoral college that chose De Gaulle as president in December, 1958 was composed of mayors and municipal councilors elected in 1953.

According to the constitution, the electoral college of the president is composed of the members of Parliament (senators and members of the National Assembly), overseas delegates who number approximately 5,200, and about 3,200 departmental councilors, who assist the prefects of the various departments in the performance of their functions as provided by law. The rest—some 73,500 members —come from among the municipal councilors and mayors of France. The constitution provides that the number of municipal councilors who enter into the presidential college depends upon the size of the municipality. For communes having up to 1,000 inhabitants, only the mayor is a presidential elector; for 1,001 to 2,000, the mayor and his first deputy; for 2,001 to 2,500, the mayor, his deputy, and one member of the council; for 2,501 to 3,000, the mayor and his two deputies; for 3,001 to 6,000, the mayor, his two deputies, and three municipal councilors; for 6,001 to 9,000, the mayor, two deputies, and six municipal councilors; for 9,000 to 30,000 inhabitants, the whole municipal council; and for communes with more than 30,000 inhabitants, one additional elector chosen by the municipal council by proportional representation for every 1,000 inhabitants in excess of 30,000. Despite this last provision, large urban agglomerations remain underrepresented.

This system gives a great advantage to the small rural communities of less than 2,000 inhabitants. The 16 million French citizens living in such communities have approximately 39,000 presidential electors, while the 27 million French who live in communities with more than 2,000 inhabitants have 33,500 electors. What is more, the communes with less than 1,500 inhabitants, representing about one third of the population of France, have a majority of presidential electors for Metropolitan France. For the small communities of less than 1,000 there was in the presidential elections of December 21 one elector for every 347 inhabitants; the ratio was one for every 713 inhabitants for the communities of 1,000 to 3,000; one elector for every 728 for the communes with 3,000 to 9,000; one elector for every 594 for the communes of 9,000 to 30,000; and for the communes with more than 30,000, one elector for every 957 inhabitants. The inhabitants of the small communes thus count from two to three times as much as those living in larger urban centers.

ELECTION OF THE PRESIDENT OF THE REPUBLIC

Reproduced from M. Duverger's *La Ve République* (1959), p. 30, with the permission of the author.

The same is true for the Senate. All the senators of Metropolitan France are elected indirectly by the municipal councils of their departments by absolute majority on the first ballot and a relative majority in a runoff. Only in the seven most populated departments —Nord, Pas-de-Calais, Rhône, Bouches-du-Rhône, Seine, Seine-Maritime, and Seine-et-Oise—do the municipal councilors elect the senators by proportional representation. Furthermore, in all the towns with more than 30,000 inhabitants the electoral college is composed of the municipal councilors and one additional delegate for every 1,000 inhabitants in excess of 30,000 elected by the council by proportional representation. This was a concession to the urban centers which, under the Fourth Republic, elected only one additional delegate for every 5,000 inhabitants in excess of 45,000 inhabitants.

The number of electors varies according to the size of the municipality, as was the case with the presidential electoral college: one elector for the communes below 1,000 to as many as seven for the communes up to 9,000 inhabitants. In the communes with 9,000 to 30,000, all municipal councilors vote. The senatorial college (about 110,000 electors), which is larger than that of the presidential college, is strikingly similar in its social composition. Again the small communes predominate. Those with less than 1,500 inhabitants

ELECTIONS OF THE SENATE

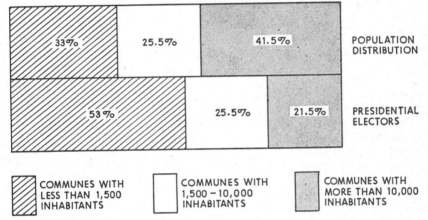

Reproduced from M. Duverger's *La Ve République* (1959), p. 92, with the permission of the author.

have a majority in the senatorial electoral college. They represent 33 per cent of the population and 53 per cent of the senatorial electors. The larger towns with more than 10,000 inhabitants, which represent more than 40 per cent of the population, have only 21.5 per cent of the senatorial electors.

It may be pointed out, at least for the election of the Senate, that a representative who owes his election to local interests—dairy farmers, beetgrowers, winegrowers—may show a great detachment when other issues are concerned and concentrate his attention on matters of national import. The case of many American senators from western and rural areas is very much in point. French political practices bear this out to some extent. There have been senators who, despite the rural character of their constituency and the indirect manner of their elections, rose to national prominence. Generally, however, the Senate, both under the Third and the Fourth Republics, was predominately a body acting on behalf of agricultural interests. The new constitution does not modify the situation. It maintains the character of this body as a "chamber of agriculture," as many of its critics pointed out.[2]

The preponderance of the rural elements of the population is especially difficult to understand in the election of the president. One reason advanced is that the framers simply returned to the old and tried ways of the Third Republic. Elections have always been indirect for the Senate and the senatorial college appeared also the best known system for electing the president. Another reason given is that the electoral college is designed to weaken the Communist vote. However, it should be pointed out that proportional representation for the designation of supplementary delegates in towns with more than 30,000 inhabitants has been introduced and that the Communist party is well entrenched outside of the urban regions. In many rural areas the Communists have shown remarkable strength ever since the Liberation. It is more likely, in fact, that alliances of the "Popular Front" type will be made in some of the rural areas than in the industrial centers where the enmity between Socialists and Communists is persistent and virulent. Michel Debré has attempted to justify the electoral system by contending that the municipal councilors are experienced in handling public affairs.[3] The same argument is made by Professor Prélot who concludes that the "term *notable* corresponds to a good name by virtue of the position held and the services rendered. . . . The senatorial college is not made up of wealthy persons. . . . Undoubtedly they are better off but this can be attributed to personal effort. . . . Communal affairs are never entrusted to persons who cannot take care of their personal affairs."[4] The argument is reminiscent of Guizot's theories in favor of property qualifications. The senatorial electoral college is perhaps the best way of creating a stable political system in which the President of the Republic becomes a national *paterfamilias*.

The framers of the constitution, however, were not looking merely for a stable government. They were attempting to create the condi-

---

[2] Maurice Duverger, *La Ve République*, p. 91.
[3] Michel Debré, in his *Refaire une démocratie, un État, un Pouvoir*, pp. 15–21.
[4] *Pour Comprendre la Nouvelle Constitution*, p. 52.

tions of dynamic and effective government in which the President of the Republic is the motor force and the source of inspiration. Does the social composition of his electoral college guarantee this? To again cite Prélot: "By definition, the senatorial support may always be presumed since the Senate, the President of the Republic, and the prime minister constitute a bloc that has the same source, the same *masse de granite*, representing the principle of force and stability for the Fifth Republic." The same author points out, however, with justice that "the electoral college of mayors, deputy-mayors, municipal councilors in choosing the president determines the overall political orientation." [5]

The center of political gravity in the Fifth Republic is to be found among the inhabitants of communes of less than 2,000 persons. Irrespective of their political affiliations—Communism and Poujadism for many of them represented a form of political protest and a means for the defense of their interests and the *status quo*—irrespective of their experience and wisdom in handling communal affairs, their occupation continues to be largely agricultural, their major concern the protection of the small farmer, the merchant, and the artisan. Their political experience lies in the accommodation of interests, the dispensing of favors, and the extraction of concessions from the central government. The industrial revolution has left them relatively unaffected, and the remarkable economic expansion France has experienced since the Liberation and the concomitant phenomena of modernization have often provoked a resentment that has been channeled into protest movements. It is paradoxical that the Gaullists, in refashioning the institutions of the Republic, sought the support of these forces. The majority has been disfranchised and dynamism has been sacrificed to the requirements of stability. Or is it simply the expression of a nineteenth century liberalism that has never been reconciled to the principles of democracy?

❖　　❖　　❖　　❖　　❖

The Constitution of the Fifth Republic is the culmination of a long revisionist movement that began under the Third Republic and which became increasingly articulate in the years preceding the fall of the Fourth Republic. Its aim was to provide for a stable and effective government. Since the political prerequisites of such a gov-

---

[5] *Ibid.*, p. 54.

ernment—cohesive majorities and national political parties—did not exist, the framers attempted to create the conditions of stability by ensuring to the government a large and autonomous sphere of action.

Their basic premise was that coherent majorities at election time were unobtainable. Hence they sought to organize the election of two of the representative organs of government—the president and the Senate—in a manner that would attenuate the divisions of the body politic. They manufactured an electoral college for the president whose social composition and orientation is very similar to that of the Senate. They established a "senatorial republic." Furthermore, the manner in which powers are organized may lead to rivalry among them. The stringency of the provisions for a motion of censure may lead the National Assembly to censure the government on its legislative texts. If legislation fails to secure a majority but is enacted simply because there is no absolute majority against the government, it is doubtful that the government will stay in office for long. It will be morally bound either to resign or to ask for the confidence of the National Assembly on its over-all program, in which case a negative vote by simple majority is enough to force it out of office. In fact, the Constitution of the Fourth Republic was violated in precisely this manner. Out of the twenty-one governments of the Fourth Republic only five were overthrown by the constitutionally prescribed absolute majorities.

A more serious weakness of the new constitution is that the people do not have a sense of participation and involvement in politics because of the indirect election of the president and the Senate. Divorce between decision and responsibility may create the same phenomenon of apathy and alienation that Gaullist revisionism deplored in the years of the Fourth Republic.

Lack of popular government and participation will not encourage the political parties to modernize their ways and organization. The highest stakes of politics—control of the organs of the government—can never be theirs under the new constitution. Since the great prizes of politics are beyond their reach, the parties will have no compelling reason to bridge their differences and effect a consolidation. As a result, they will remain isolated and continue to be permanent vehicles of protest rather than instruments of policy initiation and formulation. Multigroupism and multipartism may prove to be the rule under the Fifth Republic as it was under the previous regimes.

During the formative period of the Fifth Republic the figure of General de Gaulle is far more important than juridical subtleties relating to the interpretation of the constitution. This is due to the immense prestige of the first President of the Republic. As long as De Gaulle is in office, the presidency and the cabinet may have for a considerable period of time an overriding position vis-à-vis the other organs of government irrespective of constitutional arrangements. The constitution may work as long as there is a majority for De Gaulle, that is to say, for reasons exactly opposed to the ones that inspired its elaboration. It is only when De Gaulle's popularity declines that most of the difficulties we have discussed will appear. But by then revisionism may be in the air again.

Further References

A number of studies of the structure of the Constitution of the Fifth Republic have already appeared. The best single publication is the issue of the *Revue Française de Science Politique,* "La Constitution de la Ve République," Vol. IX, No. 1 (March, 1959), with detailed bibliography.

A succinct and balanced analysis is Stanley Hoffmann's "The French Constitution, 1958, The Final Text and its Prospects," *American Political Science Review,* Vol. LIII, No. 2 (June, 1959), pp. 332–58. Professor Maurice Duverger's *La Ve République,* cited earlier, is a comprehensive study. In addition, Marcel Prélot, *Pour Comprendre la Nouvelle Constitution* (2d ed.; Paris, 1959); Raymond Aron, *Changeante et Immuable, de la 4ième à la 5ième République;* Léon Hamon, *De Gaulle dans la République* (1958), and the preface by René Capitant; and Jean Chatelain, *La Nouvelle Constitution et le Régime Politique de la France* (Paris, 1959).

Debré's statement before the *Conseil d'État, La Nouvelle Constitution* (Tours, 1958) is an indispensable source. Also his speeches in defense of the constitution, *Refaire une Démocratie, un État, un Pouvoir* (Paris, 1958).

CHAPTER XI

Empire, Union, Community

THE HISTORY of the French Empire reflects well the paradoxes of the French political system. Justified as a source of military strength and prestige it became after World War II one of the pervasive causes of the decline of French power; dedicated to the realization of one of the most grandiose schemes of the French Revolution—the assimilation of the natives into French culture and law—it evolved in a manner which brought the incompatibilities between France and the native cultures into sharp relief. Patterned upon the Napoleonic institutions of centralization, according to which all parts of the far-flung empire were to be ruled from Paris, it allowed a situation to develop in which local French civil and military authorities became autonomous centers of power that frustrated the decisions of the government; inspiring high hopes for economic advantage, capital investment, and trade, it required substantial subsidies that turned it into a financial liability.

The principle of assimilation was based on the assumption that the fusion of the natives into French culture and language was possible and desirable and that with the passage of time "one hundred million French" would emerge. No political diversity was envisaged. The colonies were part of the Republic. Hence they were to be given increased participation in the representative institutions of the Republic—one and indivisible. During the Third Republic there were nineteen deputies and seven senators from the colonies and Algeria (nine and three respectively for Algeria). Representation was increased in the Fourth Republic.

Despite the policy of assimilation, however, the differences between France and the colonies made it impossible for the French Parliament to legislate on any colonial matters. The colonies were

THE COMMUNITY

POWERS

Foreign affairs, defense, monetary policy, common economic and financial policy, strategic raw materials. Unless there are special agreements to the contrary, also justice, higher education, foreign trade, and telecommunications.

COMMUNITY SENATE

Composition

French Republic	186	Upper Volta	12
Senegal	8	Mauritania	3
Oubangui-Chari	4	Madagascar	17
Middle Congo	3	Niger	9
Ivory Coast	11	Soudan	13
Dahomey	6	Tchad	9
Gabon	3	Total	284

Functions

Two sessions, one month each, in Paris.
Deliberates on economic and financial common policy.
"Examines" treaties.
Gives its "opinion" on parliamentary authorization to declare war.
Takes enforceable decisions—legislates on matters delegated to it by legislatures of member states.
Consulted by president on Community matters, at president's discretion.
Can take initiative for recommendations tending to harmonize legislation among member states.
Participates in revision of Community constitution jointly with French Parliament.

MEMBERS

The French Republic
Republics of French West Africa:
Ivory Coast   Niger
Dahomey   Senegal
Upper Volta   Soudan
Mauritania   Madagascar

Republics of French Equatorial Africa
Gabon   Congo
Tchad   Oubangui-Chari (Central Africa)

EXECUTIVE COUNCIL

Presided over by President of the Community.
Composed of prime minister of the Republic and heads of all member states, and all ministers of French government whose ministries relate to Community matters—Foreign Affairs, Armed Forces, Economic Affairs, Justice, Education, Transportation, Telecommunication.

Special Committees: Economic and Financial Affairs, Transportation and Telecommunication, Relations between Community and International Organizations, Justice and Higher Education, Secretariat: coordinates activities of Executive Council on behalf of President of Community.

Functions

Supreme organ of policy coordination.
Discusses matters of general policy of Community.
Deliberates on needed expenditures for the functioning of services of Community.

PRESIDENT

Election

Special electoral college composed of Parliament, Municipal Councilors, General Councilors, and representatives of parliaments and municipal councils of all member states; 90% of electors from Metropolitan France. Term—7 years.

Functions

Represents the Community.
Legislates for all Community matters.
Convenes Community Senate.
Appoints members of Court of Arbitration.
Presides over Executive Council.
Appoints high commissioners in all member states to represent him.

ARBITRATION COURT

Seven judges nominated by President of Republic. Term —6 years.

Functions

Decides on controversies arising from constitution and organic laws, agreements of Community and accords between member states and Community.
Decides contested elections for Community Senate.

placed under a special legal status. Laws made by Parliament did not apply to them unless it was expressly so stated. Instead the colonies were governed by the central administration to which Parliament had delegated virtually all powers to rule by decree. The fiction of legislative omnipotence was transformed in practice into administrative omnipotence. "The central government of the colonies in 1939," wrote a close student of French colonial policy, "is the bureaucracy. The democratic institutions of the Republic have little influence in the overseas territories." [1]

Bureaucratic centralization discouraged administrative adaptation to local conditions, the development of local self-government and the training of native elites. Colonial policy was formulated by three ministries: The Ministry of Foreign Affairs, responsible for Tunisia, Morocco, Syria and Lebanon; the Ministry of Interior for Algeria, legally a metropolitan department, and the Ministry of Colonies responsible for all the overseas colonies. A governor-general implemented the instructions from Paris in the administration of each colonial territory. This structure was buttressed by the French Army, which often had broad administrative powers. Indigenous institutions were rarely given a role to play. Local councils had only advisory powers and their members were appointed by the French administration. In the great majority of cases there were no elective institutions. By 1939 French citizenship had been granted, in the name of assimilation, to only a small fraction of the natives. Most of the colonies remained under a special regime in which administrative tutelage was the rule. Forced labor, for example, continued to be authorized.

World War II promoted a universal movement in favor of emancipation from colonial rule. The United States and the Soviet Union professed to be anticolonial. The two major colonial powers—England and France—had no alternative but to subscribe in one form or another to a statement of purpose favoring colonial emancipation. The Atlantic Charter, the United Nations' declaration on January 1, 1942, and the Dumbarton Oaks conference culminated in the United Nations Charter in which it was stated in unequivocal terms that all colonial powers should administer their colonies by recognizing the primacy of the interests of the colonial peoples and for the purpose

---

[1] H. Deschamps, *L'Union Française—Histoire, Institutions, Réalités* (Paris, 1958), p. 29.

of developing their capacity to administer themselves. The purpose of trusteeship was to encourage the progressive evolution of the trust territories towards self-government and independence.[2]

A reconsideration of both the principles and the institutions of the French colonial policy seemed therefore inevitable. Yet the intense debate that went on among the resistance groups concerning the future political regime of France hardly ever involved an earnest reappraisal of the relations between the Metropolis and the colonies. The Debré study for constitutional reform ignored the problem of the Empire. No serious debate took place over the respective merits of assimilation, federation, and independence. Lip service continued to be paid to assimilation, while at the same time pledges were made that, if carried out, would logically lead to autonomy for the colonies.

General de Gaulle's utterances reflected the general confusion that reigned on the subject. Sometimes he expressed the paternalism of the prewar years. It was the task of France to educate and elevate the natives until they were able to "conduct their own affairs." He asserted that all future developments and trends in the Empire were to take place within an institutional, cultural, and legal framework that guaranteed the supremacy of France. He talked of France's sacred trust and sovereignty, but on other occasions he referred to a federation between the colonies and France. In the Bayeux speech he had stated that "the future of 110 million men and women who live under our flag is to be sought in a federative organization."[3] In his press conference in Washington, D.C., on August 24, 1945, when asked to indicate the policy France intended to pursue vis-à-vis one of its protectorates, Indochina, General de Gaulle stated: "The position of France with regard to Indochina is very simple. France intends to recover her sovereignty over Indochina. Certainly, the reestablishment of our sovereignty will be accompanied by a new regime, but for us the recovery of our sovereignty is a capital question."[4] It became apparent later that De Gaulle contemplated only a restricted autonomy for the Indochinese states over local budgetary, social, and economic matters.

The two most significant stages in the development of a new policy

---

[2] UN Charter, Article 76.
[3] *Discours et Messages*, p. 725.
[4] *Ibid.*, p. 654.

for the Empire and the creation of new political institutions were the Brazzaville conference and the adoption of the Constitution of the Fourth Republic.

Brazzaville and After

Colonial policy was the main topic considered by a conference at Brazzaville on February 1, 1944. Even though the Free French forces included large contingents of native troops, and the seat of the provisional government was in Algiers, no representation was accorded to any of the native political leaders. The conference was composed only of the governor-generals, governors, and secretary-generals of French West Africa, French Equatorial Africa, and Madagascar, and some twenty colonial officials. Nine members of the Provisional Consultative Assembly participated and six North African *observers* were invited to attend.

The statement that was issued after six days of deliberations has often been hailed as inaugurating a new liberal policy constituting a break with the past. This, however, was hardly the case. It affirmed that "the goals of the civilizing work realized in the colonies by France preclude all ideas of autonomy, any possibility of a development of the Empire outside of the French bloc; the establishment, even in the remote future, of *self-government* (the text, to avoid all doubts, used the English term) in the colonies must be dismissed." [5] It urged that "the political authority of France be exercised with vigor over all parts of the Empire; that the colonies be accorded a large measure of economic and administrative freedom; that their responsibility be gradually developed so that they will find themselves associated in the direction of the affairs of their countries." Assimilation was not abandoned. On the contrary, in order to strengthen it, the conferees suggested that the colonies be represented in the new Constituent Assembly to be elected after the Liberation and that the representation of the colonies in the central government be in the future more effectively assured.

Yet, at the same time, the conference entertained the prospects of new institutions of a federative nature. It suggested, for instance, the creation of a colonial parliament or a federal assembly. But the purpose of this assembly was "to affirm the indissoluble unity of each of the territories constituting the Franco-colonial whole or, if one is

---

[5] For the full text see *Guetzévitch*, pp. 339–57.

willing to accept the term despite the objections it evokes, the French Federation." It suggested the suppression of the various consultative organizations and their replacement *with elected bodies* to be chosen by universal suffrage and be composed of both natives and Europeans. But their powers were to be strictly limited: "consultative" in all matters that lay within the jurisdiction of the colonial governors, "deliberative" with regard to the budget and to public works. It was also recommended that the various governors be assisted by administrative councils composed of colonial civil servants. Thus the statement issued at Brazzaville reflected the ambiguity of French political thought on the future of the Empire. Self-government was denied and assimilation reaffirmed while at the same time, curiously enough, consideration was given to a federal solution with a federal parliament and, of course, a degree of autonomy to the colonial territories.

The major part of the recommendations of the conference dealt with economic and social questions. It proposed the recruitment of natives in all administrative services on an equal basis and with the same salary as the Europeans; increased employment of native elites; extension of certain measures of social legislation and the abandonment of forced labor within a period of five years after the end of the war; economic aid to encourage industrialization; the progressive, political, and social integration of native elites with the European cadres; and the extension of education. But "education must be given in the French language and the use of local dialects must be strictly forbidden, both in private and public schools."

The French Union

After a long debate the First Constituent Assembly, in which the Socialists and the Communists had a majority and in which there were sixty-four representatives from the colonies and Algeria, produced a set of ambiguous provisions. The French Union (instead of Empire) was to be based on the free consent of the members, which by implication meant the right of secession. Territorial assemblies were to be established with the expectation that their powers would gradually develop. At the same time colonial representation in the French Parliament was increased and a common citizenship for all the colonial peoples was established. The provisions once more reflected an effort to compromise the two irreconcilable notions of assimilation and autonomy.

The Second Constituent Assembly, in which the MRP and right wing were stronger, devoted more attention to the colonial problem. No less than twenty-two articles, in contrast to the few provisions scattered throughout the text of the first draft, were required in order to define the structure of the Union. The preamble of the new constitution devoted three paragraphs to the Union. It stated that the "French Union is composed of nations and peoples who pool or coordinate their resources . . . to develop their respective civilizations, to increase their well-being and insure their security" and proclaimed that "France together with the overseas peoples forms a Union founded upon equality of rights and duties." It added that "France, faithful to her traditional mission, proposes to lead the people of whom she has assumed charge to a state of freedom in which they administer themselves and conduct their own affairs democratically."

The crucial question as to how France intended to do this— through assimilation or through a federative solution—was again evaded. Nor was it made explicit what the colonies' "own affairs" were to be. General de Gaulle stated in a speech on September 29, 1946, criticizing the new constitutional text:

[The] French Union must be a Union and must be French, that is to say that the overseas peoples who are linked with our destiny have the possibility to develop according to their proper conditions and to assume the administration of their particular affairs according to their level of development; they must be associated with France and France must maintain her pre-eminence for all matters that are common to all—foreign policy, national defense, communications, over-all economic problems. This implies on the one hand the existence of local institutions appropriate to each territory and, on the other hand, common institutions— a Council of the States, an Assembly of the French Union, a President of the French Union and ministries concerned with common affairs.[6]

The Union was composed of five distinct entities: (1) Metropolitan France; (2) the overseas "departments" of Martinique, Guadeloupe, Guiana, and Reunion. With minor qualifications, Algeria was also a Department; (3) the overseas territories, that is, all the colonies of France in Africa, Madagascar, the Pacific, and so on; (4) the "associated territories", composed of the two countries held by France under trust—Togo and Cameroun; and (5) the associated states, a new name for the old protectorates that were expected to join the

---

[6] *Discours et Messages*, pp. 744–45.

French Union in this new capacity: Tunisia, Morocco, Vietnam, Laos, and Cambodia. The constitution specified that their status would be determined by special agreements between each of them and France. Technically, they were expected to participate in the various organs of the French Union, but were not represented in the French Parliament. *Metropolitan France, overseas departments and Algeria, and the overseas territories constituted the French Republic.*

New principles were introduced. The laws made by the French Parliament were now applicable to the overseas departments, *unless it was otherwise specified in the text,* so that the competence of the Parliament was enlarged at the very time when promises of autonomy were made. This in turn called for an increase in the number of overseas deputies: 83 deputies (of whom 30 were from Algeria) and 71 senators (of whom 14 were from Algeria), out of 627 and 317 respectively. Deputies were elected for France on the basis of one for every 175,000 inhabitants. But for the overseas territories the ratio was one deputy for some 800,000 inhabitants.

New institutions were also provided for the French Union: a president, an assembly, and a high council. The President of the French Union was the President of the French Republic, elected by the Parliament in special session. The Assembly of the French Union, half of whose members represented Metropolitan France and the other half the overseas people, had only consultative powers. The decrees issued by the government for the various parts of the French Union required only the prior *"avis"* (not *"avis conforme"*) of the members of the Union. It had no power to initiate legislation. Its debates did not engage in any sense the responsibility of the government, so that members of the government rarely appeared before it.

The High Council of the French Union was composed of the President of the Republic, French ministers, and government representatives of the associated states, if they desired to participate. Conceived very much in the nature of a round-table conference of the British Commonwealth type, it was perhaps the only framework within which the various differences between the French government and the associated states could have been discussed and ironed out. It was the only institution which could initiate common policies and in which the President of the French Republic in his capacity as President of the French Union could play an important political role. Under propitious conditions, this council could have developed into something like a federal executive operating with the support and the confidence of the Assembly of the French Union. The High Council met, however, for the first time only in 1951. Boycotted by the associated states, it was ignored by the French Government and the President of the Republic.

Were the peoples of the French Union French citizens? The question taxed the ingenuity of scholars and lawyers. It was generally conceded that they were endowed with the rights of men. Forced labor was abolished. The framers of the constitution under the inspiration of the Socialist Mayor of Dakar, Lamine-Gueye, went further. They gave French citizenship to all the former "subjects" of the Empire—that is to say, to all the natives of the overseas departments and territories. Perhaps never since the days of the Roman Empire had citizenship been offered to so many diverse races and creeds, involving civil rights, political rights (under the conditions specified by law), and the public liberties guaranteed by the French Constitution and French legislation. Nor was the distinction between personal status and civil status any longer controlling. There were French citizens with a French civil status (that is, abiding by the provisions of the civil code) and French citizens with a personal or a local status (that is, whose private relations were governed by the Koranic law or local customs). Only with respect to the right to vote was the principle of equal citizenship qualified in favor of those who had opted for a civil status. But even here the corollary to citizenship—the right to vote—was progressively expanded by legislation to include in almost all areas of the Union a growing number of citizen-voters. In the best spirit of its Jacobin forefathers and in the name of the universality of the French civilization, the Assembly had made the supreme gift at its disposal: It granted French citizenship and the rights of the city to all former subjects.

Some thought that the French were trying to arrest the movement toward independence by bringing the natives into the Republic where they could be counterbalanced (as it was clear later when Algerian integration was demanded by the French settlers). Furthermore, the grant of citizenship presented a serious problem for those who did not wish to avail themselves of the rights of the city. Confronted with a policy that provided for *full citizenship and representation in the Republic,* they had no alternative other than secession. The French themselves, having increased native representation in the French Parliament and having granted citizenship to all its members, were prone to consider any federative scheme proposed by the colonial leaders as an indication of a desire to secede. This fear was of course exacerbated by the attitude of the French settlers in all parts of the Union. To them the government of the Republic was the only force that could protect their property and privileges. Within the Republic they were safe; outside of the Republic they were a small minority at the mercy of the natives. At the very moment the constitution was being drafted and as soon as it came into force, French settlers began to form associations to promote the maintenance of France—*la présence Française*—in most of the colonies and more particularly in North Africa. Together with many of the army officers and the local administrators they became powerful veto groups obstructing any gradual political development toward autonomy that would ultimately have paved the way for independence within a broader federated structure. Federalism became equated with separatism.

The central government and the Parliament remained committed to the maintenance of the Union under French sovereignty. The Empire was equated, rightly or wrongly, with France's status as one of the great powers, a symbol of strength and prestige, so that any concession was construed to be a sign of weakness. A number of factors reinforced this attitude. The inherent weakness of the various short-lived cabinets made it impossible to develop a constructive policy for the French Union; the corresponding virulence of the groups demanding the maintenance of French sovereignty contrasted sharply with vacillation of the governments of the Republic.

It was only after a long and costly war in Indochina and after the Indochinese states and Morocco and Tunisia, in 1954 and 1956 respectively, had gained their independence that the French National Assembly drafted the first constructive reform providing for autonomy. The last act was played out in 1958 when thirteen years after he had proclaimed in the most unequivocal terms France's sovereignty over Indochina, General de Gaulle promised to grant outright independence to all those who opted for it.

Reforms under the Fourth Republic

There was one basic difficulty in reforming the French Union. It could not be accomplished without a reconsideration of the definition of the Republic as "one and indivisible" composed of the Metropolis, the overseas departments, and the overseas territories.

Any suggestion to modify this magic formula would provoke an endless and futile debate. However, the loss of Indochina, the declaration of independence by Morocco and Tunisia, the Algerian fighting, and the increasingly insistent demands on the part of African leaders for self-government made reform imperative. Something had to be offered in the place of the old alternative between assimilation or independence.

The prospects of reform were not bright. It had taken four whole years to prepare a labor code for the colonies and three years for the reform of the colonial municipal institutions. To avoid similar delays the government of Guy Mollet requested, in March, 1956, the passage of a *loi-cadre* (framework law) laying down the broad principles on the basis of which the government would issue decrees to reform the institutions of the French Union. They were to be submitted to Parliament and would come into force within fifteen days unless they were rejected. The *loi-cadre* was voted on June 23, 1956 by large majorities—441 in favor and 90 against. It empowered the government to modify by decree the competence and the composition of the representative assembly of Madagascar; to establish "government councils" in all the territories; to increase the deliberative powers of the territorial assemblies, especially with reference to matters pertaining to the territorial organization and the administrative services of the various territories; to provide for a greater participation of the natives in the administration of their territories; to introduce equal and universal suffrage for the election of all representative assemblies on the basis of a single electoral college.[7]

Within five months, decrees implementing this authorization were submitted to the Parliament. They provided for the transference of considerable powers to the territories and their assemblies, the creation of "government councils" consisting of nine to twelve persons, the establishment of a federal structure for Madagascar, and the creation of two larger councils—for Equatorial and West Africa. In January, 1957, after an animated debate in the National Assembly, one of the native deputies, M. Apithy from Dahomey, proposed that the councils of government be transformed into genuine cabinets, headed by a prime minister responsible to the territorial legislature. The government countered with a compromise solution. The councils of government would be headed not by a prime minister but by a

---

[7] *Année Politique*, 1956, p. 209. For the text of the *loi-cadre*, Annex, pp. 512–16.

vice-president, who *might* resign if he lost the confidence of the territorial legislature.

The debate was even more animated when the subject of the definition of the territorial units came up. The government wished to establish a number of territories, corresponding to the old colonial administrative units. Some deputies, led by Léopold Senghor, from Senegal, argued for larger "primary federations"—one for West Africa and one for Equatorial Africa. They were in turn opposed by other African leaders, led by Félix Houphouet-Boigny of the Ivory Coast, who spoke in favor of maintaining the old territorial units.

After the Assembly's endorsement of the government decrees on February 2 and 4, 1957, legislative elections were held in the whole of Africa on March 31, 1957. Thirteen million voters (or some 50 to 60 per cent of the estimated number of those eligible) elected, in a single college in which natives and Europeans participated on an equal footing, their local legislatures.

The political map of the French Union which resulted from the *loi-cadre* and the government decrees was as follows: For West Africa the following territories were established: Senegal, Soudan, Mauritania, Niger, Upper Volta, Guinea, Ivory Coast, and Dahomey. For Equatorial Africa: Gabon, Middle Congo, Tchad and Central Africa. Each of these territories was given identical organs of government, with the exception of Madagascar, where a federal assembly was introduced. For each of the territories there was a territorial legislature elected by universal suffrage and a council of government composed of native parliamentary leaders presided over by the "chief of the territory" appointed by and representing the French government. The members of the council were to be called ministers and be headed by the vice-president of the council politically responsible before the territorial legislature. The central power (France) reserved for itself important functions: matters related to foreign affairs, defense, finances, higher education, customs, and telecommunications. All other matters came within the jurisdiction of the local legislatures and administrations.

It was an impressive and genuinely liberal reform. Yet, doubts subsisted and difficulties emerged. The movement toward the creation of larger federal structures gained momentum, and so did the demands for greater autonomy approaching genuine sovereign status. Within less than a year after the promulgation of the decrees, Africa was in a state of political ferment. Federalists and advocates of outright independence urged the modification of the decrees, the former for the purposes of creating larger federated political units within which economic and social reforms would be possible, the latter so that Africa could create its own political institutions on the basis of free participation and consent of the African leaders and populations. The conference of Bamako in the autumn of 1957 favored independence, and the conference of Kotonou in the summer of 1958 proclaimed the desirability of a United States of Africa. Were the reforms undertaken too late? The drive toward independence seemed to be as irresistible in French Africa as it had proved to be elsewhere.

Yet the reforms had modified drastically French colonial policy. Assimilation had been abandoned. Genuine self-government had been irreversibly granted. But, constitutionally, the African territories continued to be a part of the Republic and the reforms undertaken were in the nature of decentralization and delegation on the part of the sovereign authority (the French Parliament) which retained technically the plenitude of its jurisdiction. The reform of the constitution was therefore still necessary to create a new juridical structure that put an end to the supremacy of the French Parliament and excluded the fiction of the "one and indivisible Republic."

The Community

The law of June 3, 1958 granting constitutional powers to General de Gaulle's government specifically stated that the new constitution "must provide for an organization of the relations between the Republic and the peoples associated with it." [8] Like the other principles enunciated, it was broad enough to give virtually complete freedom to the framers. The alternative between assimilation and independence had to be set aside, and a new formula allowing for the particularism and the national and political autonomy of the African territories in a larger Union in which France was to be a member had to be instituted.

Gaullist revisionists had insisted upon the importance of the Union as an indispensable adjunct of French power in the world but made few specific suggestions. Both General de Gaulle and the RPF referred frequently to the notion of federal relations with members of the Empire. The content of the term "federation," however, had

---

[8] *Recueil*, p. 5.

never been clearly defined. For instance, the constitutional project prepared by one of the most articulate exponents of Gaullist revisionism in the days of the Resistance, Blocq-Mascart, stated: "The French Republic, the Metropolis, and the overseas countries, is one and indivisible." In the first congress of the RPF held in Marseilles on April 16–17, 1948, the report on the French Union envisaged an administrative reform in the direction of decentralization and urged at the same time "the establishment of a French Federation *under the aegis* of the Metropolis with a federal parliament" and postulated that "the French Union was one and indivisible." [9] In every instance the notion of a federal structure was associated with that of French supremacy. Blocq-Mascart, only a few months before the return of General de Gaulle, proposed again the establishment of a federation. He suggested a highly centralized system in which the President of the Republic was given broad lawmaking powers for all the parts of the envisaged federation.[10]

The manner in which the new constitutional framework was to be elaborated presented a number of problems. How much participation in the preparation of the constitution was to be given to the native political leaders? Was the constitution to be made in Paris and then submitted to the former colonial territories for their approval? The Communist party and the Union of Democratic Forces favored a convocation of a special congress of the colonial peoples to prepare a constitution for the Union. Given the sensitivity of the native elites, some degree of participation in the formulation of the constitution had to be envisaged.

For all of these reasons the parts of the constitutional project dealing with the Union were extremely flexible and it was understood that the Constitutional Consultative Committee was to have a free hand in reshaping it. It contained only seven brief articles under the respective titles of "The Federation" (Section XI) and the "Community of Free Peoples" (Section XII). "Between the Republic and the peoples of the overseas territories, that express the will through their territorial assemblies, a federation is created." The jurisdiction of the federation included "foreign policy, defense, monetary policy, common economic and financial policy and the exploitation of strategic raw materials, the control of justice and higher education." The President of the French Republic was the president of the fed-

---

[9] *Guetzévitch*, p. 275, and RPF, *Premières Assises Nationales* (Paris, 1948), p. 88.
[10] Blocq-Mascart, *La Prochaine République Sera-t-elle Républicaine* (Paris, 1958).

eration. The other organs of the federation were to be an executive, a federal representative assembly, and a court of arbitration. Section XII provided simply for the creation of a "community" based on agreements between the federation and other peoples "for the purpose of associating and developing their civilizations." All these provisions were to be implemented by organic laws passed at a later date by the French Parliament.[11]

The Constitutional Consultative Committee set immediately to work to modify this sketchy draft. It included a number of colonial deputies who, together with Houphouet-Boigny, a member of the De Gaulle government, played an important role in the preparation of the final draft. Lamine-Gueye, a veteran parliamentarian, became chairman of the committee's section for the French Union. He remained in constant touch with Houphouet-Boigny, Raymond Janot, the government's representative in the committee, and the Minister of Overseas France, Bernard Cornut-Gentille, former governor-general of French West Africa. Léopold Senghor from Senegal, Tsirrana from Madagascar, and Lisette from Tchad were also members. Among the French, Blocq-Mascart and Léon Noël, appointed by the government, and Coste-Floret and Pierre-Henri Teitgen, elected by the National Assembly, were known for their "federalist" ideas.

The debate in the Constitutional Consultative Committee was in essence a confrontation between the proponents of a federation, with common organs and a common jurisdiction, and a confederation. Federation, it was argued by Léopold Senghor, would freeze the juridical status of the Union and impede the evolution toward independence. Confederation, on the other hand, meant for the French representatives and many of the African leaders the disappearance of a central authority, that is, the authority of France, and the assumption of virtually an independent status by all the former territories. Common decisions would be taken only by agreements between heads of states. The Union would be transformed into a commonwealth whose members would have "dominion status."

The dialogue, confused at the judicial level, had important political meaning. The French government favored federation because it hoped to maintain through it the levers of political control on all important issues. But it made it clear that it would favor the establishment of consultative institutions so that decisions would result from

---

[11] The government draft in *Recueil*, pp. 42, 44.

common deliberations. Many of the proponents of confederation among the African leaders, however, made it equally clear that they also favored the establishment of consultative institutions through which common decisions would be reached. The more the French government leaned toward federation, the more the African leaders feared centralization and the more suspect its motives appeared to them; the more the native leaders insisted upon confederation, the more the French feared secession and the more suspect the motives of the Africans seemed to the French government officials and members of the Constitutional Committee. The legal arguments for or against federation were in essence the expression of mutual distrust.

On August 8, 1958 General de Gaulle appeared before the Consultative Constitutional Committee. He pointed out that between the two terms "federation" and "confederation" he preferred the term "association." He remarked that the alternative before the former colonies was that of association or secession. He did not object to the use of the term "self-determination" in the constitution, though he found it "awkward" (*inélégant*). He pointed out that if the African territories voted "No" to the constitution then secession "with all its consequences" would be the result. So confederation was to be excluded.[12] A federal organism with enumerated powers was to be established, but at the same time, in order to give some satisfaction to the proponents of confederation, the door was left open for an evolution toward independence. To avoid the misinterpretations to which the terms "federation" and "confederation" gave rise, the Constitutional Committee finally adopted the term "community" rather than association.

The Community is composed of autonomous states which "administer freely and democratically" their own affairs. The matters that enter within the jurisdiction of the Community are "foreign policy, defense, monetary policy, economic and financial policy, and the policy concerning common raw materials." Unless there is an agreement to the contrary, "higher education, the general organization of transportation, and telecommunications" are also included. Special agreements may intervene to provide for "the transfer of certain matters that are within the jurisdiction of the Community to the member states."[13] Thus, the common jurisdiction provided for in the original text was maintained, but a provision was inserted per-

---

[12] *Le Monde*, August 10–11, 1958, and *Paris-Presse*, August 10–11, 1958.
[13] Section XII, Articles 77, 78, and 79.

mitting the devolution of Community powers to the member states. A "common community citizenship" was established.

Some of the organs of the French Union were re-established. The President of the Republic presides over and represents the Community. There is an executive council, a Senate, and an arbitration court. The member states participate in the election of the president, and the president is represented in each state of the Community. The Constitutional Committee made a number of suggestions that were not accepted by the government. It proposed the creation of a legislature of the Community composed of delegates of the various territorial assemblies with the power to make decisions on economic and social matters and to approve all treaties. It is revealing that the government rejected the suggestion of a Community assembly with genuine powers. Instead the Community Senate (different only in name from the Assembly of the French Union) has only consultative powers. It "deliberates" on certain matters at the request of the president. It "examines" the treaties committing the Community. It takes decisions that are enforceable only when it has been authorized to do so by virtue of a delegation of powers to it by the members of the Community. In such a case its decisions are applicable to the territories of the member states only if promulgated in the form of law by legislatures of the latter.

The Executive Council is similar to the High Council of the French Union. It is a deliberative and coordinating organ composed of the President of the Community, ministers of the French Republic, and the prime ministers of the member states. The Arbitration Court decides on all differences among the member states. Finally, the part of the constitution dealing with the Community may be amended in a manner different from that provided for in the constitution of the Republic. A law must be passed in identical terms by the French Parliament and the Community Senate. This is the only subject matter over which the Community Senate has original jurisdiction.

The constitution provides, under stringent terms, for the possibility of a change of status—including, of course, complete independence. It must be requested by a member state through a resolution of its legislature and must be confirmed by a referendum "organized under the control of the institutions of the Community." The change of status must be approved by the Parliament of the French Republic and the legislature of the state concerned. Finally, the constitution provides for agreements of association "between the Community and interested states." [14] This provision is in the nature of an invitation to the former associated states to reconsider their relations with France, something that they all have declined to do thus far.

When General de Gaulle left for a visit to Madagascar and the various African capitals on August 20, the report of the Constitutional Committee had already been submitted to the government. He endorsed the term "Community." There was doubt, however, as to the exact meaning of the referendum in the former territories. He had stated before the committee on August 8 that the rejection of the constitutional text on the part of any of the territories would mean secession. But many doubted that this was his last word on the subject. Indeed, many African leaders claimed that De Gaulle was under severe pressure by members of his government not to allow the referendum to assume the character of an option between independence and community for fear that the movement for secession would be strengthened. African leaders, notably Lamine-Gueye and Senghor, claimed that De Gaulle was urged against his better judgment to announce that severe economic sanctions would be in store for the territories opting for independence. Others pointed out that the offer of independence was only a symbolic gesture on the part of De Gaulle since he was certain of the loyalty and support of all African leaders.

The search for motives in this case would be perilous and unrewarding. On the basis of the record, De Gaulle offered independence to all the colonies in the most unequivocal terms if they voted No to the constitution. It is true that he was certain that no colonial territory would vote No. In fact, some of the hostile reactions of the African leaders and people in Dakar and in Conakry took him by surprise. But independence he did offer if the Africans opted for it, and by so doing he reversed the secular trend of French colonial policy.

Speaking at Fort Lamy—in the first colony to join the Gaullist forces in World War II—De Gaulle pointed out that a new dawn was rising. "We shall build this *ensemble* of the Metropolis and the colonies and direct it toward a new destiny." [15] His speech before the assembly of Madagascar was more specific. "We shall offer to Madagascar," he proclaimed, "every conceivable alternative. The texts

---

[14] Article 88.
[15] *Le Monde*, August 22, 1958.

that are proposed to the peoples do not exclude any solution, not even secession." He also stated that France would not be opposed to the formation of federations among the overseas territories. However, he made it clear that in his opinion participation in the Community was the natural choice for the overseas territories. "Madagascar," he said, and he made the same point in every territory, "will develop and grow. Only within the Community will it find the means to realize its aspirations of becoming a modern state. Tomorrow," he said, "you will be a state as you were when this palace was built," and he pointed to the palace from which Queen Ranavalo reigned over Madagascar when General Gallieni had found it prudent to dethrone her in order to "pacify" the island.[16] At Brazzaville, Abidjan, and Dakar, De Gaulle discoursed on the same theme of free and voluntary participation in a community. At Brazzaville he went one step further.

If the peoples of the territories vote Yes to the Constitution, the Community will be established with special organs and with a division between the functions of the central government of the Community and its members. . . . [But] if one of the members of the Community feels within a given period of time capable of exercising all the burdens and obligations of independence, well then it is up to it to decide by a vote of its representative assembly and if necessary by a referendum.[17]

He never doubted that the African colonies would remain associated with France. Besides he made it clear that they were too poor and too weak to assume the burden of independence. He mentioned the subversive forces active in Africa and referred obliquely to foreign imperialisms that were eager to replace France.

In 1944 his program would have been enthusiastically endorsed. It would have perhaps altered radically the relations between France and North Africa and might have averted the long and disastrous war in Indochina. But this was 1958, after fourteen whole years in which France had been engaged in colonial wars. During this period the very intimation of independence for the colonies by a political leader was for many, as Mendès-France found out, treasonable. De Gaulle's return to power was in fact caused by a wave of nationalism provoked to a great extent by the disintegration of the Empire. Even if his personal word were accepted by the African leaders they feared the forces that were responsible for his accession to power—the army, the various patriotic organizations, the conservative politi-

---

[16] *Le Monde*, August 23, 1958.
[17] *Le Monde*, August 24–25, 1958.

cal groups, and the Algerian colons. De Gaulle's voyage was intended to reassure the African leaders. He asserted the rights of all to independence but argued in favor of the maintenance of the bonds that united the former colonies with France. The African leaders in turn accepted the Community only because it was the best step toward independence.

The nature of this misunderstanding was clearly illustrated by the dialogue between Sekou Touré, the prime minister of Guinea, and De Gaulle before the legislative assembly of Guinea. De Gaulle's visit to Conakry was the last one on his trip. He had already made his explicit pledges about independence. Yet Sekou Touré launched upon a violent speech in favor of independence. "To vote for the constitution," he said, "we must have precise pledges in its text, not only in the preamble, in favor of the right of independence *without any restrictions*. It is a matter of dignity." He continued to favor a Franco-African community, "a vast African federation associated with France." But the "Africans were Africans above all only associated on the basis of equality and freedom with France," and he asserted aggressively that military intervention was no longer possible. De Gaulle answered by repeating what he had said throughout his tour—that Guinea like any other territory could have her independence by voting No at the referendum of September 28. He promised in the most emphatic terms on behalf of France to respect Guinea's decision. He urged them to remain within the community but did not equivocate on their right to reject it.[18]

The reactions of some of the most responsible African political leaders after De Gaulle's tour were also indicative of a misunderstanding. "We shall abandon, when the time comes, the Community, without breaking our ties with France, and we shall conclude special agreements of association provided by the constitution," said Moktar Ould Daddah, president of the Mauritanian government. "Our Yes is above all a Yes to African unity which must be constituted in the form of two federations—the West French Africa and the Equatorial French Africa. . . . The Community is for us but a means and a transitional step . . . that prepares us for independence in a manner similar to that of the British territories," declared Senghor.

" 'You have a state said General de Gaulle.' This means therefore that we shall have our independence," proclaimed Tsiranana of Madagascar. "In the chain of free states which will stretch from

---

[18] *Le Monde*, August 27, 1958.

Ghana to Cameroun there is a place for an independent Dahomey that will remain by the side of France. . . . The Community properly understood ought to make room for a rapid accession to independence," stated Apithy, the prime minister of Dahomey. "Our ideal is independence in a cooperative framework with France," stated Lisette of Tchad.

But the leader of the Ivory Coast and a member of the French cabinets since 1956, Houphouet-Boigny, underlined the misunderstanding by pointing out, "Those who have entered the Community with the intention of abandoning it tomorrow are not with us." [19]

＊   ＊   ＊   ＊   ＊

The option given to the former colonies of France was the most generous ever offered by a colonial power. They could by voting No to the constitution secede and become independent. If they voted Yes they could subsequently choose for one of the following alternatives: (1) an autonomous republic with the exercise of all the powers that had not been reserved to the Community; (2) the status quo; or (3) "departmentalization," that is, to become departments of France like Martinique, Guadeloupe, Reunion, and Guiana. There was little doubt that all colonial territories that wished to remain in the Community would opt for the status of autonomous republics within the Community, and they all did.

With the exception of the No vote and the subsequent secession of French Guinea, the results of the referendum reflected the overwhelming desire of the African political leaders to remain within the Community. For a few this was a permanent solution; for most only a step toward independence. In the Ivory Coast the vote was 1,595,238 in favor of Yes and 216 No. The unanimity indicated the enormous popularity of Houphouet-Boigny and the efficiency of his political machine. In Dahomey there were 418,963 Yes against 9,246 No; in Upper Volta, 1,415,651 Yes against 11,687 No; in Mauritania, 302,018 against 19,126; in Niger, 372,383 against 102,395; in Senegal, 870,362 against 21,901; in French Soudan, 945,586 against 23,875. In Guinea the vote was against the constitution and in favor of secession by 636,281 No to 18,012 Yes. In French Equatorial Africa—Gabon, Congo, Tchad, and Central Africa—the No was below 12 per cent. Madagascar voted in favor by 1,363,059 to 302,557.

---

[19] Citations from *Cahiers de la République*, No. 16 (November–December, 1958), p. 48.

There was no manipulation of the vote. The enormous majorities in favor and, in Guinea, against, underscored the personal element that is so characteristic of the African political communities. In all cases the African voters followed the stand taken by their respective local leaders.

The endorsement of the constitution brought about a number of fundamental changes both in the theory of assimilation and in its institutions. The very notion of the Community implied an acceptance of the diversity of its members, with freedom to manage their local affairs as they saw fit. An irreversible break was made with the past. Politically, the notion of assimilation was abandoned and pluralism introduced. The French Republic and the Community were distinct entities. Within the Community there are a number of republics, each responsible for its own affairs and represented in the presidency, the Executive Council, and the Senate. There is no longer representation of the natives in the French Parliament. The possibility of a gradual transference of powers either to the Community Senate or to the member states was recognized. The Community may evolve its own Parliament or it may gradually become an association of free and independent states as in the British Commonwealth. The evolution will depend upon political circumstances, which cannot be gleaned from the constitution itself. This was explicitly recognized by Michel Debré, who stated before the *Conseil d'État*, "The evolution of this 'whole' cannot be defined by any text. It is even dangerous to demand a rigorous precision at the beginning."

Further References

There have been few publications on the French Community. The article of Marcel Merle, "La Constitution et les Problèmes d'Outre-Mer," *Revue Française de Science Politique*, Vol. IX, No. 1 (March, 1959), pp. 135–66, and the special issue devoted to French Africa, "La Vie Politique en Afrique Noire," *ibid.*, Vol. IX, No. 3 (September, 1959), pp. 577–628 are useful.

For background material, P. F. Gonidec, "Introduction à l'étude de la Communauté, *Recueil Dalloz*, January, 1959. Also H. Deschamps, *L'Union Française, Histoire, Institutions, Réalités* (Paris, 1952); *Méthodes et Doctrines Coloniales de la France* (Paris, 1953); and "Où va L'Union Française," *NEF*, June, 1955.

For the awakening of new political forces in French Africa, A. Blanchet, *L'Itinéraire de partis Africains depuis Bamako* (Paris, 1958), and E. Milcent, *L'AOF entre en Scène* (Paris, 1958).

CHAPTER XII

The Referendum of September 28, 1958

ON SEPTEMBER 28, 1958, the French were consulted for a third time since the Liberation on a new constitution. Prepared by a small group of De Gaulle's followers, debated in a closed session for only two weeks in the Constitutional Consultative Committee, hurried through the *Conseil d'État,* and finally published on September 5—in a near-record period of three months—little was known about the constitution except that it incorporated De Gaulle's ideas about a new and renovated Republic. The public had little opportunity or inclination to debate its provisions. The figure of De Gaulle overshadowed all other considerations.

Although the overt purpose of the referendum was the approval or disapproval of the constitution, many other issues were implicitly put before the electorate. At the risk of oversimplifying the French political scene, the issues may be summed up as follows: the conditions surrounding De Gaulle's return to power; the Algerian conflict, which involved two possible solutions—integration, as advocated by Jacques Soustelle, and various liberal schemes ranging from "cease-fire, elections, negotiations," as advanced earlier by Guy Mollet, to negotiations with the rebels; a liberal policy for the French Union based upon a recognition of the right of independence, as outlined by De Gaulle during his tour of Africa in August, 1958; the composition of De Gaulle's government and the delegation of full powers to it for a period of four months. Every individual voter had to balance his Yes or No for each one of the particular issues before casting his vote for or against the constitutional text submitted.

It was not a decision that could possibly be the result of reflection and deliberate choice since, on a number of these issues, De Gaulle's position was not known. Was he for integration or negotiations in Algeria? Although he had taken advantage of the conditions created by May 13 to return to power, did he bear any responsibility for them? Would he become the captive of the forces that brought about his return to power? As for the constitution itself, the doubts and uncertainties were equally present. It was a republican text in essence, but many provisions could be used against the Republic. Finally, there was the matter of De Gaulle himself. A Yes vote would give him carte blanche for four months—to govern the nation and to put the new institutions in their place. Many who retained the image of De Gaulle as the *"premier résistant"* of France had no hesitation in voting Yes. But others, even some of his followers, saw in the circumstances of his return some ominous signs.

The Political Parties

The Communist Party. On September 29, 1946, at Epinal, De Gaulle criticized sharply the draft of the Constitution of the Fourth Republic. "Frankly no," he declared referring to the proposed text. "Such a compromise does not appear to us to constitute a framework worthy of the Republic."[1] The Communist organ *L'Humanité*,[2] three days before the referendum, delivered the party's last salvo against the new constitution by using, with a sense of history if not political acumen, the same phrase, "Frankly no . . . to the Gaullist constitution."

But by appearing as the defenders of the republican tradition, the Communists risked casting themselves in the role of the defenders of the status quo. It was only in the course of the campaign that Duclos took up the theme of left-wing revisionism of the Constitution of the Fourth Republic. "It is not a question," he said, "of winning the battle of the referendum [by voting No], *which after all does not mean the simple return to what existed before De Gaulle came to power*. It is a duty to say No to the antidemocratic spirit of the constitution that they are preparing for us."[3] The party reaffirmed its traditional stand on the constitutional question. It favored a unicameral assembly with imperative mandate and the right of recall, decentraliza-

---

[1] *Discours et Messages*, p. 746.
[2] September 25, 1958.
[3] *L'Humanité*, July 24, 1958.

tion, and local assemblies to which the powers of the prefects were to
be delegated.

The Communist party attacked General de Gaulle from the very
moment Parliament voted the delegation of constituent powers.
On June 3, the Politbureau of the party called upon all democratic
forces "to stop fascism and avert the exercise of personal power." [4]
The Central Committee convened a week later and issued a long resolution condemning the envisaged constitutional reform. It accused
De Gaulle of being at the very center of the May 13 conspiracy and
called for a recognition of the right of independence of the Algerian
people and an end to colonialism.[5] In its national conference held on
July 19, the appeal for a "union of the Noes" was reiterated.

There was little that was new in the party's position. It was trying
desperately to create the conditions for a Popular Front. For this
purpose Committees for the Defense of the Republic were to be established by the party in order to attract all those who wanted to
make common cause against the constitution. "The united front,"
Duclos pointed out, "is the only way to create a movement of the
masses in favor of No to the referendum, No to the dictatorship, No
to adventure, No to war." [6] Early in September a resolution of the
Central Committee attacked De Gaulle for aggravating the war in
Algeria and pursuing a policy of social reaction leading to military
dictatorship and fascism. The No was imperative to avert a civil war.
The recipe was the same as before—a united front with the workers
and all republicans.[7]

The farthest the Communist party went, however, in suggesting
an alternative to De Gaulle's constitution was in endorsing a set of
ten principles drafted by a National University committee for the
Defense of the Republic. The text was adopted (with minor reservations) by the Politbureau and proposed as a platform of all groups
advocating a No vote. According to it a new constitution should be
drafted by a popularly elected Constituent Assembly on the basis of
the following principles: (1) popular sovereignty; (2) civil control
of military power; (3) safeguarding of individual rights; (4) safeguarding of workers' and trade unions' rights; (5) self-determination
of all peoples (Thorez preferred the term "independence"); (6) the

[4] *Ibid.*, June 4, 1958.
[5] *Ibid.*, June 11, 1958.
[6] *Ibid.*, July 25, 1958.
[7] *Ibid.*, September 8, 1958.

convening of a congress of the members of the French Union to determine their relations with France; (7) a negotiated solution in Algeria; (8) dissolution of all right-wing activist organizations; (9) reorganization of local and regional government toward more decentralization, and (10) a clear-cut provision guaranteeing the freedom and independence of political parties.[8]

Communist attacks against the person of De Gaulle were of an unprecedented violence. He was being portrayed as a former spy against the homebred resistance and a new Bonaparte. He was a new "prince-president," a *"président-moi,"* a "president-general."

It is hard to tell whether the opposition was more than verbal and whether the Communists really expected to defeat the new constitution. The party did not put all its resources in the campaign. For the most part only local meetings were held that did not require great effort or money. If there was any desire on the part of the party to achieve martyrdom it was detected only by its opponents. The tactics of a Popular Front seemed to have failed dismally. The hastily organized Committees for the Defense of the Republic were largely composed of Communists, and the announcement on June 18 of the execution of the Hungarian Premier Imre Nagy broke up the ones in which some degree of collaboration with Socialists and others had been established. In retrospect it appears that the campaign of the party was designed to assert its attachment to the Republic, to present itself as the party of legality, to undermine De Gaulle's popularity, which was considerable among the working classes, and to bide its time until evil days came upon the Fifth Republic. They also hoped to assume the leadership of the republican forces in a new Popular Front. They exploited, for instance, the Vichy reflex and constantly reminded the other parties of the fate of those who had voted for Marshal Pétain on July 10, 1940. Their efforts to identify themselves with the Republic aroused genuine concern among a number of political groups for whom a compelling reason to advocate a negative vote was to deprive the Communists of the monopoly of opposition and republicanism.

The Non-Communist Left. It has been the recurrent dream of the left-wing groups situated between the Communists and Socialists to regroup their forces. The referendum seemed to provide the occasion for creation of a broad left-wing political front. There were

---

[8] For the full text and supplementary comments by Maurice Thorez, see *L'Humanité,* September 17, 1958.

three obstacles, however: the unwillingness of its proponents to consider any form of cooperation with the Communist party, the tight control of Guy Mollet over the Socialist party, and the popularity of General de Gaulle.

A number of left-wing splinter organizations, especially *la Jeune République, la Nouvelle Gauche,* the *Mouvement de Libération du Peuple* and the *Action Socialiste* had managed to form a united group in December, 1957—the UGS (*Union de la Gauche Socialiste*). Through its two weekly organs, *France-Observateur* and *Tribune du Peuple,* the group expressed from the very start its opposition to De Gaulle. A UGS leader, Claude Bourdet, hinted at civil war in the best tradition of the Paris Commune:

We must not exclude the possibility of an open struggle, a struggle where only the forces of the masses will overcome a militarized state. . . . All the popular organizations without exception must therefore join hands in order to organize a common defense. . . . Immediately after the fall of the Gaullist regime all measures must be taken to avert the return of the adversary to the offensive. The Army must be purged. Those responsible for the liquidation of the Fourth Republic must be brought before the courts.[9]

The UGS launched an appeal to all democratic forces to hold a "vast" democratic convention in which all political parties and groups opposed to personal power would participate in order to propose a democratic constitution of a renovated republic.

The UGS was prepared to form a union with *all* anti-Gaullist forces, including the Communists. But this was not the wish of a number of left-wing Socialists and Radicals. Daniel Mayer, the former general secretary of the Socialist party and president of the *Ligue des Droits de l'Homme* (the watchdog of the revolutionary tradition), demanded a regrouping of the "non-Communist Left." It was decided accordingly to form a "common front" excluding the Communists to their left and the Socialists to their right—the *Union des Forces Démocratiques* (UFD).

The campaign of the UFD was even less vigorous than that of the Communists. It was limited to local meetings and the pronouncements of its leaders, many of whom, especially Francois Mitterand, Mendès-France, and Daniel Mayer, were widely quoted in the press. The weekly *l'Express,* which had supported Mendès-France in the elections of January 2, 1956, opened its columns to the UFD leaders.

[9] In his article "Mais l'Avenir est à Nous," *Tribune du Peuple,* June 18, 1958.

But it reached a relatively small group of persons, mostly in the Paris region, who were already receptive to a No vote.

The most important statement on behalf of the UFD was made by Mendès-France, first in a press conference and later in a long statement published in *l'Express*. It became the political charter of the non-Communist opposition to De Gaulle and to the proposed constitution.[10] He pointed out that the referendum was confusing and contradictory. It involved at least two separate sets of provisions: one on the future of the French Union and the other on the metropolitan institutions. Votes cast in the French Union for the Community with France were also to count for the acceptance of the constitution in the Metropolis. On the other hand, a No vote in France, cast by those opposed to the provisions that applied to the Metropolis would be equivalent to a No to the Community.

The Fourth Republic, Mendès-France admitted, went "bankrupt" because of the dominance of lobbies and interest groups, the dearth of political leaders, and the violation of electoral engagements. It was imperative to correct these evils and to seek a remedy by reinforcing the ties between the people and the government. The constitution would do exactly the opposite, he contended, and criticized sharply many of its provisions: the manner in which the President of the Republic was to be elected and the general emphasis upon indirect elections; the reappearance of the Senate, the reduction of the legislative powers of the popularly elected assembly, and the distinction between "law" and "rule making." De Gaulle, he continued, had made no effort to control the right-wing groups and the military. As a result the situation in Algeria was deteriorating and De Gaulle's immense prestige was dissipated.

But what if the Noes win? After protesting against the blackmail to which all democrats were being exposed, particularly the veiled threat that if the Noes won the army would intervene, Mendès-France launched his slogan for the creation of "the Contract of the Noes." To vote No, he pointed out, did not mean the return to the Fourth Republic. "The Fourth Republic is dead. We never were for it. We never appreciated the 'poisons and delights' of the system. We want something new." The Contract of Noes called for: (1) the election of a Constituent Assembly in November, 1958; (2) a vote within one month by this assembly of a simple and brief constitu-

---

[10] For the full text see *l'Express*, September 11, 1958.

tional document; (3) the convocation of a congress of the members
of the French Union to draft a new constitution for the Empire;
(4) the establishment of a genuine democracy through the discretionary power of dissolution, "as in Great Britain, so that the people
may decide"; (5) a single-member district system with runoffs;
(6) peace in Algeria by negotiations with the real Algerian spokesmen and not with "ghosts" discovered by the army or the government.

Mendès-France's statement illustrated the poverty of the political
thought of the Left. His specifications about the establishment of a
new constitution remained unconvincing. How, for instance, in an
intensely divided country could a Constituent Assembly prepare a
constitution in a period of one month? As for a "simple" constitutional text providing for the discretionary right of dissolution, a long
debate under the Gaillard cabinet had failed to produce any agreement in the National Assembly. The desperate efforts of the non-
Communist Left to provide for a constructive opposition to De
Gaulle illustrated their predicament. They rejected the Fourth Republic and proposed reforms. So did De Gaulle. They appealed to
the republican tradition and suggested the renovation of the republican institutions. So did De Gaulle. They were in favor of liberal reforms in Algeria and the French Union. Though De Gaulle's views on
Algeria were not clear, he had adopted a far more liberal policy regarding the Community than any of the left-wing leaders who had
been in power. The Left, faithful to the traditions and myths of the
Republic, wanted reform to come directly from a popularly elected
assembly. De Gaulle's reforms were ready to be submitted to the
people.

In addition to the UFD and the Communist party, an assortment of individual political leaders and groups campaigned also for
a negative vote. Most important among them were some of the
Radical Socialist leaders, notably Edouard Daladier, Bourgès-
Maunoury, and Jean Baylet. André Philip, who had been expelled
from the Socialist party, after undertaking a careful assessment of
the constitution, advocated abstention. His counsel was followed
only by the extreme right-wing weekly *Rivarol*, which asked the
voters to go to the polls but to cast blank ballots. Considerable confusion reigned among the Poujadist group. The parliamentarians
had failed to follow their leaders' instructions to vote against De
Gaulle's investiture. In a stormy congress of the party held in June,

1958, Poujade pronounced the dissolution of the parliamentary group now "that the objectives of the movement had been realized" and remained hostile to General de Gaulle and the constitution while expressing his preference for General Massu. The parliamentarians, however, seemed favorable to a Yes vote.

The Radical Socialists and the Socialists. It was among the Socialists and the Radical Socialists that the divisions became heart rending. Both parties were divided sharply over the question of De Gaulle's investiture, the Socialists voting 49 against and 42 for, and the Radicals 24 for and 18 against. This division continued into the referendum campaign.

The Socialist party was divided into three groups: the left-wing "minority" led by Edouard Depreux and Robert Verdier that had been opposed to Guy Mollet's leadership and had advocated political negotiations with a view to independence for Algeria; the ambivalent Center that had followed Guy Mollet reluctantly but had voted with the minority against De Gaulle's investiture, led by Albert Gazier, Christian Pineau, and Tanguy-Prigent; the "majority" supporting the leadership of Guy Mollet and deriving the bulk of its strength from the five largest departments, whose votes were controlled by Mollet and his lieutenants.

Early in July a special Information Conference was held in which Guy Mollet spoke in favor of the constitution and a Yes vote.[11] But Gazier managed to get a resolution accepted by the supreme organ of the party, the *Comité Directeur*, suggesting that at least two separate questions be included in the referendum. The first, asking the people whether they were in favor or not of reforming the institutions of the Fourth Republic, and the second, whether they approved or not the text prepared by the government. Two weeks later the minority and Center of the Socialist parliamentary group agreed on a strong statement that put the leadership of the party in a difficult position:

The Socialists have always denounced the coming of one-man rule [*pouvoir personnel*] as presaging fascism. . . . The revision of the constitution is necessary. But it is to a Constituent Assembly, duly elected by the people, that the task of preparing it must be entrusted. . . . To do otherwise is to open the gate wide to adventure. We are already con-

---

[11] For a detailed account see *Bulletin Intérieur du Parti Socialiste* (SFIO) Compte rendu sténographique de la Conférence d'Information, Issy-les-Moulineaux, July 6, 1958.

vinced that it is the duty of the Socialists, with the help of all the democrats, to reject it. . . . Even if the draft of the constitution could be seriously modified, the method of its preparation and the manner of holding the referendum under the intolerable pressure of a praetorian army, cannot but meet with our opposition.[12]

The alliance between the Center and the Left, however, did not last long. A delegation of Socialist leaders visited General de Gaulle and presented him with specific objections to the constitutional text under consideration.[13] They criticized the manner in which the President of the Republic was to be elected, the emergency powers granted to the president, the incompatibility between the legislative and the cabinet functions, and the limitation of the legislative powers of the Parliament. All reports indicate that they were reassured. In the meantime Guy Mollet was delaying a confrontation with the opposition until the meeting of the national congress of the party, scheduled for September 11, where he was assured of a majority.[14]

The general secretary of the Socialist party played an important role in De Gaulle's return. He appeared to be convinced that the Fourth Republic had lost all power to deal with the crisis in Algeria and that only a government led by General de Gaulle could save the Republic. Opportunistic consideration seemed also to have been taken into account. He recognized the existence of a vigorous nationalism in the country and he was fully aware of the virulence of the right-wing groups in Algeria. Mollet had also known from personal experience that the Republic's writ did not run in Algeria. His attitude, therefore, was calculated to improve the electoral position of the Socialist party by aligning it with the prevailing current of opinion.

Two important documents throw light on the attitude of the Socialist leader: the letter addressed to General de Gaulle on May 25, made public for the first time at the national congress of the party three and a half months later, and a circular addressed to all members a few days before the meeting of the party congress.[15] In his letter, Mollet wrote to De Gaulle that he was not in favor of his return to power under the then prevailing conditions, because in the

---

[12] *Ibid.*

[13] For an account see *Le Monde*, August 20, 1958.

[14] Of the five large departmental federations that have a majority in the congress of the Socialist party—Pas-de-Calais, Haute-Vienne Nord, Bouches-du-Rhône, and Seine—only the federation of Seine was in doubt.

[15] For the text see *Le Monde*, September 16, 1958.

long run it would "serve the interests of the Bolsheviks who now appear as the defenders of public liberties." The Communists are waiting for a period of "disillusionment and of difficulties that the situation renders inevitable" to "become your successors." In the meantime, he pointed out, the military and right-wing groups were on the road of pronunciamentos and military putsches in "your name." But Mollet expressed his devotion to the General and his conviction of De Gaulle's republicanism. If, however, De Gaulle were to come to power without disavowing in some fashion the military and the right-wing elements, then the future would favor the Communists. In effect he was asking De Gaulle to come to power, and promised his support if he would only use legal means. It was a masterful document. Depending on the development of the situation, it could be used either to show the republicanism of the secretary general and and his opposition to De Gaulle's return to power under the circumstances, or to take credit for the manner in which De Gaulle came to power and make it possible to become one of his confidants!

The circular addressed to the members of the party was destined to refute the arguments of the minority and Center in favor of a negative vote in the referendum. Guy Mollet confided that he was trying to decide between "resigning or continuing the struggle." [16] The situation was too grave to allow him to consider resignation.

If the Party . . . decides to vote No in the referendum there is a risk that it will disappear and perhaps provoke the disappearance of the Republic. The Party may, by aligning itself with the Communists, orient itself toward a "popular democracy." It is because of this risk that I feel that I do not have the right to abandon the struggle; I prefer to fight even if I lose.

If the party were to decide to vote No and if the constitution were rejected, what would happen, he asked? "It is good common sense that a negative vote would bring about the resignation of De Gaulle. If so . . . are you ready to take over? With whom?" Both questions, of course, could have been addressed directly to Mollet, who, in asking them, was also confessing the impotence of the party and of its leadership. With considerable insight he added:

I am telling you that, even if by error or by misfortune we decided to vote No, the majority of the people will be in favor, including many of our own voters and even the Communist voters of yesterday. If so, the Com-

---

[16] *Points de Vues et Controverses*, supplément spécial au *Bulletin Intérieur du Parti Socialiste*, No. 4 (September, 1958).

munist losses will not be obvious when the votes are counted. It will be
the non-Communist Left that will appear annihilated.

At this point, Guy Mollet undertook a detailed analysis of the constitution and concluded with a demonstration of its republican character.

The activity that preceded the Socialist party congress held at
Issy-les-Moulineaux, a suburb of Paris, between September 11 and
September 14, brought into the open the conflict within the party:
Guy Mollet in favor of the constitution and of course a Yes vote;
Edouard Depreux at the head of the opposition supported by some
important leaders of the party in favor of a No vote; and Albert
Gazier, representing a Center reluctant to accept the constitution
but unwilling to provoke a party split. The majority of the departmental federations were in favor of a Yes vote, with the exception
of the Federation of the Seine, which remained divided. The crucial
questions at the congress, therefore, were: (1) the assessment of the
exact strength of the opposition; (2) the prospects of a party split,
and (3) the type of final policy motion that would be adopted on
Algeria.

Ever since 1956 the minority group led by Depreux and Verdier
had urged negotiations and the recognition of Algeria's vocation toward independence. The leader of the important Federation of
Bouches-du-Rhône and mayor of Marseille, Gaston Defferre, consistently attempted to mediate between the minority and the leadership
of the party. He had amended the resolution presented in the 1956
congress to urge a war against two fronts: the FLN and the extreme
right-wing groups among the *colons*. At the 1957 congress he offered a compromise resolution urging immediate negotiations. Defferre's attitude was of crucial importance, therefore, especially since
he had voted against De Gaulle's investiture.

After an interview with General de Gaulle, Defferre came out in
favor of a Yes vote. Given the liberal attitude taken by the General in
promising to grant independence to the former colonies of France,
it was not likely, he contended, that he would follow a "retrograde"
policy in Algeria. He voted Yes, therefore, not because he approved
the constitutional text but because he believed that De Gaulle would
pursue a liberal policy in Algeria, which was, in his opinion, the crucial issue.

While agreeing to vote Yes to the constitution by a 70 per cent
majority, the congress adopted a resolution on Algeria by an over-

whelming vote of 3,370 mandates against 611, *which was far more liberal than any of the resolutions adopted in the past.* In fact, the text, largely inspired by the mayor of Marseille, went beyond the terms of the resolution he had introduced in the 1957 congress. The motion stated:

> . . . no reform can be operative if . . . the civil power is not re-established in Algeria; if the military and the civil functions are not again separated; if the ultras of all factions are not reduced to impotence; if the Committees of Public Safety are not dissolved; if the legality and the integrity of the electoral operations is not guaranteed, and if a political solution is not found. . . . The goal is to establish the harmonious coexistence of the two communities by the recognition of the Algerian personality and an absolute equality of rights.

After rejecting such slogans as "integration," the congress affirmed in the most unequivocal terms what had been anathema to the Algerian *colons* and perhaps to the army: the need "to seek a cease-fire with those who are fighting, accompanied with reciprocal guaranties." The solution envisaged was to be "political," stemming from negotiations with the qualified representatives from Algeria "without excluding anybody"—which meant even the members of the FLN.[17] The congress was thus voting at one and the same time for cease-fire negotiations with those who were fighting, for a political settlement in Algeria through negotiations, for the constitutional text, and for General de Gaulle.

During the debate, the opposition leaders criticized the constitution and favored a negative vote. Some reaffirmed their intention to vote No, but promised for the sake of party unity not to campaign. Only a small fraction was in favor of secession, but this included the leaders of the Seine Federation, Depreux and Verdier, who formed an autonomous group, the *Parti Socialiste Autonome.* They planned to campaign for a No vote, favored a renovated Socialist party, and called for the election of a Constituent Assembly to prepare a new constitution.

The Radical Socialist party was hopelessly divided. The discipline of the parliamentary group had never been realized and the vote on De Gaulle's investiture only served to accentuate their divisions. In the party congress Mendès-France confronted once more the con-

---

[17] For the text of the resolution see *Le Populaire,* September 16, 1958.

servative forces led this time by the former premier, Félix Gaillard. By a small majority the congress declared itself in favor of a Yes vote without, however, being in a position to enforce any discipline. In fact, a strong minority of party delegates made it clear that they intended to campaign against the referendum—Mendès-France, within the UFD, and others, notably Bourgès-Maunoury, Baylet, and Daladier as members of the party. The general policy resolution was hostile to the De Gaulle government and urged a rapid settlement in Algeria. It discarded the notion of integration, castigated the attitude of the army and the *colons,* and noted that "there was not the slightest progress" in Algeria. "The coming vote," it concluded, "will not solve anything." [18]

Center and Right.   The parties traditionally considered to belong to the Left debated their attitude toward the referendum and De Gaulle, and in so doing, very often indulged in an agonizing self-appraisal of their position and future role in the Republic. On the other hand, the conservative and center groups, satisfied with developments, confidently urged their followers to vote Yes to the new constitution and to General de Gaulle.

The MRP was perhaps the only group in doubt. The party seemed demoralized. It was an MRP leader who had the dubious honor of presiding over the liquidation of the Fourth Republic, or perhaps, as others hinted, of signing the death certificate that Guy Mollet had drafted. The mushrooming of right-wing organizations with Gaullist banners revived the specter of a resurgent Gaullist movement that, as with the RPF in 1951, might endanger seriously the MRP's electoral position. The prospect that proportional representation would be abandoned in the elections that were to follow was an additional reason for gloom. Yet there was hardly any vocal opposition to De Gaulle and the constitution. The National Committee of the party urged a Yes vote by an overwhelming majority. The electoral system preoccupied the meeting of the National Committee more than did the constitution.

The Independents and the right-wing Radical formations asserted their confidence in De Gaulle and the constitution and decided unanimously to counsel their followers to vote Yes. They expressed their satisfaction, especially with the policies of the government in Algeria, which they interpreted to be in favor of integration. Concern was voiced over De Gaulle's offer to the Africans of a choice be-

---

[18] For the full text *Information Radicale,* September, 1958.

tween "community" and "independence." Some of the extreme right-wing members went so far as to urge a No vote—but they were the rare exceptions. The Right was optimistic about the future elections, for a grand alliance was envisaged grouping the Independents, the Republican Center, the various Gaullist groups, and some of the MRP members, more especially, the former leader of the MRP, Bidault, who had formed his own group—the Christian Democrats. The new electoral system, they hoped, would sweep not only the Communists but also the Socialists out of Parliament. The satisfaction with the constitution was genuine, but for reasons somewhat different from those advanced by the Gaullists. A Senate elected by the municipal councilors was bound to be in their hands. There was also no reason why, when De Gaulle was out of the picture, the presidency would not come under their control in view of the character of the presidential electoral college.

Extreme nationalist groups felt that De Gaulle was coming to terms with the system by allowing the political leaders who had been responsible for the deterioration of the colonial position of France to participate in the government. They feared that the *élan* of the revolution of May 13 was gradually being absorbed by the "system." Royalists, Maurassians, and assorted fascists called for the establishment of a one-party system, while the various Committees of Public Safety of Algeria felt less and less inclined to support De Gaulle.

The small political group that hailed from the non-Communist resistance movement—the UDSR—broke up as a result of the investiture vote and the referendum. The two most prominent leaders of the party, Pleven and Mitterand, took opposite stands, and the latter became one of the leading members of the UFD. The virtual disappearance of the UDSR was richly compensated, however, by the sudden emergence of Gaullist organizations—all of them committed naturally to a Yes vote. They were the National Association for the Support of the Action of General de Gaulle, led by Roger Frey; the Republican Convention, led by Léon Delbecque; the Civic Union for the Referendum, led by Chaban-Delmas; and the French Union for Renovation, organized by Jacques Soustelle. These organizations, together with the Social Republicans, merged later into the Union for the New Republic (UNR).

Professional and Civic Organizations

While the parties were deliberating, a host of civic and professional associations and interest groups were taking their stand.

The National Federation of the Deported, Interned, Patriots and Re-
sistants, for instance, proclaimed its determination to vote No, while
the Civic Union of *Deux Sèvres* declared itself in favor of Yes. The
Federation of the Associations of Catholic Education opted for Yes,
and so did the Committee for the Renovation and Resistance to the
Disintegration of France and the French Union; the French section
of the Fourth International was to vote No; but the Departmental
Associations of Aid to the Aged stoutly opted for a Yes; the Association of the Bearers of Military Decorations was in favor, but the National Group of the Blind, Mutilated and Invalids of the Resistance
firmly declared that they were to vote against the "autocratic aspects
of the constitution." The French Movement for Abundance found
the constitution "totally unacceptable," but the Count of Paris was
in favor of a royal Yes. The Committee of Doctors in favor of the Republican Defense were to vote No, but the federalist periodical,
Vingtième Siècle, approved a constitution "largely inspired by its
ideas." French citizens made full use of the traditional media of political expression. All that was needed, given the state of Paris buildings, was some white paint or a piece of chalk.

   More important was the position taken by the large social, economic, and, of course, church associations. Among the trade unions,
for instance, the French Confederation of Christian Workers proclaimed its apolitical character and gave to its members full freedom to vote as they pleased. But it remained critical of the constitutional text. The Communist-controlled CGT urged a No vote, while
the Socialist *Force Ouvrière* remained neutral.

   Two important professional organizations—the National Federation of Education, representing all the educational associations, and
the Teachers Union, consisting of about a quarter of a million teachers—despite their usual profession of *apolitisme* came out against the
constitution, which they found "incompatible with the republican
tradition." [19] The same position was taken by the League of the
Rights of Man. Most of the veterans' organizations urged a Yes
vote.[20] Associations representing the artisans, the small and middle
enterprises, and the farmers were in favor of a Yes vote. The intellectuals spoke through their respective professional organizations
and divided along lines that reflected their political orientation.

----

[19] *Le Monde,* September 9, 1958.
[20] *Ibid.,* September 8, 1958.

The constitution did not refer to God. In fact it proclaimed a "lay" Republic. The question immediately arose as to whether the Catholics should vote for a document that seemed to counter their beliefs. Tracts were distributed in the Sunday masses urging the faithful to vote No. Guidance was quickly provided by a number of cardinals and archbishops. For instance, Cardinal Gerlier, of Lyon, declared at Lourdes that it would be extremely grave, given the actual circumstances, to allow French unity to be endangered. He patiently explained that *laicité* did not mean the rejection by the State of a superior moral law, nor did it imply the assertion of secular authority on religious matters. In his Pastoral Letter, Monseigneur Chappoulie pointed out that the insertion of the word "lay" in the constitution did not prevent a Catholic from voting Yes.[21] A number of other prelates openly counseled a Yes vote. On the other hand, liberal Catholics writing in the *Témoignage Chrétien* took strong exception to the manner in which General de Gaulle had come to power, to the perpetuation of military rule in Algeria, and to the plebiscitary character of the constitution. The Young Catholic Workers (JOC) urged its members to study the constitution carefully and to vote according to their conscience. But it also expressed many reservations. *Esprit,* in an editorial by its director, Jean-Marie Domenach, proclaimed the determination of liberal Catholics not to be blackmailed by the threats of a civil war. A Yes vote would be a carte blanche to one man. "It would be a gamble," he wrote, "on a man and nothing else. Our whole tradition and our reason recoil. In this century when the masses demand an answer to their anxieties and needs, the greatness of one man is an illusory protection against fate." If a civil war were to follow "we shall not miss the opportunity—perhaps the last one—to force the enemy to take off his mask." [22]

An official pronouncement was made by the Episcopate of France. In a special message, the cardinals and archbishops declared that they could not approve the inopportune propaganda in favor of a negative vote. They specified that neither the absence of any reference to God nor the term "lay republic" should prevent the Catholics from expressing themselves freely. Indeed, the obligation to vote was more imperative than ever because the major interests of France were at stake. They hoped that eventually "it will be possible with

---

[21] *Semaine Religieuse* (Angers, August 25, 1958).

[22] "Les Raisons pour le *Non,*" *Esprit,* September, 1958, pp. 294–300.

the accord of the citizens to incorporate the name of God into the Constitution of France." [23] But this pronouncement did not put an end to the divisions among the Catholics.

The Campaign

Despite the internal divisions of the parties of the Left and the Center the campaign was dispirited. The meetings lacked the animation and the discord that usually prevail in electoral campaigns. Audiences were generally small. The most tireless workers in favor of Yes were the Gaullist groups, and they received considerable help from the Ministry of Information, whose colorful posters urging a "Yes to France" they distributed. The Independents and the Republican Center were also active. Roger Duchet, the secretary general of the Independents, visited some 40 departments. Though his tour was made primarily with an eye to the forthcoming elections, he supported the Yes vote and urged the integration of Algeria. Georges Bidault spoke in a number of cities in both France and Algeria. The slogan "By voting Yes, you vote to create one nation from Dunkirk to Tamanrasset," was also that of all the Committees of Public Safety of Algeria and of General Salan, who had sent the French to their geography texts when he declared, "The Mediterranean runs through France as the Seine river runs through Paris."

The more circumspect advocates of a Yes vote—those who were for the constitution and De Gaulle but against "integration"—did little campaigning. The Radicals and the Socialists made only a few speeches in favor of the constitution. The non-Communist proponents of the No—with the exception of Baylet in the Toulouse area— remained generally inactive. The UGS, the UFD, and the Autonomous Socialists relied upon their press to reach the voters. Mendès-France, who was considered the leader of the UFD, made few appearances. Was it defeatism or the spell of De Gaulle? Or was it simply that the non-Communist Left began to feel out of tune with opinion?

The press was overwhelmingly in favor of a Yes vote. In fact, outside of the Communist newspapers, only one paper with a circulation of over fifty thousand—the *Dépêche du Midi*, in the Toulouse area —campaigned for a No. The great dailies of Paris, Marseille, Bordeaux, Lyon, and Strasbourg were all in favor of Yes. Even *Le*

---

[23] For the full text see *Le Monde*, September 18, 1958.

Monde, after giving to its readers all the reasons for voting No, in a widely quoted editorial finally favored a Yes vote.[24] The left-wing weeklies, *l'Express* and *France-Observateur,* persevered in their campaign against what they considered a repetition of Bonapartist adventures with a vehemence in which could be detected a growing sense of frustration.

The most publicized and active figure of the campaign was De Gaulle himself. His speeches in the various capitals of Africa had taken his non-Communist opposition by surprise. The option between independence and community was, on its face, the most liberal ever offered by any French political leader. It even caught the Communists off balance. It seemed to confirm the position taken by all those who, like Defferre, believed that De Gaulle symbolized the hopes for a commonwealth arrangement. But it confused the Right also. De Gaulle was opening liberal political horizons to the African people, and refused to utter the magic word of integration for Algeria. The Right was in a predicament. Radicals, left-wing Gaullists, and Socialists were to vote Yes for reasons diametrically opposed to theirs. The question that had haunted many of the Socialist and Radical leaders—"If we vote No, then what?"—was a question that many of the right-wingers were beginning to ask now. Was the shoe on the other foot? It was too late to retreat.

On September 4 (the anniversary of the proclamation of the Third Republic) De Gaulle launched the campaign. He spoke in the heart of the working class district, the *Place de la République,* where the souvenirs of the Revolution and the Commune evoke the great traditions of French Jacobinism that the working classes of Paris have made their own. "It was in the midst of a national crisis and a foreign war," he said, "that the Republic was born. It was the sovereignty of the people, the appeal to freedom and the hope of justice. It was maintained throughout the stormy adventures of our history. Today, more than ever, we want it to be safeguarded." He reminded the audience that for a long time the Republic had led the country to prosperity and ultimately to the victory of World War I, but that it had proved since then unable to provide for a stable government. It was he, however, who had proclaimed its continuity from London and who re-established it after the Liberation. He was doing it again. Referring specifically to the constitution, he pointed out, "Above the

---

[24] *Le Monde,* September 25, 1918.

political conflicts there is a national mediator, elected by the people, in charge of the regular functioning of the institutions, with the right to appeal to the supreme judgment of the electorate, and responsible in case of grave peril for the independence, the honor, the integrity of France, and the safety of the Republic." [25] He described the staggering tasks confronting France—to re-establish peace in Algeria and settle its status, to renovate agriculture, to provide for jobs, education, and housing for the ever-growing number of young people, to create an association between the workers and management, to exploit the resources of Sahara, and finally, to establish a community with Africa and Madagascar. It was all up to the people, he concluded. If they voted No, then a return to the mistakes of the past was inevitable. If the vote was Yes, a strong and effective government would be established.

As the day of the vote approached, a particularly subtle argument was advanced by a number of the leaders of the non-Communist Left, and by some well-known publicists and professors, especially Maurice Duverger. They contended that the size of the No vote would show the strength of the Left and of those opposed to a policy of integration in Algeria. A sizable No would strengthen De Gaulle's hand to deal with the extremists. It would be a great tragedy for French democracy, they argued, if the No vote at the referendum coincided with the past Communist electoral strength. All the Yes votes would be then claimed by the Right, which might compel De Gaulle to follow its policy in Algeria and elsewhere. "Vote No," urged Duverger, "because the existence of a strong opposition will help De Gaulle against the 'neo-Gaullists' who have a tendency to draw the cross of Lorraine in the form of the Nazi swastika." [26] This tenuous argument was based upon the assumption of a large majority in favor of Yes. In effect the opponents of the constitution were asking the people to vote No in order to support De Gaulle against the Right!

In Rennes, Lille, Bordeaux, and Strasbourg the week before the referendum, De Gaulle asked for a massive vote in favor of Yes:

I have to ask you to give your answer in favor of Yes in an overwhelming fashion. We must proclaim our national unity in such a fashion that we may all have confidence in France. If, on the other hand, we obtain

---

[25] For the full text see *Le Monde,* September 6, 1958; and *Année Politique,* 1958, pp. 551–52; see Appendix pp. 361–63.
[26] *Le Monde,* September 3, 1958.

only one of those small and contestable majorities, we fear that we shall not be able to overcome the obstacles that we will confront.[27]

In a last appeal on the eve of the referendum, De Gaulle urged all the people to participate in the shaping of a new republic in order to reaffirm national unity and hope.

The Results

The result of the referendum was an overwhelming victory of the Yes. In Metropolitan France, out of 26,606,948 registered voters, 22,595,703 cast their ballots—an unprecedented 84.8 per cent participation. The Yes received 17,666,828 of the ballots cast, and the No 4,624,475—79.25 per cent against 20.75 per cent. The new constitution and, with it, General de Gaulle, were overwhelmingly endorsed by the people of France. In the French Union, with the exception of Guinea which voted No, the Yes was equally overwhelming. In Algeria, the percentage of No was negligible. With the exception of the Napoleonic Constitution of 1852—an invidious comparison—no other constitution had been endorsed in France with such a show of popular approval.

The vote indicated a transformation in the electoral map of France. Traditional bastions of left-wing republicanism—the South, the Paris "red belt," the departments of the Massif Central and the South East—were swept by the pro-Gaullist current. Only in the departments of Corrèze and Haute-Vienne, strongholds of the Communists, did the No attain 36 and 34 per cent respectively. In eleven departments, including some of the most industrialized areas, the No votes amounted to between 25 and 30 per cent. On the other hand, some 21 departments returned a Yes vote of 85 per cent and more. They included the classic regions of French conservatism— the West, the East, and the region south of the Central Plains.

The Communist party went down to defeat. If one were to assume —which is entirely unwarranted—that every No was a Communist vote, even then the Communists had lost heavily. In the three legislative elections they averaged 25 per cent of the ballots cast. The percentage of the No was 20.75. The Communist party found itself abandoned by many of its voters. Since the UFD, many individual Radical Socialist leaders, a number of Socialists, the Socialist dissident groups, and even some of the extreme right-wing groups had

---

[27] *Ibid.*, September 23, 1958.

either expressed themselves or had campaigned for a No vote, the party's losses should be situated between 1.2 to 1.5 million votes.

Only in ten departments did the No vote exceed the Communist vote of the elections of 1956.[28] In a great number of departments the No was considerably below the Communist vote of 1956. In nineteen Departments the No was 7 to 10 per cent below the Communist vote, and in nineteen others, 5 to 7 per cent. The losses came from industrialized and nonindustrialized departments, from Communist proletarian and agricultural strongholds alike.

Even more convincing were the returns from Paris and the southern and eastern suburbs—the "red belt." While in Paris proper the Yes totaled 77.6 per cent of the vote, in the suburbs, it amounted to 68.1 per cent. Everywhere the No was far below the vote of the Communist party in 1956. In a number of the personal fiefs of the party leaders, the Communist vote dropped substantially. Thus, in Maurice Thorez's Ivry-sur-Seine, there were 13,039 Yes and 12,171 No, as compared to 14,583 Communist votes cast for the Party in 1956; in Montreuil, the stronghold of Duclos, there were 17,473 No as compared to 21,459 in 1956; in St. Denis, 19,144 No as compared with 24,324. In the city of Paris only in two *arrondissements* did the No total more than 30 per cent.

Important political leaders who had advocated a "No," such as Mendès-France, Mitterand, Bourgès-Maunoury, Daladier, and others with well entrenched local positions, lost heavily. In the Department of Eure, for instance, where the Radicals and the Socialists (42 per cent of the votes in 1956) campaigned for No, only some 34,-500 votes were cast against the constitution and 134,000 in favor. In Louviers, where Mendès-France was mayor, there were 3,686 Yes against 1,667 No. In Tarn-et-Garonne, a stronghold of Radical Socialism, in which the combined Communist and Radical Socialist vote in the elections of 1956 had amounted to over 38,000 votes, there were only a little over 20,000 No. In Vaucluse, where the Communist and Radical Socialist votes exceeded slightly 61,000 in the elections of 1956 and where Edouard Daladier favored a No, only 38,000 voters pronounced themselves against the constitution. In Aude, the Communists, Radical Socialists, and the Socialists under the leadership of Albert Gazier (who did not campaign actively, however), were all in favor of No. These three parties had totaled 95,000 votes

---

[28] Ariège, Aude, Aveyron, Haute-Garonne, Eure, Gers, Tarn-et-Garonne, Vaucluse, Vendée, and Loire-et-Cher.

in the elections of 1956. But there were only 35,000 No, barely 4,000 more than the Communist vote in 1956. In Hérault, despite the efforts of one of the local Radical leaders, Vincent Badie, the No amounted to 65,997, while the Communists alone had received 70,-579 in the elections of 1956. In Nord, Pas de Calais, Seine, and Bouches-du-Rhône, the Yes averaged 70 to 75 per cent. In the Bordeaux region (Gironde), the Yes was a little over 85 per cent. In other words, departments where the Socialists were traditionally strong, and in which important Socialist party leaders such as Guy Mollet, Augustin Laurent, and Defferre had favored a Yes, voted in the same way as the traditionally conservative departments.

On the following page is produced a schematic representation of the vote advocated by each party, the particular position taken by each of the parties on the issues implicit in the referendum, the internal discrepancies of the Yes camp, and the identity of the Yes and No camps. It will be seen why it is difficult to reduce the complexity of French politics into an affirmation or negation as was proposed in the referendum. In 1958, as in 1946, practically all political parties were in favor of a new Republic—a situation that naturally weakened the position of those who were arguing for a No. Thus, the broad range of agreement revealed by the overwhelming Yes was in many respects a negation—a vote against the Fourth Republic. On the other hand, the parties favoring Yes—the MRP, the Socialists, the Independents and Moderates, many of the Radicals, and the Gaullist organizations—approved of the constitution. But the nature of the popular consultation and the motives that entered into the vote were more important than the text. For instance, many liberals criticized the text but voted Yes because they favored its provisions for the Community. The vote involved other important extra-constitutional considerations: the re-establishment of the civil authority over the military and an end to the fighting in Algeria. Many who disagreed with the text voted Yes because they saw in De Gaulle the only political leader who commanded enough respect to be able to resolve these two issues. As a result the Yes represented votes of both proponents and opponents of integration of Algeria. The Defferre Yes, which accounted to a great degree for the adhesion of the Socialist party, was given for reasons diametrically opposed to the Yes of Bidault. The Radical Socialist Yes or even the Yes of the MRP followers had a different connotation from the Yes advocated by Soustelle. The overwhelming Yes cast in Algeria in the name of inte-

THE MEANING OF THE REFERENDUM

BASIC ISSUES	COMMUNIST PARTY	UFD	PSA	SFIO	RAD.-SOC. AND RGR	MRP	CHRISTIAN DEMOCRATS	IND. MODERATES	REP. CENTER	GAULLIST	POUJADIST AND COMMITTEES OF SAFETY
THE CONSTITUTION											
MAY 13 LEADING TO DE GAULLE'S RETURN											
ALGERIAN INTEGRATION											
LIBERAL POLICY IN FRENCH UNION											
DE GAULLE'S GOVERNMENT											

YES — APPROVE

NO — DISAPPROVE

gration coincided with the almost equally impressive Yes in many of the metropolitan departments and even working class districts, but its meaning was very different. Perhaps, as an astute commentator noted, the difference between Yes and No was no longer clear in the land of Descartes.

From the divisions in the Yes camp one conclusion can be drawn: The only victor was De Gaulle. The vote was a personal vote for De Gaulle—to put the new institutions in their place, solve the Algerian problem, refashion relations with the African territories, represent France with dignity and firmness in the world, curb the excesses of the military, and save the Republic. But how this was to be done remained obscure, nor was there an agreement among those who voted Yes. "De Gaulle represents the geometric point of all our differences," wrote Sartre. Did the appearance of unity camouflage these differences? Was the Yes vote merely a delegation of all political decisions to one man? If so, its significance lay precisely in its apolitical character!

Further References

No publication has appeared as yet in book form on the referendum of September 28, 1958. The reader will find some interesting reflections in Raymond Aron, *Immuable et Changeante—de la IVième à la Vième République* (Paris, 1959), and André Siegfried, *De la Quatrième à la Vième République* (Paris, 1959). For a detailed account of the events, *Année Politique*, 1958, is an invaluable source.

The periodical literature is extensive. Particularly the issues of *Cahiers de la République*, No. 15 (September–October, 1958), and No. 16 (November–December, 1958); *Preuves*, November, 1958, and January, 1959; *Esprit*, September, 1958; *La Nef*, September and October, 1958. Jean-Paul Sartre, "Les Grenouilles qui Demandent un Roi," *l'Express*, September 25, 1958, is a devastating criticism of De Gaulle and the climate of opinion that led to the referendum.

CHAPTER XIII

The Legislative Elections

THE FIRST ELECTION of the Fifth Republic took place under exceptional circumstances. The voters had approved overwhelmingly a new constitution, according to which a president was to play a preponderant role in the political system. It was obvious that General de Gaulle would be elected President of the Republic, and would shape the policies of the future, no matter what turn the election took. The election of 1958 therefore was relatively apathetic, compared to the three general elections that had preceded it under the Fourth Republic. The old parties went through the motions of the traditional campaigning, without arousing any notable enthusiasm. By and large the public seemed to view the elections as part of the process of investing General de Gaulle with the powers of the Republic.

The Electoral Law

The electoral system preoccupied all legislatures of the Fourth Republic, constituting one of the persistent controversies of the regime. The Center parties were generally agreed on the need for an arrangement that would discriminate against the extremes, but were themselves divided on the details. Each party advocated a procedure that would offer it the greatest advantages: The Radicals and most Independents favored a return to the single-member districts of the Third Republic with *ballottage*, since their "notables" would presumably benefit from local support; the MRP wished to preserve proportional representation, thus guaranteeing it a minimum representation in large areas of the nation where its electoral support was spread thin; the Socialists favored the principle of proportional representation, but with modifications. The Communists, of course, fought for a straight system of proportional representation, rigorously excluding any possibility for the Center groups to constitute alliances against them. The inability of the Assembly to agree upon a satisfactory, generally accepted electoral system was a striking illustration of its internal deadlock.

One of the major concerns of parliamentarians during their consultations with Charles de Gaulle in May, 1958 was precisely over the question whether "full powers" would extend to the electoral system. De Gaulle assured them that the new electoral system would be established by law. However, since acceptance of the constitution superceded the delegation of full powers by the National Assembly, De Gaulle made use of a special grant of power by virtue of Article 92 of the constitution to promulgate an electoral law.

The problem of the electoral system was first raised in the cabinet four days before the referendum. A study group under the direction of Michel Debré was given the task of reporting on proposals made by the groups represented in the government. Shortly after the referendum, the matter again came up for discussion. Guy Mollet spoke in favor of a modified version of the electoral system used in Germany; two thirds of the deputies would be elected from single-member districts, and one third would be selected from national lists on the basis of proportional representation. Mollet's proposal happened to suit nicely the particular needs of the SFIO, which could expect to do well in the districts and also benefit from the national lists. Soustelle, Debré (on behalf of the UNR), and some Independents advocated a departmental list system with only one ballot; the list receiving the greatest number of votes would win all seats. Such a system would encourage the Center and Gaullist candidates to form common lists, and would also cut down drastically on Communist representation. Pflimlin supported the idea of departmental lists, but wanted an absolute majority required on each of the two ballots; in the absence of an absolute majority on the second ballot, the seats would be distributed according to proportional representation. The independence and autonomy of the MRP would thus be assured, especially in negotiating agreements between the two ballots. After a long debate by his ministers, General de Gaulle pronounced himself in favor of a system that could be easily understood by the voters.[1]

---

[1] The cabinet's deliberations on electoral reform are described by *Le Monde*, September 25 and October 2 and 8, 1958. For the viewpoint of the MRP, see *Forces Nouvelles*, October 4, 11, and 18, 1958. For the electoral law see *Année Politique*, 1958, pp. 123–25.

On October 8, the cabinet decided to adopt the *scrutin d'arron-dissement* with *ballottage*. As during the greater part of the history of the Third Republic, the election was to take place in two stages: *a first ballot* in which a candidate would be elected only if he received an absolute majority of the votes cast; and a *second ballot* in which the candidate with the greatest number of votes would be elected. In the week which elapsed between ballots, the various candidates would have the opportunity to desist in favor of a better-placed rival, or simply to retire, in order to head off an even more dangerous opponent. This corresponded to the desire of General de Gaulle to have a simple, effective electoral system. It also happened to be the procedure consistently advocated by the Radical Socialists throughout the Fourth Republic. Since the Communists were completely isolated, they would be unable to negotiate alliances on the second ballot, and hence would have their representation reduced. It appeared probable at the time that the system would favor the election of independent personalities, enabling the President of the Republic to maneuver the parliamentary groups without difficulty. The single-member system was *not* applied to Algeria, however, since it would not guarantee adequate representation of Moslems. Algeria was divided into 18 districts electing 67 deputies on the basis of a list system, with only one ballot. Two thirds of the candidates were required to be of "local statute," that is, Moslems.

Several measures were adopted to discourage frivolous candidacies. A deposit of 100,000 francs (approximately $200) was required of all candidates, and was to be refunded only if they received 5 per cent of the votes on the first ballot. Candidates were also to be reimbursed for expenses incurred for bill posting, on the basis of a schedule drawn up by the prefects in each department. This applied, however, only to candidates who received over 5 per cent of the vote on either ballot. Radio and television time was made available to parties or groups presenting a minimum of 75 candidates throughout the nation, and upon proper application to the Ministry of the Interior. Each party or group was entitled to five minutes of radio time and five minutes of television time on a national network, and an additional five minutes on ten regional radio stations.

The return to the single-member district raised two immediate problems: the total number of deputies to be elected, and the exact delimitation of the boundaries of the constituencies. As is evident from American experience, the drawing of district lines in accordance with the classic principles associated with Governor Gerry of Massachusetts (gerrymandering) can frequently have an important bearing on the outcome of elections. Political commentators, as well as candidates, awaited eagerly the decrees establishing the constituencies.

The basic decision made by the government was to reduce the number of seats in France in order to increase the number allotted to Algeria, along with an approximate 10 per cent decrease in the total. The Assembly elected in 1956 was to comprise 627 deputies: 544 for France, 52 for overseas departments and territories (10 for departments and 42 for territories), 30 for Algeria, and one for the French establishments in India. However, elections were never held for the 30 Algerian seats, nor for the one seat in India; hence, the total number of deputies was 596. In France, each deputy represented an average of 79,000 inhabitants. The first legislature of the Fifth Republic was assigned 465 deputies for France (each representing a single district), 67 deputies for 18 districts of Algeria, and 4 deputies for the 2 districts of the Sahara, plus 16 deputies from overseas departments and territories.

The principle followed was to allocate seats to each department on the basis of one deputy for every 93,000 inhabitants, with a minimum of two deputies for each department. The five least-populated departments (Lozère, Ariège, Basses-Alpes, Hautes-Alpes, and the Territory of Belfort) thus received two additional deputies. The drawing of district lines within the departments was made by the Ministry of the Interior and the Office of the Prime Minister, on the basis of reports submitted by the prefects. Particular attention was paid to certain departments (for example, Mendès-France's Eure and François Mitterand's Nièvre) in order to avoid the accusation from the opposition of foul play. The preliminary recommendations were submitted to all members of the government, who in turn consulted their parties and suggested changes. The final decision regarding district lines was announced by the cabinet on October 10.

The 465 seats of France were supposed to average 93,000 inhabitants. In fact, there were several notable disparities between districts of the same department. In Rhône, the district of Villeurbanne had 137,088 inhabitants, that of Tarare only 70,260. The fourth district of Lille included 62,851 persons, that of neighboring proletarian

Roubaix-Est 117,738. The eleventh district of Nord, including all of
Dunkerque, had 117,783 inhabitants, while the adjoining twelfth
district (mainly agricultural) had only 68,860. In general, urban
districts included more residents than rural districts, but several
rural departments had their representation reduced. One of the pe-
culiar features of the districting was the division of many cities and
towns (Troyes, Perpignan, Grenoble, Le Mans, Toulouse, Limoges)
into several sectors, to which rural cantons were added. This practice
tended to dilute Communist strength, with the exception of Limoges,
where the Communist vote in the surrounding rural area was higher
than in the city itself. On the whole, however, the districting seemed
to be fair. A persistent critic of the government, *Le Monde's* Jacques
Fauvet, concluded: "The completion of a new electoral map was a
delicate operation. . . . Its authors have accomplished it honestly."

The most striking injustice involved the relative representation of
Algeria and France. Approximately one million Europeans were to
elect 21 of the 71 deputies in Algeria and the Sahara. Thus, each
European deputy from Algeria represents 48,000 inhabitants, while
each metropolitan deputy speaks for twice that many. In effect, the
Europeans of Algeria received a bonus of 11 deputies. As Maurice
Duverger plaintively observed: "The metropolitans are not even,
with regard to the Algerians, half French (Frenchmen *'à demi-
part'*)." In addition, the 50 Moslem deputies (representing 9 million
people) were obviously going to be chosen and elected under the
auspices of the army and local Committees of Public Safety. The
Moslem seats plus half the European seats, amounting to 10 per cent
of the National Assembly, constitute a vast rotten borough.[2]

The Campaign

The 1958 campaign was a relatively tame affair. Under the
Fourth Republic the basic unit of representation was the department.
The major parties held numerous mass rallies; the techniques of infiltration, heckling, contradiction, self-defense, counterattack and so
on were finely developed forms of political warfare. All this was
changed by the return to the single-member district. The 2,800 can-

---

[2] Quotations by Jacques Fauvet and Maurice Duverger are from *Le Monde*,
October 18 and November 8, 1958, respectively. The decree regulating campaign
procedures is summarized by *Le Monde*, November 1, 1958. On the drawing of
district lines, see the special articles in *Le Monde* on October 11, 12, 13, and 14, 1958.

didates instinctively reverted to the campaign tactics of the Third Republic. In the provinces, most aspirants conducted a door-to-door campaign. Antoine Pinay and Georges Bidault were among the many well-known personalities who quietly and effectively circulated in their districts, contacting "notables," and avoiding mass meetings. However, some highly publicized contests, for example, General Chassin versus Chaban-Delmas in Bordeaux, drew large audiences. In Eure, Mendès-France spoke gravely on overriding national issues before substantial gatherings. His chief opponent, Rémy Montagne, played up local questions, attacked Mendès bitterly, and cultivated the leaders of the district. Montagne ran on a ticket with the intriguing title "Rally of the Yes" (*Rassemblement des Ouis*), the Yes vote on September 28 in Eure having amounted to 79 per cent.

In Paris the leading candidates and parties held frequent rallies—almost always in a local school where perhaps one or two hundred curious residents of the *quartier* would gather to hear the hopefuls. Of course, there were exceptions. A widely publicized debate between Colonel Laure (UNR) and Jacques Féron (Independent) in a Paris right-bank district brought over a thousand noisy partisans to a schoolroom that could hold one third that number. There were relatively few incidents. While Mme. Brigitte Servan-Gros was exposing her Mendésist philosophy to a small group of voters in a popular quarter of Paris, twenty-five young men dressed as paratroopers invaded the meeting, broke benches, and administered a few blows upon the lady candidate. One of the chivalrous youths threw a bottle of acid at her face. *Le Monde* commented gravely: "The election campaign in Paris is warming up."

A few themes predominated generally in most constituences. Virtually all the candidates proclaimed their attachment to General de Gaulle. Rare was the election poster that did not contain excerpts of a letter from the General to the candidate offering congratulations on his military record, role in the Resistance, fidelity, or other service. The UNR attempted to monopolize the General, but the others embraced him just as fervently. Candidates who had never been deputies (frequently because they had been defeated in previous attempts) urged the voters to "throw the rascals out." Those who were deputies proudly described their efforts to overthrow the "system" from within. All hopefuls searched desperately to find an intimate bond (schooling, residence, place of business, relatives, and so forth) with the localities in which they ran. Apart from the Communists and Mendésists, the candidates tended to avoid issues. A number of themes cropped up continually: the Thirteenth of May was a "National Revival," Algeria is French, the Sahara a future source of untold wealth, housing a necessity, expansion of universities desirable, increased taxation a menace, and Communist China a worry. It seemed in most cases that the voter was being asked to decide which of the candidates soliciting his favors was the most authentic Gaullist, whatever that could mean in terms of specific policies.[3]

The Parties in the Campaign

The Communists (PCF). The Communist party was profoundly shaken by the outcome of the referendum, and by the certainty that its representation in the National Assembly would be reduced by the electoral system. In his report to the Central Committee on October 4, Marcel Servin admitted that the referendum was "a severe defeat" for the party. Maurice Thorez frankly stated before the same meeting that the "lies" of the bourgeoisie regarding the alleged blessings of colonialism had penetrated a part of the working class.

The basic explanation of Servin and Thorez for the defeat suffered in the referendum was that the masses had been misled by illusions regarding De Gaulle's person, past record, and present policy. The defeat of the republicans was due also to the divisions of the Left, caused by "fanatical anticommunism." The party must bring this lesson home to the Socialist and Radical masses. However, the party's liaison with the masses, observed Servin, leaves a great deal to be desired. The party must now "bathe in the masses," better understand them in order to serve as their guide.

But Thorez chided those comrades who spoke of "disaster." Referring constantly to the writings of Marx and Lenin, he demonstrated that in a class war there were defeats as well as victories, that the party remained at all times the sole instrument of the proletariat, that the line of the party had been correct, and so on. The task was clear: 4,600,000 people voted against the constitution; they, along with the former Communist supporters, must constitute the basis for a rally of all true republicans to whom it must be made clear that anticommunism leads inevitably to fascism. Under the circum-

---

[3] On the campaign in general see *Année Politique*, 1958, pp. 133–36, 139–45.

stances, the party reaffirmed its traditional tactic of "the united front from below": union of Socialist masses with the Communist party against the treason of the Socialist leaders. Guy Mollet and his "henchmen" were singled out as the chief "reactionaries" to be beaten. In a widely publicized "Letter to Socialist Workers," the Central Committee on October 22, 1958 denounced Mollet as a "strikebreaker" who plotted with De Gaulle. Socialist workers were therefore exhorted to join their Communist brethren in factories, schools, and villages to defeat reaction and launch the republican counteroffensive. Thundered Thorez as the campaign developed: "There is scarcely any difference between Guy Mollet and Soustelle: they are together in the same government. . . . The internal quarrels are a simple comedy, a way of duping a part of the masses." [4]

The emphasis on unity of action with the Socialist and Radical masses dictated Communist electoral tactics. The party undertook to present candidates in all districts on the first ballot, and hoped to attract the votes of all sincere democrats. On the second ballot it wished to bring about the union of the republican forces. The Central Committee announced: "The Party will favor agreements with the Socialists, Radicals, and Republicans who neither capitulated before the *coup de force* of the Algerian dissidents, nor called for a Yes vote, and whose political attitudes favor the rally of democratic forces against reaction."

As Maurice Thorez proudly declared shortly after the referendum, the program of the Communist party is well known and needs little repetition. It was summarized concisely by the Central Committee in its formal resolution of October 22: "In order to set up an effective barrier against the advance of reactionary forces, to reduce the effects of dictatorial power, to defend the 'small people' against the 'big,' to lay the basis for the indispensable regrouping of all republicans, it is necessary to assure the presence of an important Communist group in the National Assembly." The party leaders could have entertained no illusions, however, about the election. They had suffered serious losses in the referendum, were isolated politically throughout the country, and would be utterly unable to form effective alliances on the second ballot. In spite of all, a note of confidence was sounded by Thorez: "We can approach the new

[4] For the Communist party's position during the campaign, see *L'Humanité*, especially the issues of October 6, 10, and 23 and November 18, 1958.

phase of our struggle with resolution, and with the unshakeable certitude of final victory."

Socialists and Dissidents.   The *bureau* of the SFIO hailed the results of the referendum as marking "the beginning of the disintoxication of the working class." The party made a serious effort to reach disaffected Communists. On October 21 it was announced that two former leaders of the Communist party, Pierre Hervé and Auguste Lecoeur, along with seven other members of their group, had asked to join the SFIO. Hervé (former editor in chief of *L'Humanité*) and Lecoeur (former member of the powerful Secretariat of the Communist Party) in their letter of application for membership, denounced the Communist party's subservience to the Soviet Union. "It is only the SFIO," they concluded, "which can check reaction." The SFIO gave wide publicity to this "ralliement" as part of its campaign to recruit former Communist supporters who had voted Yes in the referendum. It is doubtful, however, that Socialist leaders really expected much success in winning over Communists. In an interview with an Italian journalist two days before the election, Guy Mollet said that the former Communist voters would most likely switch over first to the "fascists." He hoped that they would be ready for democratic socialism in time for the election of the second legislature of the Fifth Republic.

The party's main effort in the campaign was to present itself as General de Gaulle's most reliable democratic support against the ultras, the reactionaries, and the army. Every liberal move made by De Gaulle was seized upon as justification of the party's actions since May. Full support was accorded in particular to De Gaulle's Algerian policy, as defined in the Constantine speech. As one writer in *Le Populaire* put it: De Gaulle is not a Socialist, but in the Constantine speech "he uses a language that is familiar to us." The SFIO depicted itself on election posters as the "vanguard of the Fifth Republic."

During the campaign the Socialists consistently defended their record under the Fourth Republic, claiming that their attempts to bring about social progress were blocked by an unholy alliance of the Right and the Communists. The party naturally justified its actions during the difficult days of May—first by trying to defend the Republic against the insurrection, and then supporting De Gaulle's accession to power by legal means—as the only alternative to a military coup. "We were right," said Mollet during the campaign, "to have placed our confidence in the commitments accepted by General de Gaulle. Who, in effect, would have affirmed, last May 13, that six months later there would take place free elections for a renovated Parliament?" The electorate was urged to vote Socialist in order to support: a liberal policy in Algeria, as proposed by De Gaulle and contested by the ultras; a progressive, evolving French Community; and a policy of economic expansion and social justice. The Socialists then accepted the challenge laid down by the Independents. Replying to the attacks of Roger Duchet and other Independents, *Le Populaire* argued that the Right, which Mollet had earlier termed "the most stupid in the world," was the gravedigger of the Fourth Republic because of its colonial and economic policy.

The platform officially adopted by the party at the outset of the campaign reflected the usual revolutionary fervor. "Socialism is in effect a doctrine and an ethic that wishes to liberate man from all servitudes and permit him, with all respect for his personality, to develop and acquire the concrete liberties assuring the enjoyment and dignity of life." The platform warned against the dangers of recession, called for a liberal policy toward the overseas territories, flatly rejected integration in Algeria (because it does not correspond to the sincere desires of the population), and supported both the Atlantic Alliance and negotiations with Russia. The SFIO presented candidates in virtually all the districts of France. On the second ballot, departmental federations were advised to consider withdrawal when necessary to bar the route to the enemies of "republican democracy." Desistance in favor could be envisaged only for candidates supporting a "liberal policy in Algeria and overseas territories, a policy of economic expansion, full employment, and defense of purchasing power."

Guy Mollet wound up the Socialist campaign in an effective five-minute television appearance. After defending the record of his government, the Suez expedition, and past support for De Gaulle, he vaunted his nationalism. "It is normal for a Socialist to be a patriot because he must first have a free and democratic country if he dreams of enlarging that democracy tomorrow into a social democracy." Vote Socialist, he urged his audience, so that economic expansion will not be made at the expense of the workers. "I am confident. We are going to win, we, the Socialists!" [5]

---

[5] See *Le Populaire*, especially the issues of October 4–5, 14, 20, 21, and 27, and November 11, 19, 22, and 23, 1958.

As has been seen, disagreement with Mollet's policies led several Socialists to resign from the SFIO and create the Autonomous Socialist party (PSA) in September. Some of the former critics rallied to the new organization. The PSA bitterly attacked Mollet for his support of reaction in Algeria, and especially for his cohabitation with the Right under the auspices of De Gaulle. Their candidates called for a negotiated peace in Algeria, a revival of militant socialism on the home front, and severe punishment for the army officers and civil servants who challenged the Republic in May. The PSA also joined the *Union des Forces Démocratiques*. After agreement among the UFD's member organizations not to compete with each other in the same district, a total of ninety UFD candidates was presented.

The platform of the UFD [6] attempted to rally Socialists and Radicals around a central theme, which was neither nationalization nor liberalism—but *planning*. "Economic democracy is the installation of an economy functioning for and by the people. Its instrument is economic planning, that is, the conscious and selective orientation of important sectors of the economy in order to permit the satisfaction of the real needs of the nation and to assure full employment without inflation." The ideology of the UFD was of special appeal to young Socialists and Radicals who were dissatisfied with the traditional slogans of socialism and liberalism. On Algeria, the platform called for negotiations with the rebels and representative groups. The UFD entered the campaign as a kind of holding corporation whose component members preserved full liberty of action. Mendès-France, at the time anxious to avoid a break with the Radicals, emphasized that the UFD was little more than an electoral cartel. In fact, many important differences separated the chief members: the Union of Left Socialists (UGS) was militantly socialist in ideology, while the Radicals were not; the Radicals and PSA were much more hostile to the Communists than the UGS; and these groups were also far apart on foreign policy. The existence of so many internal divisions and tensions reduced considerably the UFD's effectiveness in the campaign.[7]

---

[6] The National Bureau of the UFD included Albert Chatelet, Edouard Depreux, Gilles Martinet, Mendès-France, Maurice Merlau-Ponty, François Mitterand, and Robert Verdier.

[7] *Le Monde*, November 14, 1958, and Claude Bourdet, "Voter contre le vide," *ibid.*, November 20, 1958, p. 5.

Radicals. The position of the Radical Socialist party during the campaign was formulated at a weekend meeting of the executive committee in October. Observers noted that it was one of the dullest meetings in the long history of the party. Although Mendès-France was present, his main interest was obviously elsewhere—with the UFD. His followers were in the minority. Speaking informally, he advised his friends to remain in the party in order to play the traditional role of a minority.

The president of the party, Félix Gaillard, could hardly conceal his pleasure over the adoption of the *scrutin d'arrondissement,* from which he expected "happy results." All Radical candidates were invited to conclude accords, not on the basis of party labels, but with regard to the particular candidates in each district and their attitude during the "events of May." Alliances were forbidden only with "fascists and Communists." Gaillard held out the hope that a cartel of the Center-Left (Radicals, RGR, Socialists, UDSR) might be negotiated, and he even appealed for General de Gaulle's intervention to bring it about. In a direct reference to Mendès, he declared that the party, long disrupted by futile conflicts, was now in a period of convalescence. He defined the party's true function as that of a center of gravity, a force of equilibrium, a party of government.

The "program" of the Radicals, as might be expected, was ambiguous enough to permit cooperation with both the Left and Right. On economic problems, Gaillard came out for a rise in the standard of living, to be achieved by classic economic methods. A special appeal was directed at the peasantry and youth. Jean Saint-Cyr, vice president of the party and former deputy, spoke at length on Radical plans for long-range agricultural developments and education. René Billères rekindled some of the old Radical fire in calling for a revolution in French education: by giving educational opportunities to the working class, and by making higher education more readily available to all students.[8]

The Radicals were in a poor position to take advantage of the electoral system they had so long reclaimed. Traditionally they benefited from *ballottage* because they could negotiate easily with either Left or Right, and because of the local influence of their deputies and senators. But in 1958 the party was hopelessly divided and the

[8] On the Radicals, see *L'Information Radicale-Socialiste,* November, 1958, which reprints the proceedings of the executive committee.

tide of public opinion was running strongly against all those who
had participated in the "system."

The dissident Radicals, led by André Morice, who had seceded
from the party, moved to the Right by joining forces with Bernard
Lafay's Republican Center. It was decided that the title of the national organization would be *Centre Républicain*—but each departmental federation was permitted to utilize other titles in addition. Morice selected Mendès-France as his chief target. The Center
in general campaigned vigorously on the issue of "French Algeria"
and sought its main support in the traditional middle-class clientele
of the Radical party.[9]

The Popular Republicans (MRP). The mood of MRP leaders
during the campaign was one of deep pessimism. They predicted
that the new electoral system would produce triangular contests—
between the Right, Center, and Communists—and that on the second
ballot the Center would be crushed, as happened in the by-elections
of 1956–57. Maurice-René Simmonet cried out that the single-member district sounded the end of political greatness in France. No one
could nourish the illusion, he wrote, that an Assembly elected by
scrutin d'arrondissement would vote for scientific research, investments in overseas territories, or the diffusion of French culture in
the world.

The morale of the MRP was also shaken by Georges Bidault's creation of the nationalist French Christian Democracy (DCF) in alliance with Duchet, Morice, and Lafay. Bidault attended and participated in the meeting of the MRP National Committee in October.
However, his status remained ambiguous: he accepted the final motion, but went ahead with his plans to run DCF candidates and
was not subjected to any disciplinary measures. Pierre-Henri Teitgen
pointed out that a Christian Democracy including Pinay, Morice,
Reynaud, and Pleven, as suggested by Bidault, would alienate Christian trade unionists, and move inexorably toward the Right. Shaken
by internal dissensions, the MRP seemed to enter the election thoroughly dispirited.

The National Committee met at Montrouge on October 13 to draw
up its platform. "To reconcile and conciliate devotion to spiritual
values and desire for social progress, there is the *raison d'être* of the
MRP." The party campaigned in favor of economic expansion, so-

---

[9] The special congress of the Radical dissidents is described in their journal, *La
République,* September 15, 1958.

cial and family progress, full support of De Gaulle's policy in Algeria (interpreted by the MRP as being opposed to the integration reclaimed by the ultras), and advocacy of European unity, especially the Common Market.

The MRP naturally disapproved of Duchet's attempt to convert the campaign into a straight fight between "nationals" and "Marxists," for fear that their votes would be lost to the Independents— which was precisely Duchet's intention. Under the circumstances it was impossible for the MRP to negotiate a national agreement with the other parties. Simonnet suggested that contacts be maintained with other groups, especially with a view to compromises on the second ballot. This policy was necessary because of the party's Center position: Obviously it would have to make deals on the Right or on the Left, depending upon local circumstances. After the campaign opened, the MRP vainly pleaded for an agreement among the national parties to withdraw on the second ballot in favor of the best-placed national candidate.[10]

Independents. The Independents, with Roger Duchet as their chief spokesman, took a firm grip on General de Gaulle's coattails. Algeria was Duchet's central theme in his talks around the nation. The Independents were even more extreme than the UNR, since they did not hesitate to call for complete integration and voiced apprehension over De Gaulle's liberal policy toward France's former colonies. Full approval was also expressed of the new constitution.

On economic policy, the party demanded "social and national liberalism," that is, sound money, renewal of confidence and investments by the business community, rise in the standard of living, and "genuine" social progress. Independent candidates took Western Germany as their ideal, arguing that France must likewise banish *dirigisme* and construct a new and dynamic "liberalism." The party expressed grave doubts regarding one point of the traditional Gaullist program: the association of labor and capital. Neither labor nor business, it was pointed out, supports this scheme. One Independent publicist timidly suggested that the idea could be tried out in those industries (estimated at 10 per cent of the total) in which unions and management were willing to cooperate. In its specific proposals the party favored a laissez-faire brand of liberalism, untarnished by Keynesian heresies.

---

[10] On the MRP, see the party's journal, *Forces Nouvelles*, October 4 and 18, 1958.

The main issue of the campaign, according to Duchet, was between the *dirigisme* of the Socialists and the liberalism demanded by the Independents. "I do not want Guy Mollet to be the prime minister of the next government," he declared. "France will remember that the Socialists have ruined the middle classes, crushed the taxpayers with heavy levies, killed the spirit of initiative, undermined free enterprise, multiplied the excesses of *Étatisme*, installed their members in the administrative services. She will recall that the Socialists accepted General de Gaulle only under constraint." A Socialist victory would lead to an economic recession, unemployment, and "wicked demogoguery." Besides, the Socialists were the "very men of the system." He called upon the country time and again to choose between a Socialist policy whose disastrous effects have been felt for thirteen years, and a liberal policy which has never been tried but which would assure the prosperity of the nation.[11]

As regards electoral tactics, the Independents wished to reach an agreement with Morice, Bidault, and Soustelle. Their plan was to eliminate competition among "national" candidates in order to head off the Communists and Socialists. The UNR was unwilling to accept a crusade against socialism for two principal reasons: Guy Mollet was a minister of General de Gaulle and a "national," and the party did not wish to be labelled as conservative. An accord was finally negotiated among Duchet, Morice, Lafay, and Bidault not to present candidates against each other in the same districts. The Independents were bitter over the UNR's refusal to participate in this electoral accord. In a series of sharply worded statements, Duchet accused the UNR of abusing the name of General de Gaulle and the cross of Lorraine. He was upset by the decision of the UNR to run military officers against well-known Independents (notably, Jacques Féron and Guy Petit) in middle-class districts, rather than against Communists in working-class areas. "These colonels are candidates of division," cried Duchet, who are doing harm to the national interest. They were incensed when the UNR maintained several candidates against Independents who had won on the first ballot, although, in general, satisfactory agreements were negotiated wherever there was a Communist danger.

---

[11] See Roger Duchet, "La politique des Indépendants," *Le Monde*, November 18, 1958, p. 2. Also *Ibid.*, October 21, 28, and November 14, 20, 1958, and the party's journal *France Indépendante*, especially the issues of July 28, September 22, October 6, 13, and 20, November 10, 17, and 28, and December 8, 1958.

Poujadists. On October 19, Pierre Poujade declared before his party's congress that the UDCA would *not* present any candidates in the elections, but would maintain contact with all those who wished to constitute a "Front of Liberty" against the Socialists. A week later, he changed his mind and decided to present candidates "in all the districts of France" on a "Defense of Liberties" ticket. Poujade himself ran in a district of Maine-et-Loire which voted heavily for his party in 1956. Although his campaign was marked by occasional outbursts of verbal violence, on the whole he attempted to take a moderate stand. His principal argument was that the Common Market sounded the death knell of small and family enterprise in France. It was evident that his movement was fast losing its appeal throughout the country.[12]

Union for the New Republic (UNR). The position of the UNR with respect to General de Gaulle differed radically from that of the old RPF. De Gaulle was personally in charge of the *Rassemblement*. He chose candidates, convoked and presided over meetings of the executive, supervised the functioning of all local units by means of delegates, and laid down policy. But in 1958 De Gaulle undertook emphatically to dissociate himself from *all* political parties and even from the campaign itself. He declared in his press conference of October 24: "Everyone realizes that I do not desire, that I cannot, concern myself in any direct fashion with this competition. The mission that the country has confided to me rules out the possibility that I might take a stand. . . . This impartiality obliges me to insist categorically that my name, even in the form of an adjective, not be used by any group or candidate." [13]

In spite of De Gaulle's disclaimer, his former *compagnons* of the RPF set about rapidly to create a new party of fidelity to the General. The UNR was organized immediately after the referendum by the fusion of several existing Gaullist groups.[14] On October 3, Roger Frey was elected secretary-general. The Central Committee included Jacques Chaban-Delmas, Michel Debré, Jacques Soustelle, Edmond Michelet, Léon Delbecque, Pierre Picard, and Albin Chalandon. Within a month the UNR was a national party, with local affiliates and candidates throughout France. The supporters of

---

[12] *Le Monde,* October 21, p. 5, October 22, p. 3, November 6, p. 2, and November 18, p. 3, 1958.

[13] *Le Monde,* October 25, 1958, p. 4.

[14] Soustelle's *Union pour le Renouveau Français* (the successor of USRAF), Delbecque's *Convention Républicaine,* and Chaban-Delmas' *Union Civique pour La Ve République,* and the Social Republican party.

the UNR made up a heterogeneous group: left-wing Gaullists who sought to use the General's prestige and power to implement social and economic reforms not too different from those proposed by Mendès-France, activists who helped touch off the May 13 coup, latecomers and opportunists who deserted the classic Right, and a large number of young people attracted to the UNR out of national-ist fervor. It was a hastily formed group and few expected a spectac-ular electoral success. Specialists at the Ministry of the Interior esti-mated that the party would be able to elect perhaps 75 deputies—100 at the most.

The UNR considered it unnecessary to present a precise program during the campaign. It rather sought to strike a posture: absolute fidelity to General de Gaulle. It proclaimed its "integral accept-ance" of all political positions taken by Charles de Gaulle since June 18, 1940 in all domains—foreign policy, Algeria, constitutional reform, association of capital and labor, and so on. Chaban-Delmas summed up the platform of the UNR in one concise sentence: "What is really at stake in the election of November 23 will be to elect men faithful to General de Gaulle, that is, parliamentarians determined to adopt that political behavior which is most effective in order to support the chief of the government." To illustrate its fidelity, the UNR decided not to run candidates against the men chosen by De Gaulle as his ministers, whatever their political affiliations might be.

Roger Frey studiously refused to be drawn into the ancient quar-rels of the Left and Right. "We are neither Gaullists of the Right nor Gaullists of the Left," he commented drily, "but just Gaullists." The UNR, he continued, will function as the link between Left and Right, accepting the best elements of each in order to further the work of Charles de Gaulle. The party, "anxious to be above all an effective aid for General de Gaulle, expects to be in the coming months and years that *party of government,* that republican mass of maneuver which will permit a balancing of political forces, and which will also be the great *party of movement* which France needs."

Soustelle's aggressive leadership within the UNR early led to quar-rels among its leaders. Some Social Republican parliamentarians were offended at not being consulted on investitures, and in any case were reluctant to make way for newcomers. Edmond Michelet, who represented a Left tendency, was critical of selections made by Delbecque's Republican convention, and did not wish to accord the UNR label to such activists as Jean-Baptiste Biaggi. The chief con-troversies involved the matter of alliances with other parties.

Soustelle had arrived at mutually satisfactory arrangements in investing candidates with the leaders of the Independents, Christian Democrats, and Republican Center. Other leaders of the UNR, including Michel Debré and apparently General de Gaulle himself, objected that the party would thus be identified exclusively with the classic Right. Roger Frey was then authorized to make contacts with all "national" parties on a local level, rather than to negotiate country-wide alliances with the Right. However, Soustelle had already made agreements in thirty-four districts before this decision was pronounced. At the last minute the accord between the UNR, Bidault, Duchet, and Morice broke down in the Department of Seine, and all groups immediately presented their own candidates. In the Department of Rhône, Soustelle waited until one minute before midnight of the deadline date to file his UNR list; the Independents respected the accord, and there was no competition between the UNR and Independents in that department.

The UNR was flanked on the Left by the Center of Republican Reform (CRR), whose candidates were self-proclaimed "Left Gaullists." They placed particular emphasis on the association of labor and capital. CRR candidates (80 compared to 366 UNR) denounced the "fascists of Algeria" who, they contended, did not recognize De Gaulle as their legitimate chief. On the Right the UNR found itself challenged by the "Renovation of the Republic" and "Renovation and Fidelity" together with assorted extremist groups representing the militant spirit of May 13. These rival movements of the Left and Right seemed to strengthen the UNR by affording evidence of its professed position in the Center.[15]

The Campaign in Algeria

The government created a Central Control Commission of Elections in Algeria, presided over by M. Hoppenot, with the mission of assuring a climate of large and free competition for all points of view. General de Gaulle issued specific instructions to both the commission and the army that all candidates were to be guaranteed the right to express their views and defend their program, including their positions regarding the status and future of Algeria. De Gaulle thus

---

[15] On the formation of the UNR and its electoral tactics, see *Année Politique*, 1958, pp. 129–30, 136. For the views of the leadership, see Roger Frey, "L'UNR, parti du gouvernement," *Le Monde*, November 21, 1958, p. 4, and the statements by Frey, Chaban-Delmas, and Michelet in *Voici Pourquoi*, November 20, 1958, pp. 5, 6, 11. The views of the Left Gaullists were presented by J. C. Servan-Schreiber, "La Gauche avec De Gaulle," *Le Monde*, November 19, 1958, p. 2.

hoped that out of a genuine conflict of political opinion would emerge freely elected representatives of the Algerian people. In a message to General Salan, he stated: "I consider it of extreme importance that there be a genuine competition, that is, that there can be rival lists. . . . The goal is to permit an Algerian political elite to reveal itself freely. It is thus that the political void which opened the way to the rebellion could be filled." The same message ordered officers to withdraw from the Committees of Public Safety.

Several "liberals," including Jacques Chevallier, Alain Savary, and Fonlupt-Espéraber, investigated the possibility of presenting themselves as candidates in Algeria. They all eventually renounced the attempt, contending that the conditions for free elections simply did not exist. Fonlupt-Espéraber (MRP), in a telegram to De Gaulle, requested the postponement of elections in Algeria. He declared later that the administrative and civil authorities of the department in which he considered running had constituted a list that was bound to win. In some cases, he said, the army sponsored phantom opposition lists to give the impression that the voters had a free choice. There was no point, he concluded, in flouting the democratic process by participating in rigged elections. Alain Savary (PSA) likewise found that Moslems lived in fear of being arrested for political activities. "The conditions for the functioning of a democratic system," he declared, "are not now in existence in Algeria."

The Committee of Public Safety of Algeria designated a Committee of Wise Men (*Comité des Sages*) to endorse lists and eliminate unseemly competition between "nationals." However, the withdrawal of army officers from the Committees of Public Safety brought into the open deep rivalries; the "wise men" were unable to work out satisfactory agreements among the extremists. Metropolitan observers pointed out that the "system" in Algiers was far more confused than anything under the Fourth Republic. Fifty-two lists were filed in the eighteen districts of Algeria by the deadline date, November 10. Several were disqualified by the Control Commission, including one with the intriguing title, "Crush the Rebels Above All" (*Pour l'écrasement préalable des rebelles*). Eventually the field was narrowed to forty-eight lists, almost all representing various shades of rightist opinion.[16]

---

[16] De Gaulle's instructions to General Salan are reprinted in *Année Politique, 1958*, p. 562. The statements by Savary and Fonlupt-Espéraber are in *Le Monde*, November 9–10, 1958, p. 2; and November 16–17, 1958, p. 3.

In spite of De Gaulle's instructions to the Control Commission, and even assuming that the army performed its role with scrupulous honesty (which was not the case in many districts), the campaign in Algeria was devoid of genuine political significance. The FLN boycotted and disrupted the campaign, the army was compelled to use force in assuring candidates freedom of movement and expression, and the voters in general had an extremely limited choice. In most districts the contest was between a "moderate" list favoring De Gaulle's policy, a list sponsored by the Committees of Public Safety and the army, and lists headed by ultras. The campaign was thus exclusively between assorted supporters of De Gaulle and extreme integrationists.

The Results

The results of the two ballots held on November 23 and November 30, as was the case with the referendum, at first glance appear to have transformed the structure of French politics. The UNR won 189 out of the 465 seats at stake in the Metropolis. The Communists, losing 95 per cent of their seats, were reduced to 10 deputies (compared to 145 in 1956); the Socialists retained only 40 seats (88 in 1956); all the rival factions of the once powerful Radical party held 37 seats (compared to 74 in 1956); the MRP together with the Christian Democrats did better than anticipated, retaining 57 of their 71 seats. The Independents emerged as the second largest political group in the Assembly, with 120 deputies (a gain of 24). The Poujadists, who polled over two million votes and won 52 seats in 1956, disappeared from the political scene. However, the popular vote reveals greater stability on the part of the electorate than is indicated by the results in seats won.

The main features of the first ballot in terms of the popular vote were the relative success of the UNR (17.6 per cent of the vote, making it the most favored party in negotiations for the runoff), the decline of the Communist party (which lost 1,650,000 votes, going from 25.7 per cent in 1956 to 18.9 per cent in 1958), the weakening of the Radicals, the eclipse of the Poujadists, and the relatively high number of abstentionists. Although the number of registered voters increased by half a million over 1956, the number of those who cast ballots decreased by one million. Abstentions amounted to 22.9 per cent, compared to 15 per cent in the referendum; 17.3 per cent in January, 1956; 19.8 per cent in June, 1951; 21.9 per cent in November, 1946; and 18.2 per cent in June, 1946. Thus, over four million voters or 20 per cent of the total (1,650,000 former Communists, half a million Radicals, and two million Poujadists) shifted about among

RPF VOTES
1951

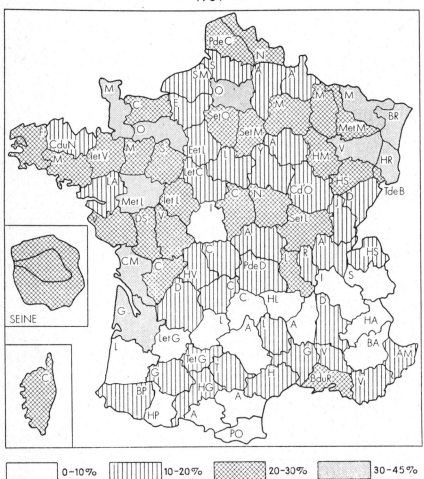

| | 0–10% | | 10–20% | | 20–30% | | 30–45% |

the parties *or into abstention* as compared with the elections of 1956.

On the national level, the Socialists and MRP (if the Christian Democrats are included) maintained their popular strength although the geographic distribution of their voting support was altered. In 1958 there were two big winners compared to 1956: the Independents and associated moderates, who gained one million votes (from 14.5 per cent to 19.9 per cent of the total); and the UNR, which won 2,550,000 votes over and above the 950,000 received by the Social Republicans in 1956. To what extent did the former

UNR VOTES
1958

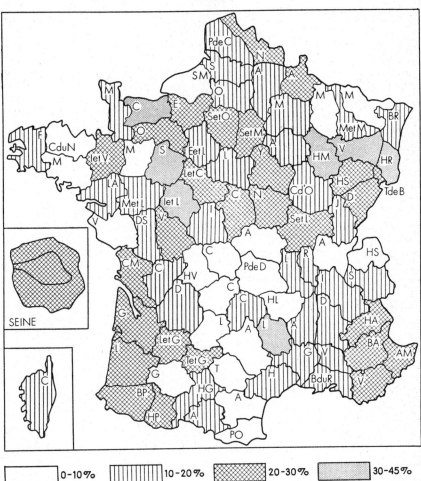

Communists, Radicals, and Poujadists go directly over to the UNR, and to what extent did they vote Socialist or MRP, an equal number of whom were displaced toward the Independents and UNR?

In the absence of reliable public opinion polls, this problem cannot be resolved with certainty. The UNR received 3,604,000 votes on the first ballot, compared to 4,266,000 for the RPF in 1951. With half a million votes fewer than the 1951 Gaullist party, the UNR spread its strength a little more evenly throughout the nation. Like the RPF, the UNR was strong in the east, west, and Paris region, but was

COMMUNIST VOTES
1956

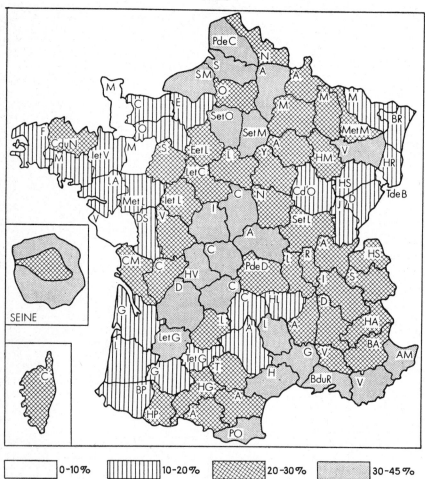

| | 0-10% | | 10-20% | | 20-30% | | 30-45% |

weaker than the RPF in traditionally conservative departments, such as Morbihan, Côtes-du-Nord, Mayenne, and Côte d'Or. On the other hand, the UNR penetrated south of the Loire more successfully than the RPF, particularly along the east coast of the Mediterranean, the Pyrénées, and the Toulouse region. In twenty-five departments (mainly in the center, south, and west) the Poujadists rolled up over 12 per cent of the vote in 1956. In six of these departments (Lot-et-Garonne, Tarn-et-Garonne, Ardèche, Isère, Yonne, and Indre-et-Loire) the UNR improved noticeably over the 1951 RPF. In gen-

COMMUNIST VOTES
1958

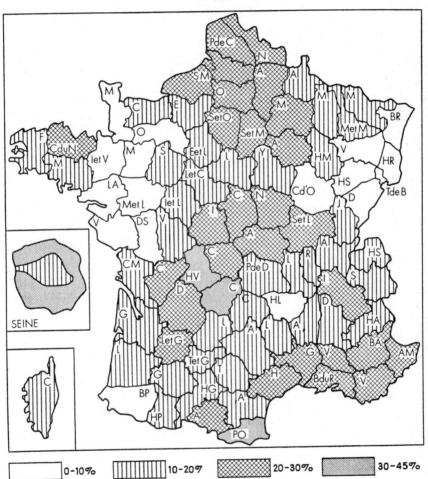

0-10%   10-20%   20-30%   30-45%

eral it appears that the former Poujadists who went to the polls in 1958 split fairly evenly between the UNR and the Independents.

No nation-wide pattern can be discerned regarding those who deserted the Communist party in 1958. Former Communists who did not abstain seem to have gone over to either the Socialists or the UNR, with variations according to local circumstances. In 19 departments the Communists lost appreciably and the Socialists gained over 3 per cent of the total. Communist losses and Socialist gains (in percentage of the total vote) in Bouches-du-Rhône were 8 and 7.2

VOTING AND POLITICAL PARTIES IN 1951, 1956, AND 1958

	1958 (First Ballot)		1956		1951	
	Votes	*Per Cent*	*Votes*	*Per Cent*	*Votes*	*Per Cent*
Registered.........	27,236,491	..	26,772,255	..	24,530,523	..
Voters.............	20,489,709	..	21,490,886	..	19,129,064	..
Abstentions........	..	22.9	..	17.3	..	19.8
Communists........	3,882,204	18.9	5,532,631	25.7	5,056,605	25.4
Socialists..........	3,167,354	15.5	3,180,656	14.8	2,744,842	14.3
Radicals *.........	2,695,287	12.9	3,325,870	15.3	1,925,976	10.0
UNR and Gaullists...	3,603,958	17.6	948,854	4.4	4,125,492	21.5
MRP.............	2,378,788	11.6	2,374,221	11.0	2,369,778	12.3
Independents and moderates........	4,092,600	19.9	3,086,414	14.3	2,656,995	13.5
Extreme Right......	669,518	3.3	2,816,805	13.1	..	..

* With dissidents, Republican Center, and diverse Left.

FIRST AND SECOND BALLOTS, ELECTION OF NOVEMBER, 1958 AND DISTRIBUTION OF SEATS IN NATIONAL ASSEMBLY

Parties	Seats in National Assembly		1958			
	1958	1956	*2nd Ballot*	*Per Cent*	*1st Ballot*	*Per Cent*
Communists..........	10	145	3,741,384	20.7	3,882,204	18.9
Socialists.............	40	88	2,484,417	13.8	3,167,354	15.5
Radicals *............	37	74	1,398,409	7.7	2,695,287	12.9
MRP and Christian Democrats..........	44 + 13	71	1,365,064	7.5	2,378,788	11.6
UNR................	189	16	4,769,052	26.4	3,603,958	17.6
Independents and moderates..............	120 + 12	95	4,250,038	23.6	4,092,600	19.9
Extreme Right........	1	52	..	..	669,518	3.3

* With dissidents, Republican Center, and diverse Left.

per cent, respectively; in Drôme, 10.4 and 8.3 per cent; in Indre, 8.5 and 7.8 per cent; in Saône-et-Loire, 6.6 and 6.1 per cent; and in Vaucluse, 6.5 and 4.7 per cent. Socialist advances in these departments were probably at the expense of the Communists.

The UNR did exceptionally well (especially as compared to the 1951 RPF vote) in six departments where both the Communists

PERCENTAGE OF SOCIALIST AND COMMUNIST VOTES, 1956 AND 1958

Departments	Communist Votes		Socialist Votes	
	1956	1958	1956	1958
Ain	24.6	15.8	10.1	2.5
Aisne	33.9	23.1	20.1	22.7
Allier	34.1	28.1	21.9	21.3
Alpes (Basses-)	28	22.1	36.3	25.5
Alpes (Hautes-)	25.1	17.2	13.5	8.6
Alpes-Maritimes	33.8	23.2	4.6	2.8
Ardèche	26.2	19.8	7.5	10.7
Ardennes	28.2	19.5	34.3	13.3
Ariège	27.4	22.5	29.7	33.2
Aube	29.1	20.5	16	15.9
Aude	23.5	18.5	31.5	33.1
Aveyron	12.1	10.2	21.5	17
Belfort (Terr. de)	35.2 *	7.6	18.2	16.1
Bouches-du-Rhône	35	27	22.8	30
Calvados	19.6	12.9	14.1	8.9
Cantal	17	12.4	21.2	16.1
Charente	29.7	23.1	11.3	6.9
Charente-Maritime	20.7	14.9	10.8	9
Cher	36.2	28.9	10.3	11.1
Corrèze	36.7	31	17.3	20.4
Corse	22.6	10.6	3.4	2.2
Côte-d'Or	18.5	9.9	17.2	14.8
Côtes-du-Nord	24.4	20.5	16.3	10.5
Creuse	47 *	29.4	21.2	28.9
Dordogne	30.4	22.7	15.5	19.3
Doubs	14.1	9.8	26.2	21.8
Drôme	29.7	19.3	12.5	20.8
Eure	19.5	15	4.9	8.6
Eure-et-Loir	20.6	14.6	9.7	10.1
Finistère	18.6	13.8	16.6	14.2
Gard	34.9	27.7	16.3	19.9
Garonne (Haute-)	23	16.3	21.8	24.3
Gers	19.9	15.8	21.3	22.6
Gironde	16.7	12.8	16.9	19.8
Hérault	30.7	24.8	16.7	23.2
Ille-et-Vilaine	13.4	7.6	8.8	4.9
Indre	32.5	24	2.5	10.3
Indre-et-Loire	23.6	17	15.4	11.9
Isère	28.9	20.3	14.4	15.2
Jura	18.3	12.9	1.7	8.7
Landes	19.7	14.3	36.3	30.1
Loire-et-Cher	27.9	18.6	15	19.5
Loire	23.4	16.6	16.5	6.8
Loire (Haute-)	14.2	9.7	14.6	17.6
Loire-Atlantique	13.5	9.1	16.7	12.4
Loiret	22.8	17.8	12.6	9.7
Lot	24.9	19.4	19.7	18.8
Lot-et-Garonne	30.4	21.9	8.3	6.6
Lozère	32.9 *	10.1	5.1	15.9
Maine-et-Loire	12.6	8.1	7.5	8.3

PERCENTAGE OF SOCIALIST AND COMMUNIST VOTES, 1956 AND 1958—CONTINUED

Departments	Communist Votes		Socialist Votes	
	1956	1958	1956	1958
Manche	8.2	4.7	21.9	11.6
Marne	29.2	20.8	10.5	11.3
Marne (Haute-)	25.6	15.8	5.9	6
Mayenne	7.8	6.4	8.6	9.9
Meurthe-et-Moselle	27.1	15.8	15.1	12.2
Meuse	21.9	12.1	15.5	12.8
Morbihan	16.2	11	17.4	12.7
Moselle	19.3	10.4	4.7	4.5
Nièvre	29.3	23.4	18.3	19
Nord	27.3	21.1	28.4	29.7
Oise	27.5	21.3	11.3	12.1
Orne	12.9	7.2	14.9	2.1
Pas-de-Calais	30.8	24.3	33.5	32.3
Puy-de-Dôme	21.3	15	17.8	27
Pyrénées (Basses-)	14.2	8.4	10.4	11.4
Pyrénées (Hautes-)	22.3	15.2	15.4	12.2
Pyrénées-Orientales	34.8	30	26.7	35
Rhin (Bas-)	11.7	7.7	5.5	6.2
Rhin (Haut-)	12	6.9	19.9	16.6
Rhône	24.4	16.7	8.1	9.8
Saône (Haute-)	16.7	9.2	4.7	2.9
Saône-et-Loire	29.1	22.5	12.1	18.2
Sarthe	20	15.2	18.1	11.9
Savoie	26.7	11.4	8.6	14.1
Savoie (Haute-)	20.6	12.3	15.9	7.8
Seine	30.1	25.2	10.3	12.1
Seine-Maritime	30.6	21.8	12.7	11
Seine-et-Marne	30.6	22	11.6	9.5
Seine-et-Oise	34.1	25.9	9.4	11.4
Sèvres (Deux-)	13.1	4.1	12	10.5
Somme	32.1	26.6	24.6	27.2
Tarn	20.1	16.2	20.5	20.8
Tarn-et-Garonne	19.6	14.2	6.7	12.7
Var	35	23.6	22.8	23.9
Vaucluse	27.6	21.1	10.6	15.3
Vendée	6.9	6.9	17.1	5.4
Vienne	22.5	15.5	5.5	6.5
Vienne (Haute-)	35.8	33.6	25.7	49.8
Vosges	33 *	7.6	...	4.8
Yonne	22.4	18.7	9.4	12.4

* Allied with *"Progressistes."*

and Socialists lost. The pattern is clear in Basses-Alpes, where the Communist share of the total vote fell by 6 per cent and the SFIO share by 11 per cent; in the Hautes-Alpes, where the percentages were 8 and 5, respectively; Doubs, 4.3 and 4.4 per cent; Landes, 5.4 and 6.2 per cent; and Hautes-Pyrénées, 7.1 and 3.2 per cent. In none of these departments was there any significant Poujadist vote in 1956. The UNR's support in these areas doubtless came from the Left.

In 26 departments (including almost the entire northeast and Paris industrial regions) the Communist vote declined sharply without any corresponding increase in the Socialist vote, yet the UNR did not score any noticeable gains as compared with the RPF. What happened in these departments to the former RPF vote from 1951 days? If the UNR had held on to the old Gaullist vote, it would have made spectacular gains in all those departments where the Communists lost and the Socialists either remained steady or lost also.

It may be inferred that many Gaullists who turned away from the RPF after 1951 remained with the Independents and the MRP in 1958. The composition of the UNR vote was thus different from that of the RPF: It included a much greater number of former Communists, Socialists, and probably Radicals, along with Poujadists—and, in general, a smaller group of traditional conservatives. The UNR was less a party of the Center than a meeting of extremes.

The Second Ballot

The specialists at the Ministry of the Interior had expected that only from 60 to 80 seats would be won by an absolute majority on the first ballot. In fact, only 39 candidates were so elected. Two former prime ministers, Mendès-France and Joseph Laniel, suffered the ignominy of defeat on the first ballot.

The electoral law provided that no new candidacy could be entered between the two ballots and maintenance of candidacies had to be signified to the authorities by Tuesday midnight. Although candidates could retire after that date, they could not present themselves on November 30 without having gone through the formality. Many well-known personalities of the Fourth Republic immediately announced their decision to withdraw.[17] The Communist party maintained most of its candidates, but carried out its previously announced decision to desist in favor of those who campaigned for No in the referendum. Among the Socialists and Radicals who benefited from Communist desistance were Mme. Lempereur (who refused the support, however), Notebart (in Nord), Tanguy-Prigent

---

[17] These included André Le Troquer (SFIO, Paris), Pierre-Henri Teitgen (MRP, Rennes), Bourgès-Maunoury (Radical, Toulouse), Edouard Daladier (Radical, Avignon), Edouard Bonnefous (UDSR, Seine-et-Oise), Guy Petit (Independent, Bayonne), Alfred Coste-Floret (MRP, Toulouse), and Charles Hernu (Radical, Paris).

and Mao (in Finistère), and the Radical Baylet, and Mitterand.
Even though their conditions were not met, Communists also de-
sisted in favor of the Socialist opponents of Paul Reynaud and Léon
Delbecque. In return, the Socialists withdrew their candidates
(who, be it noted, did *not* desist specifically in favor of the Communists) in two districts of Nord where Communists Ramette and
Musmeaux had a chance of winning. Rivalry between Communists
and Socialists was particularly intense in Bouches-du-Rhône since
the Socialist federation of that department, under Gaston Defferre's
leadership, had waged an active campaign for the Yes.

The UNR tended to maintain its candidates, frequently against
better-placed Independents and moderates, wherever there was no
danger of a Communist victory. The Independents, who were
prepared to withdraw in all cases in favor of the best-placed "national" candidate, were bitter over the UNR's reluctance to recipro-
cate. There were nonetheless a number of agreements between the
UNR and moderates, Radicals, and Socialists, and a few instances of
MRP accords with either Socialists, moderates, or the UNR. Of the
426 contests on November 30, over 50 were straight fights between
two candidates, generally a Communist versus a UNR member. In
a few cases, the battle was between a moderate and a Socialist. In
half the districts there were triangular contests, usually a UNR candidate, a Communist, and either a moderate, Socialist, or MRP candidate. A total of 1,332 candidates presented themselves on the second ballot in 426 districts, or an average of three to four competitors
for each seat.

On the second ballot the UNR victory was nation-wide. It won
all the seats in five departments, 33 out of 55 seats in Seine, 8 out of
10 in Gironde, and 12 out of 23 in Nord. In spite of the UNR success,
the Independents and moderates maintained their positions surprisingly well. The big losers were the Radicals and, above all, the
Communists and Socialists. The Assembly was literally one of the
"newest" in French history. Only one fourth of the outgoing deputies from Metropolitan France were re-elected. The new broom
swept clean. The voters seemed to be more interested in punishing
participants in the "system" than in distinguishing nicely between
those who tried to make it work and those who sought to bring about
its downfall.

The isolation of the Communists worked invariably to their dis-
advantage when the field narrowed on the second ballot. Typical

was the experience of Mme. Jeannette Vermeersch, the wife of Maurice Thorez and an important party figure in her own right, in the Goutte-d'Or district of Paris. On the first ballot she received almost twice as many votes as her nearest rival: 11,455 (a decrease of 3,000 from 1956, however), compared to 6,786 for the UNR candidate, 5,753 for the Socialist, 4,562 for the MRP, 4,194 for the Christian Democrat, and about 5,000 for diverse moderates and extremists. On the following Sunday, the UNR and Socialist maintained their candidacy while all the others withdrew in order to "bar the route to Communism." The result on the second and decisive ballot: the UNR elected with 20,160 votes, compared to 12,545 for Vermeersch and 4,985 for the Socialists. The successful UNR candidate, Jean Bernasconi, was a thirty-year-old worker in the Simca automobile factory and an active trade unionist. The massing of non-Communist votes behind UNR candidates is also illustrated by the results in the 13th, 36th and 45th districts of Paris:

13th District	*36th District*	*45th District*
First Ballot	First Ballot	First Ballot.
Garaudy, Comm...12,030	L'Huillier, Comm..17,773	Duclos, Comm.....21,049
Sanson, UNR..... 7,309	Devaud, UNR....14,139	Profichet, UNR....18,218
Independent...... 5,748	Republican Center. 7,897	Socialist..........10,416
Socialist.......... 3,460	Socialist.......... 4,071	Diverse.......... 2,538
Diverse.......... 7,700	Diverse.......... 7,700	
Second Ballot	Second Ballot	Second Ballot
Sanson..........22,181	Devaud..........29,315	Profichet..........29,662
Garaudy..........13,767	L'Huillier.........21,383	Duclos............21,252

The Socialists also beat the Communists in many straight fights, for example in the 39th and 52d districts of Paris:

39th District	*52d District*
First Ballot	First Ballot
Fajon, Comm................22,387	Vaillant-Couturier, Comm.....21,550
Privet, Soc................... 7,218	Lacroix, Socialist............11,595
Independent................. 6,536	UNR..................... 9,159
UNR................... 5,716	MRP..................... 6,150
Diverse................... 8,300	Diverse................... 4,000
Second Ballot	Second Ballot
Privet......................24,932	Lacroix.....................28,323
Fajon......................24,451	Vaillant-Couturier..........23,969

Rare Communist successes were made possible by the failure of Socialists, UNR candidates, and moderates to settle their differences and "bar the route." In the 3d district of Allier, a Communist was elected with 17,258 votes against 17,142 for a Socialist and 10,-

997 for a moderate. Similarly, in the 7th district of Bouches-du-Rhône, the Communist won with 14,266 as against 12,177 for a Socialist and 10,887 for a UNR candidate.

Communist desistance in Finistère and Nord in favor of Socialists who had campaigned for the No did little good. In the 4th district of Finistère, Tanguy-Prigent lost to a UNR candidate by a narrow 1,500-vote margin, while in the 6th district of the same department, Mao was overwhelmed by the Independent. Communist support in the 5th district of Nord did not prevent Notebart's loss to a UNR candidate by over 6,000 votes. On the other hand, Communist decisions to maintain separate candidacies prevented a number of Socialists from winning seats, especially in Bouches-du-Rhône. Thus:

5th Bouches-du-Rhône	*8th Bouches-du-Rhône*	*3d Hérault*
Ripert, Independent..15,361	Marchetti, UNR.....18,739	Cerf-Lurie, UNR....16,905
Massias, Socialist....12,761	Deferre, Socialist....18,535	J. Moch, Socalist....15,244
Communist.........10,678	Communist.........10,825	Communist.........13,676

The chief factor in the UNR success on the second ballot was its ability to outdraw the Center parties, even in districts where moderates had won on the first ballot and so would presumably benefit from republican discipline. For example:

8th Seine	*23d Seine*	*2d Cantal*
First Ballot	First Ballot	First Ballot
Vigier, Ind........18,463	Lafay, Rep. Cen...15,118	Laurens, Ind.......11,119
Lepidi, UNR......16,617	Independent...... 7,544	Sagette, UNR..... 9,182
Communist.......12,840	Vaschetti, UNR... 7,461	MRP............. 9,150
Socialist.......... 6,308	Communist...... 4,549	Socialist.......... 4,127
Radical.......... 3,972	Socialist.......... 3,349	Communist....... 4,007
Diverse Right..... 3,600	Diverse........... 1,307	
Second Ballot	Second Ballot	Second Ballot
Lepidi............22,885	Vaschetti.........17,397	Sagette...........21,698
Vigier............21,662	Lafay............15,475	Laurens..........13,111
Communist.......15,226	Communist....... 5,014	Communist....... 4,021

The runoff system precipitated an evolution of public opinion by compelling a choice from among a restricted range of candidates. In most cases the UNR was preferred over the moderates by those who had voted for non-Communist Left parties on the first ballot.

The election in Algeria produced few surprises. In Sétif a Socialist list was elected by a margin of 4,000 votes, and in Oran the UNR list defeated the list of "Renovation and French Algeria" led by General Miquel. However, lists headed by Pierre Lagaillarde and Marc Lauriol were elected in Algiers over more moderate rivals.

Most of the 71 deputies from Algeria and Sahara advocated outright integration, while some contented themselves with support of De Gaulle's policies.

The shifts in the popular vote were magnified greatly by the single-member district system. In terms of representation in the National Assembly the three members of the prewar Popular Front (Communists, Socialists, and Radicals) suffered severe losses—going from about 300 seats to 87. The drop in the total popular vote of these three parties was not as drastic: from 55 per cent in 1956 to 47.3 per cent on the first ballot in 1958.[18]

The difficulties of the Socialists, who succeeded in maintaining their popular vote, were due primarily to the system of runoffs. The pre-election hopes of the Socialists were reasonable: The SFIO was bound to emerge as the strongest competitor of the Communists and would therefore benefit throughout the nation on the second ballot as the best-placed "republican" party. But the calculation went wrong. The Communists lost so heavily that in numerous districts there was no possibility of their winning seats; moderates and the UNR maintained their candidates and beat the Socialists. In addition, the UNR, in outdistancing the SFIO, became the chief beneficiary of anticommunism wherever the danger of a Communist victory required concentration of forces.

The Communist defeat was caused only in part by the electoral system. For the first time since the war the party lost a sizable portion of its supporters. In the past, the French Communist party had little trouble in keeping the allegiance of its adherents in competition with socialists and liberals. The success of the Mendésist Radicals in 1956 was at the expense of the moderates and conservatives—the Communist bastions were altogether insensible to promises of "New Deal" reforms, a planned economy, and social justice. The election of 1958 seemed to vindicate the opinion expressed by General de Gaulle to a visiting delegation of veterans shortly before the events of May. He commented that it is fruitless to debate with Communists since they are impervious to intellectual arguments. The only way to make a dent on the Communist party, he continued, is to champion "independence for France in all domains." The

---

[18] Discrepancies in the nomenclature of political groups and their political affiliations make it difficult to compare election results. For our tabulations we have relied upon the excellent statistical summaries in *Le Monde*. We have also consulted the *Année Politique, 1958* and the relevant communications of the Ministry of the Interior.

French Communist party, unaffected by Mendès-France's liberalism and Guy Mollet's democratic socialism, was severely shaken by De Gaulle's charismatic presence and emotional brand of nationalism.

The election was a great success for the Independents and the UNR. But these parties were not given any specific mandate by the electorate. The UNR, as has been pointed out, sought only to identify itself as a loyal support for General de Gaulle. In a sense, the very absence of a program helped make possible its victory. Most electors obviously felt that a vote for the UNR was in effect an endorsement of De Gaulle, and did not trouble with details. The spirit of the referendum carried over into the legislative election. On November 23 and 30 the people said Yes once again to General de Gaulle.

As in the referendum, the Yes to De Gaulle covered a multitude of ambiguities and divisions. Some voted UNR or Independent in order to express approval of full integration, while others wished to back up General de Gaulle as the only person capable of enforcing a liberal policy in Algeria. Most of the parties vied with each other in supporting General de Gaulle—but no agreement among them was discernible on the specific issues before the nation: Algeria, role of the army, laissez faire and planning, state aid to religious schools, and so on. The army believed its role on May 13 had been vindicated by the electorate, while the liberals hoped that civilian power was once again supreme. Public opinion responded to the magnetic quality of General de Gaulle's leadership. The cleavages within the body politic—between liberals and conservatives, communists and democrats, *laiques* and the religious, nationalists and "Europeans," imperialists and anti-imperialists, republicans and antirepublicans were only momentarily transcended.

Part Three

Gaullism in Action

CHAPTER **XIV**

Launching the Institutions

THE SUCCESS of the new institutions obviously depended on the new men entering the political scene, the manner in
which the principles and the letter of the constitution were interpreted, the balance of the political forces, and above all the use of
the constitutional machinery in solving pressing national problems.
Over and above these considerations loomed the most critical test:
how to legitimize the new constitution by reintegrating into the
political process a public opinion that throughout the period of the
Fourth Republic had remained indifferent and apathetic except for
occasional outbursts of protest taking the form of strong support for
antirepublican and antiparliamentarian parties. Opinion had not
been given the opportunity to focus on national issues and enforce
responsibility upon the policy makers. The result was demoraliza-
tion and gradually alienation of the public. Was the new regime to
provide the much-needed bridge between opinion and government?

The Presidency

After the referendum and the elections in which the self-
styled Gaullist party, the UNR, won an unexpected victory, there
was little doubt that De Gaulle would assume the office that had
been tailored after him—the presidency. Past experience had shown
that he was not at home in the Assembly where criticism, questions,
and often intemperate outbursts of humor and invective were the
rule and where the art of leadership is primarily that of bargaining,
persuasion, and argument. In 1945, he had stalked out of the Assembly and he vowed never to return to "that place." In 1958, he
was forced to go through the constitutional formality of appearing
personally before it to solicit a vote of confidence. Though he seemed

on this occasion to relish his contacts with the deputies, "operation seduction" was also something in the nature of a farewell.

On the occasion of the armistice celebration the President of the Republic, René Coty, made the traditional appeal to unity—"over and above our divergences and quarrels there is France"—and declared his intention to leave the presidency. "Listen to the man who without any doubt is speaking to you for the last time," he said. "Let us unite." [1] After two meetings between De Gaulle and René Coty, it was announced on December 1 officially that the latter did not wish to run. It was also confirmed that De Gaulle intended to be a candidate, and his name was duly presented, as required by law, by fifty presidential electors. The Communists immediately countered with Georges Marrane, a senator and a former member of De Gaulle's cabinet after the Liberation. It appeared for a time that the election might be limited to the two candidates. A few minutes before midnight of December 13—the deadline for submitting nominations—the Union of Democratic Forces (UFD) nominated Albert Châtelet, a retired dean of the School of Science of the University of Paris. The UFD's purpose was to prevent the election from being a contest between "two blocs," with the Communists receiving all the anti-De Gaulle votes. All other political parties, however, including the Socialists, favored De Gaulle. The ensuing election, therefore, held on December 21, was a formality, with De Gaulle getting 77.5 per cent of the votes. There was no electoral

PRESIDENTIAL ELECTION

Registered.........81,761
Voters............81,284
Valid ballots.......79,470

	De Gaulle	Per Cent	Maranne	Per Cent	Chatelet	Per Cent
France..............	57,649	77.5	10,125	13.6	6,617	8.9
Overseas departments..	937	81.4	176	15.2	38	3.3
Algeria..............	65	100.0	..	..	..	..
Sahara..............	214	97.2	2	.9	3	1.3
Overseas territories....	204	98.0	..	..	4	1.8
Members of the community..............	3,325	96.7	51	1.4	60	1.7
Total.........	62,394	78.5	10,354	13.1	6,722	8.4

From *Année Politique*, 1958, p. 156.

[1] *Année Politique*, 1958, Appendix, p. 569. The best over-all survey of the launching of the new institutions under the Fifth Republic is Maurice Duverger, *La Ve République* (Paris, 1959).

campaign, no debate between the candidates on the manner in which they intended to use the enormous powers of the office. The French "notables" in almost all departments simply followed the irresistible trend in favor of personal leadership. Only in the Department of Seine did the Communist candidate make a strong showing, thanks to the provision for election of supplementary delegates. He received 2,126 of the 5,653 votes cast.

Speaking one week after his election, De Gaulle reaffirmed his conception of the office and his own personal role. "The national task that I have assumed," he said, "for the past eighteen years is confirmed. Guide of France and chief of the republican state, I exercise supreme power to the full extent allowed and in accord with the new spirit to which I owe it." [2]

This view of the office stems directly from French monarchical traditions. De Gaulle is the custodian of national unity, forged by some one thousand years of history—a unity that is "real" and therefore bound to be perceived by every French man and woman through the vicissitudes and squabbles of the republican regimes. He is "invested" by history and is responsible to the people only in a vague fashion. He stands above the everyday party conflicts and quarrels, intervening only to "arbitrate." Yet, in his capacity as "Guide of France" (a phrase suggestive of Burke), he can initiate, suggest, and make policy. De Gaulle's legitimacy resides in the incarnation of the permanent interests of France that no election, no popular whim and fancy, no political opposition can invalidate. It can be set aside, as in 1946, but that was an error which in no way qualified the uniqueness of his role.

As Professor Georges Vedel points out,[3] De Gaulle seems to divide the tasks of government into three major parts. The first, *la Politique*, relates to the position and the survival of the nation in the world. This includes defense, foreign policy, and the Community. The most pressing problem of *Politique* is Algeria, and more broadly, the position of France in North Africa. In all these matters the liberty of the president to initiate policy and make decisions seems to be unqualified. He may ask for advice, demand a full-dress debate in his cabinet, and rely upon the opinions and the information given to him by his ministers, notably the Minister of Foreign Affairs. But the deci-

---

[2] *Le Monde*, December 30, 1958.
[3] Georges Vedel, "Vérité de la Vième République," *Revue de l'Action Populaire*, September–October, 1959, pp. 897–911.

sion is his own. In De Gaulle's thinking a second category of matters relate broadly to economic and social considerations. These are means for the realization of over-all national objectives. Decisions for these matters are delegated to subordinate organs—the prime minister, the cabinet, and Parliament. It is for them to reach the proper decisions, subject, of course, in the case of conflicts among ministers or between the cabinet and Parliament, to the president's "arbitration." Arbitration entails an effort to reconcile varying points of view, especially in the allocation of credits. On two occasions during the preparation of the budgets of 1959 and 1960 such "arbitration" was made by General de Gaulle. Arbitration might also, under exceptional circumstances, involve the dissolution of Parliament and national elections. For example, De Gaulle made it clear in a press conference that the legislature could not, without facing the prospect of dissolution, amend the ordinances passed by his government earlier by virtue of the powers given to him.

A third category of matters is delegated to subordinate organs, yet are closely supervised by the president. These affairs change with time, but they always touch on the vital issue of internal unity. At present this category seems to include wage policy and national education, particularly with respect to the perennial controversy over Catholic schools.

Since unity is the prerequisite of national power, General de Gaulle has been anxious to impart his view of France's historical mission to the people. As after the Liberation, he has sought to renew his contact with the masses in order to create a common sense of purpose and form a solid alliance against the "sinister men" who placed their interests above the nation. Today the President frequently tours the country to strengthen the bonds between the Guide and the people. In the course of his first busy year De Gaulle undertook many trips to the provinces and to Algeria. He usually talked personally to the officials of large provincial towns, spoke to the people in passionate and eloquent terms about the destiny of France, and returned to Paris exalted by popular response and support. If again, as in the past, the selfish factions and parties interfere with *la Politique*—the great national goals and plans— De Gaulle may this time throw his popularity in the balance by taking his program to the country, rather than retire to his small village.

General de Gaulle has attempted to give to the Fifth Republic a strong presidential, if not personal, orientation. He has controlled and shaped French foreign policy with the aid of his minister, Couve de Murville, in a manner reminiscent of nineteenth century diplomacy. He has been solely responsible for all decisions concerning the French Community; he has been the sole spokesman for policies pursued in Algeria, and his statements occasionally seem to take even the members of the government by surprise. He has been the architect of the new organization for defense and the modernization of the armed forces.

The office of the presidency is no longer a mere symbol; it has become a dynamo or motor of political power. A new style characterizes the office, highlighted by vastly increased deference. General de Gaulle's personal appearances are surrounded by much pomp and circumstance. The American institution of the press conference is now used to permit the President to state policies in his own name and directly to the people. The royal "We" or the impersonal "De Gaulle has decided" or "De Gaulle believes" is a frequent formula used by the President. But the ceremony simply reinforces what is common knowledge: that power in the Fifth Republic is concentrated in the hands of Charles de Gaulle, whose legitimacy was merely "confirmed" by the election of December 21, 1958.

The "Government"

The main part of the Gaullist plan for an independent and effective executive was realized when the revamped office of the president was entrusted to De Gaulle. But it remained to put into place the most delicate piece of the new institutional machinery— the cabinet. Although De Gaulle, both by virtue of the powers of the office and his prestige, was bound to play a determining role in all matters of policy, the prime minister and his cabinet are responsible to the National Assembly and not to the president.

The constitutional provisions were fully respected in the formation of the cabinet. The President of the Republic asked Michel Debré to become the prime minister. The latter proceeded to form his cabinet and went before the National Assembly with a proposed program. He answered questions and made it clear that on this occasion an adverse vote by the National Assembly by simple majority would automatically bring about his resignation. The National Assembly adopted the general program and thus "invested" the cabinet by a vote of 453 against 56. Only the Communists and the Socialists voted against the government, while some 29 deputies from the Center and from the Independents abstained voluntarily. The "majority" included the bulk of the MRP, the Independents, the UNR, and the deputies from Algeria.

The new cabinet differed little from the one formed by General de Gaulle in June, 1958. The only notable change was the withdrawal of the Socialist ministers. The ratio between nonparliamentarians and parliamentarians (who either resigned or were expected to resign their electoral mandates) remained about the same.

	Debré Jan. 15, 1959	*De Gaulle* June 1, 1958– Jan. 15, 1959
Nonparliamentarians	9	9
UNR	5	3
Independents	3	3
MRP	2	3
Radicals	1	2
Socialists	–	3

When two ministers, an Independent and a Radical, decided after the senatorial elections to retain their senatorial mandate and resign from the government, the proportion of nonparliamentarians in the cabinet increased. The trend in favor of "technicians" was further reinforced after the resignation of André Boulloche and Antoine Pinay, from Education and Finance respectively, and their replacement by administrators. The delegate-general of the government in Algeria is a civil servant. The Ministry of Foreign Affairs and the Ministry of Defense are in the hands of nonparliamentarians, and the secretary-general of the executive council of the Community was a top civil servant, Raymond Janot. Thus, the most significant areas of what was called earlier *la Politique* were entrusted to technicians who would presumably implement the policies of the President of the Republic. The effort to "depoliticize" other vital problems under the supervision of the cabinet was also noticeable. For instance, the ministries of Construction, Labor, Public Health and Population, and Industry and Commerce were given to nonparliamentarians from the outset.

The number of "technicians" in the cabinet and the very fact that those who were parliamentarians had to resign their mandate was expected to immunize the cabinet from the feverish preoccupation with parliamentary strategy that paralyzed decision making in the Fourth Republic. The assumption that, in case of a parliamentary revolt, the president would dissolve the Assembly further enhanced the position of the cabinet. It is reported that in the first cabinet meeting De Gaulle said, "Gentlemen, you are the government of the legislature. There will be no other." [4] At the same time, the parliamentarians in the cabinet represent all parties, with the exception of the Communists and Socialists, and the ministers with their own personal staff continue to be receptive to group pressures. In the areas that concern directly *la Politique,* initiative is with the President. But in the other areas of policy, the cabinet lacks cohesiveness and purpose. Where De Gaulle has direction and control, the civil service and the technicians are agents of a superior will; where policy does not flow directly from De Gaulle, the ministers, civil servants, and technicians begin to play an independent role.

The meetings of the Council of Ministers under the presidency of De Gaulle are frequent and prolonged. Here reports prepared by the ministers or their aides are debated, various points of view expressed, and a decision made. Generally the debate revolves around the suggestions and directives of the President. In contrast, the cabinet meetings under the presidency of Prime Minister Debré are becoming rare. There is instead a tendency to set up small interministerial committees concerned with the implementation of the decisions reached in the Council of Ministers by General de Gaulle. The cabinet has become a mere instrument for the execution of policy, and in some matters—especially defense and foreign policy —the cabinet is by-passed. For instance, when on September 16 General de Gaulle announced his policy of self-determination for Algeria, the efforts of the Prime Minister to reconcile his attitude with the presidential policy became a source of amusement to deputies and the public. Again, on December 13, 1959, De Gaulle took everybody by surprise when he announced that Senegal and Soudan (grouped in the Federation of Mali) could become independent. As one commentator has put it, "Those who imagined conflicts between the two heads of the executive may be reassured; there is but one head." [5]

But De Gaulle cannot make every decision and, what is more, supervise every decision, every nomination, and every executive order. Revolving around the President are his ministers, and around them the civil servants and the spokesmen for the powerful private interests for whom Parliament has lost its former attraction. Often

---

[4] See the excellent commentary by Pierre Viansson-Ponté in *Le Monde,* July 21, 22, 23 and 24, 1959. Also April 16 and 17.

[5] *Ibid.,* January 7, 8 and 9, 1960, comments by the same writer.

they are able to thwart the decisions made by the President, qualify his utterances, even reverse his policies. Under the shelter of the presidential power they are weaving a net of personal relations. They are the "small barons" of the system catering to and ready to serve the republican monarch. But if the latter were to vacate his power or if power were vacated by accident or death, they may become the new "princes" of the Fifth Republic.[6]

The National Assembly

Elected at the height of the pro-Gaullist enthusiasm that followed the referendum, the National Assembly in its composition reflected the deep popular distrust of the former parliamentarians and ministers. Without distinction of parties and political orientation, the electors heeded belatedly Poujade's old battle cry and had "thrown out the rascals" (including, however, the Poujadists). Out of 546 members only 131 had served in the previous Assembly, and only an additional small number had parliamentary experience either in the second legislature (1951–56) or the Council of the Republic. Generally the new men came about evenly from all political parties. A 75 per cent turnover applied not only to the UNR which had some forty former parliamentarians in its ranks, but also to the MRP, and the Independents. Only on the Left could one see a greater number of familiar faces.

Never before had an election in France accounted for such a drastic reshuffling of deputies, apart from the election of the first Constituent Assembly in 1945. Despite the great turnover of personnel, however, the professional composition of the National Assembly showed little change, except for the sharp drop of workers (caused by the virtual elimination of the Communists), as the following table shows:

	1956	1958
Lawyers	59	57
Doctors	38	37
Other liberal professions	43	54
Civil servants	132	92
Cadres	46	60
Workers and employees	58	7
Agriculture	66	52
Industrialists and merchants	65	74
Military	8	8
Clergymen	2	3
Diverse	27	21

---

[6] *Le Monde* January 7, 1960.

The new deputies set immediately to work in two special sessions: first to elect their officers, and then to draft their provisional standing orders and approve the policy of the cabinet. The UNR, together with the deputies from Algeria, was only fifteen votes short of an absolute majority; this was the second time since World War II that two parties virtually controlled a majority in the National Assembly. The UNR and the deputies from Algeria immediately joined forces to elect Chaban-Delmas, a leading Gaullist, president of the National Assembly for the period of the legislature as the new constitution prescribed. In the first ballot Chaban-Delmas received 259 votes against 168 cast for Paul Reynaud, an Independent. The Socialist candidate received 89 votes (Socialists and some MRP and Radicals), and the Communist candidate 12 votes. On the second ballot, however, the alliance between Independents, UNR, and the Algerian formation gave to Chaban-Delmas an impressive victory —355 votes out of 550.

Since the standing orders were to be provisional and subject to formal ratification by the National Assembly in its first regular session scheduled for April, 1959, the more pressing business was the formation of the parliamentary groups, the six committees allowed by the new constitution and the establishment of new sitting arrangements. Republican orthodoxy calls for the distinction between Left, Center, and Right, and it was precisely this distinction that the UNR did not wish to accept for fear it might be placed to the Right.

THE NEW SITTING ARRANGEMENT IN THE NATIONAL ASSEMBLY *

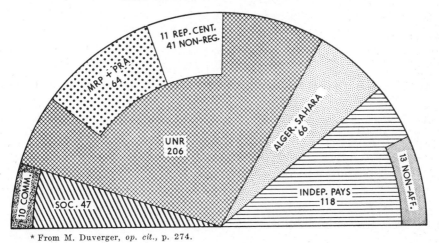

* From M. Duverger, *op. cit.*, p. 274.

One of their leaders argued in favor of the British system so that the majority would sit on one side and the opposition on the other. However, it was quickly pointed out that different majorities and different "oppositions" would materialize as the issues presented themselves before the Assembly, and that it would be extremely awkward to shift sitting arrangements for every debate. And how would one distinguish between Socialist "constructive" opposition and Communist outright opposition? After long debate a compromise was reached. As the chart on page 277 shows, the UNR is seated in a Left-Center position at the expense of the Independents, who found themselves on the extreme Right. Both because of its size and its position, the UNR engulfs the Center formations and physically dominates the Assembly.

The provisional standing orders stipulated that a minimum of thirty members was required to form a group.[7] The Communists remained isolated and therefore unable to form a parliamentary group, while the Center deputies (the old UDSR, the RGR, and fifteen Radicals) created a formation of "non-inscrits." When the Republican Center joined later they formed the *Entente Démocratique*. Thus, the number of parliamentary groups was reduced from twelve in the previous legislature to six. Whether the traditional pattern of fragmentation would be repeated under the Fifth Republic remained to be seen.

It was decided to elect members of the committees according to the numerical strength of the parliamentary groups and to elect by majority among those who did not belong to any parliamentary group. This again was a device to exclude Communist participation in the work of committees. Each committee was to consist of at least 60 and not more than 120 deputies, as follows: Foreign Affairs and Finance and Economic Plan—60 members each; National Defense and Armed Forces, and Constitutional Laws, Legislation, and General Administration of the Republic—90 members each; Production and Trade, and Cultural, Social, and Family Matters—120 members each. The suggestion that each of the six large committees be allowed to create subcommittees was finally rejected as contrary to the constitution.

The preparatory work and the provisional acceptance of the new standing orders ended on what some Gaullist commentators con-

---

[7] *Règlement de l'Assemblée Nationale* (Paris, September, 1959).

sidered an ominous note. The Assembly decided that the committees could sit while Parliament was not in session—a decision that might, under certain conditions, given their large membership, lead to a continuing effort on the part of the Assembly to interfere with the work of the executive. In addition, a provision was passed according to which "oral questions" asked by deputies could lead to a debate and a vote. Was not this the resurrection of the "interpellation" procedure that had accounted for the downfall of so many cabinets under the Third and Fourth Republics? Although the deputies argued that such a debate and vote could not force, constitutionally, the cabinet to resign, this logic was not easily accepted by those who recalled that the letter of the Constitution of the Fourth Republic had been similarly abused.

Municipal and Senatorial Elections— Return to Status Quo

On March 8 and 15 the French electors were called to the polls for the fourth and many for the fifth time in less than six months. At stake were elective offices of over 38,000 municipalities. The electoral system promulgated by the government provided for proportional representation in cities with 120,000 inhabitants or more. In smaller municipalities the traditional "winner-take-all" absolute majority system, with runoff ballot a week later in case no candidate obtained such a majority, was in effect. Generally speaking, municipal elections center around personalities and local issues. But the political element is not lacking, especially in the larger cities where the voters elect party slates on the basis of proportional representation. The municipal elections of 1947, for instance, provided the first indication of the popular strength of the RPF and led De Gaulle himself to call at the time for dissolution of the National Assembly. It was precisely the political implication of the Gaullist victory in these elections that spurred the Center parties to modify the electoral law in order to permit formation of alliances in 1951.

The municipal elections of March, 1959 had a decidedly political character. The UNR, fresh from victory in the legislative elections, pledged a vigorous campaign to "liberate" the municipalities of France from Communist domination. The elections would also provide an index of the staying power of the UNR and perhaps, as some of its leaders hoped, might even show its growing strength. The party was especially anxious to do well since the whole Senate was scheduled to be renewed a month later by an electoral college composed primarily of the municipal councilors about to be chosen. In the large cities of over 120,000 the general distribution of party vote would obviously reveal public sentiment. In the smaller cities where a second ballot was to be the rule—since few candidates or slates were expected to win an absolute majority on the first ballot —the negotiations of alliances among the candidates and parties between the first and the second ballot would provide an indication of party attitudes. For example, alliances among Communists, Socialists, and Radicals might presage a revival of the Popular Front.

The first ballot indicated that the Gaullist wave had passed, leaving in its wake the familiar electoral scene. In all the large cities the Communists held their own or improved their position, not only with reference to the November, 1958 elections, but also the municipal elections of 1953 and the legislative elections of January 2, 1956. The Communists emerged once more as incontestably the first party of France. In Paris they received 29.1 per cent as compared with 19.9 per cent in November and 27.4 per cent in 1953. The pattern was the same in Marseille, Lyon, and Le Havre. In the thirteen largest urban centers of the country the Communist vote represented 27 per cent of the total, whereas in 1953 it amounted to 26 per cent! In the suburbs of Paris they obtained 42 per cent as compared to 32 per cent in the legislative elections of November and 39.3 per cent in the legislative elections of January 2, 1956.

UNR received its worst setback exactly in those urban areas whose new dynamism it claimed to represent. In Paris it lost about 2 per cent of the votes it had received in November. In St. Etienne, Calais, and Lyon it lost 4 per cent; in Lille, roughly 20 per cent. UNR strength in the large urban centers amounted to about 21 per cent of the total—below its percentages for the legislative election and well below the strength of the RPF in the municipal election of 1947. In the Paris belt it was totally unable to prevent a Communist comeback. Out of some eighty communes, the Communists won an absolute majority on the first ballot in twenty-six. Only six went to the UNR and eight to other formations on the first ballot. It appeared that, with De Gaulle in the presidency, the electorate was going through a period of pause and reconsideration. Or as some commentators intimated, the pendulum was simply swinging from Right to Left, as it had done with remarkable monotony under all political systems in the past.

THE MUNICIPAL ELECTIONS OF 1959 (PARIS)

Parties	1959		1958 (Legislative)		1953 (Municipal)	
	Votes	Per Cent	Votes	Per Cent	Votes	Per Cent
Communists................	327,458	29.1	269,583	19.9	293,842	27.4
UNR (RPF in 1953).........	235,829	21.0	300,529	22.2	113,325	10.6
Independents..............	231,153	20.6	211,318	15.6	273,772	25.6
Republican Center and Radicals.................	97,244	8.6	50,992	3.8	42,397	4.0
Socialists.................	78,591	7.0	131,453	9.7	104,643	9.8
MRP.....................	58,426	5.2	50,868	3.7	73,687	6.9
UFD.....................	39,213	3.5				
Right groups..............	19,980	1.8	129,555	9.6	31,696	3.0
Left groups...............	9,114	0.8	56,843	4.2	10,901	1.0

The week between the first and the second ballot in the smaller municipalities where no party slate had won an absolute majority was a feverish one. From the very first it was clear that the Communists would be able to benefit from their victory, very much as the UNR had done in the legislative elections of November. Many Socialist federations were unable to resist the temptation of coming to an accord with them despite the efforts of Guy Mollet and the Central Committee to keep the Communists isolated. Some fifty such alliances were concluded, especially in the southern part of France where Socialist discipline is weak and anticlericalism strong. In Montpellier, Angers, Carcassonne, and Niort the Socialists came to terms with the Communists, and in the last two cities won —thanks to Communist support. On the other hand, the UNR in alliance with various groups—Socialists, MRP, and Independents— registered some successes, but was unable to cut into Communist strength, especially in the Paris region and the Department of Seine.

The secretary general of the UNR optimistically declared that the UNR was becoming the leader of the "national parties" and was destined to play an important role in the municipal life of France. But a certain anxiety could not be concealed. The municipal vote, he pointed out, revealed a dissatisfaction with the government's economic and social policies, and the recovery of the Communist forces "ought to furnish to the government a precious indication."[8] As for the Communists, the Central Committee in a special statement affirmed, as the RPF had done in 1947, that the National Assembly

---

[8] In *Le Monde*, March 18, 1959.

did not represent the country and urged its militants to continue the struggle for a united front with the left-wing parties. Duclos pledged the party to vote in the senatorial elections in a manner that "would defeat reaction and its accomplices." [9]

The municipal elections revealed the amazing stability of the French body politic. It seemed that Gaullism, like Boulangism or Bonapartism, might be a transient phenomenon only temporarily submerging the perennial quarrels between the French political families but unable to unite them into one political community.

Election of the Republican Senate

The mode of the election of the Senate was established by the ordinance of November 15, 1958. The 255 senators from the Metropolis were to be elected indirectly by majority with runoff ballots for all departments except the seven departments that were attributed more than four senatorial seats. Therefore, Bouches-du-Rhône, Nord, Pas-de-Calais, Rhône, Seine, Seine-Maritime, and Seine-et-Oise (accounting for sixty senators in all) elected their senators by proportional representation (in addition, twelve senators were returned from the overseas departments and territories, six represented the "French abroad," and thirty-one were elected by the Algerian municipalities). The electors in the Metropolis were the municipal councilors chosen in the March election. Cities with more than 30,000 inhabitants received one extra elector for each additional thousand inhabitants. Despite this provision the small towns and villages continued to play a dominant role—the Senate thus represents the more static regions of France rather than the dynamic departments. The "senatorial college," like the presidential college, does not reflect the movement of industrialization and urbanization that has been so marked since the war. Many political leaders who had been buried under the avalanche of Gaullism in the legislative elections were encouraged by the municipal vote to try for a comeback in the Senate. They stood a better chance with an electoral body for which past services and favors and personal influence play a very important role.

The political campaigning was restricted, as expected, to direct personal contacts and agreements between departmental party organizations. No nationwide pattern developed except for a con-

---

[9] In *Le Monde*, March 22–23, 1959.

sistent effort by the UNR and the Independents to make common lists. Attempts to extend this alliance to include the MRP and the other "government majority groups" were rarely successful. As in the municipal elections, Communist discipline, on the other hand, proved to be effective. They retired their candidates on the second ballot in more than twenty departments and helped secure the election of a number of Socialists and Radicals despite the lack of any explicit pre-election agreement.

The election constituted a virtual return to the political formations of the Fourth Republic. Six months after the legislative elections of November, the revolution of May 13 and the popular revulsion against the men of the system had left hardly any trace upon the electoral map of France. Of the 255 senators elected in France proper, only 85 were new; and among those, 35 were formerly members of the National Assembly. As for the remaining 50 seats, the incumbent usually did not run for re-election. Thus, the "new" Senate was almost an exact replica of the old. The high turnover of the legislative elections in which almost three out of four deputies were new had been reversed. In the new Senate, 84 per cent of the incumbent senators were returned, and in 35 departments there was no change at all. In 17 departments, despite changes of individual senators, the party configuration remained the same. As for the overall results, the Communists lost two seats and the Socialists five. The various Radical formations that traditionally coalesce in the Senate under the name of "Democratic Left" gained three seats, another proof that, despite their quarrels and divisions, the Radical tradition continues to be strong among the local notables and bosses; the UNR had two seats less than the RPF—an indication of its inability to establish local roots; the MRP and the Independents gained eight and five seats respectively.

The senatorial representation of a department was often diametrically opposed to the popular representation that resulted in the elections for the National Assembly. For instance, the Department of Puy-de-Dôme had one UNR and four Independent deputies, but three Socialist senators; the Lot-et-Garonne had one Independent and two UNR deputies, but two Radical senators; Vaucluse had three UNR deputies, but one Socialist and one Radical senator; Belfort had one UNR and one MRP deputy, but a Socialist senator.

The two traditional formations—Independents and Radicals— together with the rural and social action groups that were in essence the lobby of the rural interests held virtually a majority in the new Senate. The UNR could hope to maintain its national leadership only at the cost of heavy sacrifices in the Senate. This was made abundantly clear when the Senate proceeded to elect as president the man who had held this same post since 1947, Gaston Monnerville, a Radical, by 235 votes out of 276. The "Gaullists" after some ten months in office had not been able to convince the electorate of the desirability of their social, economic, and political program. In fact, the UNR had failed to evolve a program by this time and, outside of its loyalty to De Gaulle, seemed to be sharply divided by internal quarrels and ideological differences. The senatorial elections cast deep gloom on those who believed that powerful new forces had been released by the coming of De Gaulle. The Parliament represented two different tendencies. The one stemming from the electoral landslide of November and the other from a Senate which, in terms of its powers, resembled the republican senate of the Third Republic and whose political configuration reproduced the forces of the Fourth Republic. The presidency and the cabinet were in the hands of the Gaullists, or rather in the hands of De Gaulle. As Jacques Fauvet pointed out, the "three Republics" seem to be reflected in the regime which claims to be new.[10] The electoral college of the villages and the countryside continued to be attached to the traditional parties. The secretary of the UNR could not hide his bitterness when he stated that the new Senate was something of a brake to the political evolution of the country, a "revenge of the notables."[11]

There is a double irony in the composition of the Senate. The constitution gave the senators a veto power on legislation, if and when the government wished to use its powers. In view of its indirect mode of election, there was every expectation that it would be so used in order to block the National Assembly. This, however, cannot now be the case, since the UNR is strong in the popularly elected Assembly, but weak in the Senate. Secondly, the old and most experienced parliamentarians who had failed to enter the National Assembly found a haven in the Senate. Debates on the senatorial floor have taken on a solemnity and importance lacking in the National Assembly. The Senate may aspire to the role of its predecessor

---

[10] Jacques Fauvet in *Le Monde*, April 28, 1959.

[11] In *Le Monde*, April 28, 1959; the statement by Albin Chalandon, Secretary General of the UNR.

STABILITY OF SENATORIAL COLLEGE

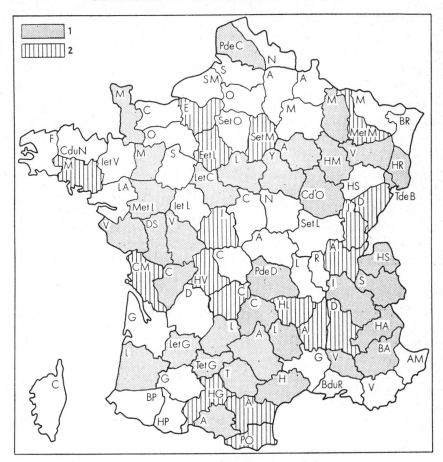

(1) Departments in which senatorial representation did not change.
(2) Departments in which, despite the changes of individual senators, the political representation remained the same. (Based on chart in *Le Monde*, April 28, 1959.)

under the Third Republic. It lacks the constitutional powers to overthrow the cabinet, but the letter of the constitution did not prevent the Senate under the Third Republic from being the censor of many cabinets.

Executive-Legislative Relations

A major purpose of the framers was to "constitutionalize" cabinet stability and leadership. During his first year in office Michel Debré was able to use the devices provided by the constitution and weather political storms which would have overwhelmed the cabinets of the Fourth Republic. Despite a number of "internal" crises that have led to cabinet reshuffling, he has retained the support of the Assembly.

The Assembly met five times between its election in November, 1958 and the end of 1959. The first, in December, 1958 was an extraordinary meeting to select its president. On January 15 it met to vote on the program of the new cabinet. These sessions lasted only three days each. The first regular session of Parliament began in the last week of April and ended three months later. Parliament devoted itself almost entirely to debate on its standing orders. Some government bills, providing for economic and social reforms, were also examined. In the months of May and June the Assembly met infrequently—in the whole month of May it sat only eight days. The second regular session opened in the first week of October and came to an official close several days beyond the constitutionally prescribed deadline of the third Friday in December. The letter of the law was respected, however, by resorting to the time-honored device of "stopping the clock." This session was virtually limited to the discussion and vote on the budget. An extraordinary session was called in the last week of December, 1959 in order to pass the education bill providing for subsidies to schools.

In its relations with Parliament the government throughout the first year of the Republic stuck firmly to the letter of the constitution. It fought hard against the introduction of any procedures that could lead, even indirectly, to an expansion of the supervisory power of the National Assembly over and beyond the vote of censure as prescribed in Article 49 of the constitution. The government has refused to permit the question period (one meeting a week is reserved for questions by members and answers by the government under Article 48) to lead to a debate or a vote. It has been equally adamant in refusing to permit Parliament to introduce and vote resolutions on any issue of policy, since this would amount to an "implicit" vote of confidence and also violate Article 34 (limiting the competence of the legislature to specified matters). The government was upheld on both counts by unequivocal decisions of the Constitutional Council.

At the same time, the government has used every weapon provided by the constitution to maintain its legislative leadership. It has controlled the agenda of the National Assembly so tightly that many deputies complained there was insufficient time to examine issues and display initiative; it has interpreted rigorously Article 40, which prohibits members of Parliament from introducing bills and amendments having as a consequence either the diminution of public financial resources or an increase in public expenditures; it has likewise made full use of Article 44, forcing the Assembly to take a single vote on "all or parts of the text under discussion, retaining only the amendments proposed or accepted by the government." This was notably the case with the budget.

The government continued the practice of the Fourth Republic in introducing *lois-programmes* (previously called *lois-cadres*) in which Parliament voted on the main principles and allowed the government large discretion in implementing these principles by decree. This was the procedure used for the reorganization of the fiscal system, the law on agricultural equipment, the law on social promotion, and the law on economic equipment of the nation (including investment and expenditures for public projects). Use was also made of Articles 34 and 37 to restrict the legislative function of Parliament to matters listed in the constitution, leaving all others to the government. Thus, the bill providing for subsidies to the Catholic schools established only the basic principle, and empowered the government to put them into execution by degrees, subject to parliamentary approval. In general, law initiation was almost the exclusive prerogative of the government and the power of the National Assembly to revise was stringently qualified.

Parliament was able to exercise only the limited powers devolved upon it by the constitution. The forms were respected. Ministers testified before the committees, and full-dress debates took place on such crucial issues as Algeria and foreign and economic policy. The debate on the budget gave deputies the opportunity to express criticism and ministers another occasion to explain policy. The procedure for a weekly question period was scrupulously adhered to by both the Assembly and government. The provision for censure was invoked for the first time with reference to the budget and, as expected, the motion failed.

But the new rules brought about growing resentment on the part of both houses. The Senate went out of its way to vote resolutions, even though they were studiously ignored by the government. Twice during the first regular session, the Senate rejected government bills. The stringent time limit imposed upon debate brought forth cries of "cabinet dictatorship." Inability of Parliament either through the committees or otherwise to scrutinize closely the activities of the cabinet increased the resentment of the parliamentarians. The traditional rivalry between Parliament and executive became increasingly sharp, and the government thought it prudent to give in on a few issues. Thus, the family allowances were increased by 10 per cent and some medical benefits reinstituted; restoration of veterans' pensions was promised; and concessions were made to rural interests, notably the wine and alcohol lobby. The government abandoned —at least for the time being—its legislative proposals to limit the privileges of the home distillers.

The essential condition of cabinet stability remained what it always had been—that of a governing majority. The new rules worked, or at least were respected, and the spirit and letter of the constitution safeguarded, because the government had the support of De Gaulle, and therefore the backing of the UNR and Independents. The government was safe as long as these two political parties stood together—not because of the constitutional rules. It could afford to ignore all the other groups—Socialists, Radicals, the deputies from Algeria, or the MRP. But this majority began to crumble at the end of 1959, less than one year after the government's formation. The two divisive factors were the same ones that had caused the downfall of many previous governments: the question of the Catholic schools and Algeria. In addition, the conservatives were restive over the drop in farm income. The revival of a strong protest movement in all rural regions of France was bound to influence many UNR and Independent deputies.

Passage of the bill in December providing for generous subsidies to Catholic schools forced Socialists and Radicals into deeper opposition to the Debré cabinet. The Independents, long unhappy with De Gaulle's policy in Algeria and ready to exploit rural discontent, proceeded once the education bill was enacted to attack the Prime Minister and the President. The official organ of the Independents called De Gaulle the "President-General" and spoke more harshly about him than had ever been the case since his investiture as prime minister in June, 1958. Thus there were signs that the government might be confronted by a "negative majority" in the Assembly—Communists, Socialists, some Radicals *and* Independents, and the deputies from Algeria—totaling some 260 deputies. A split within the UNR ranks under these conditions would put an end to the life of the cabinet regardless of constitutional provisions and devices intended to strengthen the government against the Parliament. The new rules may add a little to the government's length of time in office, but they are no substitute for a homogeneous majority.

A new type of instability has developed in the form of "small cabinet crises." Thus, in May, 1959, two ministers resigned over the manner in which the government interpreted its powers vis à vis the Parliament and particularly the Senate: Roger Houdet, the Minister of Agriculture, and Jean Berthoin, the Minister of the Interior. In December, 1959 the Minister of Education, André Boulloche, opposed a concession made by the cabinet during the debate over aid to Catholic schools, and resigned. Finally the sharp differences within the cabinet over foreign, military, and financial policy virtually forced the resignation of the powerful Minister of Finance, Antoine Pinay, and the Secretary of State for Economic Affairs, Max Fléchet, also an Independent, in January, 1960. In each case the cabinet survived and replacements came from among nonparliamentarians (except for the new Minister of Agriculture). It appears that even parliamentarians compelled to give up their mandates in order to enter the cabinet continue to be susceptible to political pressures or to have political ambitions of their own. The increasing preponderance of technicians in the cabinet is bound in turn to add to parliamentary resentment and the growing opposition.

In the last analysis, the Debré cabinet maintained its control of the National Assembly during its first year in office because the majority of the deputies were willing to follow wherever General de Gaulle wanted to go, and not because of the new procedural rules. So long as the President retains his extraordinary grip over French opinion and political leaders, his government will be able to "manage" the Assembly. But if this grip is loosened for any reason, a cabinet to survive may have to seek the shelter of the president's constitutional prerogatives: dissolution, referendum or, most probably, emergency powers.

The Finishing Touches

The Constitutional Council, whose powers are set forth in Articles 56 through 63 of the constitution, was organized by ordinances of November 7, 1958 and February 4, 1959. It was stipulated that the post of councilor is incompatible with membership in the government, Parliament, or the Economic and Social Council. With the exception of the "members by right" (the ex-presidents), the councilors are required to take an oath to perform their duties faithfully, maintain secrecy concerning deliberations and voting, and to refrain from giving advice or taking a public position on matters within the competence of the Council. Generous compensation was also provided.

On February 21, the nine members were nominated: three by the president of the Republic, three by the president of the National Assembly, and three by the president of the Senate. Former presidents Vincent Auriol and René Coty are "members by right." None of the regular appointed members have any particular competence in the field of constitutional law, though among them are two lawyers and two magistrates. The new councilors are relatively advanced in years, with five over the age of seventy. Five had been active members of the RPF or the UNR, including two close advisers of General de Gaulle: Léon Noël (the president of the Council) and Georges Pompidou. In fact, since two thirds of the members were appointed by either General de Gaulle or Jacques Chaban-Delmas, the highest court of the land is a bastion of Gaullism and can be counted upon to support the government in the event of any legal disputes with the Parliament.

The Economic and Social Council was the last domestic institution to be created. Article 71 of the constitution states that the composition and rules of operation of the Council shall be fixed by "organic law." An ordinance of December 29, 1958 defined the "mission" of the Council: "to favor the collaboration of various professional categories and to associate the economic groups with the elaboration of government policy." Under the Fourth Republic the Council had been associated also with the Parliament. The government was given the right to appoint one third of the 205 members of the Council, as compared with one twelfth of the 169 members of the old Council. The membership was to include: 45 representatives of workers, employees, and technicians; 41 representatives of industrial, commercial, and artisanal enterprises; 40 delegates from agricultural organizations; 15 persons qualified in the economic, social, scientific, or cultural domains; 15 representatives of diverse social activities (including family associations); 7 from such varied fields as cooperatives, tourism, and export trade; 2 designated by middle-class organizations; 10 specialists on economic and social problems of overseas territories or the franc zone; 20 representing economic and social activities of Algeria and the Sahara.

On June 6 the names of the members, designated by both professional organizations and the government, were made public. About three fourths of the 169 members of the former Council reappeared in the new one. Among the 70 new councilors were a number from the defunct Assembly of the French Union, and several former deputies and ministers, including notably Robert Lacoste. In addition to the councilors, about 90 "experts" were nominated by the government to advise them on matters relating to their special fields. The new Council thus resembles the old, but has a larger percentage of members appointed by the government, and much greater representation for Algeria. Its "mission" is to aid the government, rather than Parliament, in the performance of its planning and legislative tasks.

The last institution of the Fifth Republic to come into existence was the Senate of the Community, whose members are designated by the legislatures of the member states (186 for the French Republic, 98 for all the others). The president of the Community, General de Gaulle, in his opening address to the first session of the Senate on July 15, said: "The meeting of your Senate marks the end of the setting into place of the institutions provided by our constitution. . . . Thus is realized what our peoples freely decided, in full independence, by the referendum of September 28." He professed to see a great movement of the colonial elite and masses toward France, and in the name of "82 million men" extended his greetings to those assembled. At that point the institutional structure of the Fifth Republic was complete.

CHAPTER XV

The New Political Forces

GAULLISTS engineered the return of the General to power and the refashioning of the institutions of the Republic in order to construct a strong state and a stable executive authority that would be able to solve internal problems and restore French power in the world. They exploited the nationalist bent of public opinion and profited from the activities of the antirepublican groups. The left-wing forces appeared to be in a state of utter confusion both before and after the referendum and the legislative elections. As in 1945, there were signs that new political forces were ready to replace the old. It was hoped that issues would become slowly "depoliticized" within the newly found consensus and that the parties would abandon the old sterile ideological quarrels in favor of a pragmatic problem-solving approach. The defeat of the most tenacious and some thought anachronistic ideological family of the Fourth Republic—the Communist party—seemed encouraging. However, after a year and a half of Gaullist rule there were few signs of change in the party system in terms of leadership, organization, and outlook.

The Union for the New Republic (UNR)

The 189 UNR deputies in the National Assembly soon increased to 210 as a result of affiliation by a number of right wingers. The party controlled the presidency of the National Assembly, the office of the prime minister, and five ministerial posts. As a "new" party the UNR capitalized on the general reaction against the "men of the system," which accounted for the very large turnover in the personnel of the National Assembly. Yet curiously enough the UNR percentage of deputies who were returned to the National Assembly for the first time was not higher than the average. Forty out of its 189 members had been deputies or senators either in the previous legislature or in 1951. The professional composition of its members was again not different from that of the National Assembly as a whole. It included 12 "agriculteurs," 11 engineers, 22 doctors, 3 pharmacists, 22 lawyers, 7 journalists (of whom 3 were directors of newspapers), 2 generals and 3 officers, 6 notaries, 13 "cadres," 11 professors, 13 civil servants, 10 industrialists, 2 winegrowers and 2 wine merchants, 8 merchants, 15 businessmen, 2 clergymen, and a few isolated professions.

The UNR deputies were all united, at least formally, in fidelity to General de Gaulle.[1] Most of them were dedicated to creation of a strong republican state and to transformation of the economic and social structure of the country along the lines laid down by General de Gaulle. A distinct group, however, consisted of "activists" who had fought the Republic in the name of French Algeria. They were imbued with a strong nationalist spirit, wished to see many of the republican institutions, especially the party system, eliminated in favor of a one-party organization, were in favor of the maintenance of French sovereignty in Algeria and in the former colonies, and advocated state planning and controls and a dynamic expansionist economic policy. Both groups represented the lower-middle classes, who suffered most from inflation, and some of the "new" middle classes—the salaried groups in the industrial firms, the technicians, and the engineers. These two groups hoped to extend their appeal to the working classes, who, in view of the referendum and the elections, seemed disenchanted with communism. A third group was composed of notables—local men with good names and contacts who were municipal councilors, mayors, journalists, and were known in the town or district. They supported De Gaulle, but in their social, economic, and colonial policy they were generally indistinguishable from the Radicals or Independents.

After the election the party had a rudimentary organization, few

---

[1] This was the oath required of all the members of the UNR in the National Assembly:

Elected Deputy of the UNR I confirm in a solemn manner my adherence to the Union for the New Republic and to its parliamentary group. Respectful of the mandate which was given to me by the electors I will abstain during the period of the legislature from participating in or becoming a member of any other group. I take the following engagement: to remain faithful to the objectives of the UNR, to support in Parliament and in my electoral district the action of General de Gaulle, to accept the discipline of voting as decided by the majority of the group for all the important questions relating to the life of the nation and of the French community, in order to maintain the cohesion of our group and the general spirit of our movement.

members, and no program. Two diametrically opposed views about
the character of the party divided the Gaullists. One was to create
a "party of the government" sitting between the Right (the deputies from Algeria and the Independents) and the Left (Communists
and Socialists), supporting the government and General de Gaulle.
This was the attitude of Albin Chalandon, a banker and expert on
economic affairs, who became secretary-general of the party and
remained in that post until the first party congress was held in November, 1959.

On the other hand, the two main protagonists of the events of
May 13, Soustelle and Delbecque, believed that the UNR ought to
become a "mass party" and create a vast network of well-disciplined
militants, obedient to the leadership and in touch with public opinion. A mass party, by exploiting nationalist sentiment, could dis-
place the old political formations and challenge the Communists.
They too favored support of General de Gaulle—but only when he
acted in accord with their policies, notably on the issue of Algeria.

A mass party would need a dynamic and appealing program,
while a "party of government" could rely on eclecticism or equivocation. Attempts to draw up a party platform bogged down in factional disputes. Chalandon, spokesman for a "government party"
with a loose structure, favored an expansionist economic program
to attract workers and salaried employees for whom, it was argued,
the old distinction between Right and Left no longer had meaning.
This seemed to be also the attitude of the prime minister, Michel
Debré, who spoke of "depoliticization" of the old issues (including
Algeria) and their settlement on the basis of pragmatic considerations. The Soustelle-Delbecque group, while agreeing with Chalandon's economic policy, embodied the spirit of May 13. Their approach to Algeria and foreign policy was highly ideological, and
they would brook no compromise on the principle of integration.

De Gaulle steered a careful course. A mass party with a program
would inevitably make his role of "arbitrator" on national issues
difficult and would seriously limit his discretion on matters where
he had the last word—Algeria, the Community, foreign policy, and
defense. Soustelle was not given the ministry of Interior nor was he
elected president of the party. His plan to support nationalist candidates in the senatorial elections was blocked by Chalandon. A
number of self-styled Gaullist "left-wing organizations" were created
with De Gaulle's blessing, notably the UDT (Democratic Union

of Labor) in order to offset the rightist bloc headed by Soustelle. Nevertheless, the Soustelle-Delbecque group had some success within the party. In July, for instance, they managed to have a majority of their own members elected by the National Assembly to the Community Senate; they also secured modification of the composition of the Central Committee of the party to include a number of militants from the various federations. A "small committee" composed of four members (two from the Soustelle faction) was created to "assist" Chalandon in the exercise of his functions. The latter was criticized for making policy statements prior to the drafting of a program by the national congress of the party. However, the proponents of a mass party, notably Soustelle, suffered a heavy defeat in the municipal elections in the industrialized area of Lyon. Delbecque's efforts in the Department of Nord to create a mass organization brought no results. Neither faction could afford to attack De Gaulle personally or repudiate his moral leadership. The only unity possible in public was around the figure of De Gaulle and on the need of discipline that each side hoped ultimately to use for its own ends. In membership and militancy the UNR is only a pale image of the RPF which, led by General de Gaulle personally, established in a surprisingly short time a vast network of "companions" throughout the country.

The statement of September 16 by General de Gaulle offering Algeria an option between integration, independence, and local autonomy and reiterating his offer to meet with Algerian leaders for the purpose of arranging a cease-fire was the occasion for the first breach in the ranks of the UNR. Nine of its deputies,[2] all of them "activists" who had taken a leading role in the events of May 13, with Delbecque at the head, were eventually expelled from the party for refusing to accept De Gaulle's policy. Significantly enough, none of them voted against the government in the National Assembly. Five, in fact, voted in favor and the other four abstained. The breach was more symbolic than real. It gave the more intransigent party members an opportunity to come out openly in favor of a nationalist policy in Algeria. Their position was widely shared by many other members who preferred, however, not to provoke the hostility of

---

[2] The deputies were Delbecque, Arrighi, Biaggi, Brice, Cathala, Souchal, Grasset, Battesti, and Colonel Thomazo. It was rumored at the time that some type of activist operation was scheduled in Paris whose aim was to replace the Debré cabinet with one led by Soustelle or Bidault.

General de Gaulle, perhaps even the dissolution of the National Assembly.

In the first session of the National Assembly the parliamentary group of the UNR accepted a motion of the Algerian deputies in favor of integration, and pledged "to maintain French sovereignty in Algeria." The Prime Minister himself, on a number of occasions as late as August, 1959, stated that the question of French sovereignty in Algeria was an incontrovertible fact that could be modified only by a revision of the constitution. Torn between their own conception of Gaullism and their loyalty to General de Gaulle, the vast majority of the deputies opted for the second. But for how long, it remained to be seen.

The national congress of the UNR, which was held in Bordeaux in the second week of November, 1959—a year after the legislative elections—was unable to reach a genuine agreement apart from a general resolution pledging once more fidelity to General de Gaulle. The President's Algerian policy was accepted, but the general climate of opinion seemed to indicate that the delegates of the party were rather sympathetic to Jacques Soustelle's point of view. In its declaration, the congress asserted first that its fundamental doctrine stems from General de Gaulle's well-known speech of Bayeux. "Guide and arbitrator of the nation, General de Gaulle can count on us and on our Union for all the great tasks he assumes and especially when he recognizes to the Algerian people the right to fix freely its destiny." [3] On all other issues the congress accepted the line established by General de Gaulle: a summit conference well prepared in advance, membership in the Common Market, aid to underdeveloped areas, implementation of the Constantine plan. It urged also that doctrinal disputes be set aside in favor of a peaceful solution to the problem of relations between the State and Catholic schools. There was a show of independence in a resolution calling for re-establishment of the veterans' pensions in the near future. On the key question of Algeria, the congress endorsed De Gaulle's offer of self-determination. But the party pledged to carry out an active campaign in Algeria to guarantee that the eventual option would be for France and against all forms of secession. It decided

---

[3] In *Le Monde*, November 17, 1959. For the full proceedings of the congress of the UNR, *Le Monde*, November 14, 15–16, and 17. No comprehensive study of the development of the political forces under the Fifth Republic has appeared as yet. See, however, Maurice Duverger, *La V*ᵉ *République* (Paris, 1959), part II, pp. 231–98.

to create a special committee in order to follow the evolution of all problems concerning Algeria and thus be in a position to "give its aid" to General de Gaulle.

As for the leadership of the party, neither the Chalandon nor the Soustelle faction scored a victory. Chalandon resigned after defining the role of the party to be that of outright support to General de Gaulle. At the same time, he admitted that the UNR was weak because it had not been able to define a doctrine and a program. He reaffirmed his expansionist economic policy and the urgency of reform. But the Soustelle faction also emerged weakened. In its composition the new Central Committee represented the more moderate groups. The supporters of Soustelle were penalized and only one deputy from Algeria was represented in the Central Committee. The new secretary-general of the party, Jacques Richard, represented a middle-of-the-road policy. Special rules were passed so that the admission of new members would be strictly controlled with a view to avoiding the formation of a mass party and to restrict membership in various departments where the activists were strong.

The party remained what De Gaulle wished it to be: a *"masse de manoeuvre"* of some 200 deputies, without policy and doctrine, without leadership and organization, ostensibly ready to follow the President of the Republic wherever he might lead them. Yet the man to whom the UNR pledged fealty was opposed to playing the role of political leader! As President of the Republic he stood above political parties and factions. The party was thus unable to resolve the contradictions of French society through its own program and transferred all powers of decision to the providential man.

The Communist Party

The Communist defeat in the referendum and the elections was not as serious as it first appeared. The vote for De Gaulle was in the nature of a transfer of the protest vote, a phenomenon not uncommon in French politics. Bonapartism received the support of a large segment of the working classes, which are traditionally alienated from the system and constantly long for participation. In the Third Republic, General Boulanger was able to win in some of the left-wing districts of Paris. The Communists in 1958 were confronted with a strong nationalist sentiment exacerbated by the Algerian rebellion and the terrorist activities of the FLN.

Even in defeat the Communists derived some solace. They were still the largest single party in the country and continued to control a major part of the unionized workers. Despite some internal conflicts, they had the largest membership and their organization remained solid. The new conciliatory policy pursued by the Soviet leadership and Soviet technological and scientific successes also worked in their favor. Above all the French left-wing forces were literally in shambles and the Communists hoped to collect the pieces.

Ever since 1954 they had tried desperately to reconcile loyalty to the Soviet Union with an appeal for a broad left-wing front in France. The Suez adventure, the rising nationalist sentiment in the country, the Algerian war, the repression of the Hungarian uprising, the subsequent executions there and the intransigence of the Socialist leadership threw them back into isolation every time the prospects of cooperation seemed bright. But now De Gaulle was in the presidency, a right-wing majority controlled the National Assembly, the war in Algeria continued, and the stringent financial measures adopted by the new government provoked considerable dissatisfaction.

The conditions for the creation of a new popular Front were more propitious than before. Public opinion also seemed to be changing. With De Gaulle "out of politics" and his name no longer directly at stake, the political balance of forces began to swing back to the *status quo ante.* In two cases early in 1959 where the elections of two deputies were held anew after the results had been declared invalid, the Communists recovered their past strength. In Romans they received 25.6 per cent on the first ballot as compared to only 15.6 per cent in November, and in La Rochelle 28.6 per cent as compared to 19 per cent. The municipal elections held in March witnessed the return of the Communist voters to the fold and the party thus maintained its position in the Senate. Communist strength began to exert a gravitational pull on the splinter left-wing formations and on many of the Socialists. Popular Front alliances were either explicitly or implicitly accepted by many of the Socialist federations in the municipal elections. The reduction of real wages (it was estimated that within a year after the referendum real wages had dropped by about 5 per cent), the loss of income on the part of the farmers, and restrictive governmental policies in matters of medical assistance and pensions, especially among the veterans and the aged, swelled the ranks of the discontented and increased the protest vote.

Less than a year and a half after their defeat the Communists found themselves in a better tactical position. They had led the opposition to De Gaulle's return and together with some splinter formations and individual leaders—notably Mendès-France—were taking a firm stand against the Fifth Republic. The Socialist opposition to De Gaulle had been qualified and their efforts to distinguish between him and his government were too subtle for many of the voters.

It was with a note of optimism, therefore, that the party held its fifteenth congress in Ivry late in June, 1959. Maurice Thorez presented the report of the party.[4]

Since our fourteenth congress [in 1956] we have witnessed the destruction of the democratic institutions and the establishment of personal power. Our party has been the principal force to resist the reaction. . . . The Communist party predicted the fascist danger but the leaders of the Socialist party continued to divide the working class.

He proceeded in his lengthy report to identify every factor (real or imaginary) that was likely to create popular discontent and hence strengthen the party: the economic recession, the Common Market, capitalist concentration, the drop in the real wages of the workers, the lack of comprehensive social legislation, the fall in farm income, the "proletarization" of the artisans, the development of new middle classes whose interests are not reconcilable with those of the "capitalists," the intrusion of the army in politics and the creation of a "military bureaucracy," the clerical offensive, the continuation of the war in Algeria for which the party advocated negotiations, and an adventurous foreign policy based upon military strength. The party was ready to cope with all these evils by assuming the leadership in a comprehensive union of all the republican forces (socialist rank and file, liberal Catholics, Union of Democratic Forces, and Autonomous Socialists). The party morale was good, he asserted, and the membership on the increase. As of June 1, there were 425,000 members. The task of the party, Thorez concluded, was to create a vast reservoir of good will and attract the millions of prospective sympathizers.

---

[4] For the full proceedings see *L'Humanité,* June 25, 26, 27, 28, and 29, 1959.

The composition of the Congress did not differ substantially from the previous one. The average age of the delegates was 38 years as compared to 35 in 1956. Out of 507 delegates 307 had become members of the party since the Liberation. The majority of delegates were workers. But, and this, in addition to the progressive aging of the party, was a source of concern, only half the delegates were members of factory cells—the rest belonged to local and rural cells. Only about half of the delegates were active in the various front organizations of the party. Although some older members were replaced, Thorez, Duclos, Billoux, Fajon, Frachon, Waldeck-Rochet, and Servin continued to form a solid nucleus within the Politbureau. The secretariat remained firmly in the hands of Thorez and Duclos. The Party had survived. In a society whose rapid pace of industrialization should have undermined the antiquated communist slogans, it continued to prosper. It is likely to monopolize the diffused movement of protest as long as Soviet foreign policy does not change.

It was precisely a shift in Soviet foreign policy and General de Gaulle's initiative that threw the party into confusion in the latter part of 1959. The party rejected in the most explicit terms De Gaulle's offer of self-determination to Algeria. Jacques Duclos wrote that it was another "maneuver to gain time and mislead the United Nations." [5] But when De Gaulle extended an invitation to Premier Khrushchev to visit France and the latter, in a statement on October 31, 1959, declared that there were "strong ties" between France and Algeria and that De Gaulle's offer was a positive step toward peace, the Central Committee of the party reversed its position. While continuing to criticize De Gaulle's domestic and foreign policy, it nonetheless admitted that his invitation to Khrushchev and the offer of self-determination to Algeria were hopeful signs. The Central Committee stated that the higher French bourgeoisie and its government were favorably disposed toward getting out of the war in Algeria because there was an incompatibility of interests between French capitalism and the French settlers.[6] Marxist rationalization could not hide the fact that the party, as always in the past, was following the Soviet line. Soviet leadership seemed to be ready to come to terms with De Gaulle in order to undermine NATO. It was,

---

[5] Reported in *Le Monde*, September 18, 1959.
[6] *Le Monde*, November 3 and 5, 1959.

however, an about-face that the party made with great relief since its position with respect to the FLN had never been popular. But it put the party in a predicament. For the first time it had to approve *some* of the actions of General de Gaulle. Hence, it was running the risk of blunting the sharpness of its opposition, which would enable it to capitalize on the diffused protest against the regime.

The Predicament of the Socialists

Following the elections, in which the Socialist party had suffered no decrease in its electoral strength—3,167,354 as compared to 3,180,656 in 1956—but in which its parliamentary strength was reduced to just forty deputies, the position of the party appeared to be extremely difficult. The leadership had played an important role in bringing about De Gaulle's return only to find itself elbowed out. To the Right, the UNR and the Independents took over the nationalist policy that the Socialists had previously pursued when in power. To the Left, the Communists and other groups were raising the battle cries of social reforms, republicanism, and peace in Algeria. The party was being slowly demoralized by the insistence of its leader on supporting De Gaulle while providing a "constructive opposition" to the government. A number of its members and federations were beginning to look to the Autonomous Socialists and to entertain thoughts of cooperating with the Communists.

In an extraordinary party congress held in Paris early in December, 1958, Guy Mollet secured approval of his position.[7] The party pledged its support to De Gaulle as president while opposing the UNR. Late in December the economic and financial policy of the government, inspired largely by an Independent, Antoine Pinay, drove Guy Mollet and the two other Socialist ministers out of the cabinet and into the opposition. But their attacks were directed against the government of Michel Debré, not against De Gaulle. The latter's policy for Algeria was endorsed by the party leadership, while little criticism has been forthcoming against his foreign and military policy. The sharpest Socialist reaction was provoked by governmental policies that affected adversely its electoral clientele, particularly with regard to pensions, social welfare measures, wages and salaries, credits to the agricultural sector of the economy, vet-

[7] *Année Politique*, 1958, pp. 149–50.

erans' benefits, and, of course, the public schools. Halfheartedly, the
Socialists began also to ask for larger parliamentary initiative, involving scrutiny and control of the cabinet.

The most serious problems facing the party were ideological and
organizational. The first stemmed from the refusal of the party to
follow the lead of the British and German brother parties in recon-
sidering its doctrine. It is still dedicated to socialization of the means
of production and continues to employ Marxist symbols and vocabulary. Yet its electoral clientele is largely composed today of small
bourgeois, some of the workers of the nationalized industries, public
school teachers, a great part of the miners, and the workers in small
factories. The party has become increasingly "radicalized" as some
observers put it.[8] Efforts to reconsider the doctrine and give the
party a more pragmatic orientation, as André Philip had suggested,
were blocked repeatedly by the secretary-general.[9] Caught between
resurgent nationalism, to which they had virtually capitulated,
and Marxism, to which they continued to pay lip service, the Socialists, like many other parties, were unable to make an ideological and
political breakthrough and examine the new issues and problems
characteristic of an increasingly industrialized society. As a result
the "new" middle classes, the white-collar workers, the growing body
of salaried personnel in large-scale industry have not been attracted by the party. In addition its membership is declining and its
militants aging. Compared to other parties, the Socialist delegates
and deputies have the highest age average. Physical as well as political rejuvenation is badly needed.

Criticism of the party's leadership has come from many quarters.
Many of the left-wing militants had already abandoned the party
before or after the referendum and joined the Autonomous Socialist
party. On February 12, 1959, the elder statesman of the Socialist
party and former President of the Republic, Vincent Auriol, resigned and expressed in clear-cut terms his lack of confidence in
the secretary general, Guy Mollet.[10] In the municipal and senatorial
elections, party federations allied themselves in different departments with the UNR, the Independents, the MRP, the Radicals, and
Communists, with or without the blessings of the secretary general

---

[8] M. Duverger, "SFIO—Mort ou transfiguration," *Les Temps modernes*, May,
1955, pp. 1863–85.

[9] See André Philip: *Le Socialisme Trahi* (Paris, 1957).

[10] *Le Monde*, February 13, 1959, for the letter of the former President of the
Republic.

and his executive committee. The leadership of the party was losing control over the militants.

The SFIO congress of July, 1959 was an occasion for airing grievances against the party leadership.[11] The illusory character of the distinction made between De Gaulle and the cabinet was stressed by a number of speakers, and a strong plea was made for positive opposition to the cabinet *and* the President. Mollet countered by reasserting that De Gaulle was pursuing a liberal and humane policy and hence was close to the Socialists. "We must not shut our eyes however," he concluded, "to the continuing threat. There have been changes in the army, but a certain number of fascists continue to be active. If their chances are limited because of the President of the Republic, they will become great if he disappeared." But he hastened to remind the congress that "the Bolshevik danger existed also."

Guy Mollet was elected unanimously secretary-general of the party, along with an overwhelmingly loyal executive committee. In its resolution the party went from "constructive opposition" over to "vigorous" opposition. It urged negotiations with the Algerian rebels that would entail reciprocal guarantees. It concluded with a pledge to make every effort to regroup the "democratic Left," coupled with an attack against the Communists "who have played until now the unhappy role of dividing the working class." About 65 per cent of the delegates voted for this resolution, with the big federations that are controlled by the leadership providing the bulk of the votes. No new secessionist movement developed, but there was little enthusiasm about the role and the future of the party.

The Unreconstructed Left

While the Right was able, after the referendum, to coalesce behind the UNR and the Independents, the Left was fragmented to an unprecedented extent. In addition to the usual split between Communists and Socialists, there was a proliferation of left-wing formations whose leaders rejected both the pro-Soviet attitude and internal authoritarianism of the Communists and the nationalism of the Socialists.

Prior to the referendum, the Union of Democratic Forces (UFD) had developed from a loose alliance of various Left splinter groups

---

[11] For the full proceedings see *Le Monde*, July 10, 11, 12–13, and 14, 1959.

and the Autonomous Socialists. But this was only a tactical alliance—a cartel—and the Autonomous Socialists had no intention of cooperating with Mendès-France and his friends. As the PSA secretary put it, "They are Radicals and we are Socialists." [12] On the other hand, an alliance with the Union of Socialist Left (UGS) was looked upon with favor. "To the extent to which they are Socialists —that is to say, to the extent to which they wish to overthrow the capitalist regime in order to replace it with a regime of social democracy—there is every reason to believe that we could agree with them." [13] The elections and the crushing defeat of the proponents of a No produced a profound disillusionment. The last effort of the UFD was to nominate a candidate for the presidency of the Republic who received, surprisingly enough, a creditable number of votes. For several months the Left remained in a state of political shock. The municipal and senatorial elections were not encouraging since they registered a return to the traditional political formations. Only a handful of municipal councilors who ran on the UGS, UFD, or PSA tickets were successful.

Early in May the congress of the PSA voted unanimously in favor of a fusion with the UGS, but remained reticent about its relations with the UFD, that is, to Mendès-France and his political friends who had left the Radical Socialist party. The Autonomous Socialist party called for "re-establishment of a democracy based upon a real separation of powers and greater parliamentary independence," and for a negotiated cease-fire in Algeria. In a carefully worded formula, it approved of "agreement with the Communist party as the circumstances demanded on specific and limited objectives." [14] With some 15,000 to 20,000 members, they appeared to be stronger than even the leadership had expected or hoped for. The PSA was active in some seventy departments and it had considerable appeal to the young generation, particularly among intellectuals and university students. But the ideological conflict that had plagued the old SFIO persisted. This was illustrated by a debate between André Philip and Oreste Rosenfeld in which the latter argued the traditional Socialist doctrine involving the expropriation of the capitalist class, while the former urged the Socialists to establish limited objectives and confront concrete problems.

---

[12] Depreux, "Pourquoi Nous Avons Quitté la SFIO," *France Observateur*, September 18, 1958.

[13] *Ibid.*

[14] For the Congress of the PSA, *Le Monde*, May 5, 1959.

The new Socialist party announced its determination to unite with "all authentic Socialists"—a phrase hardly calculated to facilitate fusion with the Radicals. Mendès-France had taken a big step toward closing the ideological gap when he spoke in favor of "open Socialism." [15] But the word "open" evoked the flexibility and indiscipline so characteristic of the Radicals. In September, 1959, Mendès-France "Radicals"—labelled Center of Democratic Action—held a meeting in which it was apparent that they agreed with the PSA on its condemnation of the new regime, its attitude toward Algeria, its criticism of the economic and financial policy of the government, and the foreign policy pursued by General de Gaulle. The CDA agreed to dissolve and join the PSA. While acknowledging the identity of the objectives of the two groups, Mendès-France also pointed out that nineteenth century Marxism was outdated. The idea of abolishing private property is no longer valid, he stated, while the notion that private property must be qualified in favor of the general interest is widely accepted.

The union of Autonomous Socialists with the Mendès-France Radicals was consummated a month later. Mendès-France called for a total transformation of the "system" as in 1789. "We are at the gates of Bastille. It is time to find out who is governing this country —those who always act for their profit or those who have the power of numbers and feel that they have attained their 'political manhood.' " [16] Twelve former Socialist leaders and parliamentarians resigned from the Socialist party and joined the PSA. Its membership was now estimated at 25,000 and it looked as if the split within the SFIO was more than an episode in the perennial fragmentation of the Left.

Early in November, 1959, a Congress of the UGS gave its approval to the continuation of the "dialogue" with the PSA, with a view to the establishment of a single party. Although expressing its deep concern with Mendès-France and "neoradicalism," the party hoped for agreement on a clear-cut program including "complete freedom of expression" and "liberation of the workers by socialization of the means of production and commerce." [17] Thus the way seemed to be clear for unity among the small left-wing groups. But unity of the entire Left, including the SFIO and the Communist party, was as far away as ever.

[15] *Le Monde*, September 20–21, and June 23, 1959.
[16] Speech reported in *Le Monde*, October 16, 1959.
[17] *Le Monde*, November 3, 1959.

Meanwhile, another Left group—the Democratic Union of Labor —made its appearance in April, 1959. It was largely a carryover of the former Center of Republican Reform which had favored Yes because of De Gaulle's liberal record. It has been claimed that the UDT was formed under express instructions from De Gaulle. One of its leaders stated that De Gaulle was not a "man of the Right" and that it was the task of the new party to unite the Left in his support.[18] The party would eschew the old ideological divisions in favor of a policy corresponding to the real problems of the day. Any man of good will of the Left, like Mendès-France, was welcome, it was announced, provided he accepted the new institutions and the leadership of General de Gaulle. Its creation was calculated to facilitate the role of the President as an "arbiter" by creating a Gaullist group to the Left of the UNR. However, the new group aroused little response among the mass of the members of either the Left or the UNR.

The MRP

After its surprisingly good showing in the elections, the MRP seemed to enter a new period of vitality, thanks to the support of the dynamic French Confederation of Christian Workers and of liberal rural elements primarily drawn from the Catholic youth organizations. In the senatorial elections they managed to improve their position by increasing the number of their senators from twenty-one to twenty-nine—the largest net gain registered by any party.

The crisis, however, caused in part by the secession of Georges Bidault and the formation of a nationalist right-wing Christian Democracy with some fifteen deputies committed to the integration of Algeria, persisted. Some MRP leaders were willing to make concessions in order to bring Bidault and his nationalist supporters back into the fold. The MRP joined the "majority" in the Assembly, and two ministers were drawn from its ranks. But the liberal Catholic youth formations, the white-collar workers, and the more liberal rural elements forced it progressively into the opposition both in the Senate and in the National Assembly when social and economic questions were debated. The MRP parliamentarians thus voted against the budget of the government, against the bill providing for credits

---

[18] See the statement of one of the leaders of the UDT, Louis Vallon, in *Le Monde*, May 15, 1959.

to the agricultural sector of the economy, and were restive over
De Gaulle's foreign policy.

The relations between the MRP and the newly established syn-
dicalist and agricultural formations under the name of Rally of
Democratic Forces (RFD) were debated with a seriousness typical of the party in two national congresses in February and May,
1959.[19] The first congress called for the renovation of the party. The
standing rules were amended to permit the participation in the party
of "the new elements representing the live forces of the nation"; the
congress also considered the "Bidault case" settled in that he had
placed himself outside of the party. But by the time the second
congress was held, the climate of opinion had changed. The party
had shown its "staying power" in the municipal and senatorial elections, hence the need for overhauling its organization and program
seemed less pressing. The remarks of the RFD leader, Bernard Lambert, were heard with attention, and it was agreed that between the
"sclerosis" of the Socialists and the "decomposition" of the Radicals
the MRP had a great opportunity of becoming a broad *parti tra-
vailliste* (a Labor party). Despite the sympathy expressed for the
RFD, the party decided simply to continue discussions and implicitly rejected Lambert's suggestion that 50 per cent of the higher
echelons of the party be workers and farmers. In its final statement it
approved De Gaulle's Algerian policy and criticized the government's social and economic program. It counseled increased vigilance
for the preservation of European unity. It reasserted its claims that
the action of Pierre Pflimlin in May had saved the Republic and proceeded to re-elect the same leadership in all important posts.

The Ordeal of the Radicals

The Radical Socialist party has often been counted out of
the ring only to make a miraculous comeback. In 1945 it was considered moribund if not dead, yet became a key party and provided a
large number of ministers and prime ministers, among whom was
the most dynamic leader of the Fourth Republic, Pierre Mendès-
France. However, the latter's efforts to create a mass and disciplined
organization split the party into warring sections and contributed to
its defeat in the elections of November.

Since then five "radical families" have confronted the problem of

---

[19] For the full proceedings of the Congress of the MRP see *Le Monde,* February
1–2, February 3; and May 8, 9, 10–11, and 12, 1959.

burying the hatchet and agreeing on a common doctrine. A handful
of Radicals under Mendès-France resigned from the party and ultimately joined the Autonomous Socialists. A second group, representing the extreme Right led by André Morice, lost heavily in the
elections. The Center of the party was divided into two groups—
Félix Gaillard, who inherited the position of Mendès-France, led
the official Radical Socialist party, and Edgar Faure, the former
leader of the party, headed the Rally of the Left Republicans. Yet a
fifth group—the small UDSR (Socialist and Democratic Union of
the Resistance)—led by François Mitterand proudly refused to
forget the conditions under which the Fourth Republic came to an
end and advocated strong opposition to the Fifth Republic and
General de Gaulle.

The various radical families had lost few votes in the election of
November (from 15.3 per cent in 1956 to 12.9 per cent in 1958), but
their failure to unite on the second ballot reduced seriously their
representation in the National Assembly (thirty-seven instead of
seventy-four deputies). Félix Gaillard, with the tacit support of
Edgar Faure and of the conservative elements of the UDSR, hoped
that the party would be able to make a comeback by appealing to
the forces that had always contributed its principal strength—the
municipal and the departmental notables. As in the past, the party
expected to capitalize on the traditional anti-State feeling of the
French and to become the spokesman of the various interest groups
—especially the farmers, merchants, and artisans. There was no practical reason, therefore, to bring about organizational reform or to reconsider the old doctrine.

In order to qualify as a group under the standing orders of the
National Assembly, Radical deputies managed to create an *Entente
Démocratique*, which now has forty-two members. In the municipal
elections the Radicals recovered lost ground and improved their
position in the Senate by electing fifty-one senators as compared
to forty-seven in 1958. The loss of their most dynamic leader was felt
to be an advantage by those who remained in the party. "The party
has regained its wings," stated Félix Gaillard, in the congress of June,
1959. Yet the party had lost its following among the youth. It was
still sharply divided about the role it had played in the events leading to De Gaulle's return and apprehensive about the future. As in
1945, it expressed nostalgia for the institutions of the previous regime. The name of Alain, the Radical writer and critic who is a sym-

bol of individualism and anti-State philosophy, was evoked as usual, and the Republic was proclaimed to be in danger. But the old Radical battle cry of *laïcité* found little response among the delegates. Nor was the suggestion of cooperation with the Socialists warmly received. The party continued its period of convalescence. It needed no other medicine than moderate electoral success—and many considered the senatorial elections as the best sign of recovery.[20]

The Independents and Moderates

The activity among the left-wing formations in search of unity contrasted sharply with the complacency of the Independents and Moderates. A loose organization composed primarily of political bosses, the party did remarkably well in the elections of 1958. It gained about a million votes and at least 20 deputies, to bring its strength in the National Assembly to 120 deputies. Without mass membership or a coherent program, it exploited the rising wave of nationalism and Gaullism to its own electoral ends. Under the leadership of Roger Duchet, the Independents, including loosely affiliated conservative groups, received the largest number of votes—some four million—on the first ballot. It was natural, therefore, to expect friction to develop between the UNR and the Independents, the latter feeling rightly that UNR intransigence and unwillingness to form common lists on the second ballot prevented them from emerging as the largest party in the National Assembly.

The Independents became the conservative party in the National Assembly in matters of social and economic reform, the religious question, and even Algeria. They joined the UNR in the cabinet, and one of their leaders, former Prime Minister Antoine Pinay, was responsible for financial and economic policy, much to the distress of many in the UNR and particularly its secretary-general, Chalandon. However, conflicts between Independents and the UNR became sharper—on social and financial matters, as well as on De Gaulle's Algerian policy. Some Independents began to vote against the government. And unlike the UNR they continued to gain electoral strength. They did well in the municipal and the senatorial elections, gaining in the senate five seats (85 as compared to 80) to emerge as the largest group in the second chamber. As long as De Gaulle remains in office, political tactics call for caution, but with

---

[20] For the congress of the Radical Socialist party see *Le Monde*, June 14–15 and 16, 1959.

De Gaulle out, there would be no reason why an alliance between Independents and Radicals could not fetch them the most coveted office of the Fifth Republic—the presidency. The relative lack of interest on the part of many of the Radicals on the question of increased subsidies to Catholic schools may remove one of the major obstacles to the formation of such an alliance.

Activist Formations

Most of the activist groups and formations were absorbed within the UNR. The victory of the Poujadists in 1956 was short-lived. Without any supporters and without an organization, Poujade continued after the election of 1958 to speak in favor of French Algeria, to issue appeals to various military leaders to "take over," and to demand a drastic overhaul of the Fifth Republic. His most constructive suggestion was that the Fifth like the Fourth Republic ought to be blown to bits.

Most of the other right-wing groups limited themselves to specific objectives. The veterans' organizations continued to agitate in favor of "integration" and against De Gaulle's more liberal policy in Algeria; the old USRAF was reconstituted under the name of Rally of French Algeria (RAF) and reacted vehemently to De Gaulle's promise of self-determination. Fifty-two of the deputies from Algeria established a parliamentary group called Unity of the Republic, committed to integration in Algeria, led by die-hard nationalists. They were later joined by two UNR members who had been expelled from the party. The army continued to maintain a posture of legality and outward loyalty to the new regime and to De Gaulle. But extreme nationalist forces were at work. Thus, at a meeting of the reservist officers in Paris in September, 1959, a statement was issued in favor of integration of Algeria. Marshal Juin criticized sharply De Gaulle's policy in Algeria, and the commanding officer of the French forces, General Challe, reaffirmed the decision of the army to stay there in order to "protect" the Algerian and French populations. Among the colonels and the generals the attitude of open hostility to the Fourth Republic had been changed to watchful waiting.

*   *   *   *   *

Professor Goguel, in his excellent analysis of politics under the Third Republic, identified two generic categories in which the various parties could be grouped: the Party of Order and the Party of

Movement. If similar categories were applied to the Fifth Republic, the party of "order" constitutes a majority in the Parliament. The impulse to action comes from the government, in which half the ministers are nonparliamentarians, and whose inspiration is a man disdainful of political parties. In the National Assembly, despite the virtual elimination of the Communists by the electoral system, the traditional parties are strong. Out of 465 deputies for metropolitan France, 169 are Radicals and Independents. At least a third of the UNR deputies were elected because of their local attachments and past affiliations, while the 40 Socialists hardly represent any more a party of movement. Even discounting the traditionalist character of a segment of the UNR, more than half of the deputies belong in spirit and by virtue of their electoral clientele to the parties of "order." Many of the UNR and Algerian deputies represent reaction rather than movement.

Thus, the political structures of France continue to show remarkable stability and tenacity despite the industrial and economic development of the country. Efforts to disengage the political formations from the old doctrinal disputes have generally failed. "In an atomic age the conflict about Catholic schools is outdated," declared the Minister of Information and a leading Gaullist, Roger Frey.[21] Yet, in the last months of 1959 the religious question agitated public opinion more than any other issue. The victory of the proponents of support to Catholic schools, who succeeded in securing favorable amendments in an already generous government bill, has revived bitter feelings among those attached to the public schools. Nor has it been possible for the parties to attract the new social groups among the population: the managers, white-collar workers, technicians of the nationalized industries, and rural elite who have adopted modern techniques of agricultural exploitation. The MRP failed to open up the party to workers and farmers, the Left has refused to abandon doctrinal socialism in favor of a more pragmatically oriented labor party, the Communists hold to their ideology as tenaciously as ever, and the Independents gather strength with a program of inaction. In the long run, economic and social development is bound to bring about political change, but in France so far, ideologies outlive economic structures and an equation between economic progress and political change is an oversimplification.

---

[21] Quoted from the text of a speech in *Le Monde,* June 24, 1959.

CHAPTER XVI

The Vision and the Record

A YEAR AFTER De Gaulle was granted sweeping powers to refashion the Republic, the record of accomplishment looked impressive. The institutional panoply of the Fifth Republic was readied and began to function in record time. To the average Frenchman the most tangible evidence of success was the stability of the executive. With De Gaulle as prime minister and, since January, 1959, as president, surrounded by loyal ministers, continuity of thought and action was assured. Sweeping reforms were carried through in the French Empire. The former African colonies became autonomous states with the right of independence explicitly recognized, and all —with the solitary exception of Guinea—joined the Community with France. In Algeria, General Salan was replaced by a civil servant and instructor in the Institute of Political Studies of the University of Paris, Paul Delouvrier, and a number of transfers of officers gave hope of the dismantlement of the network that had defied the civil authority under the Fourth Republic. An imaginative plan for industrialization of Algeria seemed to attack the root problem of that embattled country.

At home a feverish legislative activity led to long-awaited reforms in housing, medical instruction, judicial reorganization, national defense, retail markets (at least something was being done about the scandal of *Les Halles*), tax policy, and monetary affairs.[1] The aver-

---

[1] For a general account of the major legislative reforms under the De Gaulle government see *Lois Organiques* and "Aperçu sur les Principales Réformes intervenues en France . . . du 1er juin 1958 au 5 fevrier 1959," *Notes et Etudes* (*La Documentation Française*, February 26, 1959). For the economic reforms of December, 1958 *Rapport sur la Situation Financière presenté à Monsieur le Ministre des Finances etc.* (Paris: Imprimerie Nationale, 1958), and for a discussion, Raymond Aron, "La Ve République Choisit la rigueur Monétaire," *Preuves*, May, 1959, pp. 3–13.

age Frenchman derived even greater satisfaction from France's new international prestige. After one year's intensive diplomatic effort, his country was once more reckoned a power by friend and foe. In contrast with the divisions and vacillations of the Fourth Republic, France had a stable government with a vision and a policy. In a country that will soon have the youngest population in Europe and that has made remarkable industrial and technological progress since 1950, the future looked reassuring. And it was General de Gaulle's vision and policies that shaped the future.

The Fifth Republic inherited, together with the burdens, many of the realizations left by the "princes" who governed the Fourth Republic. In several respects it simply carried on from where the Fourth Republic had left off, for example, as regards economic and colonial policy, and the Common Market. It innovated in the realm of institutions and up to a degree in foreign policy. It has been unable thus far to solve what has been generally considered the thorniest problem—the strife in Algeria—and to fashion new ties with North Africa. In an effort to eliminate uneconomic subsidies and settle the status of religious schools, it introduced measures that provoked violent disagreements.

France by 1957–58 was a prosperous country moving steadily toward economic maturity. The backward sectors of the economy were on the decline, and industrial expansion was the dominant trend. There were two basic problems that in many respects antedated the Fourth Republic—the relative low level of wages and the high level of domestic prices caused by protective tariffs and a steady inflationary trend.

The reforms undertaken by the De Gaulle government at the end of December, 1958 were made possible by the economic progress accomplished under the Fourth Republic, especially in its last five years. The purpose of the reforms was to prepare France to enter the Common Market—a decision that had been made by the leaders of the Fourth Republic and which De Gaulle promised to honor; to reduce the budgetary deficit; to increase exports and at the same time to stimulate the return of French capital from abroad and attract foreign capital. The crux of the problem was how to maintain investment at a high level, yet reduce the budgetary deficit.

In devaluating the franc by about 15 per cent, De Gaulle and the Minister of Finance, Antoine Pinay, followed in the footsteps of the Fourth Republic. In addition, the government liberalized imports up to 90 per cent with all member countries of the Organization for European Economic Cooperation. It was hoped that devaluation would stimulate exports while the liberalization of imports would provide for competition between French and Common Market products and keep prices down.

The budget for 1959 originally provided for an expenditure of 6,189 billion old francs, an increase of 658 billion (about a billion and a half dollars) over 1958. In order to keep the deficit down to manageable proportions, the government decided to reduce or eliminate certain expenditures (for example, veterans' pensions, health and social security benefits, and subsidies), while increasing taxes. Savings effected amounted to about 300 billion francs, and a similar sum was found in new revenues, so that the deficit was brought down from the 1,200 billion francs originally anticipated to about 587 billion francs (or a little over a billion dollars at the new rate of exchange)—an amount which the government planned to raise by public subscription. The reduction of expenditures did not affect important public investments—schools, housing, the French Community, and the application of the Constantine Plan. Indeed, total outlay of the government for economic development rose 10 per cent over that of 1958.

Prices of both industrial goods and agricultural products were expected to rise because of the increased cost of raw materials and the elimination of subsidies. Wages, however, were to remain stable, with only a small increase of the minimum wages contemplated. Taxes were also to go up, thus further reducing available money in the hands of the consumer. It was hoped that the devaluation of the franc would increase sales abroad and that the return of capital would lower the rate of interest, thus stimulating production. It was a bold plan of temporary economic austerity that reduced the purchasing power of the masses at a time when consumer demand was high and consumer expectations had been encouraged by the nation's prosperity.

It was estimated that about $4 billion in gold or foreign currency was "hidden" in France and that perhaps another $4 billion was owned by French and deposited in one form or another abroad. France had no dollars, but the French did. If at least part of this amount would return in the form of investment or deposits in French banks, then the experiment might succeed. Crucial to the success of the plan was the stability of the prices of raw materials and the continuation of favorable terms of trade.

Articles 91 and 92 of the constitution gave to the government sweeping powers for a transitional period of four months, which ended on February 5, 1959. It was under this grant of powers that the government proceeded to enact social, economic, and political reforms by ordinances having the effect of organic laws. It promulgated an electoral law, made arrangements for the election of the President of the Republic, set up the organs of the Community, and organized the Social and Economic Council and the Constitutional Council.

One of the most important acts of the government was to overhaul the organization of national defense by an ordinance of January 7, 1959. Two special committees, both under the chairmanship of the President of the Republic, were established: the Committee on Defense, which makes major decisions regarding the defense establishment; and the Committee of Military Defense, which concerns itself with military strategy. The President of the Republic, who under the constitution is commander in chief, is thus given broad powers of policy initiation and action in the area of national defense. The prime minister's role was restricted to implementation of general policy, despite the fact that according to Article 21 of the constitution he "is responsible for national defense." The same ordinance provided that all men are liable for seventeen years of military service. During the first five years they are available for active duty at any time, and during the remaining twelve years they form part of the reserves. This is in addition to compulsory military service for two years.

Another ordinance promulgated also on January 7, 1959 aimed, in accordance with the Gaullist doctrine, to encourage development of profit sharing by the workers in enterprises. Implementation was to result from specific agreements between representatives of industry and labor. However, virtually all trade unions have protested against this scheme and very few contracts have been concluded.

In the realm of social welfare the government compensated for cuts in some social services by providing a 4 to 5 per cent raise in the minimum wage. It also increased the existing old-age benefits by about $10 per year, provided for more comprehensive insurance against unemployment, and added to welfare benefits for children and adolescents. The government stepped up support for housing construction, one of the areas in which the French economy had lagged tragically. Fresh credits were earmarked for construction— almost 50 per cent more than the $315 million allocated in 1958.

Most of the increase was to be used exclusively for the financing of lower- and middle-income housing. Strict regulations were also passed to guarantee that lower- and middle-income housing was made available only to members of those income groups.

The government also turned its attention to reform of the public schools. Critics have long deplored the sharp distinction in French education between the academic course of study leading to *lycée* and university, and the terminal or vocational program. Children are required to undergo rigorous examinations at the age of eleven to determine their fitness to pursue academic work. Since middle- and upper-class families generally prepare their children for these tests while working-class and lower-income families do not, the two programs tend to correspond to income and class differentials in French society, and also result in a regrettable waste of intellectual talent. The government's reform was intended to reduce somewhat the differences between the two curricula and put off to a later date the point at which career decisions are made. Three stages of education are now provided: primary education consisting of an elementary cycle with one program for all students between the ages of 6 to 11; an intermediary period between the ages of 11 to 13; and secondary education (the *lycée* and complementary courses) open to all who show aptitude for it. It is to be feared, however, that enactment of half measures may forestall complete reorganization of the educational system.

Algerian Policy

At first, General de Gaulle's political policies in Algeria showed no appreciable difference from the past. He refused to pronounce the word "integration," and instead promised free elections so that Algerian spokesmen could be selected with whom he would "do what remained to be done" (*faire le reste*). Algeria was to have a "choice position" in the French "whole"—a far cry from the extremist thesis that Algeria constituted several departments of France. In his Constantine speech of October 3, 1958 General de Gaulle called for the transformation of Algeria. "This means that . . . the resources of the soil and the ability of the (Algerian) elite must be brought to light and developed; . . . that the children must be educated; . . . that all Algeria must have her share in what modern civilization can and must bring to all in terms of well-being and dignity." To achieve this "profound transformation," he laid out a five-year plan for the industrialization of Algeria, the exploitation of her resources, and the massive education of Moslem children. Among other things, he promised: distribution of over 600,000 acres of land to Moslem farmers; creation of large iron and steel production centers; the building of highways, houses, schools, and hospitals; and regular employment for 400,000 additional workers, with 10 per cent of all civil service positions in metropolitan France reserved for Moslems.[2]

Three weeks later, in a press conference, he offered the "peace of the brave" to the FLN. They could, he pointed out, raise the white flag and surrender. They would be received with honor and be granted immunity. As for the members of the "Algerian Provisional Government," they could come to Paris, if they so desired, to discuss matters with him by addressing themselves to the nearest French Embassy. Again they were guaranteed immunity and, what is more, a return ticket. When peace has settled upon the land, the way will then be prepared for a "political solution." General de Gaulle then hinted at what might come:

> The future solutions will be based—because that is the nature of things —upon that courageous personality of Algeria and upon its close association with Metropolitan France. I believe also that this ensemble, completed by the Sahara, will link itself, for the common progress, with the free States of Morocco and Tunisia.

Recognition of the distinctive "personality" of Algeria and the idea of "close association with France" pointed up again the differences between the advocates of integration and the government.

In order to implement the Constantine Plan, two administrative bodies were created: the High Council of the Constantine Plan and the Fund for the Development of Algeria. Plans were made for the construction of 2,000 classrooms and 600 social centers annually. It was also decided that between 70 and 90 per cent of the positions in the public service in Algeria would be reserved for French Moslems. A special decree made available a procedure under which foreign enterprises could work in the Sahara, on the basis of contractual agreement with the French State.

The envisaged expenditure under the Constantine Plan was both heavy and inadequate in view of the sharply rising Moslem popula-

---

[2] For the most important pronouncements of General de Gaulle on Algeria, see Appendix B. See also Bertrand Schneider, *La Ve République et l'Algérie, Documents et Confrontations* (Paris, 1959).

tion of Algeria. In 1956 the Moslems numbered ten million. It was expected that by 1970 they would be fifteen million, and would double by 1980. The average income of a Moslem is $40 per year compared to an average of $620 for a European. Given the pace of the population growth it was estimated that in order to increase the standard of living by 2 per cent annually, the French would have to invest at least $400 million a year—and double that figure by 1980. Even then, it would take fifty years to bring the average income of the Moslems up to one half that of the Europeans. In spite of inducements offered by the government, at least until the end of 1959 private business failed to be attracted by opportunities in Algeria —which is indicative of the reluctance of Frenchmen to place their capital there.

The financial problem might be eased by profits from Saharan gas and oil and industrialization of Algeria. As of 1959, no comprehensive program for industrialization of Algeria had been drawn up. Indeed, plans for utilization of Saharan energy were based more on the needs of France and the Common Market than those of Algeria. In any case, as the French completed a pipeline to the sea and increased production of both oil and natural gas, the Algerian leaders became more determined than ever to win independence and lay their hands upon a resource of their own soil.

The French hope that the Algerian masses can be won over by a rise in employment and distribution of land to the Moslems. But, given the continuation of the rebellion and the rapid increase of population in Algeria, it is doubtful that an appreciable rise in the standard of living can be accomplished despite the Constantine Plan. As of the end of 1959 only a few thousands acres of land had been given to Algerians and mass unemployment continued to be endemic.

On September 16, 1959 General de Gaulle finally defined his government's Algerian policy in a nation-wide radio and television broadcast. The President appeared to be ready to break with the past. He offered to Algeria, subject to final ratification by the French body politic, the right to choose (in a referendum to be held four years after pacification) between independence, integration with France, and home rule. Some observers saw in this statement a logical development of his liberal colonial policy, while others pointed to a number of factors that may have forced his hand: increased awareness and impatience with the war by the member-states of the Community, the meetings of the independent states of Africa early in August of the same year and their full support of the Algerian Provisional Government, the more conciliatory attitude of the Algerians who asked for negotiations without any prior conditions, the approaching debate before the United Nations, and the visit of President Eisenhower. The very prospect of independence and the promise that Algerians would freely choose their future status represented, however, a reversal of French official policy and raised hope for the settlement of the war.

However, General de Gaulle virtually ruled out independence by the manner in which the choice was presented. To opt for independence would be a catastrophe for Algeria, he stated, leading to internal chaos and ultimately to Communist domination. If Algerians wanted it, he promised to bow before the inevitable, but on two conditions: that the French settlers would remain French and be "regrouped" in certain regions of Algeria, presumably the littoral where most of them now live; and that there would be no interference with the free extraction of oil and gas by the French or with its flow some 400 miles north to the Algerian ports. Independence would thus be burdened with a double servitude.

On the other hand, integration, described as complete identification of all Algerians with France, would probably not receive the endorsement of Moslems anxious to preserve their own way of life and free to express themselves in a single electoral college. The people of Metropolitan France also would be reluctant to assume the financial burdens of complete integration. It was obvious that General de Gaulle favored the third solution: "The government of Algerians by Algerians, backed up by French help and in close relationship with her, as regards the economy, education, defense, and foreign relations." If Algerians use their universal suffrage with moderation and opt in favor of home rule, the internal regime of Algeria would be a "federal" type in which the various religious and ethnic groups —French, Arab, Kabyle, Mozambite—are protected. It would be presumably a system realizing Calhoun's dream of concurrent majorities, to the detriment, naturally, of a genuine home rule. Whatever the merits of the choice offered, it would probably not be made until four whole years elapsed after the pacification of the country. By "pacification" De Gaulle means a state of things in which there will be no more than 200 victims a year from "acts of terrorism and ambuscades." The official governmental organ *Semaine en Algérie* reported that the total number of civilian victims in the period between January 1 and August 31, 1959 was 1,613.

The whole scheme depended upon pacification, and there were two ways to bring pacification about. One was by negotiation with the Algerian Provisional Government and the FLN, and the second by an increased military effort and continued psychological warfare to wipe out the rebels and indoctrinate the Algerian masses. The army refused steadfastly to consider negotiation, and so did De Gaulle, who made his statement after a two-day visit in Algeria during which he consulted with leading army officers. He repeated his "peace of the brave" offer and urged the rebels to address themselves to the "authorities" in order to obtain "guarantees." The Algerian leaders could accept such an offer only by asking for more far-reaching concessions in the way of guarantees—even, for example, to the extent of specifying the withdrawal of the French Army—than the French were prepared to grant. The period of four years after pacification when, presumably, the referendum would be held, was also much too long to satisfy the Moslem leaders. Life, both natural and political, has a term. De Gaulle at the time was sixty-eight. In four years new elections were to take place. His proposal for a referendum split the UNR and was received with pronounced ill-humor by the Independents without rallying the Left (alienated by the government's social and economic measures and the bill to increase subsidies for Catholic schools). The course of French politics seemed unpredictable. Members of the FLN and the Algerian Provisional Government could not place their trust in De Gaulle so long as the army retained a veto over policy. Or they might have concluded that his September 16 statement was an effort to confuse the issue and gain time—a move typical of the best traditions of the Fourth Republic.

In the meantime the war continued. The army headquarters went on mentioning in communiques the staggering losses of the rebels and intimated that complete pacification of the region was a matter of weeks or months. General Challe, the commander in chief, stated early in 1959, for instance, that there was a military solution to the Algerian problem and that the solution was imminent. Marshal Juin declared then that the end of the hostilities was in sight. At the close of June, when a particularly violent raid in the vicinity of Bône—one of the larger Algerian cities—coincided with declarations of the Communist-controlled trade unions (CGT), the Catholic trade unions (CFTC), and the Radical party in favor of negotiations to end the war in Algeria, the army communique described the raid as follows: "In order to support the campaign in favor of negotiations recently launched in the Metropolis by those who support traditionally the FLN and promote the actions of the terrorists . . . a commando was sent from Tunisia . . . to operate in the town of Bône. . . ." Never before or since May 13 had the army issued a communique with such a threatening political note.

Despite De Gaulle's popularity and authority, the army was still a state within a state. A survey showed that, out of some twenty-five high-ranking officers who played a leading role in the events of May 13, the great majority continued to occupy positions of crucial importance a year later. General Salan, like General Giraud in 1943, was "promoted" to a nonexistent post, but only to be replaced by General Challe, who had been temporarily arrested after May 13 by the Minister of Defense of the Fourth Republic and ordered out of Paris. General Allard was transferred to take command of the French forces in Western Germany but was replaced by General Massu. Colonel Godard remained in his position as head of the powerful police section of the army. Colonel Gribius, whose tanks were poised in the outskirts of Paris to move into the capital a few days before General de Gaulle became prime minister, was Director of the Algerian Youth Services of the Army.

The transfer of five top rebel leaders from a prison in Paris to a fortified island (which could be interpreted as the prelude to negotiations with them), and the President's pardon of thousands of rebel prisoners, aroused deep misgivings in Algeria among the settlers and the army. Although the general officers professed their loyalty to De Gaulle, contacts were kept up between settlers' groups and key units of the army. In the event of a showdown over political policy, the anti-Gaullist conspiratorial organizations in Algiers counted on the sympathy of the army—at least to the extent that the troops would not be ordered to use force against them in the event of a repetition of the coup of May 13. The army continued to form a compact power hostile to any negotiations for a settlement of the five-year-old war. The prospect of another uprising in Algiers, countenanced or tolerated by the army, constituted a check on the government's freedom of maneuver.

As under the Fourth Republic, the Algerian lobby, consisting of high-ranking officers, activists, political leaders, and parliamentarians, tried to thwart the decisions of the central government. Some of De Gaulle's subordinates minimized the significance of his September 16 speech by asserting that negotiations would deal exclusively with cease-fire arrangements and that the French Army would continue its task of pacification and remain in Algeria in order to supervise the referendum. Debré promised the members of Parliament that the envisaged referendum would be "organized" by law, a promise which would appear to encroach upon presidential prerogative. Between September 16 and November 10, when De Gaulle put an end to attempts at interpreting his words and pledges, the Secretary of Defense, the general delegate of the government in Algeria, the commander in chief of the French forces in Algeria and the Prime Minister himself made statements calculated to appease the army and the French settlers. Thus Debré instructed the army to do its utmost in order to assure a vote favoring unity with France. The Minister of Defense declared that the army's mission in Algeria was to continue for many years to come. "In the remote future, once the political destiny of Algeria has been established, the army will remain present in order to assure its permanent mission, that is to say, the common defense of the Metropolis and Algeria against any danger that might menace it." General Challe urged his troops to continue the struggle until the victory of France was assured. "The struggle is going to be intensified even more," he warned, "up to the point of integral pacification." None of these remarks served to convince the Algerian Moslems that De Gaulle's promises would be respected.

At the height of his popularity after the referendum of September 28, De Gaulle could have done virtually what he wanted. Instead he equivocated and lost a great opportunity to change the course of events in Algeria and perhaps in the whole of North Africa. He accepted the army's idea of pacification and gave his full support to the new campaign to liquidate the FLN. He permitted an election to be held that brought into the National Assembly seventy-one diehards from Algeria—all of them committed to the idea of integration. When the old and shrewd Algerian nationalist leader Massili Hadj was asked about them, he said they represented nothing. The Fourth Republic had its *beni oui-oui*, handpicked by the French administration; the Fifth Republic had its *Garde-à-vous*, chosen by the army. Therefore, however genuine De Gaulle's intentions might have been, it remained doubtful that Algerians would accept his pledges without firm guarantees and negotiation. At this point the real issue that may pit De Gaulle against the army and the nationalists both at home and in Algeria—the issue that plagued all governments of the Fourth Republic—will be joined. Is De Gaulle willing and able to negotiate? Only in answering that question will the sincerity of his purpose and, what is more important, the balance of forces in France, be revealed.

From Community to Independence

In contrast to his treatment of the Algerian problem, there appeared to be nothing cryptic in De Gaulle's utterance concerning the future of the French colonies in Africa. The General, for whom France's presence in those regions is an incontrovertible necessity, offered independence to the African territories if they voted No to the constitution. Even if they voted Yes, they could, at a later stage, practically whenever they desired, opt for independence. Thus, for the first time France offered a vision for the future that went beyond the demands even of many of the African leaders. De Gaulle offered also a new institutional arrangement—the Community—based upon a close association between these African territories and France. Within the Community each of the former African territories (there are eleven of them) was to become an autonomous state with its own form of government (they became republics) and enjoy complete autonomy in its internal affairs.

De Gaulle had offered autonomy and promised independence in order to reinforce for the immediate future France's sovereignty in the African territories in all matters that counted most—defense, foreign affairs, and economic policy. He made a tactical retreat in order to win a major victory. In terms of international law, the Community simply perpetuated France's exclusive jurisdiction over all its members. Constitutionally, the sole legislator for all Community matters is the President of the French Republic. All decisions are issued in his name and over his signature. The French Parliament has no jurisdiction over Community affairs. Thus, De Gaulle decided that the "Marseillaise" was the national anthem of the Community; that its motto was "Liberty, Equality, Fraternity" and that its flag was the tricolor. He also ruled that the defense of the Community and its foreign policy were "one and the same" with the defense and the foreign policy of the French Republic. He nominated seven

French ministers to be ministers for the Community as well. The executive council met six times for a total of about twelve days in 1959.

Two reactions on the part of the new African states and their leaders were discernible. One favored gradual independence to be attained by the devolution of the common jurisdictions of the Community to the individual states. In this view the Community would be slowly divested of its common functions and become a mere symbol expressing only the ties that unite the African republics with France. The second favored the creation of larger federations— *fédérations primaires*—of African states, to which the functions of the Community would be gradually delegated. In January, 1959 such a "primary federation"—the Federation of Mali—composed of Senegal, Dahomey, French Soudan, and Volta, was envisaged at Dakar and its constitution drafted. It was a structure meant to put an end to what Léopold Senghor and other enlightened African leaders called the "balkanization" of Africa and to seek in larger political and territorial units the means of economic growth and development that can alone bring the French African republics to a level of relative equality with other African states and with France. By June, 1959 the fragile party organizations in French West Africa and French Equatorial Africa had been seriously undermined. A new party—the Party of African Federation—was created in June at Dakar under the leadership of powerful political leaders, including Léopold Senghor and Lamine-Gueye of Senegal. It called for the establishment of a "Negro-African nation" associated with France, and the first step in that direction was to be a primary federation composed of many states of French West Africa. It demanded a "rational and dynamic planning of the African economy," a "progressive development toward a multinational confederation," and favored independence.

In December, 1959, on the occasion of the sixth meeting of the executive council of the Community, De Gaulle gave in to the claims of independence. In the same way in which he took his associates by surprise by offering in his speeches of August, 1958 complete independence to those territories which voted No at the referendum, he now spoke of complete independence within the Community. The member states of the Community could now achieve "international sovereignty," and he pledged to see to it that the appropriate legislation and modifications of the constitution would be enacted for this purpose. In contrast to the position he had taken in October, 1958 after the secession of Guinea, De Gaulle promised French technical and economic aid to all African republics, even those who might opt for independence, and emphasized the economic, cultural, and historical ties that bound France with Africa.

Thus, the work started by the Fourth Republic was being carried to its conclusion. France's colonial policy appeared to be irreversibly altered. The African republics may become fully independent within a commonwealth framework. In following the lead of the Fourth Republic, De Gaulle was opening up new vistas of Franco-African cooperation. After many years of equivocation and half-hearted reforms, French leadership was beginning to move *with* powerful historical forces instead of trying to block them.

Foreign Policy

The origins of May 13 perhaps go back to France's costly victory in World War I and her desperate efforts to maintain the *status quo* embodied in the Versailles Treaty. Her failure to do so meant that France's position in the world inexorably followed the logic of changing power relations. The defeat of 1940 and the subsequent decline of French power, underlined by growing dependence on her Anglo-American allies, provoked a national feeling of resentment. But while the reality of the international situation altered, France's aspiration to remain a great power continued. Every loss—in the Middle East, in Indochina, in North Africa—and every concession to her allies augmented the feeling of frustration and resentment, and widened the gap between reality and aspiration. Yet the Fourth Republic failed not so much because it was unable to maintain France's status as a great power, but rather because it tried desperately to do it against all odds. The long and hopeless war in Indochina was responsible for the weakening of the French position in North Africa, which in turn accounted for France's predicament in NATO and the United Nations.[3]

The first measures taken by General de Gaulle showed a realism that contrasted sharply with his attitude immediately after liberation. Relations between Morocco and Tunisia were re-established and the French troops withdrawn from their bases in Tunisia and concentrated in Bizerte. A pledge was made to honor the agreement estab-

---

[3] On French foreign policy see Roy C. Macridis, "French Foreign Policy," *Foreign Policy in World Politics* (Englewood Cliffs, N.J., 1958), pp. 41–77.

lishing a Common Market, though it had been criticized vigorously by the Gaullists. France was also to abide by her obligations to NATO.

Within a few weeks, however, the situation changed and De Gaulle revealed that he was committed to the restoration of France as a great power within or without the Western alliances and NATO. France had a large empire even though called the Community, retained a foothold in North Africa, was the largest country of Western Europe with an agriculture capable of supporting adequately her population and with a highly developed industry, and boasted a well-trained army. She had strong bargaining power that neither friend nor foe could afford to ignore—and De Gaulle was ready to bargain with anybody, provided the bargain was to his advantage. He started his diplomatic program by demanding a drastic modification of NATO arrangements so as to give three powers—the United States, England, and France—a privileged position to formulate over-all strategy commensurate with their global obligations and military commitments. This was the essence of his letter of September 24, 1958 to President Eisenhower, Prime Minister Macmillan, and Henry Spaak, a letter whose contents "leaked" to the German press. When this demand was politely rejected by England and the United States and unfavorably commented upon by many of the NATO countries, including Germany, De Gaulle followed two courses of action. He took a number of measures aimed at underlining the fragility of NATO—he withdrew the Mediterranean units of the French fleet from NATO command, alleging as an excuse for his action the "obligations" of France in North Africa; he balked at the establishment of American launching sites in France; and, through some of his spokesmen, he demanded NATO endorsement and support of France's military effort in Algeria.

If all these steps were calculated to embarrass the United States, De Gaulle was able to follow a second course of action that was bound to embarrass the British even more. He became the champion of close European cooperation and supported the Common Market, while refusing to enlarge it by allowing for a "free-trade area" that would enable Britain and other European nations to participate. He sought to reinforce France's ties with Germany and Italy. In the course of less than a year he met with Adenauer twice, and after his state visit to Italy in June, 1959 he issued an official statement in favor of Italy's participation at the Geneva conference. All this was in line with his belief that Western Europe under French leadership could once more become a strong independent bloc—a Third Force —between the Soviet Union and the Anglo-American countries. To realize such a plan, France needed an atom bomb. With or without American secrets France planned to explode her bomb in the Sahara to demonstrate to the world her renewed military and technological strength. There was still another trump in De Gaulle's hand—the same trump he played somewhat precipitately in 1944—a trip to Moscow.

Whether De Gaulle's diplomacy can succeed and whether its success would serve the national interest remain problematic. Italy and Germany are reluctant to follow France's leadership in forming a European Third Force. Even if De Gaulle's diplomacy were to succeed, the sacrifices for France are staggering. The logic of atomic production cannot allow her to stop after she explodes one bomb, but it is doubtful that the French economy can support both bomb production and the urgent tasks of industrialization in Algeria, continuing the war there, exploiting Sahara's resources, and maintaining a competitive position in the Common Market. A great power has to make sustained military efforts, which the France of today can keep up only by exploiting the present wave of nationalism and by courting the support of an army that has shown little regard for democratic principles and republican institutions. The coincidence of a strong and rebellious army, nationalist fervor, conflict in Algeria, and aspirations to national greatness could generate a political movement that the General may not be able to control. He sees France as a civilizing and humanizing force; but to realize his vision, France in his opinion must once more be as strong as she was at the turn of the century, and the effort to achieve such strength might well release forces neither civilized nor humane.

*   *   *   *   *

Few observers doubt that the overwhelming majority who voted in favor of the new constitution essentially voted for De Gaulle. It was a personal vote that not only expressed the hopes of the French but also symbolized many of the contradictions of the French political scene. De Gaulle's most pressing historical task is to establish new institutions for the resolution of the perennial conflicts of French society. Yet the "legitimacy" of the Fifth Republic was linked with the popularity of De Gaulle and to the trust that the French put in him—a trust that showed how profound is the disaffection of the public with parliamentary, even republican, institutions, and how deep-rooted is the Bonapartist reflex.

The constitution seems to have made little impact on public opinion. Indeed, after the ritual of the referendum, the promulgation of the new constitution, and the legislative elections of November, 1958, the distrust of representative institutions by the French people became even more pronounced. The powers of the National Assembly were limited to the discussion and the enactment of program bills, introduced by the government; the question period was seriously qualified by the insistence of the government (with the blessing of the Constitutional Council) that a question cannot lead to a debate or a vote; even resolutions expressing merely the wishes of the legislature cannot be introduced. The representative assemblies were reduced to a subservient status. Above them loomed the figure of the president—with the power to appoint the prime minister, to dissolve the National Assembly, to declare a state of emergency and rule by decree, to call for a referendum on basic issues of policy, to legislate personally on all matters pertaining to the Community, and to shape and direct foreign policy. Politically, however, the president is irresponsible. He is not accountable before the legislature or the public. His policies do not stem from an electoral mandate. He is elected by some 80,000 electors, of whom the majority are mayors or municipal councilors of small villages with less than 1,500 inhabitants. As long as De Gaulle's popularity continues, these objections may be of little importance. But a constitution is not made for one man nor can its legitimacy repose on the prestige of one man. The institutions by which a future president can be invested and through which popular trust and the ultimate responsibility to the people can be kept alive are lacking. Neither the political parties nor the legislators are involved in the election of the president or in his policies. They are dissociated from the center of political power.

De Gaulle has assumed a quasi-monarchical posture—he is above political parties, exercising enormous powers because of a charisma that the impotence of the Fourth Republic and the ardor of the Gaullist groups and of some colonels and generals have heightened. His "brooding omnipresence" and the receptivity of the French to it are the distinguishing features of the Fifth Republic.

The system does not provide for any institutions to decipher the Delphic quality of De Gaulle's utterances. Debates in Parliament do not make clear his thoughts or elicit any indication of the policy he intends to follow. Thus, the personal or rather Bonapartist aspects of the regime are accentuated and the public lacks once more, as it did for different reasons under the Fourth Republic, the opportunity to appraise policies, discuss issues, and develop institutions through which it can assess responsibility. Under De Gaulle's Fifth Republic, the French are in a state of political tutelage.

Epilogue

ON FEBRUARY 2, 1960, Prime Minister Debré demanded and obtained from the National Assembly, by a vote of 441 to 75, sweeping delegations of power to govern by decree during fourteen months, "for the maintenance of law and order, the safeguarding of the State and the Constitution, and the pacification and administration of Algeria." The only limitation on this grant of power is the express injunction not to dissolve Parliament during the envisaged period of time. Thus, the Fifth Republic, which originated in a broad grant of power to General de Gaulle to govern and prepare a new constitution, had to resort to the same procedure in order to bring under control the forces that had overthrown the Fourth Republic.

On January 19, 1960, a German newspaper published an account of an interview with General Massu in the course of which he made derogatory remarks about President de Gaulle's policy in Algeria. Although the General later denied having made these comments, he was immediately summoned to Paris and then relieved of his command. In order to protest against Massu's dismissal the settlers called a general strike, staged a huge public demonstration against De Gaulle, and then set up a fortified barricade in the heart of the city of Algiers. What followed was a repetition of the previous uprising: fraternization of the army with the insurgents and the rapid mobilization of the Territorial Units. The appeals of the President of the Republic, the delegate-general, and the commander in chief in Algeria had no effect. Some political leaders, including parliamentarians, joined the rioters behind the barricades, and the loyalty of the army remained in doubt. The uprising assumed the proportions of an insurrection.

In several important respects, however, January 24, 1960 differed from May 13, 1958. General de Gaulle this time was not an alternative to the Republic; he embodied it. The Gaullists either stood firmly behind the President or refused to assume the leadership of the movement. With the exception of some UNR activists,

Georges Bidault, and a few others with limited influence, French political leaders and public opinion failed to rally to the insurgents. The crucial factor remained the army, which was faced with the choice of either obeying its commander in chief or establishing a military dictatorship. Unlike May, 1958, no third course of action was open. The army finally swung its weight against the insurrection. But it did so only after De Gaulle, in a speech addressed to the troops on January 29, pledged not to undertake political negotiations with the Algerian rebel government and promised that the army would organize the referendum after pacification had been accomplished. Thus, in order to retain the loyalty of the army, De Gaulle was compelled to offer assurances and concessions that seriously compromised his policy of self-determination for Algeria. From this moment the insurrection was doomed. The activists found themselves completely isolated and powerless without the support of the army. De Gaulle won the first battle against the forces that had provoked the shock leading to his return to power.

The situation at home was also filled with dangers. In Parliament the classic phenomenon of negative majorities was taking shape. The Independents, after Pinay's dismissal from office, were now free to challenge Debré's government, and eager to exploit social and economic unrest for political advantage. Rural syndicalists, borrowing from the arsenal of labor syndicalism, were resorting to popular demonstrations and direct action, particularly in Brittany and Normandy. Leaders of the Right, including members of the UNR, Independents, and the Algerian group in the Assembly, denounced the government's Algerian policy. Socialists, Communists, and some of the Radicals, MRP, and Independents were now permanently in the opposition. The UNR could not be counted on any longer to support the government unreservedly. The deputies from Algeria were ready to oust Debré, whose government was in real danger. Given the mood of the public, it could not be assumed that a new election would be favorable to the Gaullists. The only way out therefore was a sweeping delegation of powers to the executive.

The personal character of the Constitution of the Fifth Republic is thus further accentuated. All executive orders are to be issued under the signature of the president. The arrangement consecrates what was already known to all—that the power of the new regime resides in General de Gaulle. It is a benevolent despotism, tempered by a respect for individual freedoms and tolerated by the army. But for how long? It was only when challenged by an open insurrection eighteen months after coming to power that De Gaulle took the first steps to dismantle in Algeria some of the more subversive army services and to remove a few unreliable military commanders who sympathized openly with the Algerian activists. In February, 1960, the Psychological Services (Fifth Bureau) of the army was abolished and its functions decentralized; the separate organization of the Territorial Units was liquidated; disciplinary action was taken against a small number of army officers and police chiefs; and some leaders of the French settlers were arrested and imprisoned. But the war continued and political negotiations with the Moslem rebels were still out of the question.

The explosion of a French atom bomb was hailed by General de Gaulle as a great victory for the nation but, paradoxically, this only added to the strains under which the political system operates. In his quest for greater national strength De Gaulle is building up the very force—the army—on which his regime now so largely depends. In bypassing Parliament for a period of a year, he has ruled out the only alternative to this dependence: the creation of new political forces at home as a counterbalance. The army remains in full control in many regions of Algeria; it runs the economy, administers justice, wages the campaign of pacification, and in the event of a popular consultation will conduct the election or referendum. Intensification of the war against the rebels will inevitably increase the political importance of the army.

The measures taken after the repression of the insurrection to ensure civil supremacy in Algeria will be ineffective unless the reasons for the autonomy and ever-present defiant attitude of the army are removed, that is, unless there is a settlement of the war in Algeria accompanied by firm political guarantees acceptable to all sides. Only then can General de Gaulle turn to the most crucial task facing the Fifth Republic—the legitimization of its institutions and the development of a genuine representative democracy.

Appendixes

APPENDIX A

*The Constitution of the Fifth Republic**

PREAMBLE

The French people hereby solemnly proclaims its attachment to the Rights of Man and the principles of national sovereignty as defined by the Declaration of 1789, reaffirmed and complemented by the Preamble of the Constitution of 1946.

By virtue of these principles and that of the free determination of peoples, the Republic hereby offers to the Overseas Territories that express the desire to adhere to them, new institutions based on the common ideal of liberty, equality and fraternity and conceived with a view to their democratic evolution.

ARTICLE 1

The Republic and the peoples of the Overseas Territories who, by an act of free determination, adopt the present Constitution thereby institute a Community.

The Community shall be based on the equality and the solidarity of the peoples composing it.

Title I

ON SOVEREIGNTY

ARTICLE 2

France is a Republic, indivisible, secular, democratic and social. It shall ensure the equality of all citizens before the law, without distinction of origin, race or religion. It shall respect all beliefs.

---

* Courtesy of the French Embassy, Press and Information Division, New York.

The national emblem is the tricolor flag, blue, white and red.

The national anthem is the "Marseillaise."

The motto of the Republic is "Liberty, Equality, Fraternity."

Its principle is government of the people, by the people and for the people.

ARTICLE 3

National sovereignty belongs to the people, which shall exercise this sovereignty through its representatives and by means of referendums.

No section of the people, nor any individual, may attribute to themselves or himself the exercise thereof.

Suffrage may be direct or indirect under the conditions stipulated by the Constitution. It shall always be universal, equal and secret.

All French citizens of both sexes who have reached their majority and who enjoy civil and political rights may vote under the conditions to be determined by law.

ARTICLE 4

Political parties and groups shall be instrumental in the expression of the suffrage. They shall be formed freely and shall carry on their activities freely. They must respect the principles of national sovereignty and democracy.

Title II

THE PRESIDENT OF THE REPUBLIC

ARTICLE 5

The President of the Republic shall see that the Constitution is respected. He shall ensure, by his arbitration, the regular functioning of the governmental authorities, as well as the continuance of the State.

He shall be the guarantor of national independence, of the integrity of the territory, and of respect for Community agreements and treaties.

ARTICLE 6

The President of the Republic shall be elected for seven years by an electoral college comprising the members of Parliament, of the General Councils and of the Assemblies of the Overseas Territories, as well as the elected representatives of the municipal councils.

These representatives shall be:

—the mayor for communes of fewer than 1,000 inhabitants;

—the mayor and the first deputy mayor for communes of from 1,000 to 2,000 inhabitants;

—the mayor, first deputy mayor and a municipal councillor chosen according to the order in which he appears on the council list for communes of from 2,001 to 2,500 inhabitants;

—the mayor and the first two deputy mayors for communes of from 2,501 to 3,000 inhabitants;

—the mayor, the first two deputy mayors and three municipal councillors chosen according to the order in which they appear on the council list for communes of from 3,001 to 6,000 inhabitants;

—the mayor, the first two deputy mayors and six municipal councillors chosen according to the order in which they appear on the council list for communes of from 6,001 to 9,000 inhabitants;

—all the municipal councillors for communes of more than 9,000 inhabitants;

—in addition, for communes of more than 30,000 inhabitants, delegates appointed by the municipal council in the ratio of one delegate for every 1,000 inhabitants above 30,000.

In the Overseas Territories of the Republic, the elected representatives of the councils of the administrative units shall also form part of the electoral college under the conditions to be determined by an organic law.

The participation of member States of the Community in the electoral college for the President of the Republic shall be determined by agreement between the Republic and the member States of the Community.

The procedures implementing the present article shall be determined by an organic law.

ARTICLE 7

The President of the Republic shall be elected by an absolute majority on the first ballot. If this is not obtained, the President of the Republic shall be elected on a second ballot by a relative majority.

The voting shall begin at the summons of the Government.

The election of the new President shall take place twenty days at the least and fifty days at the most before the expiration of the powers of the President in office.

In the event that the Presidency of the Republic has been vacated, for any cause whatsoever, or impeded in its functioning as officially noted by the Constitutional Council, to which the matter has been referred by the Government, and which shall rule by an absolute majority of its members, the functions of the President of the Republic, with the exception of those provided for by Articles 11 and 12 below, shall be temporarily exercised by the President of the Senate. In the case of a vacancy, or when the impediment is declared definitive by the Constitutional Council, the voting for the election of a new President shall take place, except in case of *force majeure* officially noted by the Constitutional Council, twenty days at the least and fifty days at the most after the beginning of the vacancy or the declaration of the definitive character of the impediment.

ARTICLE 8

The President of the Republic shall appoint the Premier. He shall terminate the functions of the Premier when the latter presents the resignation of the Government.

On the proposal of the Premier, he shall appoint the other members of the Government and shall terminate their functions.

ARTICLE 9

The President of the Republic shall preside over the Council of Ministers.

ARTICLE 10

The President of the Republic shall promulgate the laws within fifteen days following the transmission to the Government of the finally adopted law.

He may, before the expiration of this time limit, ask Parliament for a reconsideration of the law or of certain of its articles. This reconsideration may not be refused.

ARTICLE 11

The President of the Republic, on the proposal of the Government during [Parliamentary] sessions, or on joint motion of the two assemblies, published in the *Journal Officiel,* may submit to a referendum any bill dealing with the organization of the governmental authorities, entailing approval of a Community agreement, or providing for authorization to ratify a treaty that, without being contrary to the Constitution, might affect the functioning of [existing] institutions.

When the referendum decides in favor of the bill, the President of the Republic shall promulgate it within the time limit stipulated in the preceding article.

ARTICLE 12

The President of the Republic may, after consultation with the Premier and the Presidents of the assemblies, declare the dissolution of the National Assembly.

General elections shall take place twenty days at the least and forty days at the most after the dissolution.

The National Assembly shall convene by right on the second Thursday following its election. If this meeting takes place between the periods provided for ordinary sessions, a session shall, by right, be held for a fifteen-day period.

There may be no further dissolution within a year following these elections.

ARTICLE 13

The President of the Republic shall sign the ordinances and decrees decided upon in the Council of Ministers.

He shall make appointments to the civil and military posts of the State.

Councillors of State, the Grand Chancellor of the Legion of Honor, Ambassadors and envoys extraordinary, Master Councillors of the Audit Office, prefects, representatives of the Government in the Overseas Territories, general officers, rectors of academies [regional divisions of the public educational system] and directors of central administrations shall be appointed in meetings of the Council of Ministers.

An organic law shall determine the other posts to be filled in meetings of the Council of Ministers, as well as the conditions under which the power of the President of the Republic to make appointments to office may be delegated by him and exercised in his name.

ARTICLE 14

The President of the Republic shall accredit Ambassadors and envoys extraordinary to foreign powers; foreign Ambassadors and envoys extraordinary shall be accredited to him.

ARTICLE 15

The President of the Republic shall be commander of the armed forces. He shall preside over the higher councils and committees of national defense.

ARTICLE 16

When the institutions of the Republic, the independence of the nation, the integrity of its territory or the fulfillment of its international commitments are threatened in a grave and immediate manner and when the regular functioning of the constitutional governmental authorities is interrupted, the President of the Republic shall take the measures commanded by these circumstances, after official consultation with the Premier, the Presidents of the assemblies and the Constitutional Council.

He shall inform the nation of these measures in a message.

These measures must be prompted by the desire to ensure to the constitutional governmental authorities, in the shortest possible time, the means of fulfilling their assigned functions. The Constitutional Council shall be consulted with regard to such measures.

Parliament shall meet by right.

The National Assembly may not be dissolved during the exercise of emergency powers [by the President].

ARTICLE 17

The President of the Republic shall have the right of pardon.

ARTICLE 18

The President of the Republic shall communicate with the two assemblies of Parliament by means of messages, which he shall cause to be read, and which shall not be followed by any debate.

Between sessions, Parliament shall be convened especially for this purpose.

ARTICLE 19

The acts of the President of the Republic, other than those provided for under Articles 8 (first paragraph), 11, 12, 16, 18, 54, 56 and 61, shall be countersigned by the Premier and, should circumstances so require, by the appropriate ministers.

Title III

THE GOVERNMENT

ARTICLE 20

The Government shall determine and direct the policy of the nation. It shall have at its disposal the administration and the armed forces.

It shall be responsible to Parliament under the conditions and according to the procedures stipulated in Articles 49 and 50.

ARTICLE 21

The Premier shall direct the operation of the Government. He shall be responsible for national defense. He shall ensure the execution of the laws. Subject to the provisions of Article 13, he shall have regulatory powers and shall make appointments to civil and military posts.

He may delegate certain of his powers to the ministers.

He shall replace, should the occasion arise, the President of the Republic as chairman of the councils and committees provided for under Article 15.

He may, in exceptional instances, replace him as chairman of a meeting of the Council of Ministers by virtue of an explicit delegation and for a specific agenda.

ARTICLE 22

The acts of the Premier shall be countersigned, when circumstances so require, by the ministers responsible for their execution.

ARTICLE 23

The office of member of the Government shall be incompatible with the exercise of any Parliamentary mandate, with the holding of any office at the national level in business, professional or labor organizations, and with any public employment or professional activity.

An organic law shall determine the conditions under which the holders of such mandates, functions or employments shall be replaced.

The replacement of members of Parliament shall take place in accordance with the provisions of Article 25.

Title IV

THE PARLIAMENT

ARTICLE 24

The Parliament shall comprise the National Assembly and the Senate.

The deputies to the National Assembly shall be elected by direct suffrage.

The Senate shall be elected by indirect suffrage. It shall ensure the representation of the territorial units of the Republic. Frenchmen living outside France shall be represented in the Senate.

ARTICLE 25

An organic law shall determine the term for which each assembly is elected, the number of its members, their emoluments, the conditions of eligibility and ineligibility and the offices incompatible with membership in the assemblies.

It shall likewise determine the conditions under which, in the case of a vacancy in either assembly, persons shall be elected to replace the deputy or senator whose seat has been vacated until the holding of new complete or partial elections to the assembly concerned.

ARTICLE 26

No member of Parliament may be prosecuted, sought, arrested, detained or tried as a result of the opinions or votes expressed by him in the exercise of his functions.

No member of Parliament may, during Parliamentary sessions, be prosecuted or arrested for criminal or minor offenses without the authorization of the assembly of which he is a member except in the case of *flagrante delicto.*

When Parliament is not in session, no member of Parliament may be arrested without the authorization of the Secretariat of the assembly of which he is a member, except in the case of *flagrante delicto,* of authorized prosecution or of final conviction.

The detention or prosecution of a member of Parliament shall be suspended if the assembly of which he is a member so demands.

ARTICLE 27

All binding instructions [upon members of Parliament] shall be null and void.

The right to vote of the members of Parliament shall be personal.

An organic law may, under exceptional circumstances, authorize the delegation of a vote. In this case, no member may be delegated more than one vote.

ARTICLE 28

Parliament shall convene, by right, in two ordinary sessions a year.

The first session shall begin on the first Tuesday of October and shall end on the third Friday of December.

The second session shall open on the last Tuesday of April; it may not last longer than three months.

ARTICLE 29

Parliament shall convene in extraordinary session at the request of the Premier, or of the majority of the members comprising the National Assembly, to consider a specific agenda.

When an extraordinary session is held at the request of the members of the National Assembly, the closure decree shall take effect as soon as the Parliament has exhausted the agenda for which it was called, and at the latest twelve days from the date of its meeting.

Only the Premier may ask for a new session before the end of the month following the closure decree.

ARTICLE 30

Apart from cases in which Parliament meets by right, extraordinary sessions shall be opened and closed by decree of the President of the Republic.

ARTICLE 31

The members of the Government shall have access to the two assemblies. They shall be heard when they so request.

They may call for the assistance of commissioners of the government.

ARTICLE 32

The President of the National Assembly shall be elected for the duration of the legislature. The President of the Senate shall be elected after each partial re-election [of the Senate].

ARTICLE 33

The meetings of the two assemblies shall be public. An *in extenso* report of the debates shall be published in the *Journal Officiel*.

Each assembly may sit in secret committee at the request of the Premier or of one tenth of its members.

Title V

ON RELATIONS BETWEEN PARLIAMENT AND THE GOVERNMENT

ARTICLE 34

All laws shall be passed by Parliament.

Laws shall establish the regulations concerning:

—civil rights and the fundamental guarantees granted to the citizens for the exercise of their public liberties; the obligations imposed by the national defense upon the persons and property of citizens;

—nationality, status and legal capacity of persons, marriage contracts, inheritance and gifts;

—determination of crimes and misdemeanors as well as the penalties imposed therefor; criminal procedure; amnesty; the creation of new juridical systems and the status of magistrates;

—the basis, the rate and the methods of collecting taxes of all types; the issuance of currency.

Laws shall likewise determine the regulations concerning:

—the electoral system of the Parliamentary assemblies and the local assemblies;

—the establishment of categories of public institutions;

—the fundamental guarantees granted to civil and military personnel employed by the State;

—the nationalization of enterprises and the transfer of the property of enterprises from the public to the private sector.

Laws shall determine the fundamental principles of:

—the general organization of national defense;

—the free administration of local communities, the extent of their jurisdiction and their resources;

—education;

—property rights, civil and commercial obligations;

—legislation pertaining to employment, unions and social security.

The financial laws shall determine the financial resources and obligations of the State under the conditions and with the reservations to be provided for by an organic law.

Laws pertaining to national planning shall determine the objectives of the economic and social action of the State.

The provisions of the present article may be developed in detail and amplified by an organic law.

ARTICLE 35

Parliament shall authorize the declaration of war.

ARTICLE 36

Martial law shall be decreed in a meeting of the Council of Ministers.

Its prorogation beyond twelve days may be authorized only by Parliament.

ARTICLE 37

Matters other than those that fall within the domain of law shall be of a regulatory character.

Legislative texts concerning these matters may be modified by decrees issued after consultation with the Council of State. Those legislative texts which may be passed after the present Constitution has become operative shall be modified by decree, only if the Constitutional Council has stated that they have a regulatory character as defined in the preceding paragraph.

ARTICLE 38

The Government may, in order to carry out its program, ask Parliament to authorize it, for a limited period, to take through ordinances measures that are normally within the domain of law.

The ordinances shall be enacted in meetings of the Council of Ministers after consultation with the Council of State. They shall come into force upon their publication, but shall become null and void if the bill for their ratification is not submitted to Parliament before the date set by the enabling act.

At the expiration of the time limit referred to in the first paragraph of the present article, the ordinances may be modified only by law in those matters which are within the legislative domain.

ARTICLE 39

The Premier and the members of Parliament alike shall have the right to initiate legislation.

Government bills shall be discussed in the Council of Ministers after consultation with the Council of State and shall be filed with the Secretariat of one of the two assemblies. Finance bills shall be submitted first to the National Assembly.

ARTICLE 40

Bills and amendments introduced by members of Parliament shall not be considered when their adoption would have as a consequence either a diminution of public financial resources, or the creation or increase of public expenditures.

ARTICLE 41

If it appears in the course of the legislative procedure that a Parliamentary bill or an amendment is not within the domain of law or is contrary to a delegation [of authority] granted by virtue of Article 38, the Government may declare its inadmissibility.

In case of disagreement between the Government and the President of the assembly concerned, the Constitutional Council, upon the request of either party, shall rule within a time limit of eight days.

ARTICLE 42

The discussion of Government bills shall pertain, in the first assembly to which they have been referred, to the text presented by the Government.

An assembly, given a text passed by the other assembly, shall deliberate on the text that is transmitted to it.

ARTICLE 43

Government and Parliamentary bills shall, at the request of the Government or of the assembly concerned, be sent for study to committees especially designated for this purpose.

Government and Parliamentary bills for which such a request has not been made shall be sent to one of the permanent committees, the number of which shall be limited to six in each assembly.

ARTICLE 44

Members of Parliament and of the Government shall have the right of amendment.

After the opening of the debate, the Government may oppose the examination of any amendment which has not previously been submitted to committee.

If the Government so requests, the assembly concerned shall decide, by a single vote, on all or part of the text under discussion, retaining only the amendments proposed or accepted by the Government.

ARTICLE 45

Every Government or Parliamentary bill shall be examined successively in the two assemblies of Parliament with a view to the adoption of an identical text.

When, as a result of disagreement between the two assemblies, it has become impossible to adopt a Government or Parliamentary bill after two readings by each assembly, or, if the Government has declared the matter urgent, after a single reading by each of them, the Premier shall have the right to have a joint committee meet, composed of an equal number from both assemblies and instructed to offer for consideration a text on the matters still under discussion.

The text prepared by the joint committee may be submitted by the Government for approval of the two assemblies. No amendment shall be admissible except by agreement with the Government.

If the joint committee fails to approve a common text, or if this text is not adopted under the conditions set forth in the preceding paragraph, the Government may, after a new reading by the National Assembly and by the Senate, ask the National Assembly to rule definitively. In this case, the National Assembly may reconsider either the text prepared by the joint committee or the last text adopted [by the National Assembly], modified, when circumstances so require, by one or several of the amendments adopted by the Senate.

ARTICLE 46

The laws that the Constitution characterizes as organic shall be passed and amended under the following conditions:

A Government or Parliamentary bill shall be submitted to the deliberation and to the vote of the first assembly to which it is submitted only at the expiration of a period of fifteen days following its introduction.

The procedure of Article 45 shall be applicable. Nevertheless, lacking an agreement between the two assemblies, the text may be adopted by the National Assembly on final reading only by an absolute majority of its members.

The organic laws relative to the Senate must be passed in the same manner by the two assemblies.

Organic laws may be promulgated only after a declaration by the Constitutional Council on their constitutionality.

ARTICLE 47

Parliament shall pass finance bills under the conditions to be stipulated by an organic law.

Should the National Assembly fail to reach a decision on first reading within a time limit of forty days after a bill has been filed, the Government shall refer it to the Senate, which must rule within a time limit of fifteen days. The procedure set forth in Article 45 shall then be followed.

Should Parliament fail to reach a decision within a time limit of seventy days, the provisions of the bill may be enforced by ordinance.

Should the finance bill establishing the resources and expenditures of a fiscal year not be filed in time for it to be promulgated before the beginning of that fiscal year, the Government shall immediately request Parliament for the authorization to collect the taxes and shall make available by decree the funds needed to meet the Government commitments already voted.

The time limits stipulated in the present article shall be suspended when Parliament is not in session.

The Audit Office shall assist Parliament and the Government in supervising the implementation of the finance laws.

ARTICLE 48

The discussion of the bills filed or agreed upon by the Government shall have priority on the agenda of the assemblies in the order set by the Government.

One meeting a week shall be reserved, by priority, for questions asked by members of Parliament and for answers by the Government.

ARTICLE 49

The Premier, after deliberation by the Council of Ministers, may pledge the responsibility of the Government to the National Assembly with regard to the program of the Government, or with regard to a declaration of general policy, as the case may be.

The National Assembly may question the responsibility of the Government by the vote of a motion of censure. Such a motion shall be admissible only if it is signed by at least one tenth of the members of the National Assembly. The vote may only take place forty-eight hours after the motion has been filed; the only votes counted shall be those favorable to the motion of censure, which may be adopted only by a majority of the members comprising the Assembly. Should the motion of censure be rejected, its signatories may not introduce another motion in the course of the same session, except in the case provided for in the paragraph below.

The Premier may, after deliberation by the Council of Ministers, pledge the Government's responsibility to the National Assembly on the vote of a text. In this case, the text shall be considered as adopted, unless a motion of censure, filed in the succeeding twenty-four hours, is voted under the conditions laid down in the previous paragraph.

The Premier shall be entitled to ask the Senate for approval of a general policy declaration.

ARTICLE 50

When the National Assembly adopts a motion of censure, or when it disapproves the program or a declaration of general policy of the Government, the Premier must submit the resignation of the Government to the President of the Republic.

ARTICLE 51

The closure of ordinary or extraordinary sessions shall by right be delayed, should the occasion arise, in order to permit the application of the provisions of Article 49.

Title VI

ON TREATIES AND INTERNATIONAL AGREEMENTS

ARTICLE 52

The President of the Republic shall negotiate and ratify treaties.

He shall be informed of all negotiations leading to the conclusion of an international agreement not subject to ratification.

ARTICLE 53

Peace treaties, commercial treaties, treaties or agreements relative to international organization, those that imply a commitment for the finances of the State, those that modify provisions of a legislative nature, those relative to the status of persons, those that call for the cession, exchange or addition of territory may be ratified or approved only by a law.

They shall go into effect only after having been ratified or approved.

No cession, no exchange, no addition of territory shall be valid without the consent of the populations concerned.

ARTICLE 54

If the Constitutional Council, the matter having been referred to it by the President of the Republic, by the Premier, or by the President of one or the other assembly, shall declare that an international commitment contains a clause contrary to the Constitution, the authorization to ratify or approve this commitment may be given only after amendment of the Constitution.

ARTICLE 55

Treaties or agreements duly ratified or approved shall, upon their publication, have an authority superior to that of laws, subject, for each agreement or treaty, to its application by the other party.

Title VII

THE CONSTITUTIONAL COUNCIL

ARTICLE 56

The Constitutional Council shall consist of nine members, whose term of office shall last nine years and shall not be renewable. One third of the membership of the Constitutional Council shall be renewed every three years. Three of its members shall be appointed by the President of the Republic, three by the President of the National Assembly, three by the President of the Senate.

In addition to the nine members provided for above, former Presidents of the Republic shall be members ex officio for life of the Constitutional Council.

The President shall be appointed by the President of the Republic. He shall have the deciding vote in case of a tie.

ARTICLE 57

The office of member of the Constitutional Council shall be incompatible with that of minister or member of Parliament. Other incompatibilities shall be determined by an organic law.

ARTICLE 58

The Constitutional Council shall ensure the regularity of the election of the President of the Republic.

It shall examine complaints and shall announce the results of the vote.

ARTICLE 59

The Constitutional Council shall rule, in the case of disagreement, on the regularity of the election of deputies and senators.

ARTICLE 60

The Constitutional Council shall ensure the regularity of referendum procedures and shall announce the results thereof.

ARTICLE 61

Organic laws, before their promulgation, and regulations of the Parliamentary assemblies, before they come into application, must be submitted to the Constitutional Council, which shall rule on their constitutionality.

To the same end, laws may be submitted to the Constitutional Council, before their promulgation, by the President of the Republic, the Premier or the President of one or the other assembly.

In the cases provided for by the two preceding paragraphs, the Constitutional Council must make its ruling within a time limit of one month. Nevertheless, at the request of the Government, in case of emergency, this period shall be reduced to eight days.

In these same cases, referral to the Constitutional Council shall suspend the time limit for promulgation.

ARTICLE 62

A provision declared unconstitutional may not be promulgated or implemented.

The decisions of the Constitutional Council may not be appealed to any jurisdiction whatsoever. They must be recognized by the governmental authorities and by all administrative and juridical authorities.

ARTICLE 63

An organic law shall determine the rules of organization and functioning of the Constitutional Council, the procedure to be followed before it, and in particular the periods of time allowed for laying disputes before it.

Title VIII

ON JUDICIAL AUTHORITY

ARTICLE 64

The President of the Republic shall be the guarantor of the independence of the judicial authority.

He shall be assisted by the High Council of the Judiciary.

An organic law shall determine the status of magistrates.

Magistrates may not be removed from office.

ARTICLE 65

The High Council of the Judiciary shall be presided over by the President of the Republic. The Minister of Justice shall be its Vice President ex officio. He may preside in place of the President of the Republic.

The High Council shall, in addition, include nine members appointed by the President of the Republic in conformity with the conditions to be determined by an organic law.

The High Council of the Judiciary shall present nominations for judges of the Court of Cassation [Supreme Court of Appeal] and for First Presidents of Courts of Appeal. It shall give its opinion, under the conditions to be determined by an organic law, on proposals of the Minister of Justice relative to the nomination of the other judges. It shall be consulted on questions of pardon under conditions to be determined by an organic law.

The High Council of the Judiciary shall act as a disciplinary council for judges. In such cases, it shall be presided over by the First President of the Court of Cassation.

ARTICLE 66

No one may be arbitrarily detained.

The judicial authority, guardian of individual liberty, shall ensure respect for this principle under the conditions stipulated by law.

Title IX

THE HIGH COURT OF JUSTICE

ARTICLE 67

A High Court of Justice shall be instituted.

It shall be composed of members [of Parliament] elected, in equal number, by the National Assembly and the Senate after each general or partial election to these assemblies. It shall elect its President from among its members.

An organic law shall determine the composition of the High Court, its rules, and also the procedure to be followed before it.

ARTICLE 68

The President of the Republic shall not be held accountable for actions performed in the exercise of his office except in the case of high treason. He may be indicted only by the two assemblies ruling by identical vote in open balloting and by an absolute majority of the members of said assemblies. He shall be tried by the High Court of Justice.

The members of the Government shall be criminally liable for actions performed in the exercise of their office and deemed to be crimes or misdemeanors at the time they were committed. The procedure defined above shall be applied to them, as well as to their accomplices, in case of a conspiracy against the security of the State. In the cases provided for by the present paragraph, the High Court shall be bound by the definition of crimes and misdemeanors, as well as by the determination of penalties, as they are established by the criminal laws in force when the acts are committed.

Title X

THE ECONOMIC AND SOCIAL COUNCIL

ARTICLE 69

The Economic and Social Council, whenever the Government calls upon it, shall give its opinion on the Government bills, ordinances and decrees, as well as on the Parliamentary bills submitted to it.

A member of the Economic and Social Council may be designated by the latter to present, before the Parliamentary assemblies, the opinion of the Council on the Government or Parliamentary bills that have been submitted to it.

ARTICLE 70

The Economic and Social Council may likewise be consulted by the Government on any problem of an economic or social character of interest to the Republic or to the Community. Any plan, or any bill dealing with a plan, of an economic or social character shall be submitted to it for its advice.

ARTICLE 71

The composition of the Economic and Social Council and its rules of procedure shall be determined by an organic law.

Title XI

ON TERRITORIAL UNITS

ARTICLE 72

The territorial units of the Republic are the communes, the Departments, the Overseas Territories. Other territorial units may be created by law.

These units shall be free to govern themselves through elected councils and under the conditions stipulated by law.

In the departments and the territories, the Delegate of the Government shall be responsible for the national interests, for administrative supervision, and for seeing that the laws are respected.

ARTICLE 73

Measures of adjustment required by the particular situation of the Overseas Departments may be taken with regard to their legislative system and administrative organization.

ARTICLE 74

The Overseas Territories of the Republic shall have a special organization, which takes into account their own interests within the general interests of the Republic. This organization shall be defined and modified by law after consultation with the Territorial Assembly concerned.

ARTICLE 75

Citizens of the Republic who do not have ordinary civil status, the only status referred to in Article 34, may keep their personal status as long as they have not renounced it.

ARTICLE 76

The Overseas Territories may retain their status within the Republic.

If they express the desire to do so by a decision of their Territorial Assemblies taken within the time limit set in the first paragraph of Article 91, they shall become Overseas Departments of the Republic or member States of the Community, either in groups or as single units.

Title XII

ON THE COMMUNITY

ARTICLE 77

In the Community instituted by the present Constitution, the States shall enjoy autonomy; they shall administer themselves and manage their own affairs democratically and freely.

There shall be only one citizenship in the Community.

All citizens shall be equal before the law, whatever their origin, their race and their religion. They shall have the same duties.

ARTICLE 78

The Community's jurisdiction shall extend over foreign policy, defense, currency, common economic and financial policy, as well as over policy on strategic raw materials.

It shall include, in addition, except in the case of specific agreements, the supervision of the tribunals, higher education, the general organization of external transportation and transportation within the Community, as well as of telecommunications.

Special agreements may create other common jurisdictions or regulate any transfer of jurisdiction from the Community to one of its members.

ARTICLE 79

The member States shall benefit from the provisions of Article 77 as soon as they have exercised the choice provided for in Article 76.

Until the measures required for implementation of the present title go into force, matters within the common jurisdiction shall be regulated by the Republic.

ARTICLE 80

The President of the Republic shall preside over and represent the Community.

The institutional organs of the Community shall be an Executive Council, a Senate and a Court of Arbitration.

ARTICLE 81

The member States of the Community shall participate in the election of the President according to the conditions stipulated in Article 6.

The President of the Republic, in his capacity as President of the Community, shall be represented in each State of the Community.

ARTICLE 82

The Executive Council of the Community shall be presided over by the President of the Community. It shall consist of the Premier of the Republic, the heads of Government of each of the member States of the Community, and the ministers responsible for the common affairs of the Community.

The Executive Council shall organize the cooperation of members of the Community at Government and administrative levels.

The organization and procedure of the Executive Council shall be determined by an organic law.

ARTICLE 83

The Senate of the Community shall be composed of delegates whom the Parliament of the Republic and the legislative assemblies of the other members of the Community shall choose from among their own membership. The number of delegates of each State shall be determined according to its population and the responsibilities it assumes in the Community.

The Senate of the Community shall hold two sessions a year, which shall be opened and closed by the President of the Community and may not last longer than one month each.

The Senate of the Community, when called upon by the President of the Community, shall deliberate on the common economic and financial policy before laws on these matters are voted upon by the Parliament of the Republic and, should circumstances so require, by the legislative assemblies of the other members of the Community.

The Senate of the Community shall examine the acts and treaties or international agreements, which are specified in Articles 35 and 53, and which commit the Community.

The Senate of the Community shall make executory decisions in the domains in which it has received delegation of power from the legislative assemblies of the members of the Community. These decisions shall be promulgated in the same form as the law in the territory of each of the States concerned.

An organic law shall determine the composition of the Senate and its rules of procedure.

ARTICLE 84

A Court of Arbitration of the Community shall rule on litigations occurring among members of the Community.

Its composition and its jurisdiction shall be determined by an organic law.

ARTICLE 85

By derogation from the procedure provided for in Article 89, the provisions of the present title that concern the functioning of the common institutions shall be amendable by identical laws passed by the Parliament of the Republic and by the Senate of the Community.

ARTICLE 86

A change of status of a member State of the Community may be requested, either by the Republic, or by a resolution of the legislative assembly of the State concerned confirmed by a local referendum, the organization and supervision of which shall be ensured by the institutions of the Community. The procedures governing this change shall be determined by an agreement approved by the Parliament of the Republic and the legislative assembly concerned.

Under the same conditions, a member State of the Community may become independent. It shall thereby cease to belong to the Community.

ARTICLE 87

The special agreements made for the implementation of the present title shall be approved by the Parliament of the Republic and the legislative assembly concerned.

Title XIII

ON AGREEMENTS OF ASSOCIATION

ARTICLE 88

The Republic or the Community may make agreements with States that wish to associate themselves with the Community in order to develop their own civilizations.

Title XIV

ON AMENDMENT

ARTICLE 89

The initiative for amending the Constitution shall belong both to the President of the Republic on the proposal of the Premier and to the members of Parliament.

The Government or Parliamentary bill for amendment must be passed by the two assemblies in identical terms. The amendment shall become definitive after approval by a referendum.

Nevertheless, the proposed amendment shall not be submitted to a referendum when the President of the Republic decides to submit it to Parliament convened in Congress; in this case, the proposed amendment shall be approved only if it is accepted by a three-fifths majority of the votes cast. The Secretariat of the Congress shall be that of the National Assembly.

No amendment procedure may be undertaken or followed when the integrity of the territory is in jeopardy.

The republican form of government shall not be subject to amendment.

Title XV

TEMPORARY PROVISIONS

ARTICLE 90

The ordinary session of Parliament is suspended. The mandate of the members of the present National Assembly shall expire on the day that the Assembly elected under the present Constitution convenes.

Until this meeting, the Government alone shall have the authority to convene Parliament.

The mandate of the members of the Assembly of the French Union shall expire at the same time as the mandate of the members of the present National Assembly.

ARTICLE 91

The institutions of the Republic, provided for by the present Constitution, shall be established within four months after its promulgation.

This time limit shall be extended to six months for the institutions of the Community.

The powers of the President of the Republic now in office shall expire only when the results of the election provided for in Articles 6 and 7 of the present Constitution are proclaimed.

The member States of the Community shall participate in this first election under the conditions derived from their status at the date of the promulgation of the Constitution.

The established authorities shall continue to exercise their functions in these States according to the laws and regulations applicable when the Constitution becomes operative, until the authorities provided for by their new regimes are set up.

Until it is definitively constituted, the Senate shall consist of the present members of the Council of the Republic. The organic laws that determine the definitive composition of the Senate must be passed before July 31, 1959.

The powers conferred on the Constitutional Council by Articles 58 and 59 of the Constitution shall be exercised, until this Council is set up, by a committee composed of the Vice President of the Council of State, as chairman, the First President of the Court of Cassation, and the First President of the Audit Office.

The peoples of the member States of the Community shall continue to be represented in Parliament until the measures necessary to the implementation of Title XII have been put into effect.

ARTICLE 92

The legislative measures necessary for the setting up of the institutions and, until they are set up, for the functioning of the governmental authorities, shall be taken in meetings of the Council of Ministers, after consultation with the Council of State, in the form of ordinances having the force of law.

During the time limit set in the first paragraph of Article 91, the Government shall be authorized to determine, by ordinances having the force of law and passed in the same way, the system of elections to the assemblies provided for by the Constitution.

During the same period and under the same conditions, the Government may also adopt measures, in all matters, which it may deem necessary to the life of the nation, the protection of citizens or the safeguarding of liberties.

APPENDIX B

Selected Documents Since De Gaulle's Accession to Power on June 1, 1958 *

1. Premier de Gaulle's Speech in Algiers on June 4, 1958

I understood you. I know what happened here. I see what you wanted to do. I see that the road you have opened in Algeria is the road of renovation and brotherhood. I say renovation in all respects. But very rightly you wanted this renovation to begin at the beginning—in other words, with our institutions—and that is why I am here. And I say brotherhood because you offer the magnificent sight of men who, from one end of the country to the other, no matter what their community, partake of the same ardor and hold each other's hands.

Well, I take note of all this in the name of France, and I declare that, from now on, France considers that in all Algeria there is only one category of inhabitant: there are only Frenchmen who have a full share, Frenchmen with a full share, with the same rights and the same duties.

This means that those paths must be opened that, until now, have been closed to many. This means that the means of livelihood must be given to those who have not had it. This means that the dignity of those whose dignity was contested must be acknowledged. This means that a country must be given to those who could doubt that they had one.

The army, the coherent, ardent and disciplined French Army, under the command of its chiefs, the army which was tried under so many circumstances and which nevertheless has accomplished here a wonderful task of understanding and pacification—the French Army has, on

---

* Unless otherwise noted, all translations are by the French Press and Information Service, New York.

this soil, been the leaven and the witness, and it is the guarantor of the movement that has developed here. It knew how to dam the torrent in order to capture its energy. I pay tribute to it. I express my confidence in it and I count on it for today and for tomorrow.

Frenchmen with a full share in a single and identical electoral college —we are going to demonstrate this no later than three months hence, on the solemn occasion when all Frenchmen, including the 10 million of Algeria, will have to decide their own destiny. For these 10 million Frenchmen, their votes will count the same as those of all the others. They will have to designate, to elect—I repeat, in a single college—their representatives for the public powers, as all other Frenchmen will do. With these elected representatives, we shall see how to do what remains to be done.

May they take part *en masse* in this immense demonstration, all those from your cities, your *douars* [villages], your plains, and your *djebels* [mountains]. May even those take part who, through despair, thought they had to wage on this soil a fight which I do recognize as being courageous—for there is no lack of courage on the soil of Algeria—which is courageous, but which is nonetheless cruel and fratricidal. To those I, De Gaulle, open the door to reconciliation.

Never more than here, never more than tonight, have I realized how beautiful, how great and how generous France is.

Long live the Republic! Long live France!

2. Excerpts from Premier de Gaulle's Radio and Television Broadcast to the Nation, June 13, 1958

French unity was breaking up. Civil war was about to begin. In the eyes of the world, France seemed on the verge of dissolution. It was then that I assumed responsibility for governing our country.

The tragedy of Algeria—upsetting the populations, putting the army to a harsh test, raising a wave of indignation there for the present, and of change and fraternity for the future—started this national crisis. But, at all events, the crisis was inevitable.

Because for twelve years the party system, insecurely based on a deeply divided people, in the midst of a terribly dangerous world, showed itself totally unfit to ensure the conduct of affairs. This was by no means due to the incompetence or the unworthiness of men. Those who held positions of power under the Fourth Republic were able people, honest and patriotic.

But, as they never represented anything but small fractions [of the population], these men who governed did not identify themselves with the general interest. Moreover—divided amongst themselves, as were their own groups, struggling against the encroachments of the Parliamentary Assembly from which they received their mandates, subjected to the demands of the parties they represented—they were doomed to live, for a few months or a few weeks, faced with huge problems which they could not possibly solve.

I said huge problems. They were indeed huge, those problems which confronted us. So are those which we shall have to brave together. To pacify Algeria. To do it in such a way that it will, forever, be body and soul with France. To organize, in a federal manner, the ties between our metropolitan country and the associated countries in Africa and Madagascar. To establish on the basis of cooperation our relations with Morocco, Tunisia, and the States of Indochina. In the Western world to which we belong—without having to confine ourselves in it—to take a place that is our own, to perform an action that is our action, with a view to serving simultaneously both peace and security. . . .

A population that is growing. An economy that has, once and for all, overcome the obstacle of routine. A technology that is forging ahead. New sources of ability that are ready to spring from the deepest layers of the population. The Sahara, which holds a fortune for us and for the territories bordering it on the north and on the south. An army that is very fine and very good. Lastly, the world which wishes—even if it sometimes pretends the opposite—to see us play the part that is rightfully ours, because it feels that this will be to the advantage of all mankind. Ah, I do not pity our youth, which sees all these resources of life, all these incentives to activity offered to it.

But there is not a single Frenchman who does not know that any future is barred to us, if France does not have to guide her a State which is capable of doing so. It is the necessary condition for everything. We have just proved this on the very brink of the abyss. It is my task, along with my Government, to propose to our people new institutions of such a kind that they will provide for the Republic powers that are strong enough, stable enough, effective enough to be responsible for its destiny. I shall do so at the beginning of the autumn. Women and men of France, it is you who will decide, at that time, through your votes, this essential reform and, thereby, the destiny of France.

The way is hard, but how glorious! The aim is difficult, but how grand! Let us go! The signal for departure is being given.

3. Excerpts from Premier de Gaulle's Speech at the Place de la République in Paris, September 4, 1958 on the Draft of the Constitution and the Forthcoming Referendum

The regime [the Third Republic] contained functional defects which might have seemed tolerable in a more or less stable era, but which were no longer compatible with the social transformations, the economic changes, and the external perils that preceded the Second World War. Had not this situation been remedied, the terrible events of 1940 would have swept everything away. But when, on June 18, the struggle for the liberation of France began, it was immediately proclaimed that the Republic to be rebuilt would be a new Republic. The whole Resistance Movement constantly affirmed this.

We know, we know only too well what became of these hopes. . . . We know, we know only too well that once the danger had passed, everything was turned over to the discretion of the parties. We know, we know only too well, what were the consequences of this. By reason of inconsistency and instability and—whatever may have been the intentions and, often, the ability of the men in office—the regime found itself deprived of the authority in internal affairs and the assurance in external affairs, without which it could not act. It was inevitable that the paralysis of the State should bring on a grave national crisis and that, immediately, the Republic should be threatened with collapse.

The necessary steps were taken to prevent the irreparable at the very moment that it was about to occur. The disruption of the State was, by a narrow margin, prevented. They managed to save the last chance of the Republic. It was by legal means that I and my Government assumed the unusual mandate of darfting a new constitution and of submitting it to the decision of the people. . . .

It is for the people we are, for the century and the world in which we live, that the proposed constitution was drafted: The country effectively governed by those to whom it gives the mandate and to whom it grants the confidence that makes for lawfulness. A national arbiter—far removed from political bickering—elected by the citizens who hold a public mandate, charged with the task of ensuring the normal functioning of the institutions, possessing the right to resort to the judgment of the sovereign people, accountable, in the case of extreme danger, for the independence, the honor and integrity of France and for the safety of the Republic. A Government made to govern, which is granted the necessary time and opportunity, which does not turn to anything other than its task and which thereby deserves the country's support. A Parliament intended to represent the political will of the nation, to enact laws and to control the executive, without venturing to overstep its role. A Government and Parliament that work together but remain separate as to their responsibilities, with no member of one being at the same time a member of the other. Such is the balanced structure that power must assume. The rest will depend upon men. . . .

A Community formed between the French nation and those of the Overseas Territories that so desire, within which each Territory will become a State that governs itself, while foreign policy, defense, the currency, economic and financial policies, use of raw materials, the control of justice, high education, long-distance communications will constitute a common domain over which the organs of the community—the President, Executive Council, Senate, and Court of Arbitration—will have jurisdiction. Thus, this vast organization will renovate the human complex grouped around France. This will be effected by virtue of the free determination of all. In fact, every Territory will have an opportunity, through its vote in the referendum, either to accept France's proposal, or to refuse it, and, by so doing, to break every tie with her. Once a member of the Community, it can in the future, after coming to an agreement with the common organs, assume its own destiny independently of the others. . . .

Here, women and men of France, is what inspires and what makes up the Constitution which, on September 28, will be submitted to your vote. With all my heart, in the name of France, I ask you to answer: Yes.

4. Excerpts from Premier de Gaulle's Speech at Constantine, October 3, 1958 *

As for Algeria, what is the future? Men and women of Algeria I have come here to tell you. This country so alive and so brave but so difficult and suffering will be profoundly transformed. This means that it is necessary that the conditions of life for each man and woman improve day by day; this means that for the inhabitants the resources of the soil, the skills of their elites must be developed; this means that the children must be educated; this means that the whole of Algeria must take its part in what modern civilization can and must bring to men—well-being and dignity.

But great projects do not amount to much except in terms of the political measures that must be taken for their realization. These then are the measures that my government will take for the coming five years by virtue of the full power that the Constitution has given to it. For the coming five years the young people who come to the Metropolis and who enter in the administrative organizations of the State—in the judiciary, in the army, in education, in the public services—will represent one tenth of the total. And this, of course, without any prejudice to a growing proportion of Algerians serving in Algeria. For the coming five years the salaries and the general remuneration in Algeria will be brought to a level comparable with that existing in the Metropolis. Before the end of five years, 600,000 acres of land will be distributed to Moslem farmers. Before the end of five years, the first stage of the plan of agricultural and industrial development in Algeria will be terminated. This stage involves the arrival and distribution of gas and oil of the Sahara, the establishment on Algerian soil of large chemical and metallurgical centers, the construction of housing for one million persons, the development of sanitary facilities, roads, ports, communications, and finally jobs for 400,000

* Translated from *Année Politique, 1958*, pp. 561–62.

new workers. In the coming five years two thirds of the boys and girls will be educated and within three years thereafter the scholarization of the Algerian youth will be complete. Throughout the coming five years the human contacts that have been established by the French army, by the officers, by the reservists, and by other forces, including the young recruits, will continue and will develop, much as will be the case in Paris and in our provinces.

Where will this profound evolution lead? . . . In two months Algeria will elect its representatives exactly on the basis of the same conditions as the Metropolis. But at least two thirds of its representatives will be Moslem citizens. . . . The future of Algeria will be built on a double basis: its personality and its close solidarity with the French Metropolis. . . . This transformation, this immense task—political, economic, social, and cultural—who can accomplish it if not France? . . . So turning to those who continue this fratricidal fight, who organize in the Metropolis those deplorable acts of terrorism, and who attempt throughout various foreign offices, through the radio, through publications in certain foreign capitals, to spread invectives against France, I ask them: "Why kill? We must live! Why destroy? The duty is to construct! Why hate? The question is to cooperate."

5. Excerpts from Premier de Gaulle's Press Conference in Paris, October 23, 1958

We have made use of [a] great popular movement to renovate our institutions. New governmental authorities will come into being, profoundly different from those of yesterday. Arbitration by the chief of State, separation of the executive and the legislative, continuity of government—that is what is provided for, that is what the people wanted. Legislative elections will be held next month to put the new Constitution into effect.

Everybody understands—I allow myself a personal word or two—everybody understands that I do not wish, that I cannot take, any direct part in this contest. The mission with which the country has entrusted me prevents me from taking sides. Thus I shall not do so on behalf of any one, even of those who always have shown a friendly loyalty to me through all vicissitudes. Of course, I shall not disapprove if groups or candidates of all shades of opinion make known their support of the action of Charles de Gaulle. Besides, others will not fail to make known their opposition, utilizing that freedom that they accuse me of wanting to destroy. This impartiality compels me to make it very clear that my name, even in the form of an adjective, must not be used in the title of any group or in the slogan of any candidate. . . .

After being suspended for a few months, the parliamentary institution will reappear, but no longer omnipotent. The lesson learned from the facts, the course of events, the judgment of public opinion, and also the civic sense of the whole of the French body politic led the people who drafted the Constitution of 1958—that is to say, the members of the Government, assisted by the work of the Constitutional Council, by the advice of the Council of State and, I should add, by the enlightened advice of the President of the Republic: all this led the drafters of the Constitution to place strict limitations and powerful brakes on future Assemblies. The nation has ratified their work. Indeed, the situation of the world, the needs of national renovation, absolutely prohibit a return to the confusion of times past.

If, unfortunately, the Parliament of tomorrow should refuse to accept the role incumbent on it, there is no doubt that the Republic would be thrown into a new crisis, the outcome of which no one can predict, except that, in any case, the parliamentary institution would be swept away for a long time to come. On the contrary, if the future assemblies rebuild their legislative functions in an objective manner, if they abstain from these rival bids, from these claims, from these partisan agitations— of which we have seen all too many examples—then, the powers of the State will function with proper balance, stability, and effectiveness and the nation will take an interest in the free debates of its representatives. In short, it is by reforming the representative system thoroughly that we have safeguarded its chance. May it not destroy this chance. . . .

Question—After the instructions you sent General Salan concerning the elections, and the order you gave the officers to withdraw from all political organizations, would you define the role you are assigning to the army in Algeria?

. . . The question is to know what is happening and what will happen as far as the French Army in Algeria is concerned. Well, the French Army in Algeria is doing what France expects it to do. Its first duty, of course, is to prevent Algeria from being lost through military action and in the field. In this respect, I believe that the hardest is done, although nothing is over as yet.

The Army is also entrusted with the security of all categories of the population, and particularly, of course, of the Moslem population. . . . How many lives, how many homes, how many crops have been protected by the French Army in Algeria! And to what slaughter would we condemn this country if we were stupid enough and cowardly enough to abandon it! That is the reason, the value, the result of so many military actions, costly in men and weariness, of so many nights and days of guard duty, of so many reconnaisances, of so many patrols and clashes. Alas, 7,200 officers and men are dead. Alas, 77,000 rebels have been killed in combat.

Another aspect of the army's mission, which it fulfills in a brilliant and moving way, can be seen in the fact that it is found throughout the country, and also that it is the army, that is to say, a devoted, disciplined, and disinterested corps. That is why it wished and it was able to establish human contact with this Moslem community which, too often and for too long, has found itself relegated to its *mechtas,* its *douars,* and its misery.

Officers and soldiers—with their hands, their hearts, their ingenuity—do not restrict themselves to protecting the population, but they help it in every way. One should see, on the spot, what they are able to do with regard to supplies, health, housing, and schools. The value of the human relationships that are established day after day must be measured. Moreover, if the referendum was what it was in Algeria, if the moving eagerness of Moslems to participate in it could be seen, this was simply the proof that a confident and reciprocal brotherhood is dawning in that unhappy land. . . .

Question—The FLN is making overtures concerning the possibilities of peace in Algeria. What attitude does the Government plan to take toward this?

The organization of which you are speaking started the fight on its own initiative. . . . However, I say unequivocally that, as for most of them, the men of the insurrection have fought courageously. Let the peace of the brave come, and I am sure that all hatred will fade away and disappear.

I have spoken of the peace of the brave. What does this mean? Simply this: Let those who opened fire cease fire, and let them return without humiliation to their families and their work.

People say to me: "But what can they do to end the struggle?" My answer is: "Wherever they are organized for combat, their leaders need only enter into contact with the French command." The old warrior's procedure, long used when one wanted to silence the guns, was to wave the white flag of truce. And I answer that, in that case, the combatants would be received and treated honorably.

As for the external organization of which we were just speaking, which, from the outside, strives to direct the struggle, I repeat openly what I have already made known. If delegates were designated to come and negotiate with the authorities the end of hostilities, they would have only to address themselves to the French Embassy at Tunis or at Rabat. Either one would ensure their transportation to Metropolitan France. There, they would be assured of complete safety, and I guarantee them the freedom to depart.

Some say: "But what would be the political conditions that the French Government would be willing to discuss?" I reply: "The political destiny of Algeria is in Algeria itself. Opening fire does not give a man the right to determine that destiny. When the democratic way is open, when the citizens have an opportunity to express their will, then there is no other way that is acceptable. Now, this way is open in Algeria."

6. Excerpts from General de Gaulle's Inaugural Address as President of the Republic and of the Community, January 8, 1959

I am deeply sensible of all that is impressive and moving in this ceremony. . . . Thus the renewed institutions of the French Republic and the new institutions of the Community come into force. Thus the man whom both the Republic and the Community have once more assigned the task of guiding them toward their destiny takes up his functions.

The destiny of France: These words bring to mind the heritage of the past, the duties of the present, and the hope of the future. Since, here in Paris, almost a thousand years ago, France took her name and the State began to function, our country has lived through many things. Now in sorrow, now in glory, it has vigorously surmounted innumerable vicissitudes from within and from without. During the last half century, it has been more gravely wounded and more sorely rent than at any previous time in its history. But now, it has suddenly been offered an opportunity to emerge from doubt, from dissensions, from humiliations. And now our country wants to seize this opportunity by giving general interest precedence over all individual interests and prejudices. Now, by the grace of God, a better life is available to the French people provided they remain true to effort and to unity.

The destiny of the Community: It is a question of giving life to this magnificent institution, which, by virture of a contract entered into in complete independence, unites on the one hand, Metropolitan France, together with the Overseas Departments and Territories, and on the other, the Republics born in the lands of Africa where liberty, equality, and fraternity have flourished under the tricolor flag. In the union thus formed, a special place is destined for the Algeria of tomorrow, an Algeria that will be pacified and transformed, developing her personality herself and closely associated with France. In the midst of a dangerous world, what a trump card for the peace of mankind, what a field that lies open to progress, what an honor for the French people and for their African brothers!

In the nation, the national interest; in the Community, the common interest—that is what, today as yesterday, it is my duty to represent, and in any case to vindicate, even to impose if this should be demanded by the public safety. In order to do this, I must have the cooperation of those who serve the Republic, the backing of the men who henceforth will be responsible in Africa, and above all the backing of the French people and of overseas peoples. Once more I ask for this cooperation, this moral backing, this support of which I was assured not so long ago in the dark days of national peril; once more I ask for this as the light of our great hope dawns on the horizon. Long live the Republic—long live France.

7. Excerpts from President de Gaulle's Press Conference in Paris, March 25, 1959

Question—How do you feel that the situation has developed in Algeria since last year when you offered the "peace of the brave" to the Algerian rebels?

There have been 130 years of vicissitudes in Algeria. For four years and more now, fighting and attacks have not ceased. We are living in an age when, on this earth, a gigantic organization is militating everywhere against the West, while the West often neglects to look after itself. We are witnessing a turmoil which, inside the Moslem world, sets many Arab countries against foreign peoples, many states and parts of states against others of the same race and the same religion, and many leaders against other leaders who, like themselves, and yet against them, claim to be champions of unity. Under these conditions, I doubt that anyone has ever been able to imagine that peace and prosperity would come all of a sudden to a torn Algeria, or that all that was necessary, at the height of a persistant fever, was to shout down one slogan with other slogans in order that all the internal and external causes of the present war should disappear as if by magic.

Personally, I do not think that, and I never say it. On the contrary, I believe and I say that the destiny of Algeria depends upon a task of long duration, the task of a whole generation performed under conditions and in a spirit that are completely new and that are aimed at enabling Algeria to reveal herself to herself and to open herself to the world as it is. I believe and I say that such a task is inconceivable without the presence and the action of France. I believe and I say that France has made her resolve, that she is now following a clear and firm plan and that, while endeavoring to achieve pacification as soon as possible, she is working for a transformation that will enable Algeria to find her new self. . . .

As this new Algeria takes shape in body and spirit, her political destiny will appear in the minds and in the votes of her children. I am sure that the Algerians want and will want this destiny to be tied to that of France and that the latter also wants and will want it, because this fits in with the nature of things, with common sense and with sentiment. This is a magnificent task which calls for the efforts of all the Algerians, of all the communities and of the French of France. By comparison, the desperate continuation of combats and attacks appears each day more absurd, because this continuation no longer seems to have any justifiable aim and therefore can lead only to hatred, misery, and death.

Yes, blood and tears still flow; yet, Algeria and France are marching together toward the future—a future which, I assert, will belong to everyone and in which no door will be closed.

8. Excerpts from President de Gaulle's Radio and Television Broadcast to the Nation, September 16, 1959

Our recovery is proceeding. . . . However, France is still faced with a difficult and bloody problem: that of Algeria. This we must solve.

We will certainly not do so by tossing at each other empty and over-simplified slogans, on one side or the other, both of which are blind to everything save their conflicting passions, interests, or daydreams. We will solve it as a great nation should do, choosing the only path worthy of being followed. I mean the free choice which the Algerians themselves will make for their future.

As a matter of fact, much has been done already to pave the way for this solution. Through pacification first of all, for nothing can be solved against a background of shooting and assassination. From that point of view, I do not claim that we have reached the end of the road. But I say that there is no comparison, in terms of the safety of persons and property, between the situation which prevailed two or three years ago and that which prevails now. Our army is accomplishing its mission both courageously and skillfully, fighting its opponents while maintaining with the population deeper and broader contacts than had ever existed before. If our soldiers, and in particular, the 120,000 Moslems among them, had faltered in their duty or if the Algerian masses had turned against France, that indeed would have spelled disaster. But since this has not occurred, the restoration of public order, although it may not be imminent, is now in sight.

The second requisite for a settlement is that all Algerians should have the means of expressing themselves through truly universal suffrage. Up to last year they have never had it. They have it now, thanks to the institution of equal rights, a single college, and the fact that the larger communities, those of the Moslems, are sure of obtaining at the polls the largest numbers of representatives elected. This was a change of the greatest significance, actually, a revolution. On the 28th of September of last year, the Algerians, by referendum, adopted the Constitution, and signified their intention that their future should be shaped along with France. . . .

Thanks to the progress of pacification, to democracy, and to social advancement, we can now look forward to the day when the men and women who live in Algeria will be in a position to decide their own destiny, once and for all, freely and in the full knowledge of what is at stake. Taking into account all these factors—those of the Algerian situation, those inherent in the national and the international situation—I deem it necessary that recourse to self-determination be here and now proclaimed. In the name of France and of the Republic, by virtue of the power granted to me by the Constitution to consult its citizens—if only God lets me live and the people listen to me—I pledge myself to ask the Algerians, on the one hand, in their twelve Departments, what, when all is said and done, they wish to be; and, on the other hand, all Frenchmen, to endorse that choice.

The question, obviously, will be put to the Algerians as individuals, for since the beginning of the world there has never been any Algerian unity, far less any Algerian sovereignty. The Carthaginians, the Romans, the Vandals, the Byzantines, the Syrian Arabs, the Cordova Arabs, the Turks, the French have, one after the other, penetrated the country without there being—at any time, under any shape or form—an Algerian State. As for the time of the elections, I will decide upon it in due course, at the latest, four years after the actual restoration of peace; that is to say, once a situation has been established whereby not more than 200 persons a year will lose their lives, either in ambushes or isolated attacks. The ensuing period of time will be devoted to resuming normal existence, to emptying the camps and prisons, to permitting the return of exiles, to restoring the free play of individual and public liberties and to enabling the population to become fully aware of what is at stake. I would like to invite, here and now, observers from all over the world, to attend, without hindrance, the final culmination of this process.

But what will this political destiny finally be, for the men and women of Algeria who will choose it, once peace is restored? Everyone knows that in theory it is possible to imagine three solutions. Since it is in the interest of all concerned—and especially of France—that the question be answered without ambiguity, the three conceivable solutions will be put to the vote:

Either—secession, where some believe independence would be found. France would then leave the Algerians who had expressed their wish to become separated from her. They would organize, without her, the territory in which they live, the resources which they have at their disposal, the government which they desire. I am convinced personally that such an outcome would be incredible and disastrous. Algeria being what it is at the present time, and the world what we know it to be, secession would carry in its wake the most appalling poverty, frightful political chaos, widespread slaughter, and soon after, the warlike dictatorship of the Communists. But this demon must be exorcised, and this must be done by the Algerians themselves. If it should appear through some inconceivable misfortune, that such is indeed their will, France would undoubtedly stop devoting so much of value and so many billions of francs to a cause shorn of any hope. It goes without saying that, on this assumption, those Algerians, regardless of origin, who might wish to remain French would do so in any case, and that France would arrange, if need be, for their regrouping and resettlement. On the other hand, everything would be arranged so that the operation of oil wells, the handling and shipping of Saharan oil—which is the result of French efforts and which is of interest to the whole western world—would be ensured in any event.

Or—out-and-out identification with France, such as implied in equality of rights: Algerians can accede to all political, administrative, and judicial functions of the State and have free access to the public service.

They would benefit, as regards salaries, wages, social security, education, and vocational training, from all measures provided for in Metropolitan France; they would live and work wherever they saw fit, throughout the territory of the Republic; in other words, they would be living, from every point of view, regardless of their religion or the community to which they belonged, by and large on the same footing and at the same level as other citizens, and become part and parcel of the French people who would then, in effect, spread from Dunkirk to Tamanrasset.

Or—the government of Algerians by Algerians, backed up by French help and in close relationship with her, as regards the economy, education, defense, and foreign relations. In that case, the internal regime of Algeria should be of the federal type, so that the various communities —French, Arab, Kabyle, Mozabite—who live together in the country would find guarantees for their own way of life and a framework for cooperation.

But since, for a year now, it has been settled that—through the institution of equal voting rights, the single college, and the emergence of a majority of Moslem representatives—the political future of Algerians is to depend on Algerians; since it has been officially and solemnly emphasized that, once peace has been restored, the Algerians will let it be known what fate they want for themselves, to the exclusion of any other, and that all of them, whatever their program may be, whatever they might have done, wherever they come from, will take part, if they wish to do so, in this vote: what then could be the meaning of the rebellion? . . .

During the few years which will pass before the deadline we have set, there will be much to do, so that Algeria, when pacified, can weigh all the factors and consequences of its own decision. I intend to concern myself personally with the task. Furthermore, the procedures of the future vote must in due course be elaborated and specified. But the road is open. The decision is taken, the stakes are worthy of France.

9. Declaration by the Provisional Government of the Algerian Republic in Tunis, September 28, 1959 *

In his declaration of September 16, 1959, the President of the French Republic, in the name of France, solemnly recognized the right of the Algerians to self-determination. The right of the Algerian people to determine freely its own destiny is finally recognized. This evolution has only been possible because, during the past five years, the Algerian people have victoriously resisted one of the most bloody wars of colonial reconquest. It has only been possible because the Front of National

---

* Translation by the Algerian Office, New York.

Liberation and the Army of National Liberation pursues, and will pursue should it be necessary, the liberating struggle. Finally, it has only been possible thanks to the support of all brother and friendly peoples, and thanks to the backing of international public opinion.

The right of peoples to self-determination, as inscribed in the proclamation of the Front of National Liberation of November 1, 1954, has always been a fundamental objective of the Algerian Revolution. It constitutes a peaceful and democratic means for the Algerian people to achieve national independence. Inscribed in the Charter of the United Nations, self-determination, that is, the right of peoples to decide for themselves their own destiny, restores to the Algerian people the exercise of their national sovereignty of which they had been temporarily deprived by a military conquest—from which no legitimacy can proceed.

The national entity which Algeria constitutes, and the sociological unity of its people are basic objective elements. An application of self-determination which would not take into account these realities, and which would aim at breaking up this entity into racial or religious communities, is delusive. Furthermore, the Provisional Government of the Algerian Republic recalls the intangible principle of the integrity of national territory, and expresses the unshakeable determination of the Algerian people to oppose any attempt at partition. It calls the attention of international opinion to the danger which any attempt against this unity and this integrity would constitute. An attempt of this nature, far from contributing to the solution of the Algerian problem, would only aggravate it and would constitute a permanent threat to international peace and security.

As for the wealth of the Sahara, its prospecting and exploitation can under no circumstances be transformed into a right of ownership. Firstly, a source of human progress for Algeria and for North Africa, these riches should only give rise to a large and fruitful cooperation in the general interest.

Moreover, to subordinate the free choice of the Algerian people to a consultation of the French people would be the very negation of self-determination and democracy. The independence which will result from a free consultation of the Algerian people will not be a source of anarchy and poverty. It will guarantee individual liberty and assure individual security. Finally, it will facilitate the building of the Maghreb and the free cooperation with all nations.

These principles being clearly defined, it is evident that the recourse to universal suffrage cannot take place without the return of peace. The "pacification," that is, the war which becomes more and more murderous, cannot restore peace in Algeria. The free choice of the Algerian people cannot be exercised under the pressure of an occupation army of more than a half-million soldiers and almost as many gendarmes, policemen, and militiamen. It cannot be exercised under the pressure of airplanes, tanks, and cannons, under the pressure of an administrative structure whose tradition of electoral frauds is known. This free choice cannot be fully accomplished when more than one fourth of the population is held in prisons, camps, or forced into exile.

All these are problems which call for discussion.

Recognized at this time by many States, the Provisional Government of the Algerian Republic is the trustee and the guarantor of the interests of the Algerian people until this people shall freely pronounce itself. It directs and controls the resistance of the Algerian people and the liberating struggle of the Army of National Liberation. Thus, there can be a return of peace only with its accord. *THIS CAN BE IMMEDIATE.* In this aim, the ,Provisional Government of the Algerian Republic is ready to enter into pourparlers with the French Government to discuss the political and military conditions of the cease-fire, the conditions and guarantees for the application of self-determination.

10. Excerpts from President de Gaulle's News Conference in Paris, November 10, 1959

[After commenting on foreign policy problems and announcing the forthcoming visit of Mr. Khrushchev to France, General de Gaulle invited questions.]

Question—Mr. President, at the United Nations, before the Political Committee, a debate is now taking place . . . on the proposed French nuclear tests in the Sahara. . . . I would like to know, Mr. President, if you could tell us what you think of this debate, and more precisely, exactly what France's position is in the atomic field.

. . . If the Anglo-Saxons and the Soviets agree among themselves to halt their tests, France can only approve. But, if anybody wished to ask France to renounce atomic weapons for herself, while others are in possession of them and are developing them in tremendous quantities, there is not the slightest chance that she would accede to such a request.

Probably the sort of equilibrium that is establishing itself between the atomic power of the two camps is, for the moment, a factor in world peace, but who can say what will happen tomorrow? Who can say, for example, whether some sudden advance in development—particularly in the field of space rockets—will not provide one of the two camps with such an advantage that its peaceful inclinations will not hold out? Who can say whether, in the future, if basic political facts should change completely, as has already occurred on the earth, the two powers that would have a monopoly on nuclear weapons might not make a deal with each other to divide the world between them. Who can say whether, should the occasion arise, while each side might follow a policy of not hurling its devices at the principal adversary, so as not to be threatened by them itself—who can say whether the two rivals might not crush others.

One can very well imagine, for example, that on such a terrible occasion, Western Europe might be destroyed from Moscow and Central Europe from Washington. And who even can say whether the two rivals, as a result of some unforeseeable political and social upheaval, will not come to the point of uniting? In truth, France, by equipping herself with nuclear armaments, is rendering a service to the equilibrium of the world. . . .

Question—Since your statement of September 16, how do you picture the development of the problem of Algeria and, in particular, the eventual prospects of a cease-fire?

As far as Algeria is concerned, one decisive fact has appeared: The Algerians will themselves have to decide their destiny. Their choice will be entirely free. It will be so because France wants the question to be settled once and for all. The choice will be free also because I have given my word that all the Algerians will be able to participate in the referendum without the slightest constraint, and even that whoever they are, wherever they come from, whatever their platform may be, they will take part not only in the voting, but also in the discussions that will precede it, so as to determine the voting procedures, when the time comes, and the regulations governing the campaign that will precede the vote. The choice will be entirely free because the Premier has several times confirmed our determination in this respect, because Parliament has given its consent and because the people approve. . . .

Therefore, I say to all the Algerians of all communities, of all political affiliations, of all ways of thinking: You can and you must take part in this transformation which is going to make Algeria a land of men who are free, dignified, proud, and prosperous. After all, that is your common lot. Why should you not have a part in this—you who have thought to serve Algeria through revolt and terror. Unless your leaders are determined to try to maintain or establish their dictatorship through violence, even if this means turning the country over to ruin and misfortune, the war you are waging there no longer has a real meaning. There are much better things to do with your zeal, your courage, and your love for your native land.

And all of you fence-sitters, you who will not budge and who are causing Algeria to lose time, when she ought to be finding her peace and her development, and finding them soon, now that it is understood that her destiny is in the hands of those who live there, why do you not form a great party for Algerian progress?

You, the French of Algeria, who for generations have done so much, if one page has been turned by the great wind of history, well, it is up to you to write another. Let there be a truce to vain nostalgia, vain bitterness, vain torments; take the future as it comes, and grapple with it. More than ever Algeria needs you. More than ever France needs you in Algeria.

And you, all the foreign peoples and States, if you believe, as one must think, that when all is said and done the only quarrel that matters is the cause of mankind, recognize that France is upholding this quarrel there in Algeria, for Algeria, with Algeria, and, if you please, respect her effort.

11. Excerpts from President de Gaulle's Address in Dakar before the Federal Assembly of Mali at the Sixth Meeting of the Executive Council of the French Community, December 13, 1959 *

Yes, in a few days France, the Federation of Mali and the states that compose it will begin negotiations to modify the status of their relations. This was implicitly and even explicitly provided for by the Constitution of the Community that we all have voted. It is nonetheless true that this will lead the federal state of Mali, and the member states of Soudan and Senegal that compose it, to a new position. The one they occupied last year was new. And it will be even more so in the immediate future. In other words, this state of Mali will assume what some call a "position of independence" and which I prefer to call that of "international sovereignty." I say that I prefer it, without contesting the attraction and the significance that the term independence may have and ought to have for all peoples and in particular for this one. I prefer, nevertheless, international sovereignty because it appears to me to correspond better to enduring necessities and more particularly to present-day necessities. Independence is a term which signifies an intention, but the world being what it is—so small, so cramped, so interfering with itself—that real independence, total independence does not truly belong to anybody. . . .

When, therefore, a country like yours will assume the international responsibility that I mentioned the whole world is looking to see in which direction it will move of its own accord. Will it choose the camp of freedom, will it choose the other camp? . . . But again, things being what they are and the world being what it is, Mali must choose the direction that it will take. In order to choose it and to follow it there is something essential. . . . What is essential for a country to play its international role is for it to exist by itself, through itself and in itself. There is no international reality which is not at the same time a national reality; for a country in order to play its role in the world must follow the paths permitting it to do so; the first of these paths is that it constitutes itself as a State. A country has never been known to exist and even more important exist internationally without a State. That is to say, an organization which directs the whole of the citizenry, which is accepted and recognized by

* Translation from the full text of the address reprinted in *Le Monde*, December 15, 1959.

all the inhabitants, and which leads the entire country toward a better life. . . .

This is a technical epoch in which we are living. There is no state with any weight which does not contribute something to the technical progress of the world. This I must recommend since I have the honor of finding myself among you. You are taking the responsibility and France accepts it with all her heart. I promise that she is ready to help you. She is ready first because of her humane nature. There have been vicissitudes in the history of France but the continuity of this history exists and goes back before the Revolution. . . . From its very inception the vocation of France, the purpose of France, have been a humane vocation and a humane purpose. She is faithful to this purpose when she offers you her loyal and friendly cooperation in the creation, establishment, and progress of your state. . . .

That is why you may count on France. In the world in which we are and in which we are going to be, no longer only linked together, but side by side—in this world let us stay together. This is the best service that we can render to ourselves, and in any case it is, in the last resort, what humanity requires of us.

12. Excerpts from General de Gaulle's Radio and Television Broadcast to the Nation on Algerian Policy, January 29, 1960

If I have put on my uniform today to address you on television, it is in order to show that it is General de Gaulle who speaks, as well as the Chief of State.

In Algeria, we are fighting against a rebellion which has lasted more than five years. France is valiantly continuing to exert the necessary efforts to put down that rebellion.

But she wants to arrive at a peace that is peace; to do what has to be done so that the tragedy does not begin all over again; to act in such a way as not—when all is said and done—to lose Algeria, which would be a disaster for us and for the West. The world, a prey to vast crises and movements which are well known, is watching this struggle which disturbs it and in which the various opposing camps seek to take a hand. It is obvious that the unity, progress, and prestige of the French people are at stake, and that the future of this people is blocked as long as the Algerian problem remains unsolved.

Taking all this into consideration, I, in the name of France, made the following decision: The Algerians shall have free choice of their destiny. When, one way or another—through the conclusion of a cease-fire or through total defeat of the rebels—we shall have put an end to the fighting, when later, after a prolonged period of restored peace, the populations will have had a chance to understand what is at stake and, moreover, thanks to us, to achieve the necessary progress in the political, economic, social, educational, and other fields—then, it will be the Algerians who will say what they want to be. This will not be dictated to them. For if their response were not really *their* response, then while for a time there might well be military victory, basically nothing would be settled. On the contrary, everything can be settled and, I believe, settled in France's favor, when the Algerians will have had an opportunity to make known their will in all freedom, dignity, and security. In short, self-determination is the only policy that is worthy of France. It is the only possible outcome. It is the policy which has been defined by the President of the Republic, decided upon by the Government, approved by the Parliament, and adopted by the French nation.

Now then, there are two categories of people who do not want any part of this free choice.

First, the rebel organization, which maintains that it will cease fire only if I negotiate with it beforehand, by special prerogative, on the political destiny of Algeria, which would be tantamount to building it up as the only valid representative and to elevating it in advance to being the government of the country. That I will not do.

On the other hand, some persons of French descent demand that I renounce the idea of self-determination, that I say that everything has been done, and that the fate of the Algerians has already been decided. That I will not do either. Self-determination is the only means by which the Moslems can themselves cast out the demon of secession. As to the terms of this or that French solution, I mean to have them worked out at leisure, when peace has been restored. After which, I reserve the right to commit myself—when the right time comes—for whatever I shall consider good. You may be sure that I will do this thoroughly.

It was then that, trying to force their pretended claims on the nation, on the State and on myself, certain people in Algiers started an insurrection; it was then that they fired on the forces of law and order and killed fine soldiers, and they are now rising up in arms against the authority of France. Aided in the beginning by the accommodating uncertainty of various military elements, and profiting from the fears and feverish passions stirred up by agitators, they have thus far obtained the support of part of the European population; they have instigated a forced strike, the halting of transportation, and the closing of stores. Because of them, there is danger that a disruption of the national unity may occur, to the indignation of the French nation and in the very midst of the struggle being waged against the rebels. There is not a man with any common sense who does not see what the inevitable consequences would be if this dreadful secession carried the day.

In face of the foul blow that has thus been struck against France, I speak first of all to the community of French descent in Algeria. . . . Frenchmen of Algeria, how can you listen to the liars and the conspirators who tell you that in granting a free choice to the Algerians, France and De Gaulle want to abandon you, to pull out of Algeria and hand it over to the rebellion? Is it abandoning you, is it wanting to lose Algeria, to send there and to maintain there an army of 500,000 men equipped with tremendous amounts of materiel; to consent to the sacrifice there of a good many of our children; to pay out there, this very year, civil and military expenditures amounting to a thousand billion [old francs], to undertake there a tremendous program of development; to draw from the Sahara, with great difficulty and at great expense, oil and gas in order to bring them to the sea?

How can you doubt that if, some day, the Moslems freely and formally decide that the Algeria of tomorrow must be closely united to France—how can you doubt that anything would bring greater joy to our country and to De Gaulle than to see them choose, between one solution or another, the one that would be the most French? How can you deny that all the work for the development of the Moslem populations, which was initiated eighteen months ago, and is now still being pursued and which, after pacification, will have to be expanded yet more —how can you deny that this work tends precisely to create new and manifold ties between France and the Algerians? Above all else, how can you fail to see that, in rising up against the State and against the nation, you are surely heading toward ruin and at the same time you are running the risk of causing France to lose Algeria at the very moment when the decline of the rebellion is becoming evident? I solemnly appeal to you to return to law and order.

Next, I speak to the army, which, thanks to its magnificent efforts, is in the process of winning the victory in Algeria; however, some of the elements of this army might be tempted to think that this war is their war, not France's war, and that they have a right to a policy which would not be France's policy. To all our soldiers I say: In your mission there is no room for any equivocation or interpretation. You must liquidate the rebel force which is seeking to drive France out of Algeria and to impose upon that land its dictatorship of want and sterility. At the same time that you are conducting the battle, you must contribute to the material and spiritual transformation of the Moslem populations so as to win their hearts and minds to France. When the time comes for the people to vote, it will be your responsibility to guarantee the complete freedom and sincerity of this vote.

Yes, that is your mission, as France gives it to you, and it is France that you serve. What would the French Army become but an anarchic and absurd conglomeration of military feudalisms, if it should happen that certain elements made their loyalty conditional? As you know, I have the supreme responsibility. It is I who bear the country's destiny. I must therefore be obeyed by every French soldier. I believe that I shall be obeyed, because I know you, because I have a high regard for you, because I feel affection for you, because I have confidence in General Challe whom I have placed at your head, soldiers of Algeria, and finally, because I have need of you for France.

This having been said, listen to me carefully. . . . No soldier, under penalty of being guilty of a serious fault, may associate himself at any time, even passively, with the insurrection. In the last analysis, law and order must be re-established. The methods to be employed so that law and order will prevail may be of various sorts. But your duty is to bring this about. I have given, and am giving, this order.

Finally, I speak to France. Well, my dear country, my old country, here we are together, once again, facing a harsh test. By virtue of the mandate that the people have given me and of the national legitimacy that I have embodied for twenty years, I ask all men and women to support me, no matter what happens.

And while the guilty ones, who dream of being usurpers, take as a pretext the decision that I have made concerning Algeria, let it be known everywhere, let it be clearly understood, that I do not intend to go back on that decision. To yield on this point and under these conditions would be to destroy the trump cards that we still hold in Algeria, but it would also be to make the State bow before the outrage that is being inflicted on it and the threat that is aimed at it. Thus France would become but a poor broken toy adrift on the sea of hazards.

Once again, I call upon all Frenchmen, wherever they may be, whoever they may be, to reunite themselves to France.

Long live the Republic. Long live France.

13. Excerpts from the Statement of Premier Michel Debré to the National Assembly, February 2, 1960

Last week, in Algiers, some Frenchmen rose up against the State and, because they rose against the State, it was even possible to fear the beginning of a civil war. The ordeal was surmounted and, thanks to General de Gaulle, surmounted quickly. But from these barricades, from this outbreak, from the actions which preceded and accompanied them, there are lessons to be learned. . . .

The events of the past week made it necessary not only to remind people of a sense of direction and purpose; it also made it necessary to remind them of the respect they owed the State. This has been done and this has been understood. But whether it is a matter of the policy in Algeria or a matter of obedience to the State, it is necessary to do more than to issue a reminder; the State must also be strengthened. For the success of any policy, the State must be in a position to meet the circumstances and the requirements of this policy. There must first of all be men, and there must even be one man. We saw this once again last week, and perhaps I saw it better than anyone else.

The choice between order and disorder, the wavering between a tragedy and perhaps a collapse, and the maintenance of the unity without which there is no nation—all this hinged, if I may venture to say so, on one man. National legitimacy has spoken, but it is one man alone who, at present, embodies this legitimacy in such a way that no one, in the long run, has or can be mistaken on this score. The nation, once again, owes a great deal to General de Gaulle. Popular opinion, moreover, has understood this perfectly.

Behind this one man there must be suitable political institutions. We can believe and we can hope that the political system, as defined in the Constitution of 1958, gives and will give the Government and, in a general way, the executive, solid foundations for its action. But there must also be means. It is in this area that experience has revealed—particularly during the past few days—the shortcomings of the State's machinery.

The maintenance of order at a time when it is disturbed, and yet more important, at a time when the Government has a presentiment that it is going to be disturbed; the direction of the civil and military services, not only to ensure normal functioning but also to secure the success of a policy in the face of hesitations or the existence of cases of ill will; the orientation of all the administrative services responsible not only for the execution of day-to-day tasks, but also for infusing these tasks with the very breath and unity of views without which theories and even law itself remain dead letters or become diverted—to meet these exigencies which, believe me, were shown during the past weeks to be very basic exigencies, and which will be still more basic in the months to come —to meet these exigencies, it is essential to strengthen the possibilities of action of the executive. This is why, in accordance with Article 38 of the Constitution, the Government asks you for these special powers, which are both defined and limited by the bill that we are asking you to pass.

Thanks to this law, ordinances can be taken in the Council of Ministers, submitted for the approval of the President of the Republic—who will therefore, in the last instance, be the judge of their opportuneness— and finally, once they are approved, applied without delay.

14. Losses by the French and Rebels in First Five Years of Algerian War *

Five Years of Algerian War	French Soliders Killed	Rebel Losses
November 1, 1954 to October 23, 1958..........7,200		77,000 (killed)
October 23, 1958 to October 25, 1959...........2,150		35,800 †
Total...............................9,350		

† Listed as *hors de combat*—no distinction made between killed and prisoners taken.

* From *Le Monde*, November 1–2, 1959, p. 2. Based on General de Gaulle's press conference statement of October 23, 1958, and on figures released by the official *Semaine en Algérie* for the following year.

15. Analysis of Important Votes in the National Assembly, Second Session, October–December, 1959

Algerian Policy

On October 15, 1959 the Assembly approved Prime Minister Debré's governmental declaration on Algeria, based on the September 16 speech of General de Gaulle. Out of a total vote of 552, the results were: for, 441; against, 23; abstained voluntarily, 28; did not take part in voting, 60.

Group	Total Number	For	Against	Abstained Voluntarily	Did Not Participate
UNR	209	205	0	0	4
Independents	118	84	13	17	4
MRP	57	52	0	2	3
Unity of Republic	43	4	0	2	37
SFIO	44	44	0	0	0
Entente Démocratique	43	38	0	4	1
Communist party	10	0	8	0	2
Dissident UNR	9	5	0	0	4
Non-inscrits	19	9	2	3	5
Total	552	441	23	28	60

From *Le Monde*, October 17, 1959, p. 4.

Fiscal Reform

On October 29, the government bill on fiscal reform passed by a vote of 380 to 95, with 61 deputies either abstaining voluntarily or not taking part in the vote.

Group	For	Against	Abstained or Did Not Participate
UNR	184	3	17
Independents	104	2	10
MRP	34	13	6
Unity of Republic	31	1	13
SFIO	0	38	4
Entente Démocratique	12	26	5
Communist party	0	10	0
Dissident UNR	4	0	1
Non-inscrits	11	2	5
Total	380	95	61

From *Le Monde*, October 31, 1959, p. 5.

The Budget

On its first reading, November 9, the budget on general estimates was carried by a vote of 198 to 63. On the second reading the vote was 224 to 172 (with 107 not voting).

In order to defeat the budget the Socialists introduced a motion of censure on November 26. According to the constitution, only the votes in favor of the censure motion are recorded. There were only 109 votes in favor, hence the budget was automatically adopted.

The vote on the Socialist motion of censure (failure of which entailed adoption of the budget for 1960), was as follows:

Group	For
Communist party	10
SFIO	44
Entente Démocratique	29
MRP	15
Independents	8
Unity of Republic	1
Non-inscrits	2
Total	109

From *Le Monde*, November 29–30, 1959, p. 3.

Status of Private Schools

On December 24 the government bill on relations between private schools and the State was passed by a vote of 427 to 71. The same bill passed the Senate on December 30 by a vote of 173 to 99.

Group	For	Against	Abstained	Did Not Take Part
UNR	193	3	5	8
Independents	114	2	2	1
MRP	52	0	3	2
Unity of Republic	30	0	1	14
SFIO	0	44	0	0
Radicals and Entente Démocratique	25	8	7	3
Communist party	0	10	0	0
Non-inscrits	13	4	0	7
Total	427	71	18	35

From *Le Monde*, December 25, 1959, p. 6.

16. Changing Composition of the Debré Cabinet *

Following is the first government of the Fifth Republic, formed on January 8, 1959.

* The following abbreviations are used for political parties and mandates of parliamentarians: Ind.—Independent Party; MRP—Popular Republican Movement;

Premier .... Michel Debré (UNR Senator)
Minister Delegate to the
     Premier .... Jacques Soustelle [1]
                    (UNR Deputy)
Ministers of State .... Félix Houphouet-Boigny [2]
                    (RDA Deputy)
                    Louis Jacquinot (Ind. Deputy)
                    Robert Lecourt (MRP Deputy)
                    André Malraux

Ministers:
     Justice .... Edmond Michelet
                    (UNR Senator)
     Foreign Affairs .... Maurice Couve de Murville
     Interior .... Jean Berthoin [3] (Rad. Senator)
     Armed Forces .... Pierre Guillaumat
     Finance and Economic
          Affairs .... Antoine Pinay [4] (Ind. Deputy)
     National Education .... André Boulloche [5]
     Public Works and
          Transport .... Robert Buron (MRP Deputy)
     Industry and Commerce ... Jean-Marcel Jeanneney
     Agriculture .... Roger Houdet [6] (Ind. Senator)
     Labor .... Paul Bacon
     Public Health and
          Population .... Bernard Chenot
     Construction .... Pierre Sudreau
     War Veterans .... Raymond Triboulet
                    (UNR Deputy)
     Post Office, Telegraph, and
          Telephone .... Bernard Cornut-Gentille [7]
                    (UNR Deputy)
     Information .... Roger Frey
Secretaries of State
     Social Affairs .... Miss Néfissa Sid Cara
                    (Algerian Deputy)
     Civil Service .... Pierre Chatenet [8]

RDA—African Democratic Rally; Rad.—Radical; UNR—Union for the New Republic. When no party affiliation is indicated, the incumbent is a nonparliamentarian.

[1] Dismissed in February, 1960.

[2] Agreed to remain in cabinet only until institutions of the Community were established.

[3] Resigned in May, 1959.

[4] Resigned in January, 1960.

[5] Resigned in December, 1959.

[6] Resigned in May, 1959.

[7] Dismissed in February, 1960.

[8] Appointed Minister of the Interior in May, 1959.

Economic Affairs .... Max Fléchet [9] (Ind. Senator)
Industry and Commerce ... Joseph Fontanet (MRP Deputy)
Budget .... Valéry Giscard d'Estaing
                       (Ind. Deputy)
Interior .... Michel Maurice-Bokanowski
                       (UNR Deputy)

The new ministers as of January, 1960 included the following:

Minister of the Interior .... Pierre Chatenet (May, 1959)
Minister of Agriculture .... Henri Rocherau
                       (Ind. Senator—May, 1959)
Minister of Finance and
  Economic Affairs .... Wilfrid Baumgartner
                       (January, 1960)
  Minister of National
    Education .... Louis Joxe (January, 1960)

During the first week of February, 1960 the cabinet was re-shuffled as follows:

Premier .... Michel Debré (UNR Sen.)
Ministers Delegate to the
    Premier .... Pierre Guillaumat *
                      Roger Frey
Ministers of State
    Scientific Research .... Louis Jacquinot (Ind. Dep.)
    Overseas Departments and
      Territories, Sahara ..... Robert Lecourt * (MRP Dep.)
    Cultural Affairs .... André Malraux
Ministers
    Justice .... Edmond Michelet (UNR Sen.)
    Foreign Affairs .... Maurice Couve de Murville
    Interior ..·.............. Pierre Chatenet
    Armed Forces .... Pierre Messmer †
    Finance and Economic
      Affairs .... Wilfrid Baumgartner
    National Education .... Louis Joxe
    Public Works and
      Transport .... Robert Buron (MRP Dep.)
    Industry and Commerce ... Jean-Marcel Jeanneney
    Agriculture .... Henri Rochereau (Ind. Sen.)
    Labor .... Paul Bacon
    Public Health and
      Population .... Bernard Chenot

---

[9] Resigned in January, 1960.
* Members of the government having changed posts on February 5.
† New members of the government.

Construction .... Pierre Sudreau
War Veterans .... Raymond Triboulet (UNR Dep.)
Post Office, Telegraph, and
    Telephone .... Michel Maurice-Bokanowski *
                   (UNR Dep.)
Information .... Louis Terrenoire † (UNR Dep.)
Secretaries of State
    Moslem Social Affairs ...... Miss Néfissa Sid Cara
                     (Algerian Dep.)
    Finances .... Valéry Giscard d'Estaing
                     (Ind. Dep.)
    Industry and Commerce ... Joseph Fontanet (MRP Dep.)
    The Community .... Jean Foyer † (UNR Dep.)

Thus, of the twenty-seven members of the cabinet of January 8, 1959, *thirteen* either resigned, were dismissed, or changed posts by February 5, 1960.

---

* Members of the government having changed posts on February 5.
† New members of the government.

APPENDIX C

Chronology of French Politics, January, 1956 to February, 1960

1956

Jan. 2	Election of the National Assembly.
Jan. 31	Assembly votes confidence in Guy Mollet, the prime minister designate.
Feb. 6	Incidents in Algiers. Resignation of General Catroux, Resident Minister in Algeria.
March 2	Recognition by France of the independence of Morocco.
March 8–15	National Assembly and Council of Republic vote special powers to government in Algeria. On question of confidence in Assembly, the Communists support the government.
March 23	Resignation of Mendès-France as Minister of State in the Mollet cabinet.
June 5	National Assembly votes confidence in North African policy of government.
July 26	Nasser announces nationalization of Suez Canal.
Oct. 22	Moroccan plane carrying several FLN leaders, including Ben Bella, forced down at Algiers.
Oct. 18–25	Debate on foreign and Algerian policy in Assembly. Government receives a vote of confidence.
Oct. 30	Declaration of government on Franco-British intervention in Egypt.
Dec. 10	Government receives confidence of Assembly on budget (Communists and Poujadists oppose, moderates abstain).
Dec. 20	Assembly approves government's foreign policy (Communists and Poujadists oppose, most moderates support Government).

386

1957

Feb. 19
: Executive Committee of Independents sharply criticizes economic and Algerian policies of Mollet.

March 29
: Mollet government receives narrow majority (221 in favor, 188 against, 110 abstentions) on vote of confidence in Assembly. Radicals are divided, moderates abstain.

May 21
: Mollet government is defeated on its financial and economic proposals by a vote of 213 in favor, 250 against (Communists, Poujadists, Independents), with 70 abstentions (including 28 Radicals).

June 12
: Maurice Bourgès-Maunoury (Radical) is invested as prime minister by a vote of 240 to 194. Most of the MRP deputies abstain.

July 19
: Government receives vote of confidence on extension of special powers in Algeria (280 for, 183 against).

Sept. 30
: Bourgès-Maunoury government is refused confidence on its *loi-cadre* for Algeria by a vote of 279 against, 253 for. The opposition includes 38 Independents and 17 Social Republicans.

Nov. 5
: National Assembly accords confidence to Félix Gaillard by 337 votes against 173.

Nov. 15
: United States and Great Britain deliver arms to Tunisia.

Nov. 29
: *Loi-cadre* for Algeria is approved by 269 votes to 200.

1958

Feb. 8
: Bombardment of Sakhiet-Sidi-Youssef.

Feb. 11
: Gaillard government receives a vote of confidence (335 to 179). The Anglo-American offer of good offices is accepted by the French government.

April 15
: An interpellation on the Anglo-American good offices leads to the overthrow of the Gaillard government by a vote of 321 to 255.

May 13
: Confidence is accorded to Pierre Pflimlin by a vote of 274 to 129. Riots in the city of Algiers. Formation of a Committee of Public Safety, which appeals to General de Gaulle.

May 14
: Message of President Coty ordering the army to obey constituted authority.

May 15
: Declaration of General de Gaulle that he is ready to assume the powers of the Republic. Entry of Socialists into the Pflimlin cabinet.

May 16
: Assembly votes to declare a state of emergency in Metropolitan France.

May 17
: Resignation of General Ely, the Chief of Staff.

May 19
: Press conference of General de Gaulle, in which he announces his readiness to assume power.

May 24	A Committee of Public Safety in Corsica seizes control of the island.
May 26	A meeting takes place between Prime Minister Pflimlin and General de Gaulle.
May 27	General de Gaulle declares that he has begun the regular procedure leading to his accession to power. Assembly votes a bill permitting a new revision of the constitution.
May 28	Resignation of the Independent ministers, followed by that of the Pflimlin cabinet. General de Gaulle meets with the presidents of the two legislative chambers.
May 29	Message of President Coty to Parliament announcing his intention to designate General de Gaulle as President of the Council.
June 1	General de Gaulle is accorded confidence as President of the Council of Ministers (309 for, 165 against).
June 2	Assembly votes full powers and modifies procedure for amendment of the constitution (350 for, 163 against).
June 3	Adjournment *sine die* of the Parliament.
June 4	Trip of General de Gaulle to Algeria.
Aug. 8	General de Gaulle appears before the Constitutional Consultative Committee and clarifies a number of points concerning the proposed text.
Aug. 14	The Constitutional Consultative Committee ends its deliberations.
Aug. 26	Trip of General de Gaulle to Madagascar and Africa, during which he offers independence to those countries which vote No in referendum.
Aug. 29	The final draft of the constitution is examined by the Council of State.
Sept. 3	The draft of the constitution is definitively accepted by the cabinet.
Sept. 4	General de Gaulle launches the referendum campaign with a public address at the *Place de la République* in Paris.
Sept. 28	Referendum on the constitutional text, which is approved: 79.25 per cent vote Yes and 20.75 per cent No.
Oct. 7	Adoption of the new electoral law and promulgation by ordinance.
Oct. 9	Instructions of General de Gaulle to General Salan on the elections in Algeria. Officers are ordered to withdraw from the Committees of Public Safety.
Nov. 23	First ballot of the legislative elections.
Nov. 30	Second ballot of the legislative elections.
Dec. 9	Opening session of the new National Assembly.
Dec. 12	General Salan is removed from his post of command in Algeria, and named Inspector General of National Defense.
Dec. 13	General de Gaulle announces his candidacy for President of the Republic.

Dec. 21	General de Gaulle is elected President of the Republic and of the Community.
Dec. 28	Announcement of the new financial measures decided by General de Gaulle and Antoine Pinay.

1959

Jan. 8	Inauguration of General de Gaulle as President of the Republic and of the Community.
Jan. 15	The government of Michel Debré is constituted and appears before the National Assembly, where it is approved by a vote of 453 to 56.
Feb. 3–4	First meeting of the Executive Council of the Community.
Feb. 20	Nomination of members of the Constitutional Council.
March 8	First ballot in the municipal elections.
March 15	Second ballot in municipal elections.
April 21	First regular session of the National Assembly.
April 26	Senatorial elections.
June 1	Senatorial elections in Algeria.
June 4	Full-dress debate in the National Assembly on Algeria.
June 9	The Senate resolves unanimously in favor of re-establishment of veterans' benefits.
June 10	National Assembly passes bill to institute budgetary unity between Metropolis and Algeria.
June 24	The Economic and Social Council is convened.
July 15	Opening session of the Senate of the Community.
July 23	Prime Minister Debré promises the National Assembly the government will introduce a bill to settle the status of the private schools before the end of the year.
Sept. 16	General de Gaulle offers the choice of self-determination to Algeria, after pacification.
Sept. 28	Algerian Provisional Government answers De Gaulle, declares itself ready to discuss political and military conditions of a cease-fire and mutual guarantees.
Oct. 8	Parliament convenes for its second regular session.
Oct. 15	Assembly approves government policy in Algeria by 441 votes to 23.
Oct. 16	The first split of the UNR parliamentary group leads to the expulsion of nine members.
Oct. 26	President de Gaulle issues a message to the civil service and armed forces in Algeria. Prime Minister Debré attaches a directive.
Oct. 30	Khrushchev cautiously supports De Gaulle's policy in Algeria.
Nov. 3	French Communist party reconsiders its position with reference to self-determination in Algeria as proposed by De Gaulle, and favors it.

Nov. 7   Minister of Defense Guillaumat sends message to General
             Challe defining mission of army in Algeria.
Nov. 9   National Assembly begins consideration of the budget
             with a favorable vote (198 to 63) on the first reading.
Nov. 10   Press conference of General de Gaulle in which he re-
             affirms his policy on Algeria.
Nov. 25   Premier Debré engages responsibility of government on
             text of budget. Motion of censure introduced by Socialists
             is not passed by Assembly on November 27, which thus
             adopts budget.
Dec. 5   Inauguration of pipe line from Hassi-Messaoud to Bougie.
Dec. 13   General de Gaulle in a speech at Dakar accepts principle
             of negotiations with Senegal and Soudan for independence.
Dec. 23   Government accepts amendment during education debate
             by defenders of the religious schools. Minister of Educa-
             tion Boulloche resigns in protest.
Dec. 24   National Asssembly adopts government's education bill,
             dealing with status of private schools, by 427 votes to 71.
             On December 30 the Senate also approves the measure,
             which becomes law.

1960

Jan. 12   General de Gaulle accepts resignation of Antoine Pinay
             as Minister of Finance, who is replaced by the Governor
             of the Bank of France, Wilfrid Baumgartner.
Jan. 22   The Ministry of the Army announces the replacement of
             General Massu by General Crépin as corps commander in
             Algeria, after the former had criticized the government
             during an interview with a German journalist.
Jan. 24   A riot breaks out in the city of Algiers during a rally pro-
             testing Massu's dismissal. Twenty-one persons, including
             eleven gendarmes, are killed.
Jan. 25   A general strike is called in Algiers. Activists throw up
             barricades, without being interfered with by the army or
             police.
Jan. 29   General de Gaulle, in a radio and television address, or-
             ders the army to end the insurrection. Next day the para-
             troopers form a cordon around the barricades and order
             the rioters to surrender.
Feb. 1   The insurgents quit the barricades; most go home, but
             some of the leaders are arrested.
Feb. 3   Parliament approves (441 to 75) a one-year grant of power
             to the government, under Article 38, to take whatever
             measures are necessary to maintain law and order, safe-
             guard the State and Constitution, and pacify Algeria.

Index

Index

A

Abbas, Ferhat, 30–34, 40, 43, 55
Africa
  Equatorial, 198–99, 324
  United States of, 200
  West, 198–99, 202, 207, 324
Alain, 308–9
Alcohol lobby, 22, 23–24, 288
Algeria; *see also* Ferhat Abbas; *Front de la Libération Nationale; and* Integration
  elections in, 38–40, 251–53, 264–65
  electoral system in, 33, 35–38, 55, 236
  French conquest of, 26
  French policy toward, since rebellion, 54–61, 316–23, 369–71, 374, 381
  and French politics, 45–61, 220–21, 296–97, 300–301, 303
  legal status of, 35–38, 54
  Moslem and European communities in, 27–39
  Moslem Independence movement, 29–35
  provisional government, 317, 320, 371–73
  rebellion, 1954, 42–44, 380
  uprisings
    January, 1960, 330–31, 376–80
    May, 1945, 34
    May 13, 1958, 62–81
Algerian Assembly, 35, 40–42, 47
Algerian lobby, 321
Allard, General, 85, 321
ALN, 43–44
Amis du Manifeste et de la Liberté, 33
Apithy, Sourou-Migan, 198, 208
Arbitrage, 149, 175, 272
Armée de la Libération Nationale (ALN), 43–44
Army, French
  and events of May, 1958, 73–77, 79, 81, 84–86, 88, 90, 92, 93, 100, 109–12
  political activities, 64, 107–13, 252–53
  Psychological Services, 103–6, 110, 332
  revolutionary warfare, theory of, 102–7, 112–13
  Sections Administratives Spécialisées (SAS), 105, 112

Aron, Raymond, 47
Arrighi, Pascal, 90, 91
Assemblies, Constituent, 126–27, 148–49, 193–94
Assembly, National, of Fifth Republic; *see also* Parliament
  committees, 277–79
  composition of, 276–77, 292–93
  general, 175, 186, 276–79, 328
  and government, 168–69, 176–79, 285–89
  procedure, 167–72, 286–89
  sessions, 286
  sitting arrangements, 277–78
Assimilation, 35, 200; *see also* Union, French
Association des Oulémas, 30
Atlantic Charter, 190
Atom bomb, 332
Aumeran, General, 49
Auriol, Vincent, 95, 99, 290, 302

B

Ballottage
  in Fifth Republic, 236–37, 261–66
  in Fourth Republic, 13, 234, 245
  mentioned, 122
  in Third Republic, 12
Bamako, conference of, 200
Barangé bill, 14, 24
Bayeux speech (De Gaulle), 16, 149–50, 153
Baylet, Jean, 216, 222, 262
Beeley, Harold, 59
Ben Badis, 30
Ben Bella, 42–43
Bernasconi, Jean, 263
Berthoin, Jean, 288
Biaggi, Jean-Baptiste, 250
Bidault, Georges, 60, 66, 77, 80, 223, 226, 231, 246, 248, 251, 306–7, 331
Billères, René, 245
Bizerte, base of, 325
Blocq-Mascart, Maxime, 127–28, 150, 201
Blum-Violette bill (1937), 31
Bonneval, Colonel de, 65
Boulanger, General, 4, 71, 121, 297
Boulloche, André, 274, 289
Bourdet, Claude, 214

393

This book has been set on the Linotype in 11 point Caledonia, leaded 2 points, and 10 point Caledonia, leaded 1 point. Chapter numbers are in Caledonia Bold; chapter titles are in Lydian Cursive. The size of the type page is 27 by 45½ picas.